What I Saw in California

What I Saw in California

By Edwin Bryant

Introduction by Thomas D. Clark

University of Nebraska Press
Lincoln and London

Introduction copyright 1985 by the University of Nebraska Press
Manufactured in the United States of America

First Bison Book printing: May 1985
Most recent printing indicated by the first digit below:
    2   3   4   5   6   7   8   9   10

This edition reproduces the original 1848 edition published by D. Appleton & Company. In the table of contents, the descriptions of chapters 23 and 27 are transposed.

Library of Congress Cataloging in Publication Data

Bryant, Edwin, 1805–
    What I saw in California.

    Reprint. Originally published: New York :
D. Appleton : Philadelphia : G. Appleton, 1848.
    1. California—Description and travel—To 1848.
2. West (U.S.)—Description and travel—To 1848.
3. Overland journeys to the Pacific. 4. Bryant,
Edwin, 1805–1869. I. Title.
F864.B815 1985   979.4   84-28003
ISBN 0-8032-6070-9 (pbk.)

∞

Introduction
By Thomas D. Clark

Few American authors have been so successful in the timing of their books as Edwin Bryant. Before *What I Saw in California* reached the public in 1848, gold was discovered on the American River. By the time this discovery was publicized worldwide, the book was being reviewed in the press. Suddenly, the former Kentucky newspaperman was recognized as an authority on how to survive the grueling passage from Independence, Missouri, to San Francisco, a passage he had made two years earlier.

To be sure, Bryant's was by no means the only journal of overland travel available to the Forty-niners. Francis Parkman had traveled almost half of the same route in 1846 and written about it in *The Oregon Trail* (1849). Lansford Hastings had published *The Emigrant's Guide to Oregon and California* in 1845 (it would be used the following year by the Donner party), and by 1849 there existed numerous other journals and guides, including two or three books on life in California.

It was Edwin Bryant, though, who set the pattern for most travelers who were to describe their experiences along the California Trail in the great rush of 1849. He made specific recordings of time, place, and weather. *What I Saw in California* may lack the flowing literary qualities of Parkman's *Oregon Trail,* but it is more penetrating and helpful as a contemporary source of information. It was widely emulated by the diarists among the Forty-niners. They realized, as Bryant did, that their accounts would reflect forms and conditions of life that would quickly disappear, and that what they wrote would mirror the image of an irrecoverable moment in American history.

When Bryant resigned his position as coeditor of the *Louis-*

ville Courier in April 1846 and looked westward, the road to California was already beginning to fill up with emigrants. At least two hundred wagons rolled that year, carrying well over a thousand men, women, and children. By now a good deal of information had circulated—by word of mouth and by letters from those who had gone ahead—to steel them on their way. All were caught up in the westering fever that had been raging since the Great Pathfinder and even greater publicist, John Charles Frémont, as well as lesser promoters, had pictured the West as a most desirable place to go. The migration was helped along, too, by outfitters and travel agents of various sorts who had an economic stake in it.

The optimism of the emigrants was not dampened by the extremely unsettled political situation in California, which in 1846 was still a foreign country, a possession of Mexico. On May 13 of that year, while Bryant's party was just getting underway, the United States, voicing grievances but mainly pressing for annexation of California, declared war on the Republic of Mexico. About the same time, American settlers in California, led by Captain Frémont, set up a short-lived republic in northern California under the Bear Flag. Late in the year the combined forces of Brigadier General Stephen Watts Kearny and Commodore Robert F. Stockton defeated the Mexican army in southern California and the American conquest, which was to be formalized in the Treaty of Guadalupe Hidalgo early in 1848, was only a matter of time.

Some of the emigrants of 1846 fought in the war weeks after they arrived in California. Among them was Edwin Bryant, who in October accompanied Captain Frémont on an expedition to assist Commodore Stockton in the fighting at Los Angeles. In fact, a number of professional men (that year's emigration was the first to attract writers, clergymen, lawyers, and physicians in any force) served temporarily as officers in the Mexican War. No one was more representative of that professional class than Edwin Bryant, although his beginnings were modest enough.

Born near Pelham, Massachusetts, seven miles west of Amherst, in 1805, the son of Ichabod and Silence Bryant, Edwin had an unhappy childhood. His parents were first cousins, and Ichabod was the profligate brother of Dr. Peter Bryant, father of the poet William Cullen. Ichabod was said to have been in and out of prison and could hardly have been a caring father. Thus Edwin was left dependent upon relatives for his unbringing. He lived briefly with his maternal uncle, Bezabiel Bryant, in Bedford, West Chester County, New York. Later he studied medicine under the tutelage of Dr. Peter Bryant.[1]

Edwin Bryant arrived in Louisville in 1830 and talked himself into a position on that city's new *Journal*. His furious anti-Jackson articles led to the editorship of the *Lexington Intelligencer* in 1834, an association that lasted ten years. During this time he helped organize the Kentucky Press Association. A popular editor and social figure in Lexington, Bryant formed a close and lasting link with Henry Clay and his family. The emotional political issues that stirred central Kentucky made this an exciting time to edit an aggressive Whig newspaper.

Late in 1844, at the urging of Henry Clay, Bryant established, with Walter N. Haldeman, another Whig journal, which would soon become known as the *Louisville Morning Courier*. Within a year his physical, or possibly political, health deteriorated, and he chose to take leave of the naggings of dog-eat-dog personal journalism.

Since his arrival in Kentucky, Bryant had been exposed to a constant flow of news about the migration of Kentuckians into the new territories beyond the Ohio and Mississippi rivers. There was the rush to Texas. Then on a much more dramatic scale Kentuckians gathered furs in the Rocky Mountains, helped open the Santa Fe Trail, established trading posts up the Missouri River, and became famous frontier scouts. They had powerful political friends in Washington who could secure for them desirable territorial appointments. These waves of migration made news back in the state, and this was especially true of the first attempts to brave the Oregon and California trails.

Even so, Bryant's decision to make the overland journey to

1. For further details of Bryant's life and career, see Thomas D. Clark, "Edwin Bryant and the Opening of the Road to California," *Essays in Western History in Honor of T. A. Larson,* University of Wyoming Publications, vol. 37, no. 3 (October 1971), pp. 29–43.

California in 1846 was surprising in view of his poor health. Much of the trail was still undefined, and the way across prairie, mountain, and desert was often treacherous. In this undertaking he was to link his name with such Kentucky wanderers as Daniel Boone, Kit Carson, the Sublette brothers, Pegleg Williams and Alexander Doniphan. Unlike his illustrious predecessors, Bryant was on a literary mission. At the outset he proposed to travel with a party organized by William H. Russell on the Oregon route as far as 121 degrees west, and then turn southwest toward the Bay of San Francisco. Later he would return to Louisville by way of Acupulco, Vera Cruz, and New Orleans.

The week before Bryant left Louisville, the *Courier* stated: "Mr. Bryant has had this trip in view for some time, and on his return he will probably write a book giving a faithful and accurate description of the 'Land of Promise.'" His colleague Haldeman expressed faith that Bryant was eminently qualified to observe the geology, botany, and advantages and disadvantages which the far western country would present to emigrants. If he did write a book it would "be reliable and of immense benefit to the thousands and tens of thousands who desire to make that country their home, but who, as yet, know so little of it. Indeed, this expedition will conclusively determine one thing—whether or not California offers inducement to settlers which the rather vague accounts that have heretofore been given of it have induced many to believe."

On April 18, 1846, Edwin Bryant, Robert T. Jacobs, and Robert Ewing departed Louisville aboard a steamboat bound for St. Louis and Independence. Passing through St. Louis, the party added a fourth member, George Louis Curry of the *St. Louis Revellie.* There were already assembled in Independence large numbers of emigrants who had responded to William H. Russell's publicity that he would lead a company from Independence to the Sacramento Valley. Among them was a former governor of Kentucky, Lillburn Boggs, who had emigrated to Missouri Territory in the great land rush of 1816.

Edwin Bryant doubtless knew Colonel Russell, another native Kentuckian and the grandson of the old Indian fighter General William Russell. He claimed to have been briefly a secretary to Henry Clay, and later had served as federal marshal and district attorney in Calloway County, Missouri.

On May 22, Bryant wrote Haldeman that the emigrant train was underway, and was then twenty-three miles beyond Independence. He described the scenery along the Missouri River, and the towns of Lexington, Booneville, and Independence. Independence, he said, had a population of one thousand and was the busiest place he had ever seen: there was a great stir of outfitting California and Oregon emigrants, and the bustle of Santa Fe traders. He told Haldeman that his small party had lingered in Independence only three days, "during which time, the streets of the town were choked up with long ox and mule teams, some of which were brought for sale, others to be hitched to wagons for the emigrating Santa Fe companies." Bryant was impressed by the fact that the companies strung as many as sixteen yoke of oxen to a single wagon, making a spectacle as "imposing as a railroad train—not so expeditious, you will readily imagine."

Spreading out beyond Independence, the great Kansas prairie entranced Bryant. He wrote, "Nothing I have ever seen in nature, can exceed the beauty and sublimity of the prairies where we now are. . . . I would go thousands of miles for no other purpose than to look upon these glorious landscapes fashioned after God's own taste. Perfumed and ornamented by myriads of brilliant flowers, and studded and relieved by beautiful parks, ponds, and rivulets, bounding in some instances the far-off horizon."

Bryant also noted that a hundred wagons were already assembled and more were arriving hourly. He thought there would ultimately be 150 with a thousand emigrants. His own party was enlarged by the addition of Nathan J. and Charles Putnam of Louisville, and B. Bosworth, W. B. Brown, and John Buchanan of Lexington.

Colonel Russell savored his moment of glory. On May 11, in a meeting conducted by the well-liked Bryant, Russell was elected to command the emigrant band. In a letter written on the trail, Russell described the Indians they met and some of the hardships the company had to endure. He concluded they were too numerous to be commanded as a single unit. A rumor was afloat that a war with Mexico had begun. He wrote, "We read it as a good joke in which even the ladies and children participate. I do not mean to be *captured*." Thus one of the most exciting folk movements in American history was inching its tedious way up a dusty trail of destiny to quarrel, split up in smaller parties, to become lost and suffer supreme tragedy, and eventually to arrive in California and Oregon.

By the end of May it became clear that the large company would have to be broken into several groups, that those who wished to travel faster beyond Fort Laramie would have to do so by pack mules, and that at the present rate of progress some emigrants would be caught in the Sierra snows. There also was indecision as to which route parties should follow beyond Fort Bridger. They could go by Fort Hall and drop down into the Humboldt Valley on the western slope of the Rockies, or gamble heavily on one of the major cutoffs, especially Hastings' by way of Salt Lake and the deadly salt flats along the southern and western shores.

Fevers and intestinal disturbances in the wagon camps caused delays, and there was an occasional death. William H. Russell himself fell ill on June 15, near the junction of the North and South Platte. At a meeting attended by Edwin Bryant, Russell resigned his post and Governor Boggs was placed in command. This meeting marked the end of Edwin Bryant's association with the great emigrant company. On June 19 he and a small party composed of Isaac Kirkendall, William B. Brown, Robert T. Jacobs, the Putnam brothers, R. H. Holder, George Law Curry, Benjamin Lippincott, Benton Burgess, and Robert Ewing rode ahead. The party apparently left its wagons behind in charge of drivers. In three days they traveled the 150 miles to Fort Laramie, where they tarried five days trading for mules, buying supplies, and awaiting the arrival of the pokey wagon train. By noon of the fifth day they considered themselves prepared to set off into the vast western country. William N. Nuttall and A. V. Brooksey joined the party. Ewing was left at Fort Laramie eventually to wander back home by way of

Bent's Fort and the Arkansas Valley, and John Buchanan re-
joined the wagon train.

Bryant referred to himself as "our captain." The entourage
now consisted of approximately thirty mules and ponies, poorly
packed by the inexperienced men. From the outset there was
the frustration of slipping packs and turning saddles. Bryant
wrote, "The mules, stupid as we regarded them, knew more
about this business than we did; and several times I thought I
could detect them in giving a wise wink and sly leer, as much as
to say, that we were perfect novices, and if they could speak,
they would give us the benefit of their advice and instruction. A
Mexican pack mule is one of the most sagacious and intelligent
quadrupeds I have ever met with."

Between June 28 and July 17, the Bryant company reached
Fort Bridger, and at that place Curry and the Putnams elected
to go to Oregon, leaving seven members with the addition of
James Hudspeth, who went briefly as a guide around the Salt
Lake. On August 30, the Bryant party reached the first outpost
of California, William Johnson's ranch on the Bear River. When
Edwin Bryant crossed the bay to San Francisco he was accompanied by Robert T. Jacobs and William B. Brown. He had lost
weight and was tanned the shade of a Digger Indian, his health
was good, and he was ready to savor the excitement being
generated on the California frontier. Abruptly his daily journal
ended at this point, indicative of the fact his interest was basi-
cally in describing the ordeals of overland travel and the changing topography of the land.

During the months from September 1846 to June 1847,
Edwin Bryant became involved in an amazing number of events
in that revolutionary land. Five days after he arrived in San
Francisco, Captains John William Livingston and William
Mervine anchored the naval vessels *Congress* and *Savannah*. A
few days later a courier arrived with news that Californians
were in revolt at Los Angeles. By October 5, Governor Robert F.
Stockton arrived in San Francisco and was greeted with pomp
in a ceremony attended by Bryant, Russell, and Jacobs. Bryant
passed the time taking meals aboard American and Russian

ships and in acquainting himself with the local businessmen. Soon after, Bryant volunteered to accompany John Charles Frémont on an expedition to assist Commodore Stockton in suppressing a rebellion at Los Angeles. Although his service as first lieutenant of Company H under the command of Jacobs was undistinguished, his notes contribute an interesting contemporary view of life in Spanish California in the middle of the nineteenth century. They both confirm and amplify Alfred Robinson's *Life in California during a Residence of Several Years in That Territory.*

Bryant and Jacobs were back in San Francisco by February 13, 1847, and Bryant noted that already the town was changing. He said that wherever the Anglo-Saxon race planted its foot, progress was inevitable. The village that he first saw had now become a bustling port with ships unloading their cargoes directly onto the ground. In the week after his return Bryant did some visiting and sight-seeing. He also began making plans to return to Louisville, plans that were disrupted when on February 20, he was asked to call on General Stephen Watts Kearny, who had come up from the south to visit San Francisco. Bryant had seen General Kearny in Los Angeles, and he knew that the year before the general had sent word by Robert Ewing to the emigrant company, warning it to be cautious of a hostile Mormon train supposedly traveling just ahead of them, and of another crossing the Missouri at St. Joseph. On February 20, Kearny asked Bryant to accept appointment as alcalde of San Francisco. He accepted the honor and was sworn into office two days later by Lieutenant W. A. Bartlett.

As alcalde of San Francisco Bryant made a modest contribution to California history. He later wrote that his magisterial decisions were founded in common sense rather than strict legal precedent. He was energetic in other matters, one of which was persuading General Kearny to proclaim as public property a considerable area of land about the mouth of San Francisco Bay. This area was to be surveyed and lots sold in order to procure funds to maintain public offices. Bryant had both knowledge and first-hand experience in assessing the desirability of waterfront property. In Louisville this had been a major issue. As a newspaperman he understood bustling riverfront activities where businessmen competed for favored locations. San Francisco appeared no different. In a proclamation, in March 1847, General Kearny authorized the sale of "beach and water lots on the east front" of San Francisco, reserving the lots that were to be used by the United States Government. Bryant advertised the terms of sale on March 16 and the sale of 450 lots took place on June 25. He purchased 14 of them himself, and was confirmed in his faith that Anglo-Saxon progress was inevitable by the *California Star,* which boasted on March 13, 1847, that San Francisco was destined to become "the Liverpool or New York of the Pacific Ocean."

When Edwin Bryant crossed the San Francisco Bay on June 2, 1847, to return to Louisville he left behind a village turning into a seaport city. Possibly he carried the manuscript of *What I Saw in California.* He learned that General Stephen Watts Kearny and Captain John Charles Frémont, among others, would depart Monterey on the following Tuesday for Sutter's Fort and was invited to join them for the return home. He had abandoned his original plan to return home by way of the Mexican cities and New Orleans. Three days after his departure from San Francisco, the *Californian* bade him farewell, saying, "We much regret his loss, both as judge and court, and as a gentleman! He goes, however, with the determination of returning to this country." The editor said Bryant had been industriously preparing material for his book on California. "Should he find at home, sufficient interest for knowledge of this country, the work will go immediately to press." This indicates Bryant prepared his manuscript for publication in California. If this is true, the boast that *What I Saw in California* was the first book published about the territory after the opening of the American period may well be true.

Obviously Bryant had kept a full trail journal. He perhaps recorded his notes in a memorandum book, or a series of the small pocket books used in those years. His wayside observations were precise and detailed, suggesting on-the-spot recordings. No one knows what became of the original notes. He may have discarded them or sent them on to the publisher in unrevised form.

Bryant's warm human qualities had impressed his associates. The editor of the *Californian* wrote of him:

> We know of no man better qualified to write such a work. He traveled from Missouri both by wagon and pack horse and will be able to give all information as to what sort of outfit is necessary. Since his arrival in California he has accepted an office in a company of volunteers and traveled by land from Sacramento to Puebles de los Angeles, he has seen the principle portions of California, and since his return from the war he has been our chief magistrate of the San Francisco District, which has enabled him to form a very correct idea of the character of the present population, and to inform himself of the resources and prospects of California.

The editor said there was a need for Bryant's book because all of those that had appeared previous to the American period were highly colored.

Accompanied by a servant, Bryant joined General Kearny's overland party at Johnson's ranch. By August 22, they arrived at Fort Leavenworth, after only sixty-four traveling days. On the return journey Bryant must have experienced some remarkably interesting incidents of travel, certainly he was witness to far more intriguing human relationships than was the case of the earlier emigrant train when William H. Russell was in command. General Kearny was exceedingly officious with Captain John Charles Frémont, who was under semiarrest for insubordination, and the conversations at the evening camps must have taken intriguing turns. If Frémont was at all communicative, and he most assuredly was, Bryant could have done a chapter of frontier history a good turn by recording the exchanges between the two generals. Frémont possessed the knowledge to give Bryant a keen insight into Rocky Mountain and Great Basin geography. Surely the Kearny entourage's quick passage east was greatly aided by Frémont's knowledge of the country and its snares. Unfortunately, Bryant did not keep travel notes on the overland trail return home. Strangely, he did not even include Frémont's name on the list of persons with whom he traveled.

Bryant left the Kearny party at Fort Leavenworth and made his way to Kentucky. Upon his return home to Louisville, he was warmly greeted, but apparently he had no immediate prospect of a job. However, he appears to have renewed the friendliest association with his former press colleagues. During his first months at home, Bryant occupied himself with lectures and seeing his book through the press. At no time did he mention a family; nevertheless he remained a close friend of Nanette Price Smith and her daughter. In fact, at no place in his travel notes had he paused, as did so many future overland travelers, to lament his absence from loved ones. None of the spectacular scenes he viewed, the luscious buffalo steaks he ate, or anything else reminded him of mother and home. Neither official Jefferson County records nor those of Christ Episcopal Church in Louisville now are explicit about his relationships with female friends. Mrs. Smith and her daughter were willed most of his estate.

Bryant seems to have lingered in Louisville only a short time before going on to Philadelphia to deliver his manuscript to the D. Appleton Company. Then he went on a lecture tour describing his overland trail experiences and the tenor of life in pastoral California. In New York he was said to have spoken before an audience that contained some of that city's most influential businessmen. In November 1847, Bryant appeared in Washington, D.C., as a witness in the court-martial of Captain Frémont. He testified that General Kearny's order authorizing the sale of bayfront lots in San Francisco did not violate the laws of Spanish territory.

What I Saw in California came from the press early in 1848. If there was doubt that it would be a success it was quickly dispelled. Before that year's end D. Appleton published two editions; the number of subsequent printings is not known. The book was given much notice and rather good reviews. Occasionally an effete magazine reviewer revealed gross ignorance of both the overland trail and California. The important North American Review published a competent and favorable review, while Thomas P. Kettle's *Democratic Review* was supercilious in its notice.

When news of the discovery of gold in California reached the East, there came a flood of letters to the *Louisville Journal* and the *Courier* seeking information about the great trail and the Far West. In reply to these letters, Edwin Bryant published on February 26, 1849, an essay on the conditions and demands of overland travel. Having made two continental crossings, and being now the author of a popular book of western travel, he considered himself competent to give advice. His essay, widely published in eastern newspapers, listed the supplies and equipment needed by a gold rush party that he proposed to assemble and lead across the plains later in the spring. He said pack mules were superior to ox teams, and he contemplated using mules accompanied by a light wagon in which more fragile supplies could be transported. Also, the wagon would serve as an ambulance. Recalling the confusion and frustrations of the emigrant train after leaving Independence and on the road to Fort Laramie, he advised using packsaddles and roping for transporting dunnage from the start. He said two pairs of alfo-jasses or large saddlebags would facilitate the daily packing and unpacking. In the way of consumable supplies he listed three hundred pounds of foodstuffs per man, these to consist of flour, bacon, coffee, sugar, dried peaches, and rice, a luxury. As equipment Bryant suggested belt pistols, knives, axes, and mallets. Companies should take certain supplies in common such as medicines, an India rubber boat, and blacksmithing and mining tools.

As for the most desirable trail to California, Bryant admonished gold-rush travelers to stick strictly to the Independence–St. Joseph–Fort Laramie–South Pass–Mary's River–Humboldt route. Vividly recalling the Donner tragedy at the Truckee-Sierra pass, he warned, "Let no emigrant accompanied by his family deviate from it, or imagine to himself that he can find a better road. This road is the best that has yet been discovered, and to San Francisco and the gold region it is much the shortest." In the remainder of his communication, Bryant dealt with the details of overland travel and the care of teams and wagons. He informed his readers that before them at the outset were 2,290 miles of rugged terrain and rigorous travel. He gave no assurances that at the end of the journey they would find gold. He only knew what he had read in the papers on this subject. On the matter of timing, Bryant recommended that emigrants be ready to start from one of the Kansas jumping-off places by April 20, and to keep moving if they wished to avoid tragedy.

What influence Edwin Bryant's letter had on gold-rush emigrants is undetermined. It is known that many of them read it, and along with his book it became a basic guide. Before he departed on his second journey across the plains and mountains, Bryant prepared a revised edition of *What I Saw in California* to which he added the *Courier* and *Journal* essay, Colonel R. B. Masons's report on the gold region, and an article from the *Washington Globe*. In 1849, D. Appleton and Company published fifth and sixth editions of the book. By 1850 there had appeared seven American printings or editions, one in Sweden, one in France, and two in England. Bryant might not have been entirely flattered by George Routledge's English edition if he read it before he left Louisville for California. It was a cheap one-shilling paperback affair containing only the trail journal, with an added chapter written by an unidentified author who made extravagant promises of sudden wealth. At the rate his book sold, Bryant had little reason to be consumed by the gamble of uncertain gold awaiting him in the Sacramento Valley.

The higher challenge was the opportunity for Bryant to revisit California. In Louisville in the spring of 1849 he had busied himself taking care of the revision of his book, organizing a trail party, and purchasing supplies. By March 26, he had assembled a company of approximately forty-two men and was ready to board a steamboat, *Pike No. 9*, for Independence. On this date, the *Louisville Daily Journal* wished them a safe journey and golden luck. The *Pike* made fast time; Bryant's party arrived in Independence on April 2, and was encamped on Neville Ross's farm, where they were buying mules from the large number of Santa Fe traders at that place. A reporter named Graham wrote the *St. Louis Republican* that the Bryant party would start for California on April 20.

On the date of Bryant's departure, more than fifteen hundred argonauts gathered in Independence to see Bryant's forty-eight-man party. It was provided with eleven tents, one wagon, an India rubber boat capable of rescuing and bearing the wagon body, a medicine chest, hospital stores and other necessaries. Each man had three mules for his own use, with three extra for each mess of four men. Each man was armed with a rifle, a pair of holster and a pair of belt pistols. The party carried sufficient staple provisions to sustain it for 120 days. A reporter observed, "For the expedition, if not for comfort, this company is better prepared than any in the field."

Again, it is a material loss from gold-rush literature that Edwin Bryant did not keep a journal of his overland journey in 1849. This time speed was his objective, and he was not now venturing into the unknown. He no doubt had in mind the fate of his property in San Francisco. Along the trail, emigrants, half-frightened and many uncertain about the wisdom of their decision to go to the gold field, noted that Bryant's party had either passed them or was camped nearby. It was the model company led by the master, and it was certain to attract attention.

Bryant showed no personal interest in the gold fields, nor did he linger there. He pushed on to San Francisco. On August 30, 1849, the *Alta Californian* welcomed his arrival. For Bryant, the return to San Francisco was a cheerful occasion. The fourteen lots, which he had either purchased in 1847 for $4,000, or had assigned to himself, had appreciated in value to $100,000. On October 17, 1849, the *Louisville Weekly Courier* rejoiced at the news: "Good fortune could not have fallen on a more deserving or estimable gentleman." In a letter to a friend, Bryant said he had fallen victim of remittent fever, and had lost thirty-seven pounds. A colleague, Jerry Cochrane, wrote that Captain Bryant was a superb trailmaster, and that he had rather have him for a guide than Kit Carson.

Bryant's 1849 visit to San Francisco was brief. However, he took time to help organize Grace Episcopal Church. From San Francisco, Bryant traveled north for a brief visit to Oregon. The *Louisville Daily Journal,* on March 22, 1850, announced that he had returned home via the Isthmus of Panama and New Orleans. The *Journal* said he planned a return to California in the immediate future, and perhaps he did return in 1853.

Reaping profits from lectures, book royalties, and sale of real estate, Edwin Bryant was able to settle down to a comfortable and leisurely way of life in the idyllic literary colony of Pee Wee Valley in Oldham County, Kentucky. Here he built a large two-story frame house, Oaklea, close to his friends, the poet W. D. Gallagher, the grammarian Henry Noble Butler, and the local historian Benjamin Casseday. His Pee Wee Valley associates said they honored him because he had traveled to far and ungodly places. Bryant quietly sat out the Civil War in his sylvan retreat, safely away from Louisville's military activities and guerrilla raids.

He ventured once more to cross the continent to California. On June 15, 1869, broken in health and prematurely aged, he arrived by train in San Francisco. The *San Francisco Alta* reported that the visitor had "published the first book on California after the conquest and many 'forty niners' brought it with them when they started on their gold hunting expedition. He was the most popular of the American alcaldes who held office before the gold discovery."

Bryant's final California visit was brief. He returned to Louisville a sick man, and in December moved from Pee Wee Valley to the Willard Hotel in Louisville, where he would be near medical aid. On December 16, 1869, while his servant was absent, Bryant jumped out of a window and ended his life. Newspapers across the land noted his passing with tributes to his fine personal qualities.

Except for his book *What I Saw in California* and his subsequent essay on overland travel, Edwin Bryant might have meant no more to western history than did the horde of nameless trailbreakers who survived the grueling passage from Independence to San Francisco. For historians of the future West, Bryant left a dependable record fixing the vivid but fleeting image of that part of the frontier expansion. Graphically, he described the hard life of negotiating the overland trail, gave one of the first accounts of the Donner tragedy, and described the kaleidoscopic life in California immediately following the American conquest. He was present to see the awakening of the Pacific Coast to its fabulous commercial possibilities. Fortunately, the Louisville editor had the newspaperman's insight and power to describe and interpret what he saw. The numerous testimonials of his dependability carried over to his book, and even yet in the face of the discovery and publication of numerous contemporary journals. The most gracious testimonials to *What I Saw in California* are the continuing stream of footnotes that cite it.

On a dreary December 17, 1869, when the Reverend Mr. James Craik intoned the Episcopal burial ceremony in Christ Church, Louisville,[2] the body of Edwin Bryant was started on a strange odyssey. Neither the minister's words nor the laudatory obituary notices ended the physical saga of Edwin Bryant. Following the funeral in Christ Church, his body was taken to Louisville's Cave Hill Cemetery to remain the next twelve years in the public receiving vault. In January 1881, the board of managers of the cemetery ordered it and eight other corpses to be buried in the company's reserve section. Seven years later, in February 1888, O. D. Bryant, a nephew, and Ira P. Rankin, a brother-in-law then living in California, received permission of J. H. Harris, secretary of Cave Hill, to have the body exhumed to be reburied in the Bryant lot in Spring Grove Cemetery in Cincinnati, where presumably it has finally come to rest permanently under a stone bearing the simple inscription BRYANT. A more vital marker, however, is Bryant Street in San Francisco, where indeed Anglo-Saxon feet daily tread the path of "progress."

Acknowledgments

Ursula Trimble of St. Matthews, Kentucky, has been diligent and imaginative in locating documentary materials relating to the personal life of Edwin Bryant in Pee Wee Valley and Louis-

---

2. The Church Book, Christ Episcopal Church, Louisville. This book gave no indication of place of burial, and because the Bryant file was removed from the active one in Cave Hill Cemetery a considerable hunt was involved in unraveling this information.

ville. It was she who finally solved the riddle of the three inter-
ments of Bryant's body. The record in the Cave Hill Cemetery
office long ago was transferred to the "dead file" and abandoned.
She has also uncovered the personal records of Nannette Price
Smith and Nannette Smith Coffin, and their Hart-McDowell
family relationships. There is an extensive legal record of the
settlement of Edwin Bryant's estate, and after a search through
the maze of court reports and executor releases, Mrs. Trimble
has determined that there still remain questions about the final
disposition of Bryant's money and property.

The archival staff of the Filson Club in Louisville generously
supplied the materials relating to Edwin Bryant's newspaper
career. The staff of the manuscript division of the Bancroft
Library of the University of California, Berkeley, generously
made available the Dulaney correspondence, and Dale L. Mor-
gan referred me to other diary material in manuscript. Christ
Episcopal Church of Louisville and the Grace Episcopal Church
of San Francisco gave me free access to their earlier records.
Finally, the Division of Communications Services of the University of Wyoming has graciously consented to my use of material from my essay, "Edwin Bryant and the Opening of the Road
to California," published in *Essays in Western History in Honor
of T. A. Larson* (Laramie: University of Wyoming Publications,
October 1971).

WHAT I SAW IN CALIFORNIA:

BEING THE

JOURNAL OF A TOUR,

BY THE EMIGRANT ROUTE AND SOUTH PASS OF THE ROCKY MOUN-
TAINS, ACROSS THE CONTINENT OF NORTH AMERICA, THE
GREAT DESERT BASIN, AND THROUGH CALIFORNIA,

IN THE YEARS 1846, 1847.

"ALL WHICH I SAW, AND PART OF WHICH I WAS."—*Dryden.*

BY EDWIN BRYANT,

LATE ALCALDE OF ST. FRANCISCO.

NEW YORK:
D. APPLETON & COMPANY, 200 BROADWAY.
PHILADELPHIA;
GEO. S. APPLETON, 148 CHESNUT-STREET.
M DCCC XLVIII.

TO

ROBERT FRAZER, SEN., ESQ.

OF LEXINGTON, KENTUCKY,

𝕿𝖍𝖎𝖘 𝖁𝖔𝖑𝖚𝖒𝖊

IS MOST RESPECTFULLY DEDICATED

BY HIS FRIEND

THE AUTHOR.

PREFACE.

In the succeeding pages, the author has endeavored to furnish a faithful sketch of the country through which he travelled—its capabilities, scenery, and population. He has carefully avoided such embellishment as would tend to impress the reader with a false or incorrect idea of what he saw and describes. He has invented nothing to make his narrative more dramatic and amusing than the truth may render it. His design has been to furnish a volume, entertaining and instructive to the general reader, and reliable and useful to the traveller and emigrant to the Pacific. If he has succeeded in this, it is as much as he can hope. The facts in reference to those military and naval operations in California which did not come under his personal observation, have been derived from authentic sources.

THE AUTHOR.

CONTENTS.

CHAPTER VII.

CHAPTER VIII.

CHAPTER IX.

CHAPTER X.

CHAPTER XI.

CHAPTER XII.

CHAPTER XIII.

CHAPTER XIV.

CHAPTER XV.

CHAPTER XVI.

CHAPTER XVII.

CHAPTER XXIV.

CHAPTER XXV.

CHAPTER XXVI.

CHAPTER XXVII.

WHAT I SAW IN CALIFORNIA, ETC

CHAPTER I.

INTRODUCTION.

Leave Louisville—Independence, Mo.—New-Mexican teamsters—Outfitting—Masonic celebration—Improbable rumors—Mormons—Indians—
Marvellous stories.

WITH my travelling companions for a journey over the Rocky
Mountains to California, (Mr. R. T. Jacob and Mr. R. Ewing,)
I left Louisville, Ky., on the 18th of April, 1846 ; and arrived
at Independence, Mo., the starting-point, on the 1st of May.

The town of Independence is situated about six miles from
the Missouri river, on the southern, or left-hand side as you
ascend it. The surrounding country is undulating, picturesque,
and highly fertile. The growth of timber is various, and all
indicative of a fat and exuberantly productive soil. Its population is about one thousand ; and, at this season, every man
seems to be actively and profitably employed. It has been
for some years the principal outfitting point for the Santa Fé
traders, and will probably so continue. Many of the houses
around the public square are constructed of brick, but the
majority of the buildings are frames. I noticed, among the
busy multitude moving to and fro through the streets, a large
number of New-Mexicans, and half-breed Indians, with their
dusky complexions and ragged and dirty costumes. They were
generally mounted on miserably poor mules or horses, and
presented a most shabby appearance. Long trains of oxen,

2

sometimes as many as ten or fifteen yokes, strung together and pulling huge tented-wagons, designed for some Santa Fé trading expedition, were moving about the streets, under the direction of numerous drivers, cracking their whips and making a great noise.   Ox-teams seem to be esteemed as preferable, in these journeys, to either mules or horses.   Following the example of others more experienced in these matters than ourselves, we determined to procure oxen, instead of mules, for our wagon, as originally we had intended.

Accordingly I purchased three yokes of oxen, which it was believed would be a team sufficiently powerful for the transportation of our baggage and provisions.   The average price paid per yoke was $21.67, which was considered very cheap. The streets were filled with oxen offered for sale by the neighboring farmers, but few of them were in good condition or well trained.   This was the case in regard to those we purchased ; but they were all young cattle, and improvable.   Young and medium-sized cattle should be selected for a journey over the plains and mountains, in preference to the heavy-bodied and old ; the latter almost invariably become foot-sore, and give out after travelling a few hundred miles.   We engaged a man, who had spent some time in the Rocky Mountains as a servant of the trading and trapping companies, for our driver and cook, and the cattle were placed under his charge to be educated.   Although we had made many purchases in St. Louis, we found upon consultation after our arrival here, that there was a long list of small articles necessary for the journey yet to be procured.   These I obtained at reasonable rates, of Messrs. WILSON & CLARKE, who keep a general furnishing store for these expeditions.   Other mercantile houses in the place were also well supplied, and sold their wares at fair prices.

The masonic lodges of Independence commemorated the departure of their brother masons, connected with the Santa Fé and emigrating parties, by a public procession and an address, with other religious exercises.   The lady-masons, that is, the wives of the members of the fraternity, walked in the procession to and from the church.   A large audience was collected to hear the address, and participate in the exercises. The address was delivered by Mr. REESE, the grand-master, or principal masonic officer in the place. It was appropriate to the occasion, except, as I thought, that it was rather over-strained in pathos. The orator, at the close of his discourse, consigned us all to the grave, or to perpetual exile. He was responded to in suitable and eloquent terms, on behalf of the Santa Fé traders and the emigrants to Oregon and California, by Col. WAUL and Col. RUSSELL. After the addresses, an original hymn, written for the occasion, as I understood, was sung with much feeling by the whole audience, to the tune of "Old Rosin the Bow." These farewell ceremonies were con-cluded by an affecting prayer and benediction. The ladies of the auditory, I thought, were the most interested in and excited by these proceedings. Some of them wept, and man-ifested strong emotions.

It rained heavily and incessantly the whole day on the 3d, and the unpaved streets of the town were so muddy and so much inundated with water, that walking about was quite out of the question. We therefore confined ourselves to our room in the hotel, where we had scores of visiters; who, finding it impossible to do any thing else, lounged and talked over the various rumors connected with the several expeditions.

One of these rumors was, that five thousand Mormons were crossing, or had crossed, the Kansas river; that they marched with ten brass fieldpieces, and that every man of the party was armed with a rifle, a bowie-knife, and a brace of large revolving pistols. It was declared that they were inveterately hostile to the emigrant parties; and when the latter came up to the Mormons, they intended to attack and murder them, and appropriate to themselves their property. Another rumor was, that the Kansas Indians had collected in large numbers on the trail, for the purpose of robbery and murder. A third was, that a party of five Englishmen, supposed to be emis-saries of their government, had started in advance of us, bound for Oregon; and that their object was to stir up the Indian tribes along the route, and incite them to deeds of hostility towards the emigrants; to attack their trains, rob, murder, and annihilate them. All these reports were sufficiently appalling to deter prudent men from incurring the dangers which they suggested, had there been any foundation for them to rest upon. Similar rumors will probably be current every year, about the time that emigrants are organizing their companies to start west.

Among the gentlemen who honored us with their company during the day, were—Mr. WEBB, editor of the "Independence Expositor," to whom I was indebted for several acts of kindness; Mr. LIPPINCOTT, a gentleman from New York, visiting California for commercial purposes; and Mr. CURRY, late one of the editors of the "St. Louis Reveille," who will be our fellow-traveller over the plains and mountains. Many tales of Rocky Mountain adventure, some of which were sufficiently dismal and tragical for the most horror-tinctured taste, others contrasting as widely therefrom as possible, were related. The merits of the countries bordering the Pacific were discussed : by some they were denounced as abodes suitable only for the condemned and abandoned of God and man; by others they were extolled, as being scarcely inferior in their attractions to the Eden described in the history of the creation, and presenting such fascinations as almost to call the angels and saints from their blissful gardens and diamond temples in the heavens. Such are the antipodes of opinion among those who rely upon second-hand testimony for their information, or are governed by their prejudices, in reference to this subject.

A story was told in regard to the climate of California, which, because it serves to illustrate the extravagances above referred to, I will endeavor to recite. It was of a man who had lived in California, until he had reached the advanced age of two hundred and fifty years! Although that number of years had passed over him, such were the life-giving and youth-preserving qualities of the climate, that he was in the perfect enjoyment of his health, and every faculty of mind and body which he had ever possessed. But he was tired of life. Having lived so long in a turbulent and unquiet world, he anxiously desired some

new state of existence, unincumbered with its cares, and unruf-
fled by its passions and its strifes. But notwithstanding all his
efforts to produce a result which he so much wished, and for
which he daily and hourly prayed to his Maker, health, and
vigor, and life still clung to him—he could not shake them off.
He sometimes contemplated suicide ; but the holy *padres*, to
whom he confessed his thoughts, admonished him that that
was damnation : he was a devout Christian, and would not
disobey their injunctions. A lay friend, however, (his *heir*,
probably,) with whom he daily consulted on this subject, at
last advised him to a course which, he thought, would produce
the desired result. It was to make his will, and other arrangements, and then travel into a foreign country. This suggestion
was pleasing to our venerable Californian patriarch in search of
death, and he immediately adopted it. He visited an adjoining
country ; and very soon, in accordance with his plan and his
wishes, he took sick and died. In his will, however, he required
his heir and executor, upon pain of disinheritance, to transport
his remains to his own country and there entomb them. This
requisition was faithfully complied with. His body was interred
with great pomp and ceremony in his own cemetery, and prayers
were rehearsed in all the churches for the rest of his soul. He
was happy, it was supposed, in heaven, where, for a long series
of years, he had prayed to be ; and his heir was happy that he
was there. But what a disappointment ! Being brought back
and interred in Californian soil, with the health-breathing Californian zephyrs rustling over his grave, the energies of life
were immediately restored to his inanimate corpse ! Herculean
strength was imparted to his frame, and bursting the prison-
walls of death, he appeared before his chapfallen heir reinvested
with all the vigor and beauty of early manhood ! He submitted
to his fate, and determined to live his appointed time. Stories
similar to the foregoing, although absurd, and so intended to
be, no doubt leave their impressions upon the minds of many,
predisposed to rove in search of adventures and Eldorados.

A party of gentlemen from Baltimore, bound for Santa Fé
on a pleasure excursion, among whom were Messrs. Hoffman,

2*

Morris, and Meredith, arrived. The small town seemed to be literally overflowing with strangers of every grade of character and condition of life, collected from all parts of the continents of America and Europe, civilized and uncivilized. On the 4th our additional purchases were made and other arrangements completed, with the exception of some fixtures to our wagon, with duplicate axletrees, ox-bows, &c. &c., which were promised to be in readiness the next morning. From the 5th, therefore, I shall date the commencement of our journey, describing as minutely as will be interesting or useful the events and observations of each day consecutively, from notes taken at the close of our several diurnal marches.

I bespeak the patience of the reader whenever these pages shall appear to him monotonous, as they doubtless frequently will. My design is to give a *truthful* and not an exaggerated and fanciful account of the occurrences of the journey, and of the scenery, capabilities, and general features of the countries through which we shall pass, with incidental sketches of the leading characteristics of their populations. The journey across the Rocky Mountains to the Pacific, is one of protracted duration, owing to the necessarily slow progress of those who undertake it, arising from the numerous difficulties and obstructions they must encounter. The scenery is neither so diversified, nor are the incident and adventure so dramatic and striking as most readers may suppose, from having perused the many unauthenticated histories, fabulous and imaginary, with which the press has of late teemed, professing to be descriptive of mountain and prairie life. The vast interior of North America, with the reputed Eldorado on the shore of the Pacific, furnishes, however, much that is worthy of the inquiry, examination, and admiration of the naturalist, and much that is calculated to awaken and please the desultory curiosity of the mass. Whatever I saw and noted at the time, with the impressions made upon my mind, will be faithfully and truthfully recorded.

CHAPTER II.

Appearance of the country—Vexatious difficulties of starting—First camp —Violent thunder-storm—Four-footed tragedian—First view of the prairies—Soil—Flowers—Emigrant camp—Frontier family—Thunder-storm on the prairie—Lodgings on the frontier—More of the Mormons—Rainbow on the prairies—Indian Creek—Place of organization—Straying of cattle and horses—Election on the prairies—Shawnee Indians.

MAY 5.—The beauties and glories of spring are now unfolding themselves, and earth and sky seem to vie with each other in presenting the most pleasing influences to the eye and upon the sensibilities. Vegetable nature in this region has arrayed herself in a gorgeous garniture, and every object that raises itself above the surface of the ground, is so adorned with verdure and all the variegated and sparkling array of floral coloring, as to challenge the admiration of the most unobservant eye.

Our wagon, which has been in the hands of the smith several days for the purpose of adapting it in all respects to our journey, we expected would be ready early this morning; but when I went to the shop to ascertain if the alterations and fixtures were completed, I found but little done. The smith made his excuses as usual in such cases, but promised to go about the work and finish it immediately. I had learned how to value his promises, and determined not to leave the spot until I saw the work finished. This was done about three o'clock, P. M. Our ox-team, which had been kept in readiness for several hours, was immediately attached to the wagon, and our luggage placed in it with all dispatch, and at four o'clock the wagon and team, under the guidance of Brownell the driver, left the town. Business detaining me a short time, I did not overtake the wagon, until it had "rolled," as the teamster's expression is, about a mile from its starting-point, where I found it firmly and immoveably stalled in the mud, so far as the power of our team could be considered an agent for its extrication. The oxen being untutored and unmanageable, could not be prevailed upon to unite their strength. I dismounted from my horse, and with the aid of Curry, McKinstry, and Nuttall, endeavored to raise the wheels and thus assist the oxen in their efforts. But all our exertions were vain. Fortunately a negro man with a well-trained yoke of oxen came down the road, while we were thus engaged, and hitching his team to ours the wagon was immediately drawn out of the mud, and, to use a nautical expression, we were "set afloat" again.

Proceeding a mile farther, I determined to encamp for the night, it being nearly sunset, on a small stream which crossed the road. Having selected the site of our camp in a grove near a log-house, the wagon, driven by Brownell, soon came up, but in attempting to cross a causeway thrown over the stream, the wheels ran off on one side, and we were stalled a second time. We were relieved finally from this difficulty by a Santa Fé teamster and his oxen, who came down the road during our labors to extricate the wagon. A Mr. Ross, of Independence, passing at the time, acted as master-teamster on the occasion, and performed his duty to admiration. The oxen seemed willing to obey him, when they would not heed the commands of others. We ascended a small elevation and encamped for the night.

Our provisions and cooking utensils, in the haste of departure, had been packed in the wagon without much regard to convenience, in case we should be obliged to make use of them ; and we were consequently compelled to remove many heavy boxes and trunks before arriving at our meal, flour, and bacon, and the pans and dishes of our kitchen and table. Upon a careful inspection, we moreover found that sundry pots, skillets, and frying-pans, which we had specially ordered and paid for, were wanting.

During the process of cooking supper, it commenced raining and blowing with great violence. Our fire was nearly extinguished by the deluge of water from the clouds, and our *dough* was almost turned to *batter*. Curry, after most persevering and praiseworthy efforts, succeeded in browning the coffee, but Jacob, when he set about grinding it, could not make the coffee-mill perform its appropriate duty, and it was voted a cheat. The rain came down so copiously at last, that our fire was entirely extinguished, and our culinary operations were suspended until nearly 10 o'clock. The violence of the storm abated at that hour. Brownell soon after succeeded in placing before us a supper of half-baked corn-bread, fried bacon, and coffee. We ate standing, with the rain falling, and our clothing completely saturated with water.

Our oxen become entangled in the ropes by which we had secured them from straying during the night, and it was not without much labor and difficulty that they were released. Jacob and myself made our bed, or rather took shelter from the storm, among the boxes in our wagon; McKinstry and Brownell bivouacked under the wagon, and Curry and Nuttall under a large tree. The suspension of the fury of the storm lasted until about 2 o'clock in the morning, when the rain recommenced falling in torrents, accompanied by peals of crashing thunder and flashes of lightning so brilliant, as to illuminate the whole vault of the heavens. Notwithstanding all these inconveniences, we rested pretty well. Distance two miles.

May 6.—The atmosphere was clear and calm, and thousands of birds were chanting their matin hymn, rendering the grove musical with their melodies.

Three Santa Fé wagons which passed our camp last night during the storm, were stalled in the road just beyond us. We purchased some corn for our oxen at the log-dwelling near by, which they devoured with a good appetite, having eaten nothing for about eighteen hours. Our breakfast, which consisted of badly-baked corn-bread, bacon, and coffee, being over, we readjusted the baggage and resumed our journey. Just as we were starting, one of our best oxen having become entangled in the rope by which he was tied, was thrown to the ground with great force, and after struggling some time he rolled up his eyes, which became fixed, and he manifested all the symptoms of

death by a broken neck, or some other fatal injury.   The rope
was cut, but he was motionless and apparently breathless.
Here, as we supposed, was a disaster, stopping further progress
until we could supply the place of the dead ox.   I was about
starting back to town to purchase another animal, when he
very calmly and deliberately rose upon his legs, and began to
feed upon the corn as composedly as if nothing had occurred.
He evidently, after struggling with the rope a long time, thought
himself dying, and made signs accordingly.

As we approached what is called the Blue Prairie, the road
became much drier and less difficult.   The vast prairie itself
soon opened before us in all its grandeur and beauty.   I had
never before beheld extensive scenery of this kind.   The many
descriptions of the prairies of the west had forestalled in some
measure the first impressions produced by the magnificent landscape that lay spread out before me as far as the eye could
reach, bounded alone by the blue wall of the sky.   No description, however, which I have read of these scenes, or which
can be written, can convey more than a faint impression to the
imagination of their effects upon the eye.   The view of the
illimitable succession of green undulations and flowery slopes,
of every gentle and graceful configuration, stretching away and
away, until they fade from the sight in the dim distance, cre-
ates a wild and scarcely controllable ecstasy of admiration.   I
felt, I doubt not, some of the emotions natural to the abo-
riginal inhabitants of these boundless and picturesque plains,
when roving with unrestrained freedom over them ; and careless alike of the past and the future, luxuriating in the blooming wilderness of sweets which the Great Spirit had created for
their enjoyment, and placed at their disposal.

The soil of these prairies is of the most inexhaustibly fertile
composition, being a black loam, usually several feet in depth.
Among the flowers which spangle the waves of this ocean of
luxuriant vegetation, were the wild pink-verbena, and the wild
indigo, with a blue bean-like blossom.   The larkspur, and myriads of smaller flowers, ornament the velvety carpet of grass.
Having alighted from my horse to gather some fine specimens

of these flowers, when I was carelessly remounting, encumbered with my gun and several other articles, the saddle turned, and my horse becoming restive or alarmed, threw me with great violence to the ground. My wrist and both shoulders were much injured, and my right side was severely bruised.

At two o'clock we reached an encampment, composed of the wagons of Colonel Russell and the family of Mr. West, of Calloway county, Mo., and some others. They were emigrating to California. The wagons numbered in all about fifteen. When our wagon arrived it was drawn up alongside the others, and our oxen released to feed upon the grass of the prairie. I visited the tents of our fellow-travellers, and found the ladies busily employed, as if sitting by the fireside which they had recently left for a long and toilsome, if not a dangerous journey, and a country of which they knew but little. Mrs. West, a lady of seventy, and her daughter, Mrs. Campbell, were knitting. Mr. West, the head of his family, was originally from Virginia, and was, he told me, seventy five years of age. His four sons and son-in-law, Major Campbell, having determined to emigrate to California, he and his wife had resolved to accompany them. Mr. and Mrs. W., although so much advanced in life, appeared to be as resolute as the youngest of their family, and to count with certainty upon seeing the Eldorado of the Pacific. The former realized this expectation, the latter did not.

A log-house, the residence of a Mr. Milliron, an emigrant to this country from Virginia, was situated about half a mile from our encampment. We visited this house soon after we encamped. The family, consisting of Mr. and Mrs. M. and several sons and daughters, have resided here, on the outskirts of civilization, four years. They have annually been afflicted with the prevailing sickness of the country, (the fever and ague,) except their eldest daughter, a very fair-skinned, handsomely-featured and graceful young woman. In a field not far from the house, one of the sons of Mr. M., with a horse-team, was plowing up the ground. I followed the plow several times backwards and forwards, and I never saw a soil indicative of a higher degree of fatness, or more productive qualities.

About five o'clock, P. M., a very black and threatening cloud, which had been gathering for some hours in the west, rose over us, and discharged rain with the copiousness of a water-spout, accompanied with brilliant and incessant flashes of lightning, and crashing peals of thunder. The scene, during the violence of the storm, was inexpressibly grand. I had never previously witnessed any meteoric displays comparable with it. The storm continuing after dark, we determined to shelter ourselves in the house for the night.

A good supper of fried bacon, eggs, fresh butter, and hot corn-bread and biscuit, with a cup of coffee, was prepared for us, to the merits of which we did ample justice. I met at the supper-table a traveller named O'Bryant. He was a young man, and last from Santa Fé, bound for Independence. He had been absent from the United States six years, during which time, impelled by the spirit of adventure and the temptations of gain, he had visited Santa Fé, Chihuahua, Mexico, the mines of Sonora, and the country of Lower California. He could, however, give us no information respecting the route we were about to travel.

The capacity of the log-house in which we had taken lodgings for the night, was confined to two small rooms; and of men, women, and children, all counted, there were some fifteen persons to be accommodated. But this, singular as it may seem to the uninitiated in frontier life, was done to the perfect satisfaction and comfort of all concerned. Such are the inventions of necessity, and so soon do our real wants and comforts overshadow and annihilate the artificial desires and luxuries of civilization to which we have been accustomed. I retired early, but the feverish and painful sensations produced by the injuries of the morning, together with the exciting impressions upon my imagination made by the remarkable aspect of the country through which we had travelled, prevented sleep. We were now on the line which divides savage life and civilization. A few miles further, and we shall pass beyond the incorporated territories of the United States into the countries inhabited by the untutored tribes of the wilderness. But notwithstanding such is our position, the scenery around us presents greater pastoral charms than I have witnessed in the oldest and most densely populated districts of the United States; houses alone are wanting to render the landscape perfect. It would seem as if in mockery of the puny efforts and circumscribed results of the labors of man to ornament the landscape by art and cultivation, the power and taste of Omnipotence had here been manifested, preparing for his children a garden as illimitable in extent as it is perfect, grand, and picturesque in appearance. Distance 10 miles.

May 7.—A rainbow formed a perfect and brilliant arch in the west, as the sun rose above the eastern horizon. A black curtain of clouds shaded the entire heavens, with the exception of a narrow fringe of yellow light above the far-off green undulations to the east. The impending masses of watery vapor soon, however, shut down, and closing this, the whole heavens were shrouded in deep gloom.

The rain fell almost incessantly during the night, accompanied by loud and continual peals of thunder, and flashes of lightning so vivid as to illuminate the apartment in which we slept, through the unchinked crevices between the logs. During these fierce bursts of the storm, I could not but sympathize with my fellow-travellers without, with no shelter but the thin covering of their tent-cloths, and no floor to rest upon but the wet, cold ground. Such are the exposures of the western emigrants.

We resumed our march in the rain, at 9 o'clock, accompanied by Colonel Russell and his wagon, leaving the other wagons encamped where we found them. We travelled about four miles to a small creek which is called "Blue Creek," and finding the waters so much swollen by the late heavy rains, that it was not fordable, we encamped in a narrow, timbered bottom, a hundred yards from the stream. About twelve o'clock the dark masses of clouds which had obscured the heavens, and poured out upon the earth such floods of water, cleared away, and the sun shone out warm and bright. We took advantage of this interregnum in the water dynasty to dry our drenched

3

clothing.   Large fires were made of the dead and fallen timber
in the bottom, and an excellent dinner of fried bacon and corn-
bread was prepared by our cook.   The severe bruises which I
had received from the accident of yesterday, aggravated by the
inclemency of the weather, were excessively painful, and rendered me quite unfit for travelling.

Ewing, who had been dispatched yesterday to Fort Leavenworth to ascertain the truth of the various rumors respecting
the numbers of the Mormons bound west, their disposition, etc.
etc., came into camp whooping, about 2 o'clock, P. M., with
a man (McClary) riding behind him on his horse.   He brought
a letter from Colonel Kearny, commandant of the fort, the
purport of which was, that a thousand Mormons had crossed the
Missouri river about four weeks since, and that a number about
equal to the foregoing were now crossing at St. Joseph's.
Others, it was reported, were soon to follow, but with proper
circumspection on our part, no difficulties with them need be
apprehended.

The emigrants with whom I have met, express generally
much apprehension in regard to the designs of the Mormons.
Many predict collisions with them and fatal results; and it is
probable that some who have started will turn back in consequence of these apprehensions.

We sounded the creek this evening, but found the depth of
water too great for fording.   We consequently resolved to encamp for the night, and pitched our tent for the first time.
Just before sunset another storm of lightning, thunder, and rain
rose in the west, and passing over us to the east, the most perfect and brilliant rainbow I ever beheld was defined upon the
face of the dark masses of clouds, displaying by a most brilliant
presentation all the colors of the prism.   Distance, four miles.

May 8.—The creek had fallen several feet during the night,
and, much to our gratification, was now fordable.   But our oxen
had strayed away, and it was not until after a long search
through the brushy and timbered bottom of the creek, that they
were found.   These difficulties in respect to cattle are always
experienced at the outset of a journey over the prairies.   At 9

o'clock we resumed our march. Fording the creek, and crossing the timbered bottom of the stream over a very deep and
muddy road, we entered another magnificent prairie beyond the
Missouri line and within the Indian territory. It is impossible
for me to convey to the reader the impressions made upon my
mind by a survey of these measureless undulating plains, with
their ground of the freshest verdure, and their garniture of
flame-like flowers, decorating every slope and hill-top. It
would seem as if here the Almighty had erected a finished
abode for his rational creatures, and ornamented it with beauties of landscape and exuberance and variety of production far
above our feeble conceptions or efforts at imitation.

Our cow, which we found it impossible to drive before us,
we secured by a rope attached to her head, and tied to the rear
of the wagon. In the course of the day she became entirely
exhausted by her own intractability, and fell down in the road.
We were compelled to leave her, and forego the luxury of milk
on our journey. Some distance to the right of our trail, about
two o'clock, p. m., we saw an encampment of several emigrant
wagons. Colonel Russell and myself proceeded to them.
Composing a portion of this party, were Mr. and Mrs. Newton,
recently from Virginia, and bound for California. Mrs. N. is a
lady of good appearance and manners, and of cultivated taste.
We dined with Mr. and Mrs. N. ; and although our dinner was
not set out in the style of the St. Charles, the Galt House, or
the Astor House, nor the viands so various, I certainly enjoyed
it more than I ever did a repast at either of those celebrated
places of luxury and resort.

Pursuing our journey, after dinner, we overtook ten emigrant
wagons, with a numerous drove of cows and other stock. Most
of these wagons are the property of Mr. Gordon, of Missouri,
who, with his entire family, consisting of several sons and
daughters, is removing to California. After some conversation
we passed them, and overtook our own wagons just as they
were driving up to the encampment on Indian Creek, where
the organization for our journey is to take place. The position
of this encampment is highly picturesque. The margin of the

small stream is fringed with a grove of timber, and from the gentle slope, where our wagons are drawn up, the verdant prairie, brilliant with flowers of every dye, stretches far away on all sides, diversified in its surface by every conceivable variety of undulation.

We found two wagons encamped here, one of which belonged to Mr. Grayson, of St. Louis. Mrs. G., an intelligent and cultivated lady, with a small child, accompanies her husband to the shores of the Pacific. A party from Michigan, under the direction of Mr. Harlan, we learned, was encamped in a grove of timber about a mile beyond us. They left Michigan in October last, and wintered near Lexington, Mo. From thence, this spring, by land, they had proceeded thus far on their journey to the Pacific. I visited them in the afternoon; and, as usual among the emigrants, found them cordial and friendly in their salutations. They had been in their present encampment more than a month, but appeared to be contented and happy, and, with the numerous women and children, who greatly outnumber the men, to possess a persevering energy and confidence in the future, that would sustain them in a journey round the globe, whatever might be its difficulties.

Returning to our camp, and accompanied by Curry and Nuttall, I walked some distance down the creek to try my luck at angling. The aggregate result of two hours' patient toil, was about fifteen small fish, with which we returned to camp. They were cooked in the pan, and our appetites were such that we enjoyed them with a relish unknown to the epicure of the "settlements."

Among the flowers and plants which I have noticed to-day, are the verbena and the indigo-plant, in larger quantities and a higher degree of perfection. Also a species of wild geranium, and the rosin-weed, the stalk of the last of which, on being broken, exudes a gum of the consistence and odor of turpentine. The lupin (not in bloom) in many places seems to dispute the occupancy of the soil with the grass. I observed, also, a plant producing a fruit of the size of the walnut, called the prairie-pea. The fruit has an agreeable taste, resembling that of the green pea of our gardens. In a raw state, it is eaten by travellers on the plains to quench thirst. It makes a most excellent pickle, as we afterwards discovered, scarcely inferior to the olive.

I killed a moccasin-snake this afternoon, when returning from our angling excursion down the creek. I had nearly stepped upon him before he was discovered, and from his attitude, he was evidently prepared to strike at me. He was about three feet in length.

The sky, since twelve o'clock, m., has been perfectly clear, and the atmosphere calm. At eight o'clock, p. m., the moon and stars are shining in all their splendor, presenting to the eye a scene of imposing sublimity, and of the most profound solitude. Distance, 16 miles.

May 9.—Immediately after breakfast I commenced the arrangement of our baggage and provisions, so as to render them convenient of access in our wagon. A party which went out in the morning to angle, brought in an abundant supply of small fish about 12 o'clock. Several emigrant wagons have arrived during the day and encamped alongside of us. The wagons at our camp this evening numbered thirty-four. We were visited by Mr. Harlan and a number of his party.

It was proposed to-day, and there was a general concurrence to the proposition, that the party for California should be organized and officered by the free choice of those concerned, on Monday next. Singular as it may appear, there is as much electioneering here for the captaincy of this expedition, as there would be for the generalship of an army, or for the presidency of the United States. The many interests of the ambitious aspirants to office, and the vehemence with which their claims are urged by their respective friends, augur unfavorably to harmony on the journey.

Our camp this evening presents a most cheerful appearance. The prairie, miles around us, is enlivened with groups of cattle, numbering six or seven hundred, feeding upon the fresh green grass. The numerous white tents and wagon-covers before which the camp-fires are blazing brightly, represent a rustic village ; and men, women, and children are talking, playing, and

3*

singing around them with all the glee of light and careless hearts. While I am writing, a party at the lower end of the camp is engaged in singing hymns and sacred songs.

The dew is very heavy, the grass being as wet as if a hard shower had fallen during the night. This diurnal condensation of dampness, and the great difference between the temperature of the day and the night, are doubtless strong agents in producing the prevailing diseases of this country,—the ague and bilious fevers.

Several of the oxen and horses belonging to ourselves and others of the party encamped, strayed away and could not be found this morning. A general hunt to recover this valuable property became necessary, and it proved successful. Emigrants cannot be too watchful of their cattle and horses when first starting upon this journey. They are all more or less disposed to stray and return to the settlements, and frequently they range to such a distance, that they cannot be recovered.

Numerous parties of ladies and gentlemen from the neighboring villages visited our camp in the course of the day, and attended divine service, the exercises of which were performed by the Rev. Mr. Dunleavy of the Methodist Episcopal church, one of the emigrants to California.

Six additional wagons came into our camp in the course of the afternoon, one of which, drawn by mules, belonged to Mr. Lippincott of New York, whom I have already mentioned. The sun, until late in the afternoon, shone with scorching intensity. Just before sunset I took a stroll over the verdant plain to gather flowers for preservation. I strayed to a stone monument erected by an emigrating company, commemorative of their departure for Oregon, on a commanding position of the prairie.

Ex-governor Boggs, of Missouri, who, with his family, designs to emigrate to California, came to our camp this evening, and soon after left, returning to Independence, his residence. He stated that it was impossible for his wagons to come up with us until Thursday.

May 11.—This day had been appointed for the organization of the emigrant company bound for California, the choice of officers, &c. Mr. HARLAN and his party came over, and at nine o'clock, A. M., all the men were assembled in the grove to proceed to business.

EDWIN BRYANT was chosen chairman, and Mr. CURRY appointed secretary of the meeting. Mr. Harlan, after the organization of the meeting, moved a postponement of the election of officers, until the emigrants had passed the Kanzas river. This motion was rejected. Mr. H. then requested leave to withdraw from the meeting, and by a vote his request was granted. He then withdrew, stating, however, before he left, his belief that companies of moderate size would travel with much more convenience and celerity than large companies, and that his party added to those on the ground, he believed, would render the train too unwieldy for convenience and progress. This view was afterwards found to be entirely correct.

Colonel W. H. RUSSELL was then chosen captain of the party encamped around us. A committee was appointed, of which Governor BOGGS was chairman, to draft rules or laws for the government of the party during their journey. They reported in the afternoon, and it was further resolved that we should recommence our journey in the morning. A guard was set over our cattle to-night, for the first time, to prevent them from straying.

A male and female of the Shawnee Indian tribe came into our camp this afternoon. Their age apparently was about fifty. They were mounted on ponies, and the female rode sidewise on the saddle. They were dressed in the costume of the whites of the frontier. They were very taciturn, and soon left us.

CHAPTER III.

MAY 12.—All the wagons and teams were this morning inspected by a committee appointed for that purpose. It appeared from their report that the number of wagons belonging to the company was 63; of men 119; of women 59; of children, male and female, 110; pounds of breadstuffs 58,484; of bacon 38,080; of powder 1,065; of lead 2,557; number of guns, mostly rifles, 144; pistols 94. The number of cattle was not reported, but I estimate it at 700, including the loose stock, and 150 horses.

The scene of "catching up," as the yoking and attaching of the oxen to the wagons is called in emigrant phraseology, is one of great bustle and confusion. The crack of the ox-goad, the "whoa-haws" in a loud voice, the leaping and running about of the oxen to avoid the yoke, and the bellowing of the loose stock, altogether create a most Babel-like and exciting confusion. The wagons commenced moving at nine o'clock, and at ten the camp was entirely deserted. In consequence of there being no order of march to-day, the train of wagons was strung out two or three miles in length. The views of this long procession, occasionally sinking into the depressions of the prairie, and then rising therefrom and winding along the curves of

the ridges to avoid the wet and soft ground, were highly picturesque.

Our journey has been over a prairie entirely destitute of
timber, or shrubbery of any kind. The soil is generally composed of a black argillaceous loam, several feet in depth. The
summits of the highest elevations exhibit a more sandy composition of soil, with a debris of flint and porous sandstone. The
grouse, or prairie-hens, have been frequently flushed during our
march. Smaller birds are not very numerous. The heat of the
sun has been extremely oppressive.

At one o'clock, P. M., we reached a small grove, composed of
a few oaks, cotton-wood, maple, and hickory trees, on the banks
of a small branch, (head of Blue Creek,) where we encamped
for the day. The wagons, in forming the encampment, were
what is called *corraled*, an anglicised Spanish word, the significance of which, in our use of the term, is, that they were formed
in a circle; constituting a wall of defence in the event of an
attack from the Indians, and a *pound* for the confinement of the
cattle and horses, whenever necessary or desirable. A Spanish
corral is a common cattle or horse pound. The area of this
circle is sufficiently large to graze, during the night, such horses
and cattle as are most likely to stray, if not thus confined. On
the outside of the *corral* the tents are pitched, with their doors
outwards; and in front of these the camp-fires are lighted, and
the culinary operations for the several families, or messes, performed.

This afternoon the company was divided into four sections,
and a leader for each was appointed, to superintend their order
of march. Several subordinate or staff officers were appointed,
as assistants to the captain, etc., etc. Regular guard-duty was
established, and our organization, theoretically, appeared to be
very perfect, and entirely sufficient for all the purposes required
of it. Distance, six miles.

May 13.—Brownell, our driver, having left camp last night,
to ride a distance of ten or twelve miles on some business, did
not return until after we had commenced our march. It was
not without great trouble that we collected our oxen, and suc-

ceeded in attaching them to the wagons. Nuttall volunteered
to act as driver *pro tem.* for the day, or until Brownell returned.

Our march was along the Santa Fé trail, through an undulating prairie-country, occasionally dotted with a few trees and
clumps of small hazel-bushes. But generally there was no
object for the eye to rest upon but the green and flowery slopes
and gentle and ever-varying irregularities in the surface of the
prairie. About one o'clock we passed what is called the "Lone
Elm," a solitary tree, standing near a pool of water.

I met, this afternoon, three returning Santa Fé trading-com-
panies; two of them with three or four wagons, and the other
with twelve wagons, all drawn by mules. They were driving
before them several large herds of mules, in the aggregate about
one thousand. The mules were so lean that the ribs of most
of them were defined with precision, and the bones of some of
them appeared to have worn through the flesh. I never saw a
more ghostly collection of animals. The operative men composing these companies were principally New-Mexicans; the
chiefs of the parties, however, were Americans. They all presented a most fagged and worn appearance.

I stopped and conversed some time with one of the leading
men of these companies. He was intelligent, notwithstanding
his soiled and ragged costume, and appeared to be very candid
in all his statements. He said that the principal part of the
mules had been driven from Chihuahua, and cost there twenty
dollars per head; that they were taken in exchange for such
commodities as had been carried out with them, and he expected to dispose of them at a profit on his arrival in the
settlements of Missouri. He said that the journey to Santa Fé
and Chihuahua was one of great fatigue and hardship, as he
knew, but that the journey to California was infinitely more so;
that our lives would be shortened ten years by the trip, and
before we returned, if we experienced such good fortune, our
heads would be white, not with the frosts of age, but from the
effects of exposure and extreme hardships. This was not very
cheering information, and bidding him a polite good-day, we
left him.

About 4 o'clock, P. M., I reached the point where I supposed the Oregon trail diverged from the Santa Fé road. It was raining copiously. At some distance in the prairie, I saw a man mounted on a horse, with a loose mule feeding near him. Supposing him to be a member of some of the front emigrating parties, I rode up to him and inquired the probable distance to the next camping-ground. He was a man of that non-committal order sometimes met with, from whom no satisfactory or explanatory information can be drawn by any inquiry, however pointed. He appeared to be afraid of exposing his own ignorance by committing himself in any direct reply; and in a vain effort to seem eminently wise and discreet, his affirmative responses were rebutted by such a volume of negative qualifications and reservations, that he was entirely incomprehensible.

The rain had abated before this unsatisfactory colloquy was ended, and a bright rainbow was formed in the east, the arch of which was not raised more than one degree above the horizon. Our train of wagons coming up, we continued on the Santa Fé trail four miles farther, when we left it on the right hand, and soon afterwards crossing a small creek with high and steep banks, we encamped on the western side of it, in a small grove which fringes the margin of the stream. Large quantities of wild onions were gathered by many of our party to-day, and being cooked with their bacon, composed the vegetable portion of their evening meal. Their odor is rank, and any thing but agreeable. The rain recommenced falling before we could pitch our tent, heavily and steadily, with every prospect of a stormy night. Distance 16 miles.

May 14.—The rain of yesterday and last night has again so much saturated and softened the ground, as to render travelling with wheels very difficult.

The first mile and a half of our route was through the timbered bottom of the branch on which we had encamped. Our progress through this was very greatly obstructed by the unevenness of the ground and its soft and miry condition. We were frequently obliged to fell trees and to cut down large quantities of small brush and throw them into the muddy ravines, in order to enable our animals and wagons to pass over them. These difficulties operate as serious discouragements upon the energies of mai y, but I look for a better road before we advance a great distance. Throughout the day the travelling has been very fatiguing to our oxen, the wagons frequently stalling in the mud-holes and the *crossings* of the small branches. Three or four hours were occupied in fording a diminutive tributary of the Wakarusa creek. The banks on the eastern side are so steep, that the wagons were let down with ropes, and the teams were doubled, sometimes quadrupled, in order to draw them up on the other side.

The largest portion of our train reached the banks of the Wakarusa about 5 o'clock, and encamped on a sloping lawn in a curve of the stream, carpeted with verdant and luxuriant grass. A grove of small trees (oak, hickory, dogwood, and willows) nearly surrounds our camp. Their foliage is of the deepest green, and flowers of all the brilliant, and the softer and more modest hues, enliven the landscape around us. The face of the country over which we have travelled to-day, has been more broken and picturesque than yesterday. We passed during our march an elevated conical swell of the plain, which I ascended ; and the view from it was one of commanding extent and great richness and beauty. The configuration of the vast diameter of the plain which can be observed from this, presents all the graceful and gentle curves, and the delicate shading and coloring that would charm the enthusiastic landscape artist in his dreaming sketches.

A number of wagons being behind at dark, a party was formed and returned on the trail to their assistance. We found two or three of the wagons stalled in the deep mud, and the tongue of one of them, belonging to some highly worthy young men from Lexington, Ky., named Putnam, was broken. After great exertions they were all drawn out and up to the camp, but it was near midnight before this was accomplished. Distance 15 miles.

May 15.—-A Potawattomie Indian, accompanied by a half-breed who spoke English correctly, came to our camp early this morning. The Potawattomie was a tall, athletic young man of a symmetrical figure, and rode a fat and handsome Indian pony, which several of our party made overtures to purchase, but they were not successful. He was dressed in a calico shirt, with buckskin pantaloons, gaiters, and moccasins. He brought with him several pairs of moccasins, some of them second-hand, which he wished to trade for meat. He soon sold out his small stock of wares and left us. The morning was spent in cleaning our rifles and pistols, which had become rusty and foul from the frequent rains.

In the afternoon we were joined by Ex-governor Boggs, of Missouri, and Colonel Thornton and another gentleman from Illinois. The general reason assigned for emigration to the Pacific, by those from the frontier settlements of Illinois and Missouri, is the extreme unhealthiness of those districts. They state that during the summer and autumnal months they are afflicted with the ague and fever; and of late years, in the winter season, the congestive fever prevails, and sometimes it is so fatal in its ravages as nearly to depopulate whole neighborhoods. They emigrate to the Pacific in search of health, and if they can find this with a reasonable fertility of soil on their arrival, they will not only be satisfied but feel thankful to Providence for providing them such a retreat from the miseries they have endured.

In the afternoon we crossed the Wakarusa creek, and encamped on the opposite bank in a grove of large timber. Several Shawnee Indians came to our camp in the evening; one of whom, calling himself John Wolf, spoke English. They begged for whiskey. Distance 1 mile.

May 16.—Several Potawattomie Indians, male and female, visited our camp this morning. None of them spoke English. They could, however, pronounce the word " whiskey," and uttering this and at the same time exhibiting small pieces of silver, was the common salutation of these miserably-clad, half-starved creatures. They excited mingled emotions of loathing and commiseration. John Wolf, the Shawnee, whose acquaintance I made yesterday, applied to me to indite for him a letter, and

4

to carry it westward to some gi :at Indian captain of his tribe. The letter, written from his detation, was only four lines in length. It informed his friend that two Shawnee chiefs, named Henry Clay and Ben Kiasas, and a sister of the Indian addressed, named Black Poddee, were dead. I folded, sealed, and superscribed the letter, but I could never hear of the friend of John Wolf, and consequently the brief epistle was never delivered.

The grove in which we were encamped presented, this morning, a most noisy and animated scene. The oxen belonging to our teams, and in daily use, now number about seven hundred; and the mules, horses, and other loose animals, amount to three hundred, numbering, in the aggregate, one thousand head of cattle and horses. "Gee-up!" "gee-haw!" and "whoahaw!" with incessant cracks of the whip, resounded on all sides, as soon as the word to "catch up" was given. As usual, a portion of the cattle could not be found when wanted, notwithstanding a guard had been placed over them during the night; and it was ten o'clock, A. M., before the rear division of the train left the encampment.

Our route, with the exception of the low rich bottom of the Wakarusa, has been over the high rolling prairie. In the far distance we could see the narrow dark lines of timber, indicating the channels of the small water-courses, stretching far away, until lost in the haze, or concealed from our view by the interposition of the horizon. Some of the slopes of the plain, in the perspective, were beautifully ornamented with clumps and rows of trees, representing the parks, avenues, and pleasure grounds of some princely mansion, which the imagination was continually conjecturing might be hidden behind their dense foliage. Not a living or moving object of any kind appears upon the face of the vast expanse. The white-topped wagons, and the men and animals belonging to them, winding slowly over the hill-tops and through the hollows, are the only relief to the motionless torpor and tomblike stillness of the landscape. A lovelier scene was never gazed upon, nor one of more profound solitude.

A short time before we encamped, this afternoon, a small party of Indians were seen in a hollow about a mile to our right.

We rode to them. and ascertained them to be Kachinga, a chief of the Kansas tribe, two warriors, and two squaws, with their families of children. They were here encamped, their tents being smoke-colored skins sewn together, and raised on small sticks, about two feet from the ground. Kachinga carried a rifle, which appeared to be new. He did not seem to understand very well the use of it. He was rouged with vermilion paint, and his hair was shorn to the skin, except a small tuft on the crown of his head, and under his chin. He wore, suspended by a buckskin string from his neck, two medals, one representing, in *alto relievo*, the likeness of Thomas Jefferson, President of the United States. The other medal, the device on which I do not recollect, purported, from the inscription, to have been presented to him by a citizen of Hartford, Ct.,—evidently a "Yankee notion." Kachinga appeared to be a man of about sixty, and the expression of his countenance and his general appearance were prepossessing. The two squaws were miserable-looking objects in their features, figures, and clothing. The Indians broke up their encampment when we left them, and soon overtaking our train, travelled along with us. The two squaws had each a pony, heavily laden with baggage. The children were in a state of nudity, and the infants were carried by their mothers, being fastened to their backs by closely-drawn blankets. They came around us while eating supper, and begged something to eat, which we gave them. Their appearance was extremely wretched.

We were overtaken to-day, during our march, by a man belonging to one of the forward trains, but who left the settlements since we did. He brought with him a late number of the "St. Louis Republican," from the columns of which we derived intelligence of the first overt acts of hostility between Mexico and the United States. The paper contained an account of the defeat and capture of a company of dragoons on the Rio Grande, under the command of Captain Thornton, by the Mexicans, and also of the supposed critical situation of the United States troops composing the command of General Z. Taylor. Notwithstanding this warlike demonstration, none of the emigrants to California, so far as I could learn, manifested a disposition to turn back in consequence of it.

That discordance, arising from many trifling circumstances and unavoidable inconveniences, which I had heard mentioned as inevitable concomitants of this journey, was displayed in several instances to-day. Many of the men manifested much petulance, incivility, and the want of a spirit of accommodation. In short, there appears to be considerable wrangling and intrigue in camp, which will probably result in a division of our party. Distance, 12 miles.

May 17.—The morning was so delightful and the atmosphere so bracing, that I started on foot in advance of the train ; and noticing on the right some attractive objects at a distance of two or three miles, I left the trail, and proceeding towards them, passed over two or three elevated swells of the prairie and through several deep and lonely hollows. In one of the latter I saw two horses grazing. My first conjecture, seeing no signs of emigrants or Indians about, was, that these horses had strayed either from our own camp or from some of the forward emigrating parties, and I attempted to drive them before me ; but they were not to be controlled, running off in a contrary direction, prancing and snorting.

In the next hollow, through which flows a small spring branch, I saw the embers of an Indian camp-fire, with the low, rude frame upon which their tent-skins had been spread surrounding it. I stirred the ashes and discovered a few live coals, showing that the camp had been occupied last night. The diminutive bottom bordering the miniature stream was covered with hazel brush, with a few alders and larger shrubbery. I crossed through the brush, and was commencing the ascent on the other side, when six Indians, mounted on horses, came in sight on the top of the hill, and began to descend it. They did not discover me immediately, but as soon as they did, they halted on the side of the hill. I was sufficiently near to see that one of them carried in his hand a broadsword, with a bright metal scabbard, which glittered in the sunbeams. This Indian, the foremost of the party, was leading a horse. When

4*

he saw me he gave the horse in charge of another. I had very carelessly, in order to be unincumbered by weight, left all my arms in the wagon, except my hatchet. I was now several miles distant from our train and entirely concealed from them, and there was no probability of any of our party passing this way. Not liking the manœuvres of the Indians, or knowing what might be their designs, I never felt more regret for any misadventure, than for not bringing my gun and pistols with me. Ascertaining that my hatchet was in a right position for use, if necessary, I advanced up the hill to the place where the Indians had halted, and stopped.

I ascertained that the party was composed of three men and three squaws. The men were armed with bows and arrows and tomahawks. The leader spoke to me in English, and said, "How do?" I replied and reciprocated the inquiry in the usual manner. He then asked, in his broken English, if there were more white men with me? I replied that there was a great number just behind. He nodded his head and looked at his companions with an expression of disappointed intelligence. I asked him if he was a Kansas? His reply was, "No,—Sac." I then passed, leaving them standing and apparently in earnest consultation.

I was glad to be relieved of their company, for I felt doubtful of their intentions, and my arms were insufficient for a successful defence against them, if they had made an attack,—from which I believe they were deterred by the supposition that my fellow-travellers would immediately be upon them. I rose the hill, and saw, at a distance of about two miles, a man on horseback riding in such a direction across the prairie that I could easily intercept him. I soon came up to him and found it to be Mr. Grayson, one of our own company, out hunting. We walked onward. and came up to the caravan while our party were nooning.

After procuring from our wagon some refreshments, and resting an hour, accompanied by Mr. Curry I again started a pedestrian, in advance of the train of wagons, for a walk of twelve or fifteen miles, the nearest point in our route, to water. The fresh breeze which had fanned us during the forenoon, died away entirely, and the sun shone with an almost scorching fervency of heat, unmitigated by a solitary cloud on the face of the sky. The trail is smooth and hard, running over the high table-land of the prairies. Clumps and rows of timber could be seen at long distances, giving to the background of the scenery a cultivated and inhabited aspect. The effects of the intense heat, aggravated by the severe exercise of fast walking, became intolerably oppressive, and produced a thirst and faintness such as I had not before experienced. We hunted along the roadside for even a puddle of water to moisten our mouths and throats, but could discover none. Finding some prairie peas, we filled our pockets with them, and their juice afforded a little relief to our thirst. At length we arrived within the distance of two miles of a line of timber on the left, indicative of water. Leaving the trail we marched directly towards it, and reaching its banks we found it to be a small creek which empties into the Kansas river, about five miles distant. We satisfied our thirst with long draughts of the tepid water, and then plunged into the current of the stream to cool our almost broiling flesh and purify our bodies from the dust accumulated upon them by the day's march.

Refreshing ourselves, in the manner above described, for an hour, the invigorating effects of which were most salutary, we returned again to the trail, just as the train of wagons was coming up and passing. Many of the oxen were so much exhausted that they could with difficulty move forward at a very slow pace. Their tongues were hanging out, and several had fallen down, being unable to proceed. One had died on the march. The order had been given to encamp on the opposite side of the stream, and several of the front wagons when they reached it attempted to cross; but the oxen, mad with thirst and heat, when they came in sight of the water, became uncontrollable, and ran down the steep bank into the stream, threatening destruction to the wagons and their contents. All efforts to prevail upon them to leave the water and ascend the opposite bank, for a long time, were unavailing. Such being the difficulties, the order was countermanded, and our camp formed on the southeastern bank of the stream.

Near our camp there is a crescent-shaped chain of elevated mounds, the natural undulations of the prairie, which I had plainly seen this morning when we commenced our march. These mounds stretch some four or five miles, and their bases being precipitous and wall-like, but for their extent, in outline they would represent the foundations and the fallen and ruined superstructure of some vast temple or overthrown city.

This evening, after we had encamped, it appeared from a speech delivered by Mr. Dunleavy, that a portion of the company had determined to separate from the main party, being dissatisfied with its present organization. Distance 24 miles.

May 18.—Mr. Jacob, who had been appointed sub-captain of one of our divisions ; Mr. Kirkendall, who had been appointed quartermaster; and Mr. Greenbury, our pilot, were dispatched early this morning to a mission about ten miles distant up the Kansas river, to ascertain if the river was fordable at that point. Colonel Russell, our captain, rode to the Kansas ferry, five miles distant, to ascertain if the ferry-boats were disengaged, and could, if we deemed it expedient to cross here, ferry our wagons over the river.

Although the morning was fine and pleasant, it clouded up before eight o'clock and commenced raining, accompanied by thunder. After considerable labor and difficulty we succeeded in crossing the creek without any accident, except the breaking of an axletree of one of the wagons in descending the steep bank. Colonel Russell met us on the opposite bank, and, some conversation ensuing with the leaders of the disaffected party, it was proposed that the company should divide, it being too numerous and cumbrous for convenient progress. Those who were in favor of remaining with the originally organized company were requested to move towards the ferry. Thirty-five of the wagons moved forward, and the remainder separated from them.

The signs were so strongly indicative of a heavy rain, that it was thought imprudent to delay crossing the Kansas until the

return of the gentlemen dispatched up the river this morning,
but that we should proceed to the ferry and cross forthwith.
The Kansas, at the ferry, which is owned by two half-breed
Indians, is about two hundred yards in width at this time; but
at some seasons of the year, from its banks, it evidently is much
narrower. The approach to it, on either side, is through a
timbered bottom about three-fourths of a mile in width. The
trees are chiefly oak, linden, and hickory. Hazel and a variety
of underbrush and grapevines, make up the small shrubbery
of the bottom.

The labor of ferrying our wagons over was commenced at
one o'clock. The wagons were hauled as near the boat-landing
as they could be by the teams, and then with their loads in
them were lifted and pushed into the boats by the united
strength of the men. By hard and unremitting toil the thirty-
five wagons, which now constituted our train, were safely trans
ported to the other side; and all our oxen, horses, and loose
stock swam over, by six o'clock, P. M. The fee for ferriage,
per wagon, was one dollar. Two boats are employed, and they
are large enough to transport two wagons each trip. They are
pushed across the stream with long poles handled by Indians.
All being over, we moved forward about three miles and encamped on the bank of Soldier Creek, a small stream emptying
into the Kansas.

While on our march from the Kansas to our encampment,
Mr. Branham and myself, being in advance of the main party,
discovered an abundance of ripe strawberries. We stopped
and gathered several quarts, and, carrying them to camp, they
were served up by Mrs. B., with rich cream and loaf-sugar, a
genuine luxury in this wild region.

This morning, before we commenced our march, a Mrs. Hall,
the wife of one of the emigrants, was safely delivered of a pair
of twins. Thus two were added to our number. These young
natives of the wilderness were appropriately named. The
mother and children were doing well this evening.

Mr. Webb, editor of the "Independence Expositor," accompanied by Mr. Hay, a great-grandson of Daniel Boone, arrived

at our camp, direct from the settlements, just after dark. They came express to communicate to us the last intelligence we shall receive from the United States, before reaching the Pacific. They brought with them all the letters at the Independence and Westport post-offices addressed to emigrants, and several files of papers to the latest dates. These gave positive information of the existence of hostilities between Mexico and the United States on the Rio Grande, and confirmed the rumor respecting the perilous situation of Gen. Taylor. How this important event is to affect us upon our arrival in California, it is impossible to foresee. No one, however, is in the least disposed to turn back in consequence of it. Distance 10 miles.

CHAPTER IV.

Methodist Mission on the Kansas—Soldier Creek—Lustration—A ruined Indian town—A rose in the wilderness—Another division—Kansas Indian towns—Ki-he-ga-wa-chuck-ee—Prairie potato—Mountain trappers—Beauty of scenery and fertility of soil—Vermilion Creek—Brilliant meteor—Big Blue River—Prairie-pea—Legislation on the prairies.

MAY 19.—We remained encamped to-day, in order to enable Mr. Boone, a grandson of Daniel Boone, and his family and party, who wish to join us, to come up. Messrs. Kirkendall, Jacob, and Greenbury, reached camp this morning about seven o'clock, relieving me of some uneasiness on their account. They had found a ford, near the mission, about twelve miles up the Kansas; but when they returned to the ferry, finding that our train had all passed over, and it being late, they remained during the night with the party that separated from us this morning. The mission which they had visited, and at which they were well received and entertained, is an establishment for the education and christianization of the Indians, supported in part by the United States government, and under the patronage and superintendence of the Methodist Episcopal Church of the United States. There is a blacksmith's shop at the mission, and an extensive farm under cultivation.

The stream on which we are encamped is called "Soldier Creek," from the circumstance, as I learned, that, some years since a company of traders having smuggled into the Indian territory a quantity of whiskey, were pursued by a detachment of United States soldiers, and overtaken at the spot where our wagons are formed into a *corral*. Their whiskey was taken and emptied into the stream; and the soldiers having encamped here during these proceedings, gave its present name to the creek. The bank of the small rivulet was lined at an early hour after breakfast with fires, kettles, washtubs, and piles of unwashed linen, showing conclusively that a general lustration was to be performed by the female portion of our party. The timber on the creek consists of oak, linden, and some maple trees. They are of good size, and in several places the bends of the stream are well covered with them. I had heard reports of the creek being richly stocked with a variety of fish; but after two trials of several hours each, without a single nibble at my hook, I was compelled to entertain strong doubts of the accuracy of the reports. The whiskey poured into the stream may have poisoned the fish, as it would have done the Indians, had the traders been successful in their designs.

The soil of the Kansas bottom, and where we are encamped, is a rich argillaceous loam, of great depth, and capable of producing any crop adapted to this latitude. The natural grasses grow with great luxuriance, but they are of a coarse species, and when matured must be rather tough, and not very nutritious.

A new census of our party was taken this morning, and it was found to consist of 98 fighting-men, 50 women, 46 wagons, and 350 cattle. Two divisions were made of the wagons, for convenience in marching. We were joined to-day by nine wagons from Illinois, belonging to Mr. Reed and the Messrs. Donner, highly respectable and intelligent gentlemen, with interesting families. They were received into the company by a unanimous vote.

A Kansas Indian village was visible from our camp on the plain to the south, at a distance of two or three miles. As soon as the sun was sufficiently low in the afternoon, accompanied by Jacob, I visited this village. The walk was much longer and more fatiguing than we expected to find it. While on the way we counted, for a certainty, on our arrival, to be received and entertained by the female *élite* of the Kansas aristocracy, clad in their smoke-colored skin costumes, and with their copper complexions rouged until they vied, in their fiery splendors, with the sun, seen through a vapor of smoke. We carried some vermilion and beads along with us for presents, to ornament the most unadorned, in accordance with the taste of the savages. But, alas! after all our toil, through the rank and tangled grass, when we approached the village not a soul came out to welcome us. No Kansas belle or stern chief made her or his appearance at the doors of any of the wigwams. We entered the village, and found it entirely deserted and desolate, and most of the wigwams in a ruinous state.

A large wigwam, or cabin, near the centre of the village, had recently been burnt to the ground. The whole number of the buildings standing was fourteen. They varied in dimensions, from twenty to thirty-six feet in length, by fifteen in breadth. The cabins are constructed by inserting in the ground hickory saplings, and bending them so as to form an arch about eight or ten feet in height at the top. These saplings are bound firmly together by willow twigs, making a strong, though light framework. This frame is shingled over with bark, peeled from the linden and other large trees, in strips of about twelve inches in breadth and five feet in length. Over this is another frame of saplings and willow-withes, securing the roof and walls, and binding the whole building together. Each cabin has one small entrance, about four feet in height, and three feet in breadth. We passed through, and examined four or five of them. The bark-walls, on the inside, were ornamented with numerous charcoal-sketches, representing horses; horses with men mounted upon them, and engaged in combat with the bow and arrow; horses attached to wagons; and, in

one instance, horses drawing a coach. Another group represented a plow, drawn by oxen.   There were various other
figures of beasts and reptiles, and some which I conjectured to
be the Evil Spirit of the Indian mythology.   But they were all
done in a style so rude, as to show no great progress in the fine
arts.   None of the cabins which we entered contained a solitary
article of any kind.   I returned to our camp, disappointed in
my expectations of meeting the Indians at their village, and
saddened by the scene of desolation I had witnessed.

In reference to the present number of the Kansas tribe of
Indians, I could obtain little satisfactory information.   They
appear to be wretchedly poor.   The country they claim as
theirs, and inhabit, affords little or no game ; and so far as my
observation has extended, they give no attention to agriculture.
The number of warriors which the tribe can assemble, I heard
estimated at three hundred ; but I have no means of judging of
the accuracy of this estimate.

May 20.—Our driver was helplessly sick this morning from
the effects of an over-night's drunken frolic, upon some wretched,
adulterated whiskey which he had procured somewhere in the
camp.   We were compelled to employ a new driver for the day,
and to haul our old one in the wagon.

We travelled several miles over a flat plain, in some places
wet and boggy.   The Kansas river skirted with timber, with a
rich and extensive landscape beyond, could be seen on our left ;
and on our right Soldier Creek, with scenery equally attractive.

I saw near the trail this morning, a solitary wild rose, the first
I have seen blooming in the prairies, the delightful fragrance of
which instantly excited emotions of sadness and tenderness, by
reviving in the memory a thousand associations connected with
home, and friends, and civilization, all of which we had left
behind, for a weary journey through a desolate wilderness.   It
is not possible to describe the effect upon the sensibilities produced by this modest and lonely flower.   The perfume exhaled
from its petals and enriching the " desert air," addressed a
language to the heart more thrilling than the plaintive and im-
passioned accents from the inspired voice of music or poesy.

We encamped at 3 o'clock, P. M., in a heavy rain, accompanied by thunder and lightning, which had been pouring down upon us three hours. Our camp is on the high ground of the prairies, a mile from wood and water, which necessary articles have to be hauled to it in the rain and through the deep mud.

The Indians have, thus far, made no attempts to steal our cattle. They generally keep a respectful distance, showing themselves in small numbers on the summits of the prairie, adjacent to the route of our train. I watched to-night until one o'clock. The howls and sharp snarling barks of the wolves; the mournful hootings of the owl, and the rush of the winds through the tree-tops of the neighboring grove, are the only sounds disturbing the deep solitude of the night. Distance eight miles.

May 21.—The views from the high elevations of the prairie, have, as usual, been strikingly picturesque. The country we have passed through for the last one hundred miles, presents greater attractions to the eye than any that I have ever previously seen. What the climate may be in winter, or how it may effect the health of settlers in summer and autumn, I have no means of judging. Its elevated and undulating surface, however, would seem to indicate salubrity.

About noon we arrived at another small creek, the banks of which on both sides are steep, and very difficult to pass. Our wagons were lowered down by ropes, and by doubling teams, they were all finally drawn out of the bed of the stream, and up the opposite bank. It was four o'clock when this was accomplished. We encamped in a bend of the stream, about a mile from where we crossed it.

The day has been delightful, and a more cheerful spirit seems to prevail in our party than usual. Mr. Boone, whom we have been expecting several days, came up and joined us this afternoon. The men amused themselves, after we encamped, by firing at a target. The distances were 80 and 200 yards. Among the best shots, with the rifle, were those of Brown of Lexington, Ky. At dark our cattle were driven into the corral

5

to prevent them from straying, and from being stolen by the Indians.   Distance 6 miles.

May 22.—This morning thirteen wagons, about half of which belonged to Mr. Gordon, of Jackson county, Mo., separated from the main party, assigning as a reason therefor, that the company was too large, and that as a consequence of this, our progress was too slow for them.   This is the second division in our party which has taken place since we started, and there is a strong probability that soon there will be others.   A restlessness of disposition, and dissatisfaction from trivial causes, lead to these frequent changes among the emigrating parties.

The trail along which we have travelled to-day, has been dry, compact, and easy for our teams.   It runs over a high undulating country, exhibiting a great variety of rich scenery.   As the traveller rises the elevated swells of the prairie, his eye can frequently take in at a glance, a diameter of 60 or 80 miles of country, all clothed at this season with the deepest verdure, and the most luxuriant vegetation.   We encamped for the day on what was called by some " Black Paint" Creek, by others " Sandy," a tributary of the Kansas river.   The bottom on either side of the creek, is timbered with large and handsomely-shaped oaks

Mr. Kirkendall and myself were two or three miles in advance of our train, when we commenced winding through the ravines of the bluffs, in order to descend to the bottom-lands bordering the stream.   We were met here by four young Indians, apparently riding a race.   They were mounted on fat ponies, which they urged forward at their highest powers of speed, until coming up to us they drew their horses in, and passing by a short distance, wheeled about and rode along at our side to the bank of the stream.   Here we met some forty or fifty more Indians, and we soon discovered that about two miles below there were two large Kansas villages.

One of those whom we met at the creek was a very hand some young man, (a chief,) whose dress was much more cleanly and of better materials than his followers or associates.   He carried in his hand a small looking-glass, which he consulted with great frequency and earnestness, evidently much pleased with his personal appearance. A profusion of bone and tin trinkets ornamented his ears, and nose, and neck. A medal with the likeness on one side of " John Tyler, President of the United States," was suspended on his breast. On the other side there was a device of a pipe and a tomahawk, and the following inscription, " Peace and Friendship." This Indian appeared to have great influence over the young men of his tribe. I did not learn his name.

Our train came up and encamped, and it was not long before the two villages appeared to be entirely emptied of their men, women, and children. The camp was filled and surrounded by them. They numbered probably some four or five hundred. Those who last came from the villages were mostly in a wretched condition, so far as their clothing was concerned. An exceedingly foul blanket, more than half worn, and sometimes in tatters, with a pair of leggins, constituted their suits of garments. A large portion of the men were well-proportioned and above medium stature; and the countenances of many were prepossessing and intelligent, if not handsome. Some of them wore their hair long, and it presented a tangled and matted appearance. The heads of others (probably warriors) were shorn close to the skin, except a tuft extending from the forehead over the crown of the head down to the neck, resembling the comb of a cock. The faces of many were rouged,—some in a fanciful manner, with vermilion. The eyelids and lips only, of several, were painted; the cheeks and ears of others, and the forehead and nose of others. There appeared to be a great variety of tastes and no prevailing fashion. I noticed that the ears of a great number of the men were bored with four large holes in each, so large that the finger could be passed through the perforations, from which were suspended a variety of ornaments, made of bone, tin, and brass. Small globular and hollow metal buttons, with bàlls in them, were strung around the neck or fastened to the leggins of others, so that every motion of their bodies created a jingling sound.

Such as rode ponies were desirous of *swapping* them for the

American horses of the emigrants, or of trading them for whiskey. They all appeared to be most unblushing and practised beggars. There was scarcely an object which they saw, from a cow and calf to the smallest trinket or button upon our clothing, that they did not request us to present to them. Bread, meat, tobacco, and whiskey, they continually asked for; and the former we gave to them, the last we had not to give— and if we had had it, we should not have given it. Among these very troublesome visiters was Ki-he-ga-wa-chuck-ee, (words importing "the rashly brave," or "fool-hardy.") This personage is a principal chief of the Kansas tribe. His wife accompanied him. He appeared to be a man of about fifty-five years of age, of commanding figure, and of rather an intellectual and pleasing expression of countenance. I presented his squaw, whose charms were not of the highest order, with a dozen strings of glass beads, with which she and her spouse seemed to be much delighted. They both spoke and said, "Good! very good!" A turban; a soiled damask dressing-gown of originally brilliant colors, but much faded; buckskin leggins and moccasins, composed the dress of Ki-he-ga-wa-chuck-ee. He wore the usual quantity of bone and tin ornaments about his ears and neck, and the little jingling buttons or bells on his legs. His face was painted with vermilion.

The reputation of the Kansas Indians for honesty is far from immaculate among the emigrants, and a strong guard was placed around the camp and over our cattle, notwithstanding the pledge of Ki-he-ga-wa-chuck-ee, that none of his people should steal from or molest us in any manner. About 10 o'clock at night, two Indians were taken prisoners by the sentinels on duty. They were greatly alarmed when brought to the guard-tent, expecting immediate punishment. An investigation took place, and it turned out, that they had come into the camp by appointment with some individual of our party, who had promised to trade with them for a horse, for which they were to receive four gallons of whiskey. Their motive in coming late at night was, that they wished to conceal the trade from the Indians generally, as in the event of its being known, they would be compelled to divide the whiskey among the whole tribe, whereas they wished to drink it themselves. The trade was broken off, and the Indian captives, much to their relief, were discharged. Several of the young men from our camp visited the nearest Kansas village after dark. They had not been in the village long, before the cry of " Pawnee ! Pawnee !" was raised by the Indians, and several guns were discharged immediately. This alarm was probably raised by the Indians, to rid themselves of their white visiters, and the *ruse* was successful. The Pawnees, as I learned, had a short time previously made an attack upon the Kansas, and besides killing a number of the latter, had burnt one of their villages. Distance 18 miles.

May 23.—The Indians were in and around our camp before we were fairly aroused from our slumbers, begging with great vehemence for bread and meat. Ki-he-ga-wa-chuck-ee, and his wife, took their seats upon the ground near our tent, it being headquarters, and there remained until the train was ready to move. In consideration of the fulfilment of the promise of the chief that nothing should be stolen from us by his people, a general contribution was made, of flour, bacon, and sundry other articles, amounting in the aggregate to a large quantity, which was given to the chief to be divided as he saw fit among his people. This appeared to give general satisfaction to our visiters, and we left them in the full enjoyment of their luxuries.

The ford of the small creek on which we encamped last night was difficult, owing to its steep banks and muddy channel. We were obliged to fell small trees and a large quantity of brush, and fill up the bed of the stream, before the wagons could pass over. Our route for several miles was through a highly fertile valley, bounded on the east by a chain of mound-shaped elevations of the prairie, on the west and in front by " Hurricane Creek," the timber skirting which is plentiful and large. The most enthusiastic votary of agriculture and a pastoral life, could here, it seems to me, realize the extent of his desires—the full perfection of rural scenery, and all the pleas-

5*

ures and enjoyments arising from the most fruitful reproduction in the vegetable and animal kingdoms. Granite, flint, and sandstone are exhibited in boulders and a debris on the slopes of the highest elevations.

Several of the Kansas Indians followed us from our last encampment. One of them presented to me a root or tuber, of on oval shape, about one and one-half inch in length, and an inch in diameter. This root is called the prairie potato. Its composition is farinaceous and highly nutritious, and its flavor is more agreeable than that of the finest Irish potato. I have but little doubt, if this plant was cultivated in our gardens, it would be an excellent and useful vegetable for ordinary consumption; and very probably it would be so improved as to form a substitute for the potato. The wild rose, which is now in full bloom, perfumes the atmosphere along our route with a delicious fragrance. The wild tulip, (yellow and variegated,) a plume-shaped white flower, and several flowers of the campanella or bell-shaped classification, have ornamented the prairie to-day.

We crossed the creek on our left at 12 o'clock, M. Two hours were occupied in passing our wagons over it. Our route from the creek continued over an open and rolling prairie, broken by small branches and ravines;—the last of which are now dry, but seem to serve as aqueducts to convey the water from the rolling plains to the principal streams in rainy seasons, or during the melting of the snows early in the spring.

In the afternoon, near a small pond of water, we met four trappers from the Rocky Mountains, returning to the "settlements." They were accompanied by several Delaware Indians, all of whom spoke English so as to be understood. There were suspended from the saddle of one of the trappers, a wild turkey, a racoon, and several squirrels, which they had taken last night. To acquire the trapper's art, a long apprenticeship is evidently requisite. Although the country through which we are travelling abounds in all the natural vegetable riches which a most generous soil can be supposed to produce without cultivation, we have rarely seen signs of game of any description, beast or bird. By the mystery of their art, however, these hunters of the mountains have contrived to supply themselves with a sufficiency of meat to keep themselves from starvation. They were packing several large sacks of fur-skins. They reported that on the Platte, some one or two hundred miles in advance of us, there were large herds of buffaloes, and that we should experience no difficulty while in this region in supplying ourselves with fresh meat. The costume of these men was *outré* surpassing description.

We encamped this afternoon in a small depression of the prairie, near a fine spring of cold pure water, surrounded by a few trees. The water of this spring was as grateful to us as nectar to the fabled deities of heathen mythology. Several of the Kansas Indians followed us all day, and are with us to-night. Distance 12 miles.

May 24.—The first five miles of our march was over a rolling prairie country, dotted with occasional clumps of timber. We then crossed a creek with a rapid and limpid current, flowing over a rocky and gravelly bed. This stream would afford fine water-power for mills. The banks above and below the ford are well supplied with oak, elm, and linden trees, of good size ; and the land, which on the western side rises from the creek in gentle undulations, is of the richest composition, and covered with a carpet of the greenest and most luxuriant vegetation. We found here, gushing from a ledge of limestone rock, a spring of excellent water, from which we refreshed ourselves in draughts that would be astonishing to the most fanatical cold-water advocate.

Rising from the bottom of this stream, upon the table-land, the scenery for a long distance to the north and the south is surpassingly attractive. On the eastern bank of the rivulet, a chain of mound-shaped bluffs stretches far away to the right and the left, overlooking the gentle slopes and undulations on the western side. It is impossible to travel through this country with the utilitarian eye and appreciation natural to all Americans, without a sensation of regret, that an agricultural resource of such immense capacity as is here supplied by a bountiful Providence, is so utterly neglected and waste. The soil, I am persuaded, is capable of producing every variety of crop adapted to this latitude, which enters into the consumption, and conduces to the comfort and luxury of man, with a generosity of reproduction that would appear almost marvellous to the farmers of many of our agricultural districts on the coast of the Atlantic. This fair and extensive domain is peopled by a few wandering, half-naked and half-starved Indians, who have not the smallest appreciation of the great natural wealth of the country over which they roam in quest of such small game as now remains, to keep themselves from absolute famine. Having destroyed or driven farther west all the vast herds of deer, elk, and buffalo which once subsisted here upon the rank and nutritious vegetation, they are now starving, and have turned pensioners upon the government of the United States, and beggars of the emigrants passing west, for clothing and food. Beautiful as the country is, the silence and desolation reigning over it excite irrepressible emotions of sadness and melancholy.

Passing over the undulations, in a few miles we discovered, on the right-hand of the trail, another spring of cold water, from which again we refreshed ourselves. At this point the country becomes much more elevated, and the view on all sides still more extensive, bounded by the far, far-off green hill-tops, without a solitary tree in the vast expanse. Where timber exists on these plains, it is usually in the ravines and bottoms, and along the water-courses, frequently entirely concealed from the eye of the traveller when surveying the country from the ridges.

I noticed this morning, in a ravine near our camp, a species of honeysuckle. Its blossom was white, and without fragrance. The wild rose, perfuming the atmosphere with its delicate and delicious fragrance, the sweetbrier, tulip, and the usual variety of other flowers, have exhibited themselves on our march.

The oxen, overcome by the extreme heat of the sun during the marches, are beginning to perish. I saw two dead oxen by the wayside, this morning, which belonged to some of the forward companies.

We encamped, this afternoon, in a hollow where there is a fine spring of cold, pure water, but no timber, with the exception of three elm-trees. A dead and fallen elm has been drawn to our camp, and divided among the several messes for fuel. This tree was entirely consumed by us, and the next three emigrating parties will consume the three standing elms. Our progress is very slow. But notwithstanding this, many of the wagons are late in reaching camp, and the train is frequently strung out several miles. I am beginning to feel alarmed at the tardiness of our movements, and fearful that winter will find us in the snowy mountains of California, or that we shall suffer from the exhaustion of our supply of provisions. I do not fear for myself, but for the women and children of the emigrants. Singular as it may seem, there are many of our present party who have no just conceptions of the extent and labor of the journey before them. They appear to be desirous of shortening each day's march as much as possible, and when once encamped are reluctant to move, except for the benefit of fresh grass for their cattle, and a more convenient and plentiful supply of wood for the purposes of cooking. There are several persons in camp ill with bilious complaints. Distance 10 miles.

May 25.—Our route to-day has been over a more broken country than I have seen since entering upon the prairies. The timber fringing the margin of Vermilion Creek, seen in the distance, has been the only relief to the nakedness of the country, with the exception of two or three solitary trees, standing isolated on the verdant plain. We reached the Vermilion about noon. The bank of this stream on the eastern side was so steep, and the ford in other respects so difficult, that we were detained several hours in crossing it. The Vermilion is the largest watercourse we have crossed since leaving the Kansas. Its current is more rapid than has been usually exhibited by the streams of these prairies, and would afford very good water-power. The timber at this point on its banks, is about a quarter of a mile in width, and consists chiefly of oak and elm. It has been reported to be abundantly supplied with a variety of fish. Ewing and Nuttall, who encamped with an emigrant party here last night, caught two good-sized catfish, but none of a different species.

Between this and the Big Blue, on the trail, there was said to be neither wood nor water, and consequently our water-casks were filled, and a supply of wood placed in our wagons, sufficient for fires at night and in the morning. We encamped this afternoon on a high elevation of the prairie, about five miles west of the Vermilion. Just as our wagons were forming the corral, a storm of thunder, lightning, rain and wind, burst upon us, drenching us to the skin, and nearly upsetting some of our wagons with its furious violence. The cloud rose from the west, and soon passing over to the east, within a hundred yards of us the most brilliant rainbow I ever beheld was formed, the bases of the arch resting upon two undulations between which we had passed. No Roman general, in all his gorgeous triumphal processions, ever paraded beneath an arch so splendid and imposing. The clouds soon cleared away, the rain ceased, and the brilliant meteor faded, leaving nature around us freshened and cleansed from the dust and impurities, which for two days past have been excessively annoying.

The ridges over which we had marched to-day, have generally exhibited a coarse gravel of flint and sandstone, with boulders of the latter, and of granite. Distance 15 miles.

May 26.—Our route to-day has continued over a rolling, and rather broken country, compared with former marches. We crossed a small stream about three miles from our encampment, the limpid waters of which flow merrily over a gravelly bed, and a few straggling trees ornament its banks. From this we continued to ascend over elevated ridges, until we reached the bluffs which overlook Big Blue River. Descending from these, and ascertaining that from the late rains the stream was so much swollen as not to be fordable, we encamped on a slope of the prairie, near the timber, at one o'clock, P. M.

The Big Blue in its present state, at the ford, is a stream about one hundred yards in width, with turbid water and a strong and rapid current. A large quantity of drift is floating on its surface. The timber on it at this point is about half a mile in width, and is composed of oak, cotton-wood, walnut, beach, and sycamore. The trees are large, and appear to be sound and thrifty. A small spring branch empties into the main river, which here runs nearly from the north to the south, just above the ford. The waters of the branch are perfectly limpid, and with a lively and sparkling current bubble along over a clear bed of gravel and large flat rocks. In the banks and the bed of this small stream, there are several springs of delicious cold water, which to the traveller in this region is one of the most highly-prized luxuries. Should our government determine to establish military posts along the emigrant trail to Oregon, a more favorable position than this, for one of them, could not be selected. The range of bluffs on the eastern side of the river, about two hundred yards from it, overlooks and commands the entire bottom on both sides, forming a natural fortification.

The river has continued to rise rapidly since our arrival here, and at sunset the muddy waters were even with its banks. It is not probable that we shall be able to ford it for two or three days. The two companies immediately in advance of us, were so fortunate as to reach the stream last night before the great rise took place, and we saw them on our arrival wending their way west, over the high and distant ridges.

A fruit called the prairie pea, which I have previously noticed has been very abundant along our route. The plant which produces it is about eight inches in length, and has a leaf similar to that of the wild pea vine. The fruit, which varies from half an inch to an inch in diameter, has a tough rind, with a juicy pulp, the flavor of which resembles that of the green pea in its raw state. In the heart of the fruit there are a number of small seeds. Mrs. Grayson, having the necessary spices, &c., made of the prairie pea a jar of pickles, and they were equal if not superior to any delicacy of the kind which I have ever tasted. The wild rose with its delicate perfume, and the wild tulip, have been the most conspicuous flowers.

The afternoon has been devoted, by the female portion of our party, to the important duty of " washing." I noticed that the small branch was lined with fires, kettles, tubs, and all the paraphernalia necessary to the process of purifying linen. The Big Blue is said to abound in fish, but its extreme height, has prevented much success with our anglers. A catfish about three feet in length was taken this evening by one of our party.

While I am writing, a public meeting is being held in the area of the corral. There is much speaking and voting upon questions appertaining to the enforcement of by-laws, and regulations heretofore adopted, but rarely enforced. We are a pure democracy. All laws are proposed directly to a general assembly, and are enacted or rejected by a majority. The court of arbitrators, appointed to decide disputes between parties, and to punish offenders against the peace and order of the company, does not appear to have much authority. The party condemned is certain to take an appeal to an assembly of the whole, and he is nearly as certain of an acquittal, whatever may have been his transgressions.

The day has been delightful. No disagreeable incident has marred the general harmony and good feeling. The new moon exhibited its faint crescent above the tree-tops contiguous to our camp, soon after the sun sank behind the western horizon. She was recognised as an old and familiar acquaintance of the great family of Adam, with whom our friends of the orient might be shaking hands at the same time that we were gazing upon her pleasing features. Distance 10 miles.

CHAPTER V.

Terrible storm—More legislation—Alcove spring—Honey—A death and funeral—Boat-launch—Blue River Rover—Soil and scenery along the Blue—Fresh graves—Pawnee country—Quarrels in camp—Withdrawal of the Oregon emigrants—Indian hunters—Indian appetites—More fighting—Antelopes—False buffalo chase—Blacksmithing on the plains.

MAY 27.—A terrific thunder-storm roared and raged, and poured out its floods of water throughout a great portion of the night. But for the protection against the violence of the wind, afforded by the bluffs on one side and the timber on the other, our tents would have been swept away by the storm. The whole arch of the heavens for a time was wrapped in a sheet of flame, and the almost deafening crashes of thunder, following each other with scarcely an intermission between, seemed as if they would rend the solid earth, or topple it from its axis. A more sublime and awful meteoric display, I never witnessed or could conceive.

The river since last night has risen several feet, and there is now no hope of fording it for several days. At eight o'clock, A. M., an adjourned meeting of the company was held in the *corral*, to hear and act upon a report of a committee, appointed by the meeting last night, to draw up additional regulations for our government during the journey. As usual in these assemblies, violent language was used, producing personal altercation and much excitement. A motion having been made by one of the company, to appoint a standing committee to try the officers, when charged with tyranny or neglect of duty by any individual of the party, it was carried; whereupon all the officers announced their resignations, and we were thrown back into our original elements, without a head and without organization. I felt fully satisfied that a large majority of the emigrants composing our party were in favor of order, and a restraining exercise of authority on the part of their officers, and that they had voted without understanding the effects which must follow the measure adopted. Not having participated in the proceedings of the meeting previously, I moved a reconsideration of the vote just taken, and explained the reasons therefor. My motion was carried by a large majority; the resolution raising the standing committee was rescinded, and the officers who had just resigned were re-elected by acclamation! These matters I describe with some minuteness, because they illustrate emigrant life while on the road to the Pacific, where no law prevails except their will. So thoroughly, however, are our people imbued with conservative republican principles, and so accustomed are they to order and propriety of deportment, that with a fair understanding, a majority will always be found on the side of right, and opposed to disorganization. " Our glorious constitution," is their motto and their model, and they will sanction nothing in derogation of the principles of the American constitution and American justice. There are, however, men in all emigrating parties, desperate and depraved characters, who are perpetually endeavoring to produce discord, disorganization, and collision ; and after a proper organization of a party, as few public assemblages as possible should be convened for legislative purposes.

This afternoon, accompanied by several of the party, I strolled up the small branch, which I have previously mentioned as emptying into the river just above the ford. About three-fourths of a mile from our camp we found a large spring of water, as cold and pure as if it had just been melted from ice. It gushed from a ledge of rocks, which composes the bank of the stream, and falling some ten feet, its waters are received into a basin fifteen feet in length, ten in breadth, and three or four in depth. A shelving rock projects over this basin, from which falls a beautiful cascade of water, some ten or twelve feet. The whole is buried in a variety of shrubbery of the richest verdure, and surrounded by small mound-shaped inequalities of the prairie. Altogether it is one of the most romantic spots I ever saw. So charmed were we with its beauties, that several hours unconsciously glided away in the enjoyment of its refreshing waters and seductive attractions. We named this the " *Alcove Spring ;*" and future travellers will find the name graven on the rocks, and on the trunks of the trees surrounding it.

There are indications of the existence of mineral coal on the Big Blue. Mr. Grayson and others went out in search of honey this morning, and returned in the afternoon with several buckets full of the pure and delicious product of the labors of the bee. Our hunters and fishermen met with no success. Some of them discovered a large, but deserted Indian encampment, about four miles up the river, which they conjectured had been occupied by the Pawnees.

May 28.—The river having fallen only fifteen inches during the night, after breakfast the whole party capable of performing duty were summoned to repair to a point on the river about half a mile above us, to assist in the construction of a raft to ferry our wagons over the stream. The response to this call was not very general; but a number of the men armed with their axes, adzes, and a variety of other mechanical tools, immediately assembled and repaired to the place designated. We labored industriously the entire day, in making "*dug-outs.*" Two large cotton-wood trees were felled, about three and a half or four feet in diameter. From these canoes were hollowed out, twenty-five feet in length. The two canoes are to be united by a cross-frame, so as to admit the wheels of our wagons into them. Lines are then to be attached to both ends, and our water-craft is thus to convey our wagons over the river, being pulled backwards and forwards by the strength of the men.

I strolled up another small branch, which empties into the Big Blue not far distant from our encampment. The water is abundant, and of the finest quality, and the scenery most picturesque and romantic. I procured in my rambles a plentiful supply of the prairie pea for pickling, and I would recommend all emigrants travelling this road to do the same. A man belonging to one of the forward companies returned back this afternoon, in search of some lost cattle or horses. He reported that a child of Judge Bowlin, one of the emigrants to Oregon, died yesterday. The man in crossing the river was thrown from his horse, and it was with great difficulty that he could save himself from drowning. He sank several times, and was carried down the stream by the rapid current; at last he succeeded in grasping the tail of his horse, and was thus kept above water until he was drawn to the shore.

May 29.—Last night Mrs. Sarah Keyes, a lady aged 70, a member of the family of Mr. J. H. Reed of Illinois, and his mother-in-law, died. Mr. Reed, with his family, is emigrating to California. The deceased Mrs. Keyes, however, did not intend to accompany him farther than Fort Hall, where she expected to meet her son who emigrated to Oregon two or three years since. Her health, from disease and the debility of age, was so feeble, that when she left her home, she entertained but faint hopes of being able to endure the hardships of the journey. Her physicians had announced to her that she could live but a short time, and this time she determined to devote to an effort to see her only son once more on earth. Such is a mother's affection! The effort, however, was vain. She expired without seeing her child.

The event, although it had been anticipated several days, cast a shade of gloom over our whole encampment. The construction of the ferry-boat and all recreations were suspended, out of respect for the dead, and to make preparations for the funeral. A cotton-wood tree was felled, and the trunk of it split into planks, which being first hewn with an axe and then planed, were constructed into a coffin, in which the remains of the deceased were deposited. A grave was excavated a short distance from the camp, under an oak-tree on the right-hand side of the trail. A stone was procured, the surface of which being smoothed, it was fashioned into the shape of a tombstone, and the name and age, and the date of the death of the deceased, were graved upon it.

At 2 o'clock, P. M., a funeral procession was formed, in which nearly every man, woman, and child of the company united, and the corpse of the deceased lady was conveyed to its last resting-place, in this desolate but beautiful wilderness. Her coffin was lowered into the grave. A prayer was offered to the Throne of Grace by the Rev. Mr. Cornwall. An appropriate hymn was sung by the congregation with much pathos and expression. A funeral discourse was then pronounced by the officiating clergyman, and the services were concluded by another hymn and a benediction. The grave was then closed and carefully sodded with the green turf of the prairie, from whence annually will spring and bloom its brilliant and many-colored flowers. The inscription on the tombstone, and on the tree beneath which is the grave, is as follows: "Mrs. Sarah Keyes, Died May 29, 1846: Aged 70."

The night is perfectly calm. The crescent moon sheds her

pale rays over the dim landscape; the whippoorwill is chanting its lamentations in the neighboring grove; the low and
mournful hooting of the owl is heard at a far-off distance, and
altogether the scene, with its adjuncts around us, is one of
peace, beauty, and enjoyment.

May 30.—The river having remained stationary during the
night, and from the frequency of rains there being no present
probability of its falling so as to be fordable, the business of
completing our ferry-boat was resumed with energy at an early
hour. This work being finished, the nondescript craft was
christened the "Blue River Rover," and launched amid the
cheers of the men. She floated down the stream like a cork,
and was soon moored at the place of embarkation. The work
of ferrying over was commenced immediately. Much difficulty,
as had been anticipated, was experienced in working the boat,
on account of the rapidity of the stream and the great weight
of many of the wagons. The current was so strong, that near
the shore, where the water was not more than three or four feet
in depth, the strength of a man could with difficulty breast it.
One of the canoes was swamped on the western side in drawing the third wagon from it. The damage, however, was soon
repaired and the work resumed. Nine wagons and their contents were safely ferried over during the afternoon.

May 31.—The business of ferrying was resumed at an early
hour, and continued with vigor until nine o'clock at night, when
all the wagons, oxen, and horses were safely landed on the
western bank of the river, where our *corral* was formed. The
labor has been very severe, and sometimes dangerous; but was
rendered still more disagreeable by a very sudden change in
the temperature. A chilling wind commenced blowing from the
northwest at four o'clock, P. M. Soon after dark masses of
clouds rolled up, and it rained violently. At six o'clock the
thermometer had fallen to 48°; and our men, many of whom have
been standing in the water the whole day, when they came into
camp were shivering as if under the influence of a paroxysm of
the ague.

A fisticuff fight, in the progress of which knives were drawn,

6*

took place near the river bank, between two drivers, who ordinarily were very peaceable and well-disposed men. Fortu-- nately, by the interposition of those standing by, serious results were prevented. The pugnacious and belligerent propensities of men display themselves on these prairie excursions, for slight causes and provocations. The perpetual vexations and hard- ships are well calculated to keep the nerves in a state of great irritability.

Jacob was taken quite sick this evening from the effects of the wet and the cold. He was relieved, however, in a short time. The growth of timber on the western bank of the river, is oak, walnut, elm, a few poplars, cotton-wood, the black haw, (in bloom,) dog-wood, and a variety of small shrubbery. Grape- vines cover many of the trees. Distance one mile.

June 1.—Cloudy, with a cold, raw wind from the northwest. The great and sudden change of the temperature, connected with the heavy fall of rain last night, completely drenching every thing exposed to it, is exceedingly distressing to the women and children, who generally are thinly clothed, and unprepared to resist the effects of exposure and atmospheric eccentricities. Many of them suffered greatly last night, and this morning and during the entire day the wind has blown with the rawness and bleakness of November, rendering over- coats necessary to the comfort of those who have been constantly exercising themselves by walking or otherwise.

We resumed our march after a detention of four days. As we rose from the bottom of the Blue, upon the high and rolling prairie, a vast diameter of country spread itself before us in all directions, presenting a landscape surpassingly attractive. Springs of cold, pure water, gushing from the cliffy banks of the small branches and ravines, are abundant on all sides. These delightful watering-places are usually shaded by small clumps of trees; and their existence and locality are thus indi- cated to the thirsty traveller in quest of the delicious and indis- pensable beverage which they so generously supply.

The general features and characteristics of the country over which we have travelled to-day, are not very dissimilar from

the descriptions previously given. There is a paucity of timber. The soil is exuberantly rich, and productive of the most
luxuriant grass and a great variety of plants, few of which,
however, are now in bloom. The surface of the country is high
and undulating. There are no stagnant pools or boggy marshes
to produce malaria. All the aspects are indicative of a healthful
climate ; but whether this conclusion is experimentally correct,
I have no means of judging.

The strongest objection to the territory we have passed
through, since we left the Missouri line, is the sparseness of timber. With this single objection, the country appears to be the
most desirable, in an agricultural point of view, of any which I
have ever seen. It possesses such natural wealth and beauties,
that at some future day it will be the Eden of America. When
that epoch arrives, he who is so fortunate as to be then a
traveller along this route, may stand upon one of the high
undulations, and take in at a single glance a hundred, perhaps
a thousand villas and cottages, with their stately parks, blooming gardens and pleasure-grounds ; their white walls seen
through the embowering foliage, and glittering in the sunbeams
from every hill-top and slope of these magnificent plains.

I saw a solitary cluster of a pure white flower, of the poppy
family, which previously I have not seen. The lupin is abundant,
but not in bloom. At four o'clock, P. M., we reached a small
branch, a tributary of the Blue, which presented so many difficulties in crossing, that the remainder of the day was laboriously
occupied in passing our wagons to the opposite bank, where we
encamped, forming our *corral* in the bottom, to avoid the
ground so often occupied by emigrant companies which have
preceded us. The grass, for a long circumference, has been
cropped in many places to the roots, showing that large herds
of cattle are in advance of us.

Near our camp there is a dead ox, and two graves of
children, which have died and been buried within the last four
days. A stone with the inscription, " May 28, 1846," stands
at the head of one of the graves ; at the head of the other,
there is a small wooden cross. The bones of these children

will sleep in their nameless graves, in this remote wilderness, unless disturbed by the cupidity of the savage, or the hunger of the wolf, until the last trump shall summon them from their repose.

We are now in the territory of the Pawnees, reported to be vicious savages, and skilful and daring thieves. Thus far we have lost nothing of consequence, and met with no disaster from Indian depredation or hostility.

Several unpleasant difficulties and altercations have occurred to-day, from the perverse obstinacy of some of the men, who refuse obedience to the orders of our captain. The standing committee appointed to adjust such matters, have been in session the whole of this evening. The result of their investigations I have not heard. There has been, for several days, a very troublesome dispute between two Oregon emigrants, partners for the journey, one owning the wagon and the other the oxen. The claimant of the oxen insists upon his right to take them from the wagon. The proprietor of the wagon denies this right. The difference was brought to a crisis on the road to-day, by a personal rencounter produced by an attempt of the ox claimant to take the oxen from the wagon, and thus to leave it to move along by the best mode that could be invented for such an exigency. If a man is predisposed to be quarrelsome, obstinate, or selfish, from his natural constitution, these repulsive traits are certain to be developed on a journey over the plains. The trip is a sort of magic mirror, and exposes every man's qualities of heart connected with it, vicious or amiable. Distance 14 miles.

June 2.—The temperature continues unseasonably cool, and there is much suffering and some sickness among the women and children in consequence of it.

A scene of angry altercation, threatening to terminate in violence and blood, occurred last night about eleven o'clock, during the sitting of the committee of arbitration on the oxen and wagon controversy which I mentioned yesterday. Happily, through the interposition of those roused from their slumbers by the loud threats, epithets, and language of defiance, which passed between the parties at variance and their respective friends, the affair was quieted without more serious consequences. This morning the men composing the company were summoned, at an early hour, to meet at the guard-tent for the purpose of adopting measures for the prevention of similar outbreaks, disturbing the peace and threatening the lives to an indefinite extent, of the party.

The two individuals at variance about their oxen and wagon, were emigrating to Oregon, and some eighteen or twenty wagons, now travelling with us, were bound to the same place. It was proposed, in order to relieve ourselves from the consequences of disputes in which we had no interest, that all the Oregon emigrants should, in a respectful manner and a friendly spirit, be requested to separate themselves from the California emigrants, and start on in advance of us. This proposition was unanimously carried, and the spirit in which it was made prevented any bad feeling, which otherwise might have resulted from it. The Oregon emigrants immediately drew their wagons from the *corral* and proceeded on their way.

Many of them, especially the females, separated from us with much apparent reluctance and regret. When making their adieux, several of them were affected to tears. Doubtless tender ties of affection and friendship, formed between the young men and young women of the two parties, were then sundered, an' will never be reunited. Such are the stern and inflexible decrees of Fate in the delicate affairs of the heart.

Our march to-day has been for the most part over a smooth inclined plane, in some places wet and marshy. We encamped on another small affluent of the Blue. Just before we encamped, we saw, at the distance of about three miles, some moving objects, which being inspected through a glass proved to be Indians. They were a party of four Shawnee Indians, one or two of whom spoke English, and had been out on a trapping and hunting expedition. They were now returning to their homes. Two of them by invitation came to the camp, supped and remained all night with us. We purchased of them some dried buffalo tongues and jerked meat, which they packed in skins on their horses. Distance 12 miles.

June 3.—A bitter wind blows from the northeast, chilling as the blasts of November. Flannels, overcoats, and all the clothing of winter are necessary to comfort. The day has been the coldest and most disagreeable that I ever experienced in the month of June.

The two Shawnee Indians parted from us on their homeward journey, at the same hour that we commenced our march. They carried with them a large budget of letters, which had been written during the night by those composing our party, addressed to their friends at home. We also supplied them with bacon, flour, coffee, and sugar, sufficient for the remainder of their journey. They supped and breakfasted with our mess, and I never saw men swallow food with such apparent enjoyment and in such prodigious quantities. Each of them consumed as much at one meal, as a man with ordinary appetite and pow·ers of digestion would eat at six. Our cook this morning, in order that there should be no deficiency, prepared five or six times the usual quantity of bread, and fried bacon, and coffee, but it all disappeared, besides nearly a quart of lard in which the bacon was swimming.

A few scattering trees on a small branch which we crossed this morning, are all that we have seen during our day's march. Our route has been over ascending ground nearly the whole day. Late in the afternoon we reached the summit of a ridge, overlooking a valley, through which winds a small rivulet, the banks of which are fringed with timber. The view from the ridge of the beautiful valley below, appeared almost like a creation of enchantment. Involuntary exclamations of pleasure and admiration escaped from the lips of the whole advance party as soon as the scene became visible.

Descending into the valley and crossing the stream, we encamped in a grove of oak on the western side. Vegetation here is much more backward than it has appeared generally on our route. The grass is not so high, and many of the oaks display no foliage and are still in the bud. I account for this by supposing the country to be much more elevated than that which we have passed over. I noticed, on a gravelly bluff overlooking the valley, the cactus or prickly-pear, and some beautiful specimens of the flower called " Adam's Needle," and a bell-shaped flower of variegated colors. Two elk, a panther, and some wild turkeys have been seen during our march, but they were beyond the reach of our rifles.

Two men, who joined us a few days since, had a violent quarrel in camp this evening. Blows were exchanged, knives and pistols drawn ; and but for the interference of Mr. Kirkendall, who was standing near at the time and rushed between the parties, one or both would probably have been killed. A wagon belonging to a German emigrant named Keyesburgh, whose wife carried in her arms a small child, and was in a delicate situation, was upset, and the woman and child precipitated into a pool of water. The tongue of the wagon was broken, and all its contents were thoroughly wet and plastered with mud. Fortunately, however, no other damage was done. The · woman and child escaped without material injury. Distance 18 miles.

June 4.—Our march, as usual, has been over the high tableland of the prairie, occasionally dotted with one or more small trees, indicating the localities of springs or pools of stagnant water. The undulations and ravines have been less frequent, the surface of the country presenting before us an expansive inclined plane, which we have been climbing the entire day. We crossed several affluents of the Blue, with sandy and gravelly beds ; the waters having ceased to flow, stand in pools of considerable depth. The soil as we advance is becoming sandy and less fertile, and the grass and other vegetation is much shorter and thinner. Vegetation appears to be very backward, many of the trees being bare of foliage ; and the flowers which one hundred and fifty miles back were dropping their blossoms, are here budding and bursting into bloom.

About noon a number of antelopes were seen grazing, about two or three miles. A party started out immediately on the best horses to hunt them. We spread out to the right and left, and the antelopes did not discover us until we had approached within the distance of half a mile. They then raised their heads, and looking towards us an instant, fled almost with the fleetness of the wind. I never saw an animal that could run with the apparent ease, speed, and grace of these. They seem to fly, or skim over the ground, so bounding and buoyant are their strides, and so bird-like their progress. A chase was commenced immediately, but it ended as might have been expected; the antelopes were very soon two or three miles distant, notwithstanding we rode fleet horses, and as if in derision of our slow progress, would stop occasionally and look around until we came near to them, when again they would bound off, and in a few minutes be out of sight. In shape they resemble in many respects the goat; their size is considerably below that of the common deer. Their limbs are very small and sinewy. Their hair is coarse, and of a light chestnut color mingled with white. Beneath the tail on the thighs behind, there is a small oval-shaped spot of white hair. All our efforts to approach them within gunshot were entirely fruitless. The sport, however, was very good for us, but not so agreeable to our horses.

We encamped this afternoon on the Little Blue, in sight of the timber skirting which we have travelled most of the day. The trees are chiefly oak, cotton-wood and hickory. Mr. Grayson brought in a fine fat doe, which he had succeeded in shooting after a day's hunt. This is the first game of consequence, that has been killed since we commenced our journey, and it was a luxury highly appreciated after subsisting so long upon salt meat.

We are beginning now to look for buffalo, with great curiosity and interest. Every dark object descried upon the horizon is keenly scrutinized, and manufactured into one of those quadrupeds, if its shape, color and proportions, can be tortured into the slightest resemblance. So eager and excited are our men in this respect, that two of them in advance, discovering two others at a distance of three miles, were so certain that they were buffaloes, that they commenced a chase, which lasted several hours, the distance between the parties being maintained for some time by nearly equal speed. The pursuers were greatly chagrined when they discovered their mistake. The day has been highly favorable to our cattle, being so cool that over-coats were comfortable. Distance 22 miles.

June 5.—Our march to-day has been along the bottom, or in sight of the Little Blue, which is skirted by a few large trees, chiefly oak and cotton-wood. We crossed the dry gravelly beds of several streams, which in rainy seasons, or during the melting of the snows, flow into the Little Blue. In passing over one of these, our wagon was so much injured that we were compelled to stop several hours to repair it. A fire was lighted, irons heated, and the "art and mystery" of blacksmithing, without anvil, and with axes and hatchets for hammers, in the course of two hours repaired the injury. The train in the mean time had moved on, and we were left far in the rear.

The composition of the soil continues to exhibit fewer fertile qualities. It is sandy, and the vegetation is scattered and short. I noticed to-day a beautiful crimson, five-leafed flower, produced by a small vine. The shape of the flower resembles the holly-hock, but its leaves are much more delicate, and its color more deep and brilliant.

We encamped this afternoon in a handsome bottom of the Little Blue, with good water and grass, and a plentiful supply of dry wood. The scenery is attractive, and the evening, although cool for the season, is not unpleasant. Distance 21 miles.   7

CHAPTER VI.

Sickness among the emigrants—Effects of travel and exposure upon the appearance and habits of our party—Method of travel—The Little Blue River—Change in the soil—A break-down—Platte River—Soil of the Platte bottom—Human bones—Buffalo bones—Post-offices—Islands of the Platte—Bois de Vache—Mackinaw boats—Prairie-dog town—Rocky Mountain hunters, and boatmen—The bluffs of the Platte—Immense fungi—First buffaloes—Men in search of a doctor—Disposition among emigrants to take large doses of medicine—Effects often fatal—Barbarous surgical operation—Distressing scene—Funeral—Wedding—Birth.

June 6.—There has been considerable sickness in camp during the past ten days; resulting, as I believe, from imprudent exposure and indulgence. The complaints are chills and fevers, and diarrhœa. The cases have, however, generally yielded to medicine. Few of our company have been accustomed to the fatigues, exposures, and privations of a camp-life, and on the whole it is rather surprising that the outset of the journey has not affected us more seriously than it has. Many have decidedly improved in health, and are now becoming so inured to our present mode of life, that the usually deleterious effects of exposure to dampness, cold and heat, are not a subject of much consideration.

Our faces are nearly as dark, from the effects of the sun and the weather, as those of the copper-colored inhabitants of these plains whom we have so often met. Before our evening ablutions, after encamping, are performed, and the black dust of the prairie is laved from our skins, if a friend from the "settlements" were to meet us, clad as we are in our grotesque and careless costume, he might very naturally mistake us for a company of the savages who roam over this wide wilderness. Once a week is as often as the most particular and fastidious exquisite of the party consults his pocket-mirror and admires his physiognomy; and the not very delicate nerves of most of them, it must be admitted, are then often severely shocked; and they regard their own images with feelings of terror and aversion, rather than with emotions of admiration. The anecdote of the very ugly man who, after surveying himself in the glass, exclaimed, "Not handsome, but *d—d* genteel!" is not applicable to any of us. No one is either genteel or handsome.

Our system of travel is thus: The whole encampment is roused by the sound of a trumpet at or before sunrise. Breakfast, which hitherto has consisted of bread, fried bacon, and coffee, is prepared and discussed as soon as possible, usually by six o'clock, when the morning cattle-guard is summoned to drive the oxen into the *corral* preparatory to "catching up" or yoking. This occupies an hour or more, and at seven or half-past seven o'clock, our march commences. Between 12 o'clock and one o'clock the train is halted in the road for the oxen to breathe. There is a delay of an hour, during which each person partakes of such refreshment as has been provided for him before leaving camp in the morning. The march is then resumed, and continued according to circumstances in reference to grass, water, and wood, until 5 or 6 o'clock in the afternoon, when our *corral* is formed, our tents pitched, and our evening meal provided.

Until last night the oxen have been driven into the *corral* at 8 o'clock, to guard against Indian thefts; but now that we have approached so near the buffalo region, where cattle are of no value in the estimation of the savages, this practice has been discontinued. We have seen no Indians, except the Shawnees mentioned, since we left the Big Blue River. The Shawnees reported that there was an encampment of 300 Pawnee warriors, at a point now about five days' journey in advance.

Our route has been up the Little Blue, which runs in a southeast direction. We have generally travelled upon its bank. The waters of the stream at present are confined to a channel about ten yards in width, but during high-water, or freshets, they overflow the most of the bottom. The deposite of sand and detritus from an overflow of the present year, is so deep in many places that the grass has not penetrated through it. The soil of the bottom appears to be of a fertile composition, but that of the table-land or prairie undulations is sandy and grav-elly, producing but little grass. Among the flowers which I noticed to-day were the foxglove, and a plume-shaped flower, the petals of which are pink, purple, and blue. The wild pea, in bloom, is quite abundant in places ; and the lupin disputes the tenantry of the ground with the grass.

The *mirage* has displayed itself several times to-day with fine effect, representing groves of waving timber and lakes of limpid water. Our amateur hunters, several of whom have been out all day, brought in no game. They saw large numbers of ante-lope, but never were so successful as to approach within rifle-shot of them. We are encamped to-night on a handsome bot-tom, between the Little Blue and a small branch emptying into it. The moon is shining brilliantly, and the evening is more pleasant than any we have enjoyed for some time. The trail has been dry and firm, and, with the exception of the ravines we are compelled to cross, a better road could not be desired. Distance 20 miles.

June 7.—We continued along the banks of the Little Blue until noon, when the trail diverged from the stream to the right, ascending over the bluffs, into the high table-land of the prairie, in order to strike the Platte river, the estimated dis-tance of which from this point is twenty-seven miles. We supplied ourselves with water and wood, expecting to encamp to-night where neither of these could be obtained. The soil of the prairie is thin, and the grass and other vegetation presents a blighted and stunted appearance. I did not notice a solitary flower in bloom, between the Little Blue and our encampment.

About two o'clock, P. M., in crossing a ravine the bank of which was steep, one of the axletrees of our wagon broke down entirely, and our progress consequently was suspended. This would have been a most serious disaster, detaining us probably a whole day, but for the fact that we had brought with us from Independence duplicate axletrees. The train " rolled" past us, but a number of men sufficient to assist in repairing the damage to our vehicle remained. The tools with which we had provided ourselves in the event of accidents, consisting of a saw, shaving-knife, augers, chisels, hammers, etc. etc., were now found indispensable. With the aid of these, Mr. Eddy, a carriage-maker by trade, was soon as busily at work in adjusting the new axletree to the size of the irons appertaining to the wheels, as if he had been in his own shop at home. The damage was fully repaired, and our wagon as strong if not stronger than before at sunset, when we started for camp.

The twilight soon melted into moonlight, and the evening was serene and beautiful. As we jogged along at our leisure over the smooth road, objects indistinctly observed in the dim distance were shaped according to the taste or fancy of the several individuals of the party, to represent buffaloes, bears, elk, and Indians. We came in sight of our encampment about half-past ten o'clock. The tents and wagon-covers at the distance of a mile, appeared in the moonlight like a cluster of small white cottages composing a country village. Some trees near the tents strengthened the agreeable illusion. To my surprise, when I approached nearer the encampment, I found the *corral* formed on a handsome sloping lawn near the brink of a chain of small pools of clear water, shaded by ash and elm trees. This was unexpected, as we had been informed there was no water between the Little Blue and the Platte. The scene was peaceful and pleasing, awakening such emotions as are felt when revisiting some favorite haunt of boyhood, engraven upon the memory and consecrated by juvenile affection. Being a mile or two in advance of our wagon, I sat down under a tree on the bank of the first pool, and contemplated the scene of peace and solitude until my companions came up. We then drove into camp, unharnessed our team, and pitched our tent for the night. Distance 16 miles.

June 8.—The prairie over which we travelled, until we reached the bluffs that overlook the wide valley or bottom of the Platte, is a gradually ascending plane. The soil is sandy; the grass is short, and grows in tufts and small bunches. I saw no flowers.

We reached the bluffs bordering the valley of the Platte, about three o'clock, P. M., and from these we had a view of the valley beyond and the river winding through it. We encamped late in the afternoon on the river bank, about four miles above the point where we entered the valley. Opposite to our camp is Grand Island, which extends up and down the river farther than the eye can reach, but its exact dimension I do not know.

The Platte here (its waters being divided by Grand Island) is about one hundred and fifty yards in breadth. Its current is sluggish and turbid. The timber consists of a few cotton-wood trees, and these principally are on the island. The bottom on the southern side is about three or three and a half miles in width. The soil near the river appears to be fertile, but next to the bluffs it is sandy, and the grass and other vegetation present a stunted and blighted appearance. Small spots in the bottom are covered with a white efflorescence of saline and alkaline substances combined.

While marching across the valley this afternoon, I saw numbers of antelopes, and of the curlew, a large and fine bird. One of the former was killed by Mr. Grayson, and brought into camp. The flesh is coarser than that of the deer, but I thought it more juicy and tender.

We met this morning a man belonging to a company of Oregon emigrants, which had encamped last night about five miles in advance of us. He stated, that a party of twenty or thirty Pawnee Indians had attempted to break into their camp, and that they had much difficulty in keeping them off. This company, to-night, is about three miles from us; and the report of fire-arms being heard in that direction, it was conjectured that their difficulties with the Indians had been renewed. A party of our men volunteered to march to their assistance. They returned, and reported that no Indians had been seen in the vicinity.

The wood for our camp-fires, to-night, has been obtained (by wading the river) from the island opposite. Although the turbid water, rolling in eddies, appears, by a glance at its surface, to be of great depth, yet when sounded, in no place is it more than four feet deep. Distance 25 miles.

June 9.—The morning air is pleasant and invigorating. The
dew, heretofore, has wet the grass as much as a fall of rain;
and usually it has not been evaporated until eleven or twelve
o'clock. This morning the grass was not perceptibly damp;
and from this time forward, I am informed, we shall rarely
witness the phenomenon of copious dew.

Our route, to-day, has been along the bank of the Platte;
the general course of which is nearly from the west to the east.
After passing the head of Grand Island, about eight miles
above our encampment, the river expands in breadth, presenting
a surface of water two miles wide; and resembling the Missouri
or the Mississippi. Although the channel is so broad, indicating to the eye a large volume of water, the stream is, nevertheless, so shallow, that in many places it can be forded without
wetting the pantaloons, if well rolled up above the knees. The
bed of the river is composed of sand. This is constantly shifting
its position by the action of the current, and fresh deposites are
made. The banks of the Platte are low, not rising more than
four feet above the present surface of the water. The bottom,
at this point, I do not think, is often inundated; such is the
breadth of the channel, that an immense body of water would be
required to raise the stream above its banks. For all the purposes of navigation the Platte is a nullity.

The soil of the Platte bottom appears to be indurated by
drought. Occasionally there are marshy places, but these are
easily avoided; and the trail in general is dry and hard.

One of our party who left the train to hunt through the
valley, brought into camp this evening a human skull. He
stated that the place where he found it was whitened with
human bones. Doubtless this spot was the scene of some
Indian massacre, or a battle-field where hostile tribes had met
and destroyed each other. I could learn no explanatory tradi-
tion; but the tragedy, whatever its occasion, occurred many
years ago. The bones of buffalo, whitened by the action of
the atmosphere, are seen every few yards.

A sort of post-office communication is frequently established
by the emigrant companies. The information which they de-

sire to communicate is sometimes written upon the skulls of buffaloes,—sometimes upon small strips of smooth planks,—and at
others a stake or stick being driven into the ground, and split
at the top, a manuscript note is inserted in it.   These are conspicuously placed at the side of the trail, and are seen and read
by succeeding companies.   One of the last-described notices
we saw this morning.   It purported to be written by the captain of a company from Platte county, Mo., a portion of which
was bound for California, and a portion for Oregon.   It consisted of sixty-six wagons.   They had travelled up the Platte a
considerable distance, passing through the Pawnee villages,
with which Indians they had had some difficulties.   They had
also suffered much from the rains and high waters.   They were
now one day in advance of us.   The number of emigrants on
the road for Oregon and California, I estimate at three thousand.

We encamped late this afternoon on the bank of the Platte.
From our position I counted twenty-five islands, varying in
dimensions, generally from a rod to a quarter of a mile in diameter.   The green herbage, trees, and shrubbery upon them,
assume many singular and rather fantastic shapes, representing
in the distance, ships, gondolas, elephants, camels, flat-boats,
etc. etc.   The landscape composed of these objects in the river,
is fairy-like and highly pleasing to the eye.

At this time there are but few flowers in bloom in the valley
of the Platte.   I have noticed none varying from those of the
prairies which we have travelled over, and rarely any of these.
Our fuel for cooking is what is called " buffalo chips," which is
the deposite of manure made by the herds of buffalo that have
roamed over this region in years past, and has become perfectly dry, burning with a lively blaze and producing a strong
heat.   The " chips" are an excellent substitute for wood.   Some
ducks, plover, and curlews, were killed to-day.   Distance 18
miles.

June 10.—Our route the entire day has been up the bottom
of the Platte, frequently near its bank.   The river maintains its
expansive width, and is dotted with numerous small green islets

The valley on the opposite side appears, from the distance at which we view it, to be a plain of sand. The vegetation of last year not having been burnt off, is still standing, and hides with its brown drapery the fresh growth of the present year, and hence the barren aspect.

We saw from our encampment this morning eight small boats, loaded, as we ascertained by the aid of a glass, with bales of furs. The boats were constructed of light plank, and were what are called "Mackinaw boats." The water of the river is so shallow, that the men navigating this fleet were frequently obliged to jump into the stream, and with their strength force the boats over the bars or push them into deeper water. We watched them from sunrise until 8 o'clock in the morning, and in that time they did not advance down stream more than a mile.

I rode to-day through a village of prairie-dogs. The village covered several acres. Scattered over this space there were, perhaps, five hundred small conical elevations raised by these animals in excavating their subterraneous dwellings. I saw large numbers of the diminutive residents of this populous town. They are about the size and of the proportions of the Norway rat, and their hair is a mixture of light brown and black. When I approached their habitations a multitude could be seen scampering about, and hard barking with a shrill but rather playful and pleasing sound, or tone of voice. The whole of them, however, soon ceased their music, and ran into their holes, from whence they peered their heads with a very timid and innocent expression of countenance. The rattlesnake and the owl are said to be the associates of these singular and orderly little animals, but whether this statement is or is not true, I could not, from what I saw, determine. Some of our party shot several of them, and the meat is said to be tender and of a good flavor.

We encamped this afternoon on a small creek emptying into the Platte, the waters of which are brackish and disagreeable to the taste, and not conducive to health. This remark is applicable to many of the small affluents of the Platte. The mosquitoes, morning and evening, have been very troublesome since we entered this valley. They collect about our animals and ourselves in immense swarms, and bite with the most ravenous eagerness. The slightest puncture of their probosces, inflames the skin and produces a most painful sensation. Distance 18 miles.

June 11.—The soil and scenery of our day's march have presented few varieties worthy of notice. The breadth of the river bottom on the southern side, is from two and a half to four miles. The bluffs, as we advanced up the stream, become more elevated and broken. Sometimes they present a sloping, grassy surface, blending gently with the level plain ;—at others, they assume the form of perpendicular, or overhanging precipices, with a face of bare and barren sand, so compact as to appear like solidified rock.

The tracks and other signs of buffalo have been seen frequently during the day, but none of the animals have yet been discovered. It is probable that the large number of emigrants who have preceded us, have driven the few buffaloes which descend the Platte so low as this, into the hills. The bleaching skeletons of these animals are strewn over the plain on all sides, ghastly witnesses deposited here, of a retreating and fast perishing race. At some future epoch in geological history, they will claim the attention of the curious scientific naturalist.

I observed the cactus, or common prickly-pear, in bloom, frequently on the march. The flower is a pale yellow. Many antelopes have been seen, but it seems almost vain to attempt to hunt them. Their timidity and fleetness are such, that they cannot be approached except by stealth, and to do this on the level and bare plain, is very difficult.

About 11 o'clock this morning, being considerably in advance of our train, I discovered a man at the distance of half a mile, standing in the trail leaning upon his rifle. He was dressed in the hunting costume of the mountains,—buckskin shirt, pantaloons, and moccasins. After the ordinary salutations, he informed me that his name was Bourdeau ;—that he was from St. Charles, Mo., and was one of a party which left a small trading-post on the Platte, a few miles below Fort Laramie, early in May. They were navigating two " Mackinaw boats" loaded with buffalo skins, and were bound for the nearest port on the Missouri. He stated that they had met with continual obstructions and difficulties on their voyage from its commencement, owing to the lowness of the water, although their boats, when loaded, drew but fifteen inches. They had at length found it impossible to proceed, and had drawn their boats to the shore of the river, and landed their furs. Their intention now was to procure wagons if they could, and wheel their cargo into the settlements.

To meet men speaking our own language, in this remote wilderness, was to us an interesting incident. Our train coming up, we determined to proceed as far as the place where the party of Mr. Bourdeau had landed their furs, (about four miles,) and there to noon, in order to give all interested an opportunity of making inquiries, and to write letters to their friends in the United States, to send by this conveyance. The company of *voyageurs* consisted of Mr. Bourdeau, Mr. Richard, Mr. Branham, formerly of Scott county, Ky., a half-breed Mexican, an Indian, and several creole Frenchmen, of Missouri. The Mexican and the Indian were engaged in frying bread in buffalo tallow for dinner. Their cooking apparatus and arrangements did not present the most cleanly aspect, but the results of their culinary operations were such as to excite the appetite of the epicure of the mountains. The whole party presented a half-civilized and half-savage appearance in their dress and manners. The Americans were all well-formed, athletic, and hardy young men, with that daring, resolute, and intelligent expression of countenance which generally characterizes the trappers, hunters, and traders of the mountains. Their avocation, position, and connections force them to be ever watchful, and ever ready to meet danger in its most threatening forms.

We traded with them for their buffalo skins, giving in exchange flour, bacon, sugar, and coffee, which they needed. Sugar and coffee were rated at one dollar per pound, flour at fifty cents, and buffalo-robes at three dollars.

Messrs. Bourdeau, Richard, and Branham accompanied us to our encampment this afternoon, and remained with us during the night. They procured a horse and such other articles as they needed for their journey into the settlements. Our camp is on the south bank of the Platte, which at this point presents a sheet of turbid water, between two and three miles in breadth, dotted with numerous small green islets, which give a most pleasing relief to the monotonous landscape. Distance 17 miles.

June 12.—The mornings are uniformly delightful and the atmosphere elastic and bracing, in this region. The sun shines with great power in the middle of the day, but usually a fresh breeze mitigates the intensity of its heat.

The banks of the river, like those of the Mississippi, are considerably higher than the surface of the plain next to the bluffs. There is a very gradual descent from the stream to the point where the bluffs connect with the plain. This is produced by the deposite of detritus when the water from the melting snows above overflow the banks of the river, and partially inundate the valley.

This afternoon, accompanied by Mr. Kirkendall, I left the train for the purpose of crossing the valley and exploring the hills or bluffs, in search of buffalo. We saw grazing on the plain, near the foot of the bluffs, numerous herds of antelopes ; but could never approach them within rifle-shot. We entered the bluffs through a gorge or ravine, which we followed for about two miles, when we ascended to the summit of one of the highest elevations. From this, on one side, we could see the Platte and its broad valley for a long distance. On the other side were the innumerable sandy peaks, assuming every variety of rude and misshapen configuration ; and separated from each other by deep hollows and ravines and impassable gulfs, hollowed out by torrents of water, or the action of the winds upon the dry and sandy composition of the ground. More wild, desolate, and rugged scenery than is presented by these bluffs, after you enter them, is rarely seen. Our attempt to reach the prairie, where, from the signs, we expected to find buffalo, was abortive. After winding over the steep ridges and through the deep hollows for several hours, we at last became so entangled, that for some time we felt doubtful of forcing our way out, without returning by the same route which we had come. This, at the risk in several instances of our horses' necks, we finally accomplished, reaching the valley in safety.

I noticed numerous fungi, of a globular shape ; some of which were ten inches in diameter, and perfectly white. Indications of iron and copper ores were seen in several places.

We encamped this afternoon on a small branch, the waters of which, when they flow, empty into the Platte. At present, the water stands in stagnant pools. A few cotton-wood trees are scattered along the stream. The dead limbs of these, with "buffalo chips," compose our fuel. Mr. Reed shot a large elk to-day, and brought the carcass into camp. The flesh of the elk is coarse, but this was tender, fat, and of a good flavor. Distance 16 miles.

June 13.—The wood-work of many of the wagon-wheels have contracted so much from the effects of the dry atmosphere on the Platte, that the tires have become loose, and require re-setting. There being sufficient wood to make the fires necessary for this purpose at this encampment, it was determined that we should remain for the day.

Messrs. Grayson and Boggs, who crossed the Platte yesterday afternoon for the purpose of hunting, returned this morning with their horses loaded with the choice pieces of a buffalo cow which they had killed about fifteen miles below our camp. The meat was tender and juicy, but not fat. They reported that they saw large numbers of buffalo on the opposite side of the river ; and that they could approach them within rifle-shot without difficulty. The day has been pleasant, with a most agreeable temperature under the shade of our tents.

June 14.—An Indian was discovered last night by one of the guard, lurking in the bushes ; no doubt intending to steal some of our horses. He ran off with great speed when the alarm was given.

We resumed our march at the usual hour. About five miles

8

from our encampment we were met by three men belonging to
an emigrant company, which they had left last night about
twenty-five or thirty miles in advance. They were in search
of a doctor. A boy eight or nine years of age had had his leg
crushed by falling from the tongue of a wagon, and being run
over by its wheels; and besides, there were in the company a
number of persons ill with fevers and other complaints.

There being no physician in our party, and possessing, from
my former studies and later experience, some pathological and
anatomical knowledge, together with such a knowledge of the
pharmacopœia and materia medica as to be fully sensible that
many patients are killed, rather than cured, by the injudicious
use of medicine, I had consented on several occasions, when
persons belonging to our company were seized with sickness, to
give them such advice and to prescribe and administer such
medicines as I thought would be beneficial. I informed the
patients in all cases that I was no "doctor," but acted rather
in the character of the "good Samaritan." By using this phrase
I would not be understood as assuming to myself the merits and
virtues of the individual who, under that name, has been rendered forever memorable and illustrious for his humanity by
the impressive parable of our Saviour. In all cases of sickness
in our party where I was called, I have the satisfaction of knowing that no one died. This I do not attribute to any medical
skill or science of my own, but to the fact that medicines were
exhibited in small quantities, and such as would not crush the
recuperative powers and sanative impulses of nature. On this
long and toilsome journey, during which it is impossible to suspend the march for any length of time, doses of exhausting
medicines should never be administered to the patient. If they
are, the consequences most frequently must result in death.
The fatigues of the journey are as great as any ordinary constitution can bear; and the relaxing and debilitating effects of
medicines injudiciously prescribed in large quantities, are often,
I believe, fatal, when the patient would otherwise recover.

It so turned out that I had acquired the undeserved reputation of being a great "doctor," in several of the emigrant

companies in advance and in our rear, and the three men who
had met us, above noticed, had come for me. I told them,
when they applied to me, that I was not a physician, that I
had no surgical instruments, and that I doubted if I could be
of any service to those who were suffering. They stated in
reply that they had heard of me, and that they would not be
satisfied unless I accompanied them in all haste to their encampment. I finally consented to their urgent demands, feeling desirous of alleviating as far as I could the miseries of the
sick and disabled, which here are more dreadful than can be
imagined.

Making my arrangements as soon as I could, I mounted the
horse which had been brought for my conveyance—one of those
hard trotters whose unelastic gait is painfully fatiguing to the
rider. You are obliged to protect yourself from the concussion
caused by the contact of his feet with the earth, by springing
from the saddle at each stride. We crossed, in a few miles, a
small branch shaded by some oak-trees. In the bank of this
we found a spring of cool water. There was, however, such a
multitude of mosquitoes and gnats surrounding it, that we had
but little enjoyment in its generous supply of refreshing waters.
The air is in places filled with these troublesome insects, and the
venom of their bite is frequently seriously afflictive. At the
spring above alluded to, the trail recedes from the river, and
runs along under the bluffs, which, to-day, seemed to shut from
us every breath of air, rendering the heat of the sun oppressive
almost to suffocation. I observed that some of the bluffs which
we passed were composed of calcareous rock, and the debris
below was of the same composition. I shot with my pistol,
while riding this morning, an antelope, at a distance of 150 yards.

After a most fatiguing and exhausting ride, we reached the
encampment to which I had been called about five o'clock, P. M.
The men who had been sent for me had given no description of
the case of fracture, other than that which has above been stated.
I supposed, as a matter of course, that the accident had occurred
the preceding day. When I reached the tent of the unfortunate
family to which the boy belonged, I found him stretched out

upon a bench made of planks, ready for the operation which they expected I would perform. I soon learned, from the mother, that the accident occasioning the fracture had occurred nine days previously. That a person professing to be a "doctor," had wrapped some linen loosely about the leg, and made a sort of trough, or plank box, in which it had been confined. In this condition the child had remained, without any dressing of his wounded limb, until last night, when he called to his mother, and told her that he could *feel worms crawling in his leg!* This, at first, she supposed to be absurd; but the boy insisting, an examination of the wound for the first time was made, and it was discovered that gangrene had taken place, and the limb of the child was swarming with maggots! They then immediately dispatched their messengers for me. I made an examination of the fractured limb, and ascertained that what the mother had stated was correct. The limb had been badly fractured, and had never been bandaged ; and from neglect gangrene had supervened, and the child's leg, from his foot to his knee, was in a state of putrefaction. He was so much enfeebled by his sufferings that death was stamped upon his countenance, and I was satisfied that he could not live twenty-four hours, much less survive an operation. I so informed the mother, stating to her that to amputate the limb would only hasten the boy's death, and add to his pains while living; declining at the same time, peremptorily, all participation in a proceeding so useless and barbarous under the circumstances. She implored me, with tears and moans, not thus to give up her child without an effort. I told her again, that all efforts to save him would be useless, and only add to the anguish of which he was now dying.

But this could not satisfy a mother's affection. She could not thus yield her offspring to the cold embrace of death, and a tomb in the wilderness. A Canadian Frenchman, who belonged to this emigrating party, was present, and stated that he had formerly been an assistant to a surgeon in some hospital, and had seen many operations of this nature performed, and that he would amputate the child's limb, if I declined doing it, and the mother desired it. I could not repress an involuntary shudder when I heard this proposition, the consent of the weeping woman, and saw the preparations made for the butchery of the little boy. The instruments to be used were a common butcher-knife, a carpenter's handsaw, and a shoemaker's awl to take up the arteries. The man commenced by gashing the flesh to the bone around the calf of the leg, which was in a state of putrescence. He then made an incision just below the knee and commenced sawing; but before he had completed the amputation of the bone, he concluded that the operation should be performed above the knee. During these demonstrations the boy never uttered a groan or a complaint, but I saw from the change in his countenance, that he was dying. The operator, without noticing this, proceeded to sever the leg above the knee. A cord was drawn round the limb, above the spot where it was intended to sever it, so tight that it cut through the skin into the flesh. The knife and saw were then applied and the limb amputated. A few drops of blood only oozed from the stump; the child was dead—his miseries were over!

The scene of weeping and distress which succeeded this tragedy cannot be described. The mother was frantic, and the brothers and sisters of the deceased boy were infected by the intense grief of their parent. From this harrowing spectacle, I was called to visit the father of the dead child, who was lying prostrate in his tent, incapable of moving a limb, with an inflammatory rheumatism, produced, as I supposed from his relation, by wading streams and exposure to rains during the commencement of the journey, while under the influence of large doses of calomel. He was suffering from violent pains in all of his bones, which, added to his mental affliction from the death of his child, seemed to overwhelm him. He told me that he had been unable to walk or sit upright for four weeks. He begged that I would prescribe something for his relief. I comforted him with all the encouragement in reference to his case that I could conscientiously give, and left some medicines, enjoining him, however, not to deviate the thousandth part of a scruple from my directions, unless he wished to die at once.

8*

The propensity of those afflicted by disease, on this journey, is frequently, to devour medicines as they would food, under the delusion that large quantities will more speedily and effectually produce a cure. The reverse is the fact, and it is sometime dangerous to trust a patient with more than a single dose.

From this family I was called to visit a woman, the wife of one of the emigrants, who had been ill for several weeks of an intermittent fever. She had taken large quantities of medicine, and her strength and constitution appeared to be so much exhausted, that I had no hopes of her recovery, unless the company to which she belonged could suspend their march for a week or more, and give her rest. This I communicated to her husband, and left such medicines, and gave such advice in regard to nursing as I thought would be the most useful in her case. A young man applied to me for relief, who after I had examined him, I believed to be laboring under a disease of the heart. I told him that I could do nothing for him ; that the journey might effect his cure, but that no medicine which I possessed would have any other than an injurious effect.

After visiting some four or five other persons more or less indisposed, and prescribing for them, by invitation of Col. Thornton I walked from this encampment to his, about three-fourths of a mile distant. Col. T., it will be recollected, was a member of the Oregon party, which separated from us about two weeks since. In crossing the Platte bottom to his encampment, we forded two small streams flowing into the main river. Their waters are brackish and bitter with saline and alkaline impregnation. On our arrival at Col. T.'s camp, my old acquaintances and late fellow-travellers were rejoiced to see me. They evinced their pleasure by many kind and cordial manifestations. Mrs. Thornton, a lady of education and polished manners, received me in her tent as she would have done in her parlor at home. I was most hospitably and agreeably entertained, by these my respected friends.

Between eight and nine o'clock in the evening, I was invited to attend a wedding which was to take place in the encampment. The name of the bridegroom I did not learn, but the bride was a Miss LARD, a very pretty young lady, who, I doubt not, will be the ancestress of future statesmen and heroes on the shores of the Pacific. The wedding ceremonies were performed by the Rev. Mr. Cornwall, and took place in the tent of her father. The candles were not of wax nor very numerous, nor were the ornaments of the apartment very gorgeous or the bridal bed very voluptuous. The wedding-cake was not frosted with sugar, nor illustrated with matrimonial devices, after the manner of confectioners in the "settlements;" but cake was handed round to the whole party present. There was no music or dancing on the occasion. The company separated soon after the ceremony was performed, leaving the happy pair to the enjoyment of their connubial felicities. This was the first wedding in the wilderness, at which I had been a guest.

After we left the bridal tent, in looking across the plain, I could see from the light of the torches and lanterns the funeral procession that was conveying the corpse of the little boy whom I saw expire, to his last resting-place, in this desolate wilderness. The faint glimmer of these lights, with a knowledge of the melancholy duties which those carrying them were performing, produced sensations of sadness and depression. While surveying this mournful funeral scene, a man arrived from another encampment about a mile and a half distant, and informed me that the wife of one of the emigrants had just been safely delivered of a son, and that there was, in consequence of this event, great rejoicing. I could not but reflect upon the singular concurrence of the events of the day. A death and funeral, a wedding and a birth, had occurred in this wilderness, within a diameter of two miles, and within two hours' time; and to-morrow, the places where these events had taken place, would be deserted and unmarked, except by the grave of the unfortunate boy deceased! Such are the dispensations of Providence!—such the checkered map of human suffering and human enjoyment!

I saw numbers of buffalo to-day, and large numbers of antelope. The grass surrounding the encampments is green and luxuriant, but more distant from the river it is short and thin, and has a blighted appearance. Buffalo chips constitute the only fuel. Having left my thermometer in the wagon, I could not make an observation to-night. Wind east, with clouds and flashes of lightning. Distance 30 miles.

CHAPTER VII.

Country becomes more arid and sterile—Return party from Oregon—
Herds of buffalo—Dead oxen—Chalybeate spring at the ford of the
Platte—Killing buffaloes—Buffalo meat—Resignation of Colonel Rus-
sell and other officers—Determination to change our mode of travel—
Ash Hollow—General post-office.—Grave opened by wolves—Chimney
Rock in the distance—Court-House Rock—Fœtid water and tainted
atmosphere—Quicksands—Near view of Court-House Rock—A man
in a fright—Near view of Chimney Rock—Scenery at Chimney Rock
—Horse-trading—Furious storm—Scott's Bluff—First view of Rocky
Mountains—Horse Creek—Fort Bernard—Fort Laramie—Sioux In-
dians—Beauty of the Sioux women—Sioux Lodges.

JUNE 15.—Accompanied by two men, I started back on the trail to meet the train to which I was attached. We came in sight of the advance party after travelling about four miles, and I stopped until the wagons came up,—the two men leaving me in pursuit of their own party. When our train came up, I ascertained that they had travelled yesterday 23 miles, and about three miles this morning.

Colonel Russell, our captain, had been seized during the night with a violent attack of chills and fever, and I found him in his wagon quite ill.

As we advance up the Platte, the soil becomes less fertile. The vegetation is thin and short. The river to-day has generally been eight or ten miles from us on our right. Ledges of calcareous rock frequently display themselves in the bluffs. The heat of the sun during the day's march, has been excessively oppressive. Not a cloud has exhibited itself on the face of the heavens, nor a tree or a shrub on the surface of the plain over which we have travelled, or in the distance as far as the eye could reach.

We encamped this afternoon about a mile from the junction of the north and south forks of the Platte, near a spring of cold pure water, than which to the weary and thirsty traveller in this region nothing can be more grateful and luxurious. Nature, in this region, is parsimonious in the distribution of such bounties, and consequently when met with, their value is priceless to those who have suffered through a long day's march under a burning sun, and whose throats are parched with dust and heat. Several of our party who have been hunting to-day, reported that they saw large droves of buffalo on the plains to the south of us, numbering from five hundred to one thousand. Distance travelled from my place of encampment last night 18 miles.

June 16.—A number of our party were seized with violent and painful sickness, brought on no doubt by indulging too freely in the cold water of the spring. Our route to-day has been up the south fork of the Platte, the trail generally running through the bottom near the river. The bottom is much narrower than on the main Platte, and the bluffs are more gentle and sloping. The grass near the bank of the stream is green and luxuriant, but near the bluffs it is very thin; and the soil still farther back is, in many places, quite bare of vegetation.

About 12 o'clock we met a party of five men, from Oregon, returning to the United States. They were a portion of a company which originally numbered eighteen, and which left Oregon city on the first of March. They stopped at the Wallawalla mission one month, and the residue of the time they have been marching. Their baggage and provisions are packed on mules and horses, and they average from twenty-five to thirty miles per day. One of the party having dislocated his shoulder, with three others stopped at Fort Laramie until the injured man could recover sufficiently to travel. The remainder of the company, they stated, were about fifteen miles in their rear. They had not been molested in any manner by the Indians on their route, although they had met them in various places. They had kept an account of the emigrant wagons, as they met them, and reported the number at 430, which, added to our own, make a total of 470. These are about equally divided between California and Oregon. They gave a flattering description of the fertile portions of Oregon. After visiting the United States, they intend to return and settle permanently on the Pacific.

We saw, in the course of the day, several herds of buffalo grazing on the plains two or three miles distant from the trail. A large and fat cow was chased and shot near our camp this afternoon, by Mr. Grayson, supplying us with an abundance of excellent fresh beef. Cacti, tulips, and the primrose, have displayed their blossoms along the trail during our march.

Soon after we encamped, this afternoon, nine men belonging to the Oregon party, reported by those we met this morning, came up, and, by our invitation, encamped with us. Among this party is an intelligent young man by the name of Wall, from St. Louis, who has been on the Pacific coast of South and North America, and among the islands, for some years, and is now returning home by this route. We learned from Mr. Wall that some of the forward emigrant companies had lost their cattle and horses by Indian depredations. We pass, every day, several cattle which have been left behind, too much crippled, or exhausted by fatigue, to proceed. The Platte rose five inches last night. Distance 17 miles.

June 17.—We reached the ford of the Platte about two o'clock, P. M., and ascertained by an examination that, although the river was still rising, our wagons could pass over without much difficulty. While waiting at the river for our party to come up, I discovered, a short distance above where the trail enters the stream to cross it, a large spring of cold water, strongly impregnated with iron, and slightly with sulphur. I drank freely of the water of this spring during the afternoon, and found its effects upon me beneficial. I would advise those emigrants passing this way, who are afflicted with the ordinary complaints on this portion of the route, to visit this spring, and when they leave it to fill their casks with the water, for use on the road.

Our wagons were all passed safely over the river before sunset, an event thought to be worthy of general congratulation. The stream was rising rapidly; and when so high that it cannot be forded, owing to the absence of timber, it forms an impassable barrier to the progress of emigrant parties. Their only course, in such a case, is to halt until the water falls. Two or three buffaloes were killed near our camp this evening. Distance 17 miles.

June 18.—The trail to-day has run along the north bank of the south fork of the Platte, and we encamped at that point where the road diverges from the stream to cross over the prairie to the north fork. The soil of the bottom is sandy; and the grass, which appears to have been blighted by drought, is short, thin, and brown.

We saw large herds of buffalo during our march, some of which approached us so nearly that there was danger of their mingling with our loose cattle. The buffalo-hunt is a most exciting sport to the spectator as well as to those engaged in it. Their action when running is awkward and clumsy, but their speed and endurance are such, that a good horse is required to overtake them or break them down in a fair race. Although the uninitiated in this sport may without much difficulty wound one of these animals with his rifle or pistol, it requires the skill and practice of a good hunter to place the ball in those parts which are fatal, or which so much disable the strong and shaggy quadruped as to prostrate him or force him to stop running. I have known a buffalo to be perforated with twenty balls, and yet be able to maintain a distance between himself and his pursuers. Experienced hunters aim to shoot them in the lungs or the spine. From the skull the ball rebounds, flattened as from a rock or a surface of iron, and has usually no other effect upon the animal than to increase his speed. A wound in the spine brings them to the ground instantly, and after a wound in the lungs their career is soon suspended from difficulty of breathing.

They usually sink, rather than fall, upon their knees and haunches, and in that position remain until they are dead, rarely rolling upon their backs.

The flesh of the bull is coarse, dry, tough, and generally poor. The beef from a young fat heifer or cow, (and many of them are very fat,) is superior to our best beef. The unctuous and juicy substances of the flesh are distributed through all the muscular fibres and membranes in a manner and an abundance highly agreeable to the eye and delightful to the palate of the epicure. The choice pieces of a fat cow, are a strip of flesh along each side of the spine from the shoulders to the rump; the tender-loin; the liver; the heart; the tongue; the hump-ribs; and an intestinal vessel or organ, commonly called by hunters the "marrow-gut," which, anatomically speaking, is the chylo-poetic duct. This vessel contains an unctuous matter resembling marrow, and hence its vulgar name. No delicacy which I have ever tasted of the flesh kind can surpass this when properly prepared. All parts of the buffalo are correspondingly palatable with those of tame cattle; but when they are abundant, the principal part of the carcass is left by the hunter to feast the beasts and birds of prey.

This evening, after we encamped, Colonel Russell, who has been suffering for several days from an attack of bilious fever, tendered his resignation of the office of captain of our party. His resignation having been accepted by a vote of the company assembled, Ex-governor Boggs was called to the chair. A motion was then made by E. Bryant, and unanimously adopted, that the thanks of the company be expressed to Colonel Russell for the manner in which he has discharged his duties since his election to the office of captain. The other subordinate officers then resigned their places. These were Messrs. Kirkendall, Donner, Jacob, and West. A similar vote of thanks was adopted in regard to them. Mr. F. West was afterwards appointed captain pro tem., and the meeting adjourned. Distance 12 miles.

June 19.—A party of eight or ten persons, including myself, had determined, on our arrival at Fort Laramie, to change our mode of travel, provided we could make suitable arrangements. If mules could be obtained for packing, our design was to abandon our oxen and wagons, and all baggage not absolutely necessary to the journey. This would enable us to proceed with much greater expedition towards the point of our destination.

The distance from the south to the north fork of the Platte, by the emigrant trail, is about twenty-two miles, without water. The country between the two streams is elevated and rolling. The soil is poor, and the grass and other vegetation thin and short. The bloom of the lupin in many places gives a blue coloring to the undulations of the prairie. No trees or shrubs are visible.

While halting at noon, midway of our day's march, we were overtaken by Messrs. Lippincott and Burgess, two gentlemen who left us at the Kansas, and had joined some of the advance companies. They had been out six days in search of some mules composing their team, which they supposed had at first strayed from their encampment, and then been driven off by the Indians. In their excursion, they had been as high up as the head-waters of the Little Blue, where, as they stated, they found the soil of the country sandy and sterile, and vegetation parched by the drought. Their search had been unsuccessful.

We descended into the valley of the north fork of the Platte, through a pass, known as " Ash Hollow." This name is derived from a few scattering ash-trees in the dry ravine, through which we wind our way to the river bottom. There is but one steep or difficult place for wagons in the pass. I saw wild currants and gooseberries near the mouth of Ash Hollow. There is here, also, a spring of pure cold water. We met at this spring the four members of the Oregon party which had been left at Fort Laramie. The man with the disabled arm, by resting two or three days, had recovered sufficiently to be able to travel. He informed me that he was returning to Ohio for the purpose of disposing of his property there, which he should invest in sheep and cattle, and drive them to Oregon next year.

We found near the mouth of "Ash Hollow," a small log-cabin, which had been erected last winter by some trappers, returning to the "settlements," who, on account of the snows, had been compelled to remain here until spring. This rude structure has, by the emigrants, been turned into a sort of general post-office. Numerous advertisements in manuscript are posted on its walls outside; descriptive of lost cattle, horses, etc. etc.; and inside, in a recess, there was a large number of letters deposited, addressed to persons in almost every quarter of the globe, with requests, that those who passed would convey them to the nearest post-office in the states. The place had something of the air of a cross-roads settlement; and we lingered around it some time, reading the advertisements and overlooking the letters. Distance 22 miles.

June 20.—Having made my arrangements for the purpose, last night, with a view of carrying into effect the design of changing our method of travel I left the encampment early this morning, accompanied by Messrs. Kirkendall, Putnam, Holder, and Curry, for Fort Laramie, about one hundred and fifty miles distant. In the course of the day we were joined by Messrs. Lippincott, Burgess, Brown, and Ewing.

For several miles, after leaving our encampment near the mouth of "Ash Hollow," the wagon-trail passes over a sandy soil, into which the wheels sink eight or ten inches. The surface of the ground, however, becomes gradually more compact; and the bottom of the river occasionally exhibits patches of green grass. The bluffs which wall in the river valley, are becoming rugged and sterile, exhibiting barren sands and perpendicular ledges of rock. The general aspect of the scenery is that of aridity and desolation. The face of the country presents here those features and characteristics which proclaim it to be uninhabitable by civilized man. The light sands, driven by the bleak winds, drift across the parched plain, filling the atmosphere, and coloring the vegetation with a gray coating of dust. The Platte preserves the same general features as below the forks. Its width is not so great; but still it is a wide stream with shallow and turbid water, the flavor of which is, to me, excessively disagreeable. But we are forced to make use of it to quench our thirst.

I noticed several times to-day, on the bluffs, a few stunted cedars, the deep-green foliage of which was some relief to the dreary monotony of the scenery. We found a grave which had been opened by the wolves or the Indians, and the corpse exhumed. Some of the bones were strewn around the excavation from whence they had been taken.

About four o'clock, p. m., we overtook a train of twenty-one emigrant wagons, under the command of Captain Dickinson. This company is the same that separated from us soon after crossing the Kansas river. We accepted Captain D.'s invitation to encamp with him for the night; and travelling along with him, we passed another small emigrant party which had halted for the day. Our camp is near the bank of the river, and the grass immediately surrounding it is green. Another emigrant party is in sight, about three miles in advance of us. A thunderstorm rose from the southwest about five o'clock, and there was a copious and refreshing fall of rain. A beautiful bow, of the most brilliant colors, displayed a perfect arch in the east immediately after the shower had passed over. Our party were distributed among the tents of the emigrants for the night. I was most hospitably entertained at the tent of Mr. Gordon, an intelligent and highly respectable gentleman, with an interesting family of sons and daughters. Distance 30 miles.

Sunday, June 21.—The shower of last evening has washed the grass and laid the dust. The landscape wears a greener and more attractive drapery.

The atmosphere this morning being clear, we saw distinctly the "Chimney Rock," at a probable distance of thirty-five or forty miles. Some ten or twelve miles this side of it we also saw an elevated rock, presenting an imposing and symmetrical architectural shape. At this distance its appearance was not unlike that of the capitol at Washington; representing, with great distinctness of outline, a main building, and wings surmounted by domes. This, I believe, has been named by emigrants the "Court-house."

As we approached this large rock, it assumed still more definitely the regular proportions of an artificial structure. At times its white walls and domes would appear in a state of perfect preservation; in other views they appeared partially ruinous, like some vast edifice neglected or deserted, and mouldering and falling under the influence of time. Desirous of examining this object more closely than could be done by an observation from the trail, accompanied by Mr. Lippincott, I left our party, turning our horses in a direction towards it. After riding about four miles we ascended the bluffs, the view from which, over the plain to the south, was one of sterile desolation. The wind was blowing fresh, and the white sand and dust were driving through the air and drifting in heaps, like freshly-fallen snow in a furious storm. A fœtid odor, highly offensive, probably arising from some stagnant lake at a distance, impregnated the atmosphere. While riding at full speed we came suddenly upon a stream of clear running water. It appeared so inviting to the eye, that we dismounted for the purpose of drinking from its limpid current; but a single swallow was sufficient to produce nausea. In attempting to cross the stream, which is about two rods in width, Lippincott's horse sank into the quicksands so that his body became entirely covered. After some difficulty he was extricated, and farther down the stream we found a safe ford with a compact bottom of bluish clay. I noticed along the bank of this stream several round rolls of clay and sand, combined in layers from one and a half to two feet in diameter, and about the same in length. These singular formations appear to have been produced by the action of the wind, forcing a small lump of soft clay forward until by accumulation its size is increased to the above dimensions.

We continued our course towards the rock about three miles farther, when its distance from us appeared to be still so great, that we concluded we could not visit it and overtake our fellow-travellers before night. The rock appeared, from the nearest point where we saw it, to be from 300 to 500 feet in height, and about a mile in circumference. Its walls so nearly resemble masonry, and its shape an architectural design, that if seen in an inhabited country, it would be supposed some collossal edifice, deserted and partially in ruins.

Turning our course towards the river we kept along over the bluffs for several miles, from which we had an extensive view of the arid plain to the south, with clouds of dust and sand flying over it. The " Chimney Rock" has been in sight the whole day. About five miles before we reached it a very amusing incident occurred. A man on horseback appeared in front coming towards us. He was about two miles distant when we first saw him. He appeared to be riding leisurely along the trail, and did not discover us until he had approached within the distance of half or three-quarters of a mile. He then suddenly halted, turned his horse partly round, and seemed in doubt whether to advance or retreat. In the mean time we continued to approach him ; and several of the party starting their horses suddenly forward on a gallop, gave a loud Indian whoop. This appeared to operate with electrical force. He fled with all the speed that his horse was capable of. Whip and spur were applied with an energy indicating that the rider supposed his life dependent upon their influence over the animal he rode. He would occasionally look back, and then renew with increased zeal the lashes upon his poor beast. Away and away he went, almost with the fleetness of the wind, and was soon lost to our sight in a distant depression of the plain. He evidently supposed us to be a party of Indians, whom he did not wish to encounter, and seized with a panic, fled with the precipitation I have described. I did not see him afterwards. He was an emigrant probably in search of lost cattle.

We encamped about five o'clock, P. M., on the bank of the Platte, about three miles from the " Chimney Rock." This remarkable landmark derives its name from some resemblance which it bears to a chimney. Its height from the base to the apex is several hundred feet, and in a clear atmosphere it can be seen at a distance of forty miles. It is composed of soft rock, and is what remains of one of the bluffs of the Platte, the fierce storms of wind and rain which rage in this region, having worn it into this shape. The column which represents the chimney, will soon crumble away and disappear entirely.

The scenery to the right of the rock as we face it from the river, is singularly picturesque and interesting. There are four high elevations of architectural configuration, one of which would represent a distant view of the ruins of the Athenian Acropolis ; another the crumbling remains of an Egyptian temple ; a third, a Mexican pyramid ; the fourth, the mausoleum of one of the Titans. In the background the bluffs are worn into such figures as to represent ranges of castles and palaces. A black cloud which has risen in the west since three o'clock, hangs suspended like a sable curtain over this picture of nature in ruin and desolation. A narrow bright line of lurid light extends along the western horizon beneath the dark mass of vapor where the sun is setting, casting huge and lengthened shadows over the plain, from pyramids, spires, and domes, in the far distance.

The illusion is so perfect that no effort of the imagination is required to suppose ourselves encamped in the vicinity of the ruins of some vast city erected by a race of giants, contemporaries of the Megatherii and the Ichthyosaurii.

An emigrant party is encamped about two miles below us on the bank of the river. Two of them, after having visited the " Chimney Rock," rode over to our camp. We invited them to partake of our humble fare, and if they thought proper, a bed in our spacious chamber. The first consisted of bacon broiled on a stick over a fire of buffalo chips ; and the last was the illimitable canopy of the heavens. What was wanting in variety and sumptuousness of fare, was fully made up in the dimensions of our sleeping apartment. They declined our invitation, but were resolutely bent on making a horse-trade before they bade us good-evening. This duty was performed to their satisfaction by my friend Lippincott. Horses were traded and exchanged, but which party had the advantage, it would require one more learned than myself in horseflesh to decide. Were I to give an opinion, I should go so far as to intimate that both parties were sufferers by the contract.

Our party being small, every individual composing it was

compelled to stand a watch during the night, for the protection of our animals and ourselves. My watch come on in the early part of the night. The dark masses of clouds which had been rising from the west for many hours, continued to become more and more threatening. I never witnessed more brilliant displays of electricity, or heard more deafening crashes of thunder. While standing in our camp with a pistol in my hand, sparks of electricity rolled along the barrel and dropped to the ground. I was several times sensibly but not violently affected by electrical shocks. Distance 35 miles.

June 22.—The rain poured down in torrents about one o'clock this morning, and the storm continued to rage with much violence for several hours. A great change had taken place in the temperature during the night, and when I rose from my bivouac, my clothes were dripping wet, and I was shivering with cold. The buffalo chips being too wet to ignite, we were forced to leave our encampment without our coffee, a great deprivation under present circumstances.

If I could I would endeavor to describe to the reader by the use of language, a picture presented this morning, at sunrise, just as we were leaving our encampment, among these colossal ruins of nature. But the essay would be in vain. No language, except that which is addressed directly to the eye, by the pencil and brush of the artist, can portray even a faint outline of its almost terrific sublimity. A line of pale and wintry light behind the stupendous ruins, (as they appeared to the eye,) served to define their innumerable shapes, their colossal grandeur, and their gloomy and mouldering magnificence. Over us and resting upon the summits of these, were the black masses of vapor, whose impending weight appeared ready to fall and crush every thing beneath them. The cold winds blew with the force of a tornado, and the dark drapery which obscured the heavens was wrapping its sable folds, as if to shelter and protect the skies from the fury of the storm. The sublime conceptions of Martin, representing infernal scenery, were vividly brought to mind by these phenomena; and nothing which previously I have witnessed in nature, has so nearly resembled those extraordinary imaginative sketches of this artist.

About twenty miles distant from our encampment of last night is " Scott's Bluff," a very elevated and remarkable formation.   It derives its name, as I have been informed by one who was in part cognizant of the facts, from these circumstances :—A party of some five or six trappers, in the employment of the American Fur Company, were returning to the " settlements," under the command of a man—a noted mountaineer—named Scott.   They attempted to perform the journey in boats, down the Platte.   The current of the river became so shallow that they could not navigate it.   Scott was seized with a disease, which rendered him helpless.   The men with him left him in the boat, and when they returned to their employers, reported that Scott had died on the journey, and that they had buried him on the banks of the Platte.   The next year a party of hunters, in traversing this region, discovered a human skeleton wrapped in blankets, which from the clothing and papers found upon it, was immediately recognised as being the remains of Scott.   He had been deserted by his men, but afterwards recovering his strength sufficiently to leave the boat, he had wandered into the bluffs where he died, where his bones were found, and which now bear his name.

The bluff is a large and isolated pile of sand-cliffs and soft sandstone.   It exhibits all the architectural shapes of arch, pillar, dome, spire, minaret, temple, gothic castle, and modern fortification.   These, of course, are upon a scale far surpassing the constructive efforts of human strength and energy.   The tower of Babel, if its builders had been permitted to proceed in their ambitious undertaking, would have been but a feeble imitation of these stupendous structures of nature.   While surveying this scenery, which is continuous for twenty or thirty miles, the traveller involuntarily imagines himself in the midst of the desolate and deserted ruins of vast cities, to which Nineveh, Thebes, and Babylon were pigmies in grandeur and magnificence.

The trail leaves the river as we approach " Scott's Bluff,"

and runs over a smooth valley in the rear of the bluff seven or eight miles. From this level plain we ascended some distance, and found a faint spring of water near the summit of the ridge, as cold as melted ice. I need not say that we refreshed ourselves from this beneficent gift of nature to the weary and thirsty traveller. We reached the extreme height of the dividing ridge about three o'clock, P. M., and from it we had the first view of the peaks of the Rocky Mountains. Laramie's Peak, and several other elevations about one hundred or one hundred and fifty miles distant, were very distinctly visible, and I think I saw the summits of the Wind River Mountains, about four hundred miles distant. The atmosphere was very clear, and the summits of the last-named mountains appeared like small white clouds, resting upon the horizon. I may be mistaken in my supposition.

Descending from the ridge, we passed over a barren country, broken by deep chasms and ravines hollowed out by the winds and the torrents of water pouring from the hills in wet seasons, for twelve miles, when we reached Horse Creek, where we expected to encamp. But the grass being very indifferent, although it was near sunset we determined to find, if possible, a better encampment on the river some five or six miles distant. We accordingly laid our course for the nearest point on the Platte, passing over a plain, the prevailing growth being the cactus, the thorns of which were very troublesome to the feet of our animals. We reached the bank of the river just before dark, and encamped, although the grass around us was very indifferent. Dark clouds had been rising for some hours from the south and the southwest, and we had scarcely completed the labor of unsaddling our animals when a strife of the elements commenced. Lightning, thunder, and wind seemed to vie with each other for predominance. We succeeded, after much difficulty, in striking a fire in the hurly-burly of the storm, and preparing as hastily as possible a cup of coffee and a slice of broiled bacon, we made our beds upon the ground, and accommodated our philosophy to a thorough saturation by water before morning, which expectation was not disappointed.

The rain fell in torrents about ten o'clock, and in a short time my blankets and all my clothing w are as wet as if they had been submerged in the river.   Distance 45 miles.

June 23.—My physical sensations when I rose this morning were not agreeable.   Every article of bedding and clothing which I possessed was perfectly saturated with water.   A thick driving mist concealed from our view all distant objects, and seemed almost to penetrate the pores of the skin.   It was a long time before we succeeded in striking a fire for the preparation of breakfast, of which we all stood much in need, having fared indifferently for the last thirty-six hours.   A faint blaze, sufficient to boil water for coffee and to broil a slice of bacon for each, was at last raised, and as soon as our hasty morning meal was over, we resumed our march.

We found two emigrant encampments in a few miles, from one of which I purchased a tin cup, (a great prize,) having been so unfortunate as to lose my own on the march since leaving the wagon.   The channel of the Platte has become much compressed; during our march to-day its average breadth has not been more than three hundred yards.   The soil of the bottom is sandy and barren; there is but a scant vegetation upon it, owing to drought or other causes.   I noticed, in several places, clusters of small islands ornamented with willows and occasionally a cotton-wood tree.   Looking down upon these islands from the bluffs, they presented a cultivated appearance; the green foliage of the willows, in contrast with the white sand, represented circular and serpentine walks of shrubbery in the distance, and the barren soil, cultivated ground.   These appearances were numerous and very pleasing just below a small trading-post, called "Fort Bernard," about eight miles from Fort Laramie.

We reached "Fort Bernard," a small building rudely constructed of logs, about two o'clock, P. M.   While approaching it, I saw a large herd of mules grazing on the plain and guarded by Mexican Indians.   One of these had a small looking-glass, with which he conveyed the reflected rays of the sun into our faces, by way of a distant salutation.   The mules (animals of

which we were in quest) were objects more agreeable and interesting to us than their keepers.   I had a letter of introduction to Mr. Richard, the principal of this trading-post, from his
brother, one of the party which we met on the Platte.   Mr. R.
received us with mountain cordiality, inviting us to remain with
him over night.   We declined the invitation, having determined
to proceed as far as Fort Laramie.   An inhabited house, although of the rudest construction and with accommodations far
inferior to an ordinary stable, was nevertheless a cheering sight.
Several traders from Taos and the head-waters of the Arkansas in New Mexico were collected here, to whom the herd
of mules we saw belonged.   They had packed flour, some four
hundred miles, for the purpose of trading with the Sioux Indians.

We arrived at Fort Laramie in the midst of a violent storm
of rain, thunder, and lightning, just before sunset.   About three
thousand Sioux Indians were encamped in the plain surrounding the fort.   The lodges, as I understood, numbered about six
hundred; and the whole plain, at a distance, appeared like a
vast cultivated field, from which the crop had been gathered
and secured in stacks.   An immense number of horses, belonging to the Indians, were grazing on the plain.   The Sioux had
collected here to this number for the purpose of organizing a
war-party to attack the Snakes and Crows.   They held a grand
war-dance in the fort to-day, which had just concluded when
we arrived.   Many of them, I could perceive, were intoxicated
with the excitement of the dance, or from the effects of whiskey.
The females especially appeared to be under the influence of
this excitement.   Notwithstanding the rain, a large number of
them were outside the walls of the fort, dancing, singing, and
throwing themselves into a variety of grotesque and not very
decent attitudes, according to our notions of feminine delicacy
and decorum.   Many of these women, for regularity of features
and symmetry of figure, would bear off the palm of beauty
from some of our most celebrated belles.

A portion of the Sioux women are decidedly beautiful.   Their
complexion is a light copper color, and, when they are not

rouged artificially, the natural glow of the blood is displayed upon their cheeks in a delicate flush, rendering their expression of countenance highly fascinating. The dress of the higher orders (for there is an aristocracy among them) is graceful and sometimes rich. It consists usually of a robe or shirt of buckskin, with pantaloons and moccasins of the same, tastefully embroidered with porcelain beads of various colors. The material of their dress is so prepared, that frequently it is as white as the paper upon which I write, and as flexible as the muslin which envelops in its misty folds the forms that float in our ballrooms. Their feet are small and exquisitely formed. The student of sculpture, when he has acquired his trade at Rome or Florence, should erect his studio among the Sioux for his models.

The Sioux are one of the most powerful tribes of Indians on the continent of America. Their warriors number, as I understand, about eight or ten thousand, and they claim a district of country of great extent. These claims and pretensions are disputed by other tribes surrounding them, and the consequence is, that they are engaged in perpetual wars with their neighbors. The men are powerfully made, and possess a masculine beauty which I have never seen excelled. Conscious of their superior strength, of course, like all savage nations under the same circumstances, they are arrogant and exacting towards their more feeble neighbors; and have thus, probably, acquired a reputation for cruelty and duplicity. But, having passed twice through them without injury or insult of any kind, I have little reason to suppose that this reputation would be sustained by any facts, after a full and fair investigation. The men, as well as the women, are generally well clothed in skins and blankets, and they have every appearance of being well fed. The numerous herds of buffalo which roam over the plains and mountains within the Sioux territory, afford a bountiful supply of meat; and by an exchange of their skins with the traders they obtain blankets, and sometimes flour, sugar, and coffee, and other luxuries. They have among them a few muskets and rifles, but their principal weapons are the bow and arrow, tomahawk, and hunter's knife.

Fort Laramie, or "Fort John," as it is otherwise called, has been the principal trading-post of the American Fur Company. Its distance from Independence, by the route we travelled, is *six hundred and seventy-two miles.* Its latitude is about 42° 40″ north. It is situated on Laramie river, near its junction with the Platte, and is surrounded by an extensive plain. Timber in the vicinity is very scarce. Not a foot of ground around the fort is under cultivation. Experiments have been made with corn, wheat, and potatoes, but they either resulted in entire failures, or were not so successful as to authorize a renewal. The Indians, who claim the soil as their property, and regard the Fur Company as occupants by sufferance, are adverse to all agricultural experiments; and on one or two occasions they entered the small enclosures, and destroyed the young corn and other vegetables as soon as they made their appearance above the ground. The Fur Company raise cattle and poultry, make butter, and have an abundance of milk for their own consumption. They also have herds of horses and mules, which they either breed themselves or purchase from the Indians. The Indian horses are the most hardy animals of the kind I have ever seen. Many of the breeds higher up in the Rocky Mountains have powers of endurance nearly equal to the Mexican mule; an animal which I regard as superior to any other on the continent of America for long, toilsome, and difficult journeys.

"The Fort," as it is called, is a quadrangle, the walls of which are constructed of *adobes*, or sun-dried bricks. The area enclosed is, I should suppose, about half or three-fourths of an acre of ground. Its walls are surmounted by watch-towers, and the gate is defended by two brass swivels. On three sides of the court, next to the walls, are various offices, store-rooms, and mechanical shops. The other side is occupied by the main building of the Fort, two stories in height. The Indians have permission to enter the Fort during the day; at night, they encamp in their lodges on the plain.

Their lodges are constructed of poles, erected in a conical shape, for a framework, over which is thrown and fastened a roof or covering of buffalo skins, so prepared as to resist the

10

rain.   The diameter of the lodges at the base is usually about ten feet; some of them are larger.   In cold or stormy weather, the fire is lighted in the centre of the lodge.   In warm and fair weather, the fire for cooking is lighted near the entrance, on the outside.   The floor of the lodge is covered with buffalo skins, forming an excellent carpet.   When the Indians decamp for the purpose of removing to another place, the poles are fastened to their pack-horses on each side, one end dragging behind on the ground.   Short crosspieces are strapped on these, in the rear of the horse, forming a framework, upon which the baggage, and sometimes the children, are placed during the march.   The small children are confined in cages, composed of willows, in the form of a common crockery crate, except that the door for ingress and egress is at the side.   In this manner, these Indians travel fifty or sixty miles a day, according to circumstances; the women always taking charge of the luggage, pack-animals, and children.

The numerous herds of horses belonging to the Indians having grazed off all the grass from the plain surrounding the fort, and it being unsafe to trust our animals with theirs, we determined to proceed and encamp for the night about five or six miles further, at a point where we were informed there was good grass.   Distance from our last encampment to Fort Laramie, 40 miles—to this camp, 46 miles.

CHAPTER VIII.

Procession of the Sioux—Purchase of mules—Extreme high prices for coffee, sugar, tobacco, flour, etc.—Shooting-match with the Sioux Indians —A return party from California—Denunciation of the country by them —Resume the journey on pack-mules—Vexations of mule-packing— Cañon of the Platte—First appearance of wild sage—View of the Rocky Mountains—Another Oregon return party—Swarms of crickets—An extinct volcano—Green peas—A good supper—Frost in the mountains— Effects of earthquakes—Hunters and trappers: their numbers, habits, etc. —Celebration of the 4th of July—Gnats and mosquitoes—Joined by Mr. Buchanan—Alkaline lakes—Impure water, its effects—Sweet-water Mountains.

JUNE 24.—About 8 o'clock I started alone to return to Fort Laramie. I had not travelled far when I met processions of the Sioux Indians, who this morning broke up their encampment. Having resolved upon and organized an expedition against the Snakes and Crows, their design was to conduct their women and children to a point on the Platte about fifty miles above the Fort, where they intended to leave them in the care of the old men, until the war party returned.

In marching, as I met them, they seemed to be divided into numerous parties, at the head of each of which was a beautiful young female gorgeously decorated, mounted upon a prancing fat Indian horse, and bearing in her hand a delicate staff or pole, about ten feet in length, from the point of which were suspended, in some instances, a gilt ball and a variety of large brass trinkets, with brilliant feathers and natural flowers of various colors. The chiefs, dressed in their richest costumes, followed immediately in the rear of this feminine ensign-bearer, with their bows and arrows in hand. Next succeeding them were the women and children, and pack-animals belonging to the party; and in the rear of all, the warriors. The whole, as I met them, party after party, was a most interesting display of savage pageantry. The female standard-bearers appeared to me more beautiful and fascinating than any objects connected with savage life which I had ever read of or conceived. It appeared as if this was a most solemn occasion, for not one of those composing the long column, some three or four miles in length, as I passed them, seemed to recognise any object or to utter a word. They marched at a slow pace, in perfect silence, with their eyes gazing steadfastly upon the vacancy in front. I bowed many times, but they took no notice of my salutations. Doubtless this stern deportment was expressive of their determination not to look to the right or the left, until they had penetrated into the country of, and wreaked their vengeance upon their enemies, the Snakes and Crows.

Arriving at Fort Laramie, the business I had to transact detaining me some hours, I was invited by Mr. Bourdeau and other officers of the American Fur Company, to dine with them. The dinner consisted of boiled corned beef, cold biscuit, and milk. These gentlemen (and some of them are *gentlemen* in manners and intelligence) informed me that this was their usual fare, when they could obtain flour, which was not always the case. In the absence of bread, they subsist upon fresh buffalo-meat, venison, salt beef, and milk. Mr. Bourdeau, the principal of the Fort, who is a man of about thirty, informed me that he left the settlements of the United States fifteen years since, and had never returned to them. Most of the others with whom I dined, had been absent from their homes and civilization several years.

From Laramie, I proceeded back to the small trading-post, known as "Fort Bernard," where I ascertained that arrangements could be made with the traders from Mexico for mules, by exchanging for them our oxen and wagons. I was joined here by the other members of the party which accompanied me from the wagons, and here we determined to encamp until the wagons came up.

June 25.—The mountain traders and trappers are not rich in luxuries ; but whatever they possess they are ever ready to divide with their guests. In a trade, however, they are as keen as the shrewdest Yankee that ever peddled clocks or wooden nutmegs. Coffee, sugar, and tobacco, are valued here at one dollar per pound ; whiskey at a dollar per pint, and flour at fifty cents per pint. The last-named article is sometimes a dollar per pint, according to the supply, payable in buffalo or deer skins, buckskin shirts and pantaloons, moccasins, etc., etc. Money is of no value among the Indians. The traders, however, who come here from New Mexico and the United States, whenever they see their advantage, extort money from the emigrants.

Several emigrant companies which we have passed in the last day or two, arrived this evening, and encamped near the fort. A party of Sioux Indians, headed by two chiefs, on their way to join the main body in their expedition against the Snakes, halted here for the night. The two chiefs had recently returned from a victorious expedition against the Pawnees ; bringing with them twenty-five scalps, and a number of horses. They held a "talk," and smoked the pipe of peace and friendship at the camp of Capt. Cooper. A contribution of flour and meat was then made by the emigrants for their benefit.

June 26.—Our wagon reached Fort Bernard this afternoon. We entertained at supper, this evening, all the trappers and traders at the fort. The banquet was not very sumptuous, either in viands or the manner in which it was served up ; but it was enjoyed, I dare say, with a higher relish than many a feast served in a thousand dishes of porcelain and silver. The mountaineer who has subsisted for months on nothing but fresh meat, would proclaim bread, sugar, and coffee to be high orders of luxury.

June 27.—I concluded, this morning, a trade with Mr. New, a trader from the head-waters of the Arkansas, by which Mr. Jacob and myself realized seven mules with pack-saddles and other trappings for packing, for our wagon and three yokes of oxen and their appendages. The whole of the day has been busily occupied in selecting such articles from our baggage as we cannot dispense with, and in the arrangement of our packs.

Just before sunset we had a shooting-match at a target, with a number of Sioux Indians, in which the bow and arrow, rifle,

and pistol were introduced. These Indians shoot the arrow
with great accuracy and force, at long distances. One of them
handled the rifle with the skill of a marksman and hunter. The
rapid repeating discharges of Colt's revolving-pistol astonished
them very much. They regarded the instrument with so much
awe as to be unwilling to handle it.

A party of eight or ten persons, some of whom were returning from California, and some from Oregon, to the United
States, encamped a small distance below on the Platte. One
of these came up to the fort to purchase provisions. He gave a
most discouraging description of California; representing it as
scarcely habitable. He stated, that he had resided in that
country four years, during which time not a drop of rain had
fallen; that no crops had been raised; that vegetation had
perished, and that the population there must necessarily perish
for want of food. His account of the people in California was
not more flattering than that of the soil and climate. According
to his statement, there was not a man in the country, now that
he had left it, who was not as thoroughly steeped in villany as
the most hardened graduate of the penitentiary. This man
made himself very busy among the emigrant parties for California, who had halted here, or who were passing; and many
of them, I have reason to suppose, were credulous enough to
believe him. It was easy to perceive, however, that he had a
motive for his conduct, more powerful than his regard for the
truth.

June 28.—By hard labor all the arrangements for our new
mode of travel were completed this morning; and our mules
being brought up, saddled and packed, we resumed our march
about 12 o'clock. The party which started consisted, including
myself, of Messrs. Russell, Jacob, Kirkendall, Brown, Curry,
Holder, Nuttall, and Brookey. Not one of us had ever seen a
mule packed before this morning. Some New Mexicans who
came in with the trading-party gave us our first lesson, and it
was a very valuable one, although experience and necessity,
the best of tutors, instructed us afterwards, so that many
became adepts in the art of handling and packing mules. We

had not proceeded more than two miles, before several of our packs, which at the start were very bulky, and not well balanced, were swinging under the bellies of the animals. These being re-arranged, to the best of our poor skill, (and very poor skill it was,) in a short time other packs would be in the same condition. Although these incidents were vexatious, they nevertheless afforded us occasionally with matter for laughter and amusement, chiefly at our own ignorance. The mules, stupid as we regarded them, knew more about this business than we did ; and several times I thought I could detect them in giving a wise wink and sly leer, as much as to say, that we were perfect novices, and if they could speak, they would give us the benefit of their advice and instruction. A Mexican pack-mule is one of the most sagacious and intelligent quadrupeds that I have ever met with. After much trouble of the nature described, we reached our old camp, six miles beyond Fort Laramie, where we halted for the night. We passed a company of Oregon emigrants, from one of whom I learned that Ewing had joined a party of traders, bound for Taos or the head-waters of the Arkansas. I did not hear from him after this.

June 29.—Colonel Russell and myself left our party in the valley of the Platte, in order to visit Governor Boggs's train, which we could see moving on another trail along the crest of the bluffs to our left, about three miles distant. We followed this trail, after bidding adieu to our late fellow-travellers, some ten or twelve miles, and then struck across the country for the Platte, expecting to intercept our party. We travelled several hours over a broken country covered with wild sage, and reached the Platte about three o'clock, P. M., near a grove of cotton-wood trees, and just below a *cañon* of the river, formed by perpendicular walls of red sandstone 200 or 300 feet in height. A small creek flows into the Platte at this point, the banks of which are dotted with occasional clumps of timber. The trees, although not large, are the largest and most symmetrical we have seen for 300 miles. A few stunted pines show themselves on the hills bordering the Platte, above and below the *cañon*.

Contrary to our expectation, we found no trail near the river. Following the bank of the creek, we struck the path which we had left; and ascertaining, by an inspection of the footprints in the road, that our party had not passed, we halted under the shade of a small tree, and struck a fire to keep off the mosquitoes and gnats until they should come up. Our mules appeared to understand the object of the fire, and instead of grazing, as usual, they took their positions close to the blaze and smoke, by our side. Being much fatigued, we fell fast asleep. Just before sunset our party came up, and roused us from our slumbers. They had experienced great difficulties with the packs. Some of the mules had become unmanageable, and had to be reduced to discipline and subjection by the usual process of roping, throwing, etc., etc., which occasioned long delays. Hence their slow progress. We encamped on the bank of the creek. Distance travelled on the trail, 20 miles.

June 30.—Crossing the creek a few miles above our camp, we entered the dry bed of one of its branches, which we followed some six or eight miles to the summit of an elevated dividing ridge. The dust from the disturbance by our mules of the deep, light sand along the trail, has been at times almost suffocating. We descended from the ridge through a narrow ravine plowed out between the hills by the melting snows or torrents of water in rainy seasons, and entered a narrow valley through which flows another small stream of pure, limpid water. From this valley we ascended by a steep and difficult defile another ridge of hills, of greater elevation than the last described. The view from this ridge, to one unaccustomed to mountain scenery, is strikingly picturesque, although the extensive landscape presents a wild, desolate, and inhospitable aspect. On our left are numerous mountain-peaks of great altitude, composed of barren rocks, and rising one behind another in spiral forms. To the right and in front there is a vast prospect of low conical hills far below us, ornamented with occasional groves of small pines, which, from their linear and curvilinear shapes, appear in the far distance like immense armies drawn up in battle array. We have passed to-day Laramie's, or

James's Peak, and what are called the Black Hills. We encamped at a small spring-branch, in a depression of the ridge. The atmosphere has an autumnal feel, and the wind blows fresh and cold from the northwest. Distance 25 miles.

July 1.—Leaving our camp this morning, we crossed a country exhibiting a surface of conical sand-hills, and furrowed with deep chasms and ravines. In the course of our morning march we had a view, at a distance of some twenty miles, of the waters of the Platte. The diameter of the landscape exhibited to the eye from several positions during the day's march, was at least 100 miles. It presented a broken, barren, and desolate appearance.

We met this afternoon, just after crossing a creek upon which we had nooned, a company of sixteen men, driving before them about thirty horses, returning to the States from Oregon. I conversed with several members of this party. They manifested considerable curiosity and anxiety in reference to the Oregon negotiations in progress with Great Britain. They expressed themselves as highly pleased with the country on the Pacific, from whence they came, and avowed their determination to return to it and make it their residence for life.

I noticed, to-day, in the trail, immense numbers of insects, in color and motion resembling the common cricket. They are much larger, however, and their bodies more rotund. In places, the ground was blackened with them, and they were crushed under the feet of our animals at every step.

We encamped, this afternoon, in a small, oval-shaped valley, through which flows a rivulet of pure, limpid water. The valley is surrounded on all sides by high, mountainous elevations, several of which are composed of granite-rock, upheaved by the subterranean convulsions of nature : others are composed of red sandstone and red clay. A volcanic debris is thickly scattered in places. Many ages ago, the spot where we are encamped, and where the grass is now growing, was the crater of a volcano ; but its torch is extinguished forever. Where then flowed the river of liquid fire, carbonizing and vitrifying the surrounding districts, now gurgles the cool, limpid current of the brook, in its laughing and fertilizing career towards the great Father of Waters. The thunders of its convulsions, breaking the granite crust of the globe, upheaving and overturning mountains, and "crushing the waters into mist," are now silenced; and its volumes of sulphurous vapor and heated cinders, darkening the atmosphere and affrighting the huge monster animals which then existed, when gazing from afar, are dissipated, and will never more be seen. Instead of these, the sweet chirp of the wren, and the chatter of the magpie, are heard among the trees bordering the stream, and light, fleecy clouds are floating through the azure vault of the heavens. Such are the beneficent changes ordered by that Power whose wisdom can render perfection more perfect.

A company of emigrants, composed chiefly of those who had belonged to our original party, at its organization, encamped near us. I was invited by Mr. Branham, whom I have before mentioned, to take supper in his tent. He had gathered, during the day, a mess of green peas from the wild pea-vines along the trail. These had been prepared under the superintendence of Mrs. B., and were a genuine luxury. But, that the epicure of the "settlements" may not sneer at our mountain entertainment, I will state, that in addition to the dish just named, there were on the table smoking biscuits, fresh butter, honey, rich milk, cream, venison steaks, and tea and coffee. With a hearty welcome, what more could a man with an appetite desire? Distance 20 miles.

July 2.—Mr. Kirkendall, whom I expected would accompany us, having changed his destination from California to Oregon, in consequence, as I suppose, of the unfavorable representations made at Fort Bernard in reference to the first-named country, we were compelled to strengthen our party by adding to it some other person in his place. For this purpose we remained encamped during the day, waiting for some of the rear emigrant parties to come up. None appearing during the forenoon, in the afternoon, accompanied by Brookey, I rode back some five or six miles, where I met Governor Boggs's company, and prevailed upon Mr. Hiram Miller, a member of it, to join us.

July 3.—The buffalo-robes (which compose a portion cf our
bedding) were hoary with frost, and the grass through the
whole valley was stiffened and white with the congealed moisture which had been condensed upon it during the night.
As we gradually ascend towards the summit of the Rocky
Mountains, the face of the country on our right and left becomes more and more sterile and broken. We passed, this
morning, through a deep, circular hollow, surrounded on all
sides by masses of rocks of great altitude, thrown up by earthquakes. In the centre of this valley, the bottom of which is a
flat plain, there rises a conical mass of loose rocks, piled one
upon another, about one-eighth of a mile in diameter at the
base, and rising to the height of several hundred feet. This
pyramid has evidently been raised by subterranean combustion,
but at a remote period of geological history.

We encamped this afternoon at one o'clock on Beaver creek,
an affluent of the Platte. The grass and water are good, and
the wood is abundant. The timber which fringes the margin
of the stream is chiefly box-elder and large willows. I noticed
scattered among and enlivening the brownish verdure of the
grass, many specimens of handsome and brilliantly colored
flowers. One of these was of the lily family, presenting peculiarities distinguishing it from any flower of the same genus I
have before seen. The prevailing vegetation during the day's
march, except immediately along the water-courses, has been the
wild sage, (artemisia.) In this region this shrub grows frequently to the height of two or three feet. Its stalk is ligneous, and
is sometimes of a diameter of two or three inches.

We were joined to-day by Capt. Welles and Mr. McClary,
the first a mountain-trapper, intending to accompany us as far
as Fort Bridger, and the last an emigrant bound for California.
Capt. Welles, as he informed us and as I was informed by
others, had once held a commission in the British army. He
was in the battles of Waterloo and New Orleans. He was a man
of about sixty, vigorous and athletic, and his manners, address,
and general intelligence, although clothed in the rude buckskin
costume of the wilderness, confirmed the statements in regard

to him, made by himself and others. The Rocky Mountains have their white as well as their copper-colored population. The former I should estimate at from five hundred to one thousand, scattered among the Indians, and inhabiting, temporarily, the various trading-posts of the Fur Companies. Adventure, romance, avarice, misanthropy, and sometimes social outlawry, have their influence in enticing or driving these persons into this savage wilderness. After taking up their abode here, they rarely return, to remain permanently, to civilized life. They usually contract ties with the Indians which are sufficiently strong to induce their return, if they occasionally visit the "settlements." Many of them have Indian wives and large families. Polygamy is not uncommon. They conform to savage customs, and from their superior intelligence have much influence over the Indians, and frequently direct their movements and policy in war and peace. Distance 18 miles.

July 4.—Gov. Boggs's emigrant company having arrived and encamped just above us last night, it was resolved, out of respect to the birthday of our National Independence, to celebrate it in the usual manner, so far as we had the ability so to do. Mr. J. H. Reed had preserved some wines and liquors especially for this occasion—an anniversary, by the way, which in this remote and desert region crowded our memories with reminiscences of the past, pleasurable from the associations which they recalled, and painful from the position which we now occupied.

At nine o'clock, A. M., our united parties convened in a grove near the emigrant encampment. A salute of small-arms was discharged. A procession was then formed, which marched around the *corral*, and returning to the grove, the Declaration of American Independence was read, and an address was delivered by Col. Russell. A collation was then served up by the ladies of the encampment, at the conclusion of which, toasts suitable to the patriotic occasion were given and drunk with much enthusiasm, a discharge of musketry accompanying each sentiment. Songs were sung, patriotic and sentimental, and I thought, on the whole, that the "glorious fourth" was celebrated here in this remote desert with more spirit and zest, than it usually is in the crowded cities of the States. The pageantry, of course, was not so imposing.

After participating in these ceremonies and festivities, in the afternoon we resumed our journey, making a short march over a country exhibiting greater fertility than has been presented for several days past. The wild sage is the prevailing vegetation on the table-land and on the sides of the hills, giving to them a dark and shaggy aspect. Occasionally there are patches of bunch-grass, which is heavily seeded and appears to be highly relished by our animals. The cactus continues to display its yellow and sometimes crimson blossoms on all sides.

We encamped this afternoon near a grove of box-elder, willows, and alders, on the bank of a creek fifteen or twenty feet in width, with pure limpid water running over a gravelly and sandy bed. The grass surrounding our camp is more abundant and luxuriant than I have seen for several hundred miles. Our mules as well as ourselves suffer much from the myriads of buffalo-gnats and mosquitoes, which take up their abode near all the water-courses and every fertile spot. The evening is perfectly calm and very beautiful. The howling of the wolves and the low hum of the insects, are the only sounds which disturb the profound solitude. We have seen but few birds or signs of animals since we left the Platte bottom. I noticed several magpies this afternoon. Distance 12 miles.

July 5.—The sun rose clear, with dark banks of clouds in the west, which soon disappeared. The little grove near our camp was rendered musical by the notes of the wren and other feathered choristers. The buffalo-gnats and mosquitoes, as usual, were excessively annoying just after sunrise.

The face of the country for several miles of our march this morning, presented more habitable indications than I have observed since leaving Fort Laramie. Deer and antelope were frequently seen grazing at a distance, and birds of various plumage and notes were flitting across our path and perching themselves upon the low shrubbery. These moving objects relieve the death-like torpor and silence which generally prevail. Crossing two small branches we struck the Platte once

11

more about ten o'clock, A. M.   The channel of the Platte here is not more than two hundred feet in breadth.   We travelled up the south bank of the river until we encamped for the day.

Our camp is in a handsome bottom covered with green, luxuriant grass, and ornamented with a grove of tall, straight cottonwood trees.   Jacob brought into camp a specimen of coal taken from the bank of the Platte by one of the emigrants. It resembled our commom bituminous coal, but when placed on the fire it did not seem to ignite or blaze freely.   This is the first positive indication of the existence of coal I have noticed during our journey.   A shrub called grease-wood, about three feet in height, with a bright green foliage containing a fetid, oily substance, in places disputes the occupancy of the soil with the wild sage.   The sun-flower, wild daisy, and a flower emitting an odor resembling the heliotrope, have exhibited themselves. We found here two emigrant companies, one for Oregon and one for California.   One of them was encamped on account of the illness and expected death of one of its members, a woman.   No rain appears to have fallen in this vicinity for a long time.   The ground is so hard that it is with difficulty that we can force our mule-pickets into it.   While on the march, we are frequently enveloped in clouds of dust.   Distance 28 miles.

July 6.—Travelling up the river seven or eight miles, on the south bank, we forded it just below a grove of cotton-wood trees.   From the ford the trail ascends the high bluffs overlooking the valley of the river, from which we had a view of several green islands, one of which resembles a *heart* so nearly in shape that we named it *Heart Island*.   Vegetation over the expanse of table-land on our right is brown and dead with drought.   After a march of several miles on the bluffs, we crossed a deep ravine or chasm, through which we descended again to the bottom of the Platte, where we found Capt. West's company of emigrants encamped for the day.   Several of the emigrating parties have, been encamped here, and have *jerked* buffalo meat.   By invitation, Mr. John C. Buchanan, of Lexington, Ky., joined us at this place.

After halting a short time, our party, with the exception of myself, moved on. I waited for Mr. Buchanan to complete his arrangements for separating from those with whom he had heretofore travelled. We left the emigrant encampment, both of us much encumbered with his baggage, about five o'clock, P. M. The trail here finally leaves the Platte river. Ascending the bluffs on the right, we pursued our way over an arid plain, the only vegetation upon which is the wild sage, grease-wood, and a few perishing plants. We passed immense piles of rocks, red and black, sometimes in columnar and sometimes in conical and pyramidal shapes, thrown up by volcanic convulsions. These, with deep ravines, and chasms, and widespread sterility and desolation, are the distinguishing features of the landscape. We reached our camp at a spring impregnated with salt and sulphur, about ten o'clock at night. An emigrant company had made their camp here. In the course of the march we have passed several small lakes or ponds, incrusted with the carbonate of soda or common saleratus. Their appearance resembles congealed water. A few buffaloes have been noticed at a distance during our march. On our right, this afternoon, at a very great distance, I observed the summits of several high mountains covered with snow. Distance 28 miles.

July 7.—I was seized, during the night, with a violent and exhausting sickness. The soil and water of the country through which we are now travelling, are strongly impregnated with salt, alkali, and sulphur; rendering the use of the water, in large quantities, deleterious to health, if not dangerous. I was scarcely able to mount my mule when we commenced the day's march.

A ride of fourteen miles, over an arid, undulating plain, with a growth of stunted wild sage, brought us to a small grassy hollow, through which runs a faint stream of limpid water. Nothing, in my condition of extreme thirst and feverish excitement, much aggravated by the hot sun and dust, could be more cheering than this agreeable sight. Dismounting from my mule, in an almost fainting state, I hastened to the stream, and sitting down beside it, filled my cup with the water ; but great was my disappointment, when raising the cup to my lips I found the liquid bitter with salt and alkali, and undrinkable. I dug several holes with my hand and cup in the sand, close to the stream, hoping to obtain water less impregnated with these disagreeable substances, but without success.   Some one of our party in searching about, however, discovered at the lower end of the little valley, in the side of a bank, a small spring and a basin of fresh cold water.   To describe the deliciousness of this, as it tasted to me in my diseased and feverish condition, would be impossible.   I drank draught after draught, and then making a shade from the sun with my blankets, laid down to rest while our mules were grazing.

The cooling water of the spring, and an hour's rest, revived my strength ; and at three o'clock we resumed our march. Five miles from this we passed another spring of cold water ; the purest I have tasted since leaving the Blue River.   It is on the right hand of the trail, and surrounded by clumps of witch-hazel and alders.   Ascending from this spring several miles, we mounted the summit of a dividing ridge, from which we had a view of the Sweetwater River Mountains, raising their bald rocky pinnacles at a distance of some twenty or thirty miles. Descending from this ridge, we reached, about sunset, a small stream, and encamped upon its grassy banks.   A number of small herds of buffalo have been seen during our day's ride. We have passed several dead oxen, and others alive, but exhausted by the journey.   Distance 30 miles.

CHAPTER IX.

Independence Rock—Sweetwater River—Devil's Gate—A solitary traveller
—Distant view of Wind River Mountains—Chalky Lakes—Deleterious
effects of milk—Sickness in emigrating parties—Another return party from
California—Buffalo-chase—Mortality among the oxen of the emigrants—
Wolves in chase of diseased oxen—South Pass of the Rocky Mountains—
Pacific Springs—Last view of the Atlantic slope—Jacob's Tower—Little
Sandy River—Troublesome visiters—The Mirage—Big Sandy River—
Greenwood's Cutoff—Curious incident—Snake Indian hunting-party.

JULY 8.—We reached about noon a well-known landmark of the
mountains, called "Independence Rock;" from the circumstance
of the celebration of the fourth of July here by one of the first
emigrant companies to Oregon.   It is an isolated elevation,
composed of masses of rock, about one hundred feet in height,
and a mile or more in circumference, standing in a central and
conspicuous position near the northern bank of the Sweetwater
river, and between the ranges of mountains which border the
valley of that stream.   A multitude of names, to the number,
I should suppose, of several thousand, are painted and graven
upon this rock.   I did not follow the example of those who have
preceded me, and my name is not there.   Near this place are
several small lakes, the waters of which having evaporated,
have left a deposite or incrustation of the carbonate of soda.
They resemble ponds of frozen water.   Col. Russell and myself
supplied ourselves with saleratus, for culinary purposes, from
this bountiful natural manufactory of this article, without price.
    Proceeding up the Sweetwater river about five miles, we
passed what is called the Devil's Gate ; a remarkable fissure in
the rocky mountain-wall, which, above this point, runs parallel
with and within a short distance of the stream.   The fissure is
about thirty feet in breadth, and the perpendicular walls on
each side of the channel of the stream which flows through
it, are, by estimate, between two and three hundred feet in
height, perhaps more.

11*

We encamped just above the Devil's Gate about twelve
o'clock, M. The camp of Captain Cooper's emigrant company
was a short distance from us. By invitation, Colonel Russell
and myself dined at the tent of Captain C., who, with a large
and interesting family of sons and daughters, is destined for
California. Wild currants have been quite abundant along the
trail in several places to-day. A few buffalo were seen. Distance 16 miles.

July 9.—The Sweetwater mountains, on the north side of the
stream, are composed of bare granite rocks, entirely destitute of
vegetation. These rise abruptly to a high elevation. The
mountains on the left are more sloping, and have a soil sustaining vegetation. The Sweetwater river at this time is at this
point not more than thirty feet in breadth, and so shallow that
it can be waded without wetting the knees. The grass covering
its bottom seems to have been blighted by drought before it
reached maturity, and is for the most part brown and crisp.
Following the wagon-trail we left the river about nine o'clock,
A. M., and returned to it again after a ride of four hours. We
nooned upon the bank of the stream, near a clump of small
willows. The trail diverges again from the river, and crosses a
broken and arid plain, the vegetation upon which is the sage
and grease-wood, with a few straggling blades of dead grass.
The flinty gravel mingled with the sand is very destructive
to the feet of our animals. I noticed this afternoon two remarkable dome-shaped rocks of great elevation, between which
there is a gap in the right-hand range of mountains, affording a
view to the north of great extent, bounded by some high mountain-peaks which seem almost to mingle their summits with the
clouds.

Myriads of the insect before described, resembling the cricket,
blackened the ground in places. We encamped this afternoon
on the river, near a narrow gap between the ranges of mountains through which the Sweetwater forces its way. Distance
30 miles.

July 10.—When the sun rose it shone upon and illuminated
a dense bank of fog resting at the base of the mountains to the

southeast, giving it the appearance of an immense mass of snow. An Oregon emigrant company having encamped near us last night, we were visited by them this morning; and one of them, (Dr. Davis,) originally from Montgomery county, Kentucky, and, as he informed me, a relative of the Hon. Garrett Davis, the distinguished member of Congress of Kentucky, invited Colonel Russell and myself to breakfast with his family. We accepted the invitation, and partook with strong appetites of his good cheer. This company had been successful in hunting deer, and we obtained from one of the party a supply of fat venison.

Just before we were leaving camp for the day's march a solitary horseman rode up. From his own account, which I have no reason to doubt, his name was Bonney, from Oregon, and he had travelled from Fort Hall to this place by himself, and intended to make the journey into the settlements of the United States alone. He travelled, I believe, in the night, and concealed himself and horse in the ravines during daylight. He emigrated to Oregon last year from Ohio, and was now returning to take out his family next year. There must have been a powerful motive to induce an experienced man to risk the hazards of such a journey ; and whether he ever reached the end of it or not I can scarcely conceive to be doubtful. Mr. Bonney brought with him an open letter from L. W. Hastings, Esq., of California, dated on the head-waters of the Sweetwater, and addressed to the California emigrants on the road. The main contents of the letter I will not recite. It hinted, however, at probable opposition from the Californian government to the ingress to that country of American emigrants; and invited those bound for California to concentrate their numbers and strength, and to take a new route which had been explored by Mr. H., from Fort Bridger via the south end of the Salt Lake, by which the distance would be materially shortened.

Passing through the gap between the two ranges of granite mountains which here approach each other within a few hundred yards, we had our first view of the Wind River Mountains. They were hoary with a drapery of snow more than halfway from their summits to their bases, and appeared, from the distance we saw them, like white clouds resting upon the horizon. It was a satisfaction to know that we were in sight of the crest of the Rocky Mountains, the point where the waters of the continent divide, taking different courses—the one flowing into the Atlantic, the other into the Pacific.

We passed through a narrow valley several miles in length, the surface of which is white with an alkaline efflorescence. A small stream flows through this valley, the water of which is bitter with alkaline impregnation. Several numerous flocks of antelope have been in sight to-day.

Returning to the Sweetwater about four o'clock, P. M., we encamped near a cluster of small willows, after a continuous march of nine hours. The ranges of hills running parallel with the river have, at this point, lost in some degree their rocky characteristics. They are not so elevated, and more gentle and sloping. The bottom on which we are encamped is covered with the common thistle, and there is but little grass. The mules, however, crop the thistle-blossoms, and seem to relish them. The atmosphere is filled with swarms of mosquitoes, which bite with a fierceness far greater than their civilized brethren of the "settlements." Colonel Russell complains of severe and painful sickness to-night. Brown shot an antelope in the sage near our camp; but leaving the carcass where it fell, in order to obtain a mule to pack it on, before he could return to it again the wolves had devoured it. Distance 33 miles.

July 11.—We continued our route up the valley of the Sweetwater, occasionally leaving the bank of the stream and striking over the rolling and arid table-land to cut off the bends, We nooned near some small lakes or ponds, the water of which is so saturated with a cretaceous substance as to be unfit for use. Some of our mules drank of it,—others refused. Brown's Oregon emigrating-company, consisting of about thirty wagons, nooned at the same place. They supplied us with milk and buttermilk—frequently used by the emigrants as substitutes for water. But I am inclined to the belief that the large quantities of milk drank by the emigrating parties, are productive of the fatal febrile complaint known among them as "camp-fever."

Most of the emigrant families drive along with them several cows which are regularly milked, and in a thirsty state the milk is frequently drank in quarts, and sometimes gallons, in the course of a few hours. It also composes a portion of every meal, being used as water or coffee during the hearty repasts upon fat middling of bacon and buffalo meat. The cow which yields the milk, from being constantly exercised in the hot sun, with little rest day or night, is frequently in a diseased or feverish state. It is more than probable that the disease afflicting the animal is communicated, through the use of its milk, to those who drink it in the quantities which I have named. Besides this, the cows are frequently forced to subsist upon herbage, the poisonous qualities of which are imparted, in some extent, to their milk, and thus communicated to those who use it too freely. This conclusion may be erroneous, but it has subsequently been confirmed by Dr. SAUNDERSON, a surgeon of the army, who accompanied General KEARNY's expedition to New Mexico and California, for whose opinion I entertain great respect.

There were in Mr. Brown's company several persons prostrated with fevers and other diseases. I was called upon as usual, when passing emigrant parties, to prescribe and give advice in these cases, and the short time I remained here was busily employed among the sick. One of the cases of fever was a young man about twenty-one years of age. He had been ill ten or twelve days. I found him in the wagon in a state of half stupor. His pulse was slow and irregular, sometimes rolling with a throbbing volume, then sinking to a wiry feel. A cold perspiration stood on his forehead.

Another case to which I was called, was that of a woman of about thirty-five or forty. She was of a naturally vigorous constitution, and inclined to corpulency. I found her prostrate in a close-tented wagon, upon the covering of which the sun was pouring its almost scorching rays. A burning fever had flushed her face to the color almost of scarlet, except small circles of corpse-like pallor around the lips and eyes. Her respiration was so difficult, that frequently she gasped to recover her breath. She could not speak audibly, but made known her wants in whispers. I felt a shudder of painful horror when looking upon her, distorted as her features were with agonizing suffering. Her daughters, three interesting girls from twelve to seventeen years, gathered around me with anxious and inquiring looks, watching every expression of my countenance while I was making the examination.

I learned from her husband, that some two or three weeks ago, after having labored hard in washing during a hot day exposed to the sun, she had imprudently bathed in very cold water. The consequence was, a severe cold with a high fever. The affection had increased, until she had been brought to the condition in which I saw her. Calomel and other medicines had been administered in large quantities without any beneficial result. She continued to get worse every day. The woman was fearfully attacked with pneumonia, and the violence of the disease, with the exhausting medicines she had taken, had reduced her to a state of helpless feebleness. She begged me in whispers to give her something to relieve the pressure upon her lungs, and restore her breathing. Poor woman! I thought her breathing hours were nearly over!

The daughters, with anxiety and grief depicted upon their countenances, questioned me: "Do you think she is better?" "Do you think she will get well?" "What will you give her?" I shook my head, and told them that there was hope while there was life, but that they alone could save their mother. They regarded me with an expression of hopeless sorrow and disappointment. I then explained to them, that any medicines which I possessed, would only aggravate the disease and render her more feeble than she now was; that they must make warm teas and prevail upon her to drink them in large quantities every hour in the day, and with this treatment and good nursing, it was possible for her to recover. With this advice I left them, fully persuaded that the woman would not live twenty-four hours. But I have since learned that my advice was followed, and that the patient recovered and is now a healthy woman.

Proceeding on our journey, we crossed in the course of the afternoon two small creeks, near one of which we encamped about 5 o'clock, P. M., for the day. Two or three miles before we halted, we passed the camp of a party of four men returning to the United States from California. They were Messrs. Sublette, Taplin, Reddick, and ———. Messrs. Taplin and Reddick had been members of Captain Fremont's exploring party. They left California with a party with which they travelled as far as Fort Hall, and from thence have proceeded on by themselves, expecting, as I understood, to fall in at Fort Laramie with some party of traders bound to the frontier towns of Missouri. Mr. Reddick is a nephew of an old friend and neighbor of mine, CHARLES CARR, Esq., of Fayette county, Kentucky, and had been absent from his friends two years.

A number of buffaloes were seen at a distance of a mile or two from the trail, just before we encamped, and a member of this party was in full chase of one of them. I watched the chase with interest and no small degree of excitement, until man, horse, and buffalo disappeared in one of the ravines of the plain. Brown, discovering that a buffalo had run into the willows bordering the stream upon which we encamped, started towards the place on his mule. Leaving his mule on the plain, he succeeded in approaching and killing the buffalo at a single shot. This, to us, important feat, being performed, (for we were much in want of fresh meat,) he remounted his mule and rode into camp swinging his cap and shouting with exultation. Two pack-mules were soon saddled, and a party went out to slaughter the fallen animal and bring in the meat. The animal was a cow, and although not fat, the flesh was tender and juicy, and we had a sumptuous supper.

The lawn surrounded by willows, upon which we are encamped, is ornamented with the lupin and its blue blossoms, and several other more brilliantly-colored flowers. We have passed to-day some eight or ten dead oxen which belonged to emigrant companies in advance of us. Oxen, when foot-sore or exhausted by fatigue, are left by the emigrants, and immediately become the victims of the wolves, who give them no rest until they fall.   I have sometimes traced an ox pursued by wolves along the trail for ten or twenty miles, and noticed the places where he would turn and give battle to his remorseless pursuers.   The result in every instance was, that I found the dead carcass or the skeleton of the ox, upon which the wolves and ravens had been feasting.   Domesticated animals, unprotected, cannot resist the persevering attacks of the wolves, urged on as they are by their appetites, and conducting their warfare with all the skill of instinct, sharpened often by famine.   The deer and antelope are compelled frequently to shelter themselves from the attacks of these animals, under the strong protection of the buffaloes, and you sometimes see herds of buffaloes and antelopes mingled and grazing together.   Distance 25 miles.

July 12.—Leaving our encampment, in a few miles we crossed another small stream, about four miles from which we again struck and crossed the main Sweetwater river, and left it finally, making our way up a very gentle ascent to the SOUTH PASS OF THE ROCKY MOUNTAINS, or the dividing ridge separating the waters of the Atlantic and the Pacific.   The ascent to the Pass is so gradual, that but for our geographical knowledge and the imposing landmarks on our right, (the snow-capped peaks of the Wind River Mountains raising their cold, spiral, and barren summits to a great elevation,) we should not have been conscious that we had ascended to, and were standing upon the summit of the Rocky Mountains—the *backbone*, to use a forcible figure, of the North American Continent.

There is, I believe, considerable misconception in regard to the South Pass of the Rocky Mountains.   The general supposition is, that it is a difficult and narrow passage by steep ascent and descent, between elevated mountain-peaks.   This conjecture is very far from the fact.   The gap in the mountain is many miles in breadth, and as will have been seen from the daily description of our marches, the ascent up the Platte and Sweetwater has been so gradual, that although the elevation of the Pass above the sea is, according to some observations, between seven and eight, and others, nine and ten thousand feet, yet from the surface we have travelled over, we have been scarcely conscious of rising to the summit of a high ridge of mountains. The temperature has given us the strongest admonitions of our position. The Pass, where the emigrant trail crosses it, is in latitude about $42\frac{1}{2}°$ north and longitude $31\frac{1}{2}°$ west from Washington City. The wagon trail, after we reach the summit, passes two or three miles over a level surface, between low sloping elevations composed of sand and clay, and covered with a vegetation now brown and dead, when it descends by a gentle declivity to a spring known to emigrants as the "Pacific Spring," the water from which flows into the Colorado River of the West, and is emptied into the Gulf of California. The upper waters of the Colorado of the West, are known to travellers and trappers in the mountains as Green River. The stream assumes the name of Colorado, (or Red,) farther down towards the Pacific. The distance from Fort Laramie, by the route which we travelled, to the "Pacific Spring," according to our estimate, is *three hundred and eleven miles.* It is stated at twenty miles less by some travellers. According to this estimate the distance from Independence to the "Pacific Spring," two miles west of the South Pass, is *nine hundred and eighty-three miles.*

The health of Col. Russell being very feeble, we encamped for the day as soon as we reached the spring on the west side of the Pass. The water of the spring is very cold, and the grass surrounding it has been much fed down by the emigrant parties which have preceded us. We found here a solitary emigrant wagon, and its proprietor, wife, and two or three children. From his own account, he had had a difference with the company in which he had been travelling, and this morning he had determined to separate from his former fellow-travellers, and unite himself to some of the rear companies when they came up.

Just before sunset, accompanied by Jacob, I ascended one of the highest elevations near our camp ; and we took a farewell look of the scenery towards the Atlantic. The sun went down in splendor behind the horizon of the plain, which stretches its immeasurable and sterile surface to the west as far as the eye can reach. The Wind River Mountains lift their tower-shaped

and hoary pinnacles to the north.   To the east we can see only
the tops of some of the highest mountain elevations.   The scene
is one of sublime and solemn solitude and desolation.   The
resolution almost faints when contemplating the extent of the
journey we have already accomplished, and estimate the ground
which is yet to be travelled over before we reach our final
destination on the shore of the Pacific.   Illimitable almost as
the prospect seems to the eye, the vision can penetrate to the
distance of a few marches only on our toilsome journey through
the barren and inhospitable wilderness.   To the left of the
"Pacific Spring," at a distance of eight or ten miles, there is a
spiral elevation, resembling a Gothic artificial structure.   This
I named "Jacob's Tower."   Distance 20 miles.

July 13.—Our route to-day has been over an arid undulating plain, in a west-by-north course.   The plain, where any
vegetation exhibits itself, is covered with wild sage, with a few
occasional blades of dead bunch-grass between the sage-hillocks.

Far in front, rising solitary from the face of the plain, are
elevated *buttes*, of singular configuration.   The plain appears at
some geological era to have been submerged, with the exception of these *buttes*, which then were islands, overlooking the
vast expanse of water.   Some of these *buttes*, far to the northwest, present castellated shapes.   Others resemble vast structures,
surmounted by domes.   As we approached "Little Sandy river,"
an affluent of Green river, we came in view of a plain of white
sand or clay, stretching to the southeast a vast distance.   We
crossed the deep channels of two streams, about midway of our
day's march ; but the waters which flowed through them
during the melting of the snows on the mountains, were absorbed by the sands, and unseen.   Their beds were dry as
ashes.

We encamped on Little Sandy about three o'clock P. M.,
among the small willows along its margin.   The stream, at this
season, has a shallow, limpid current, running over a bed of
yellowish sand and gravel, through a channel about fifteen or
twenty feet in breadth.   The grass among the willows is sufficient for our animals.   The mosquitoes manifest an almost

invincible courage and ferocity. We were obliged to picket our mules and light fires, made of the wild sage, around and among them, for their protection against the attacks of these insects. An antelope and sage-hen were killed during our march to-day. The hen was the mother of a large brood of chickens. The mother and protector of this family was killed by the rifle-ball; but the children escaped by hiding in the sage.

The *mirage* has deceived us several times during the day's march. When thirstng for water, we could see, sometimes to the right, sometimes to the left, and at others in front, representations of lakes and streams of running water, bordered by waving timber, from which a quivering evaporation was ascending and mingling with the atmosphere. But as we advanced, they would recede or fade away entirely, leaving nothing but a barren and arid desert. The lupin is blooming on our camp-ground. Distance 28 miles.

July 14.—The mosquitoes, with an untiring perseverance, and a chivalry and courage equalling if not surpassing the valor of the hosts which met and fought our generals and armies in Mexico, disturbed our repose and kept us awake nearly the whole night. Although frequently defeated by *fire* if not by sword, still they remained unconquered, and would listen to no propositions of peace. We determined, therefore, early this morning, to adopt a " masterly *activity*," and the " *line* of march" policy, leaving them in full possession of the territory which they claimed, and which they are welcome from me to hold to the end of time.

Our route this morning was across the plain some ten or twelve miles, when we struck the Big Sandy river, another affluent of the Green, or Colorado. The emigrant trail known as " Greenwood's Cut-off," leaves the old trail via Fort Bridger to Fort Hall at this point. It is said to shorten the distance on the Fort Hall route to Oregon and California some fifty or sixty miles. The objection to the route is, that from Big Sandy to Green river, a distance of forty-five or fifty miles, there is no water. We nooned on the Big Sandy, under a high bluff, down

which we descended to the water; but there was no grass for
our mules. A curious incident occurred here. Colonel Russell,
who has been suffering from disease for several days, when we
dismounted to noon, was placed under the shade of a clump of
small willows on the bank of the stream. In his unquiet state,
produced by a periodical fever, he threw his hands around him
on the grass, whereon his blanket had been spread. In doing
this he accidentally grasped something which had a metallic
feel, that upon examination proved to be a pair of silver-mounted
spectacles. There were no signs of any encampment at this
place during the present year. Who could have left or lost
these spectacles, so singularly recovered ?

During our afternoon's march we fell in with a party of some
sixty or eighty Soshonee or Snake Indians, who were returning
from a buffalo-hunt to the east of the South Pass. The chiefs
and active hunters of the party were riding good horses. The
others, among whom were some women, were mounted generally
upon animals that appeared to have been nearly exhausted by
fatigue. These, besides carrying their riders, were freighted
with dried buffalo-meat, suspended in equal divisions of weight
and bulk from straps across the back. Several pack-animals
were loaded entirely with meat, and were driven along as we
drive our pack-mules.

They struck the wagon-trail a short distance only before we
came in sight of them, and their advance party, consisting of
some six or eight, were the first we saw and the first who discovered us. They appeared to manifest some uncertainty and
irresolution when they saw us pursuing them; but they finally
halted in the trail and waited for us to come up. We held out
our hands in token of friendship, and they did the same, giving
a most cordial shake, which ceremony with Indians is not usually
expressive of a high degree of warmth or gratification. It is one
of the signs between the whites and themselves which they have
learned from the former, and they make use of it without fully
understanding its significance, as I believe. But these Snakes
seemed truly glad to see us, and really friendly. Whether these
manifestations prepossessed me unduly in their favor I cannot

say, but I was much pleased by their civil deportment, and the kind and amiable expression of their countenances.

Our conversation, of course, was carried on altogether in signs, except a few words and names of things which the Snakes themselves had acquired from the English and American traders and trappers at the posts of the fur companies. The Sioux, in the Snake language, when translated into ours, are called "*cutthroats*," and the sign for their name is a motion with the hand across the throat. We conveyed to them all the information we had, in the best manner we could, in regard to the warlike movements of the Sioux. They appeared to comprehend us; and I noticed that a party of four or five, mounted on good horses, started off in advance of the others at a great speed. The rear of the hunting party continued to overtake us as we moved slowly along, and several of them when they came up to shake hands, said, "How do?" and asked for "tobac." I had a pound or two of tobacco in a small bag suspended from my saddle, which I distributed among them, and it appeared to give them great satisfaction. They made signs inquiring if we had whiskey, by forming their hands into a cup-shape, putting them to their mouths, and throwing their heads back, as if in the act of drinking a long and refreshing draught. I shook my head, in token that we had none.

Among the party I noticed a very beautiful young female, the daughter of one of the chiefs of the party, who sat upon her horse with the ease and grace almost of a fairy. She was clothed in a buckskin-shirt, pantaloons, and moccasins, with some really tasteful ornaments suspended around her neck and delicate waist. It will be a long time before I forget the cheerful and attractive countenance, graceful figure, and vivacity of feature and language of this untutored child of nature.

The Soshonees or Snakes occupy the country immediately west of the South Pass of the Rocky Mountains; and their principal places of trading are Fort Hall, a post of the Hudson's Bay Company, and Fort Bridger, the establishment of an individual trader. There are other white traders among them, who, having intermarried with the Indians, change their posi-

12*

tions according to circumstances. They are one of the most powerful tribes of Indians west of the Rocky Mountains, and have hitherto on all occasions manifested a most friendly disposition towards the emigrants passing through their territory. Many of the men we saw were finely formed for strength and agility, with countenances expressive of courage and humanity. They evinced fine horsemanship, and a skilful use of the bow and arrow, their principal weapon in hunting and war. I do not know that the United States government has made treaties with the Snakes. The Indians rode along with us to our place of encampment for the day.

We encamped on the bank of the Big Sandy, in a handsome bottom formed by a bend of the river. The general aspect of the country through which we have passed to-day is much the same as yesterday. The table-land of the plain produces little vegetation except the wild-sage, and this is stunted and seems to be dying from drought or the poverty of the soil. On the narrow bottoms of the river there is grass ; and immediately on its banks there are clumps or thickets of small willows, from half an inch to an inch in diameter, and from five to ten feet in height. The lupin is in bloom around our camp. Distance 30 miles.

CHAPTER X.

Green River—Terrific storm—Desolate scenery—Black's Fork—Rainbow bluffs—Remarkable butte—Arrival at Fort Bridger—Messrs. Hastings and Hudspeth—Traders and trappers from Taos—Capt. Walker—Californian horses—Snow showers on the mountains—Resume our march by the new route via the Great Salt Lake—Cold weather—Ice in July—Bear River—Difficult passage through the mountains—Elephant statue.

JULY 15.—About eight miles from our last encampment we struck and forded Green river, the head of the Colorado or Red River of the West, which empties into the Gulf of California.

The river at the ford is between fifty and one hundred yards in breadth, and the water in the channel is about two and a half feet in depth. The bed of the channel is composed of small round stones. The stream runs with a clear rapid current. Cotton-wood and small willows border its banks as far as we travelled upon it. These, with some green islands, afford an agreeable and picturesque contrast to the brown scenery of hill and plain on either side. Continuing down the river we halted at noon to rest our animals under the shade of some large cotton-wood trees. There was but little grass around us. A dark cloud, across which there were incessant flashes of lightning, rose in the west soon after we halted.

At half-past two o'clock, P. M., resuming our march we travelled about two miles farther down the stream, and left it near a point where I saw the ruins of several log-cabins, which I have since learned were erected some years ago by traders and trappers, and have subsequently been deserted. The trail here makes a right angle and ascends over the bluffs bordering the valley of the stream, in nearly a west course. We had scarcely mounted the bluffs when we were saluted by a storm of rain, lightning, thunder, and wind, which raged with terrific fury and violence over the broken and dreary plain, for several hours.

It is scarcely possible to conceive a scene of more forbidding dreariness and desolation than was presented to our view on all sides. Precipitous and impending cliffs of rock and concrete sand and clay, deep ravines and chasms plowed out by the torrents of water or by the fierce tornadoes which rage with unrestrained force and fury over this desert, with a few straggling and stunted sage-shrubs struggling for an existence in the sandy and gravelly soil, were the prominent objects that saluted our vision. Far to the left of us, the Utah mountains lift their summits covered with perpetual snows, presenting to the eye a wintry scene in the middle of July.

While travelling onward at a slow pace, being some hundred yards in advance of the main party, (the storm having in some degree subsided,) with skins thoroughly wet and in no **very** cheerful mood, one of the party behind struck up in a sonorous voice the serio-comic elegy of "Lord Lovell and Lady Nancy." Shouts of merry laughter succeeded the rehearsal of each stanza, and the whole party, from being in a most gloomy and savage state of mind, were restored to the best possible humor. The strong contrast between the sublime which they had seen and felt, and the ridiculous which they heard, operated upon them something like a shock of galvanism on a dead body.

Just before sunset, we reached the summit of the ridge between Green river and Black's Fork, a tributary of the former. From this, at a distance of six or eight miles, we could see the last-named stream, and the smoke rising from the fires of an emigrant encampment. We reached Black's Fork of Green river, and encamped upon it some time after dark. There was no wood except some small green willows which resisted ignition; and weary and wet, we soon made our beds and fell asleep. Distance 35 miles.

July 16.—Black's Fork is a stream varying in width from fifty to one hundred feet. Its waters are limpid and cold. The trail crosses this stream several times during the day's march, leaving it as often to cut off the bends, and returning to it again. The scenery along our route to-day has been interesting, although the soil of the country for the most part is frightfully sterile.

The bluffs, assuming the forms and elevation of *buttes*, which border the valley of the stream through which we are travelling, are composed of soft sandstone and a concrete combination of sand and clay. Their perpendicular walls are colored with nearly all the hues of the rainbow, in stratified lines. Red, green, blue, yellow, and purple are distinctly represented. These bluffs are worn by the action of water and wind into almost every conceivable shape. A very remarkable isolated elevation or *butte*, rises abruptly from the flat surface of the plain, about eighteen miles from our last encampment. Its shape is irregularly oval. It is about two or three miles in circumference, and its extreme height is probably five hundred feet above the level of the plain. In general shape and ornament it presents the appearance of a magnificent structure erected by human labor, but crumbling into ruins. Surrounding it there are a multitude of columns of unknown architectural orders, (orders of nature,) and grotesque figures in statuary, and carvings in *alto* and *basso relievo*. Some of these would be substitutes for the sphynxes of Egyptian architecture ; others for caryatides, etc., etc. But it is useless to multiply similitudes, for there is scarcely a prominent animal figure in nature, or a distorted and unnatural shape conceived by man for architectural ornament, that has not some feature represented here, sculptured and carved upon the soft rock by the winds and the rains. A well-defined cornice surrounds the western and southern sides of this temple of nature, and its roof is surmounted by three immense domes, in comparison with which those of the Capitol, St. Peter's, and St. Sophia are toys. A few miles beyond this, there is a labyrinth of columns formed in the bluffs by the action of water and wind, through which when you enter it, the voice and sound of footsteps are echoed and re-echoed a long distance.

The *mirage* displayed here its illusory invitations with great distinctness. The presentations of this phenomenon were not, however, different from those previously noticed. Just before sunset, we once more struck the stream on which we were travelling, and had a view of the landmarks which, we supposed, were near Fort Bridger. The trail at this point diverged again from the stream, and we travelled over a barren plain, with no vegetation upon it except the wild sage. We were overtaken by darkness some miles before reaching our destination for the day. The trail was lost by my mule, upon the natural instinct of which I relied more than upon myself, in the dark. We proceeded onward, and finally saw the faint light of camp-fires, apparently very near, but really at a long distance. Striking in a direct line for them, we met many obstacles and obstructions, some of which were imaginary, others real. We were at last successful in crossing, in the dark, a ravine, bordered on each side by timber, and entering upon the bottom of grass where the lights appeared that we had so intently watched.

Proceeding on, we reached the encampment of Mr. Hastings about eleven o'clock at night. A shower of rain, which fell during the afternoon, had wet us to our skins, and shivering with the dampness and cool temperature, we let our mules loose, and gathered around a miserable fire, the fuel of which was composed of small, green willows. Distance 40 miles.

July 17.—We determined to encamp here two or three days, for the purpose of recruiting our animals, which, being heavily packed, manifest strong signs of fatigue. We pitched our tent, for the first time since we left Fort Laramie, near the camp of Messrs. Hastings and Hudspeth. These gentlemen left the settlements of California the last of April, and travelling over the snows of the Sierra, and swimming the swollen water-courses on either side, reached this vicinity some two weeks since, having explored a new route, via the south end of the great Salt Lake, by which they suppose the distance to California is shortened from one hundred and fifty to two hundred miles. My impressions are unfavorable to the route, especially for wagons and families; but a number of the emigrant parties now encamped here have determined to adopt it, with Messrs. Hastings and Hudspeth as their guides; and are now waiting for some of the rear parties to come up and join them.

"Fort Bridger," as it is called, is a small trading-post, established and now occupied by Messrs. Bridger and Vasquez. The buildings are two or three miserable log-cabins, rudely constructed, and bearing but a faint resemblance to habitable houses. Its position is in a handsome and fertile bottom of the small stream on which we are encamped, about two miles south of the point where the old wagon trail, via Fort Hall, makes an angle, and takes a northwesterly course. The bottom produces the finest qualities of grass, and in great abundance. The water of the stream is cold and pure, and abounds in spotted mountain trout, and a variety of other small fish. Clumps of cottonwood trees are scattered through the valley, and along the banks of the stream. Fort Bridger is distant from the Pacific Spring, by our estimate, 133 miles.

About five hundred Snake Indians were encamped near the

trading-post this morning, but on hearing the news respecting the movements of the Sioux, which we communicated to them, most of them left immediately, for the purpose, I suppose, of organizing elsewhere a war-party to resist the threatened invasion. There are a number of traders here from the neighborhood of Taos, and the head-waters of the Arkansas, who have brought with them dressed buckskins, buckskin shirts, pantaloons, and moccasins, to trade with the emigrants. The emigrant trade is a very important one to the mountain merchants and trappers. The countenances and bearing of these men, who have made the wilderness their home, are generally expressive of a cool, cautious, but determined intrepidity. In a trade, they have no consciences, taking all the "advantages;" but in a matter of hospitality or generosity they are open-handed—ready, many of them, to divide with the needy what they possess.

I was introduced to-day to Captain Walker, of Jackson county, Missouri, who is much celebrated for his explorations and knowledge of the North American continent, between the frontier settlements of the United States and the Pacific. Captain W. is now on his return from the settlements of California, having been out with Captain Fremont in the capacity of guide or pilot. He is driving some four or five hundred Californian horses, which he intends to dispose of in the United States. They appear to be high-spirited animals, of medium size, handsome figures, and in good condition. It is possible that the trade in horses, and even cattle, between California and the United States may, at no distant day, become of considerable importance. Captain W. communicated to me some facts in reference to recent occurrences in California, of considerable interest. He spoke discouragingly of the new route via the south end of the Salt Lake.

Several emigrant parties have arrived here during the day, and others have left, taking the old route, via Fort Hall. Another cloud, rising from behind the mountains to the south, discharged sufficient rain to moisten the ground, about three o'clock, p. m. After the rain had ceased falling, the clouds **broke away**, some of them sinking below and others rising above the summits of the mountains, which were glittering in the rays of the sun with snowy whiteness. While raining in the valley, it had been snowing on the mountains. During the shower the thermometer fell, in fifteen minutes, from 82° to 44°.

July 18.—We determined, this morning, to take the new route, via the south end of the great Salt Lake. Mr. Hudspeth—who with a small party, on Monday, will start in advance of the emigrant companies which intend travelling by this route, for the purpose of making some further explorations— has volunteered to guide us as far as the Salt Plain, a day's journey west of the Lake. Although such was my own determination, I wrote several letters to my friends among the emigrant parties in the rear, advising them *not* to take this route, but to keep on the old trail, via Fort Hall. Our situation was different from theirs. We were mounted on mules, had no families, and could afford to hazard experiments, and make explorations. They could not. During the day I visited several of the emigrant *corrals*. Many of the trappers and hunters now collected here were lounging about, making small trades for sugar, coffee, flour, and whiskey. I heard of an instance of a pint of miserable whiskey being sold for a pair of buckskin pantaloons, valued at ten dollars. I saw two dollars in money paid for half a pint.

Several Indians visited our camp, in parties of three or four at a time. An old man and two boys sat down near the door of our tent, this morning, and there remained without speaking, but watchful of every movement, for three or four hours. When dinner was over, we gave them some bread and meat, and they departed without uttering a word. Messrs. Curry and Holder left us to-day, having determined to go to Oregon instead of California. Circles of white-tented wagons may now be seen in every direction, and the smoke from the camp-fires is curling upwards, morning, noon, and evening. An immense number of oxen and horses are scattered over the entire valley, grazing upon the green grass. Parties of Indians, hunters, and emigrants are galloping to and fro, and the scene is one of almost holiday liveliness. It is difficult to realize that we are in a wilderness, a thousand miles from civilization. I noticed the lupin, and a brilliant scarlet flower, in bloom.

July 19.—Bill Smith, a noted mountain character, in a shooting-match burst his gun, and he was supposed for some time to be dead. He recovered, however, and the first words he uttered upon returning to consciousness were, that " no d—d gun could kill him." The adventures, hazards, and escapes of this man, with his eccentricities of character, as they were related to me, would make an amusing volume. I angled in the stream, and caught an abundance of mountain trout and other small fish. Another shower of rain fell this afternoon, during which the temperature was that of a raw November day.

July 20.—We resumed our march, taking, in accordance with our previous determination, the new route already referred to. Our party consisted of nine persons. Mr. Hudspeth and three young men from the emigrant parties, will accompany us as far as the Salt Plain.

We ascended from the valley in which Fort Bridger is situated, on the left of a high and rather remarkable *butte* which overlooks the fertile bottom from the west. There is no trail, and we are guided in our course and route by the direction in which the Salt Lake is known to lie. The face of the upland country, after leaving Fort Bridger, although broken, presents a more cheerful aspect than the scenery we have been passing through for several days. The wild sage continues to be the principal growth, but we have marched over two or three smooth plains covered with good grass. The sides of the hills and mountains have also in many places presented a bright green herbage, and clumps of the aspen poplar frequently ornament the hollows near the bases of the hills.

We crossed a large and fresh Indian trail, made probably by the Snakes. Many of their lodge-poles were scattered along it, and occasionally a skin, showing that they were travelling in great haste. As usual for several days past, a cloud rose in the southwest about three o'clock, P. M., and discharged sufficient rain to wet us. The atmosphere during the shower had a

13

wintry feel.   On the high mountains in sight of us to the left, we could see, after the clouds broke away, that it had been snowing.

We reached a small creek or branch called "Little Muddy" by the hunters, where we encamped between four and five o'clock.   Our camp is in a handsome little valley a mile or more in length and half a mile in breadth, richly carpeted with green grass of an excellent quality.   An occasional cotton-wood tree, clumps of small willows, and a variety of other shrubbery along the margin of the stream, assist in composing an agreeable landscape.   The stream is very small, and in places its channel is dry.   The wild geranium, with bright pink and purplish flowers, and a shrub covered with brilliant yellow blossoms, enliven the scenery around.   The temperature is that of March or April, and winter clothing is necessary to comfort.   Many of the small early spring flowers are now in bloom, among which I noticed the strawberry.   Large numbers of antelopes were seen.   Distance 15 miles.

July 21.—Our buffalo-robes and the grass of the valley were white with frost.   Ice of the thickness of window-glass, congealed in our buckets.   Notwithstanding this coldness of the temperature, we experience no inconvenience from it, and the morning air is delightfully pleasant and invigorating.   Ascending the hills on the western side of our camp, and passing over a narrow ridge, we entered another grassy valley, which we followed up in a southwest course, between ranges of low sloping hills, three or four miles.   Leaving the valley near its upper end, or where the ranges of hills close together, we ascended a gradual slope to the summit of an elevated ridge, the descent on the western side of which is abrupt and precipitous, and is covered with gnarled and stunted cedars, twisted by the winds into many fantastic shapes.   Descending with some difficulty this steep mountain-side, we found ourselves in a narrow hollow, enclosed on either side by high elevations, the bottom of which is covered with rank grass, and gay with the bloom of the wild geranium and a shrub richly ornamented with a bright yellow blossom.   The hills or mountains enclosing this hollow, are composed of red and yellow argillaceous earth.   In the ravines there are a few aspen poplars of small size, and higher up some dwarfish cedars bowed by winds and snows.

Following up this hollow a short distance, we came to an impassable barrier of red sandstone, rising in perpendicular and impending masses, and running entirely across it. Ascending with great difficulty the steep and high elevation on our right hand, we passed over an elevated plain of gradual ascent, covered with wild sage, of so rank and dense a growth that we found it difficult to force our way through it. This ridge overlooks another deeper and broader valley, which we entered and followed in a southwest course two or three miles, when the ranges of hills close nearly together, and the gorge makes a short curve or angle, taking a general northwest direction. We continued down the gorge until we reached Bear river, between one and two o'clock, P. M.

Bear river, where we struck and forded it, is about fifty yards in breadth, with a rapid current of limpid water foaming over a bed so unequal and rocky, that it was difficult, if not dangerous to the limbs of our mules, when fording it. The margin of the stream is thinly timbered with cotton-wood and small willows. The fertile bottom, as we proceeded down it, varying in width from a mile and a half to one-eighth of a mile, is well covered with grasses of an excellent quality; and I noticed, in addition to the wild geranium, and several other flowers in bloom, the wild flax, sometimes covering a half acre or more with its modest blue blossom. Travelling down the stream on the western side, in a course nearly north, six miles, we encamped on its margin about 3 o'clock, P. M.

The country through which we have passed to-day, has, on the whole, presented a more fertilized aspect than any we have seen for several hundred miles. Many of the hill-sides, and some of the table-land on the high plains, produce grass and other green vegetables. Groves of small aspen poplars, clumps of hawthorn, and willows surrounding the springs, are a great relief to the eye, when surveying the general brownness and sterility of the landscape. I observed strawberry-vines among the grass in the hollows, and in the bottom of Bear river; but there was no fruit upon them.   We have passed the skeletons of several buffaloes.   These animals abounded in this region some thirty years ago; but there are now none west of the Rocky Mountains.

Brown shot three antelopes near our camp this afternoon. A young one, which was fat and tender, was slaughtered and brought to camp; the others were so lean as not to be considered eatable.   The sage-hens, or the grouse of the sage-plains, with their broods of young chickens, have been frequently flushed, and several shot.   The young chickens are very delicate; the old fowl is usually, at this season, lean and tough.

McClary has been quite sick with a fever which has prevailed among the emigrants, and frequently terminated fatally. This afternoon he was scarcely able to sit upon his mule, from weakness and giddiness.   Distance 25 miles.

July 22.—Cold, with a strong wind from the snowy mountains to the southwest, rendering the atmosphere raw and uncomfortable.   We rose shivering from our bivouacs, and our mules picketed around were shaking with the cold.   McClary was so much relieved from his sickness, that he considered himself able to travel, and we resumed our march at seven o'clock. Crossing the river bottom on the western side, we left it, ascending and descending over some low sloping hills, and entering another narrow, grassy valley, through which runs a small stream in a general course from the southwest.   We travelled up this gradually ascending valley about twelve miles, to a point were the stream *forks*.   Near this place there are several springs of very cold water.   Following up the right-hand fork some miles farther, in a northwest course, we left it by climbing the range of hills on the right hand, passing along an elevated ridge, from which we descended into a deep mountain gorge, about one o'clock, P. M.

The mountains on either side of the *cañada* or gorge are precipitous, and tower upwards several thousand feet above the level upon which we are travelling.   At 3 o'clock we crossed a small stream flowing into the *cañada* from the northeast.   Continuing down, the space between the ranges of mountains becomes narrower, and choked up with brush, prostrate trees, and immense masses of rock (conglomerate) which have fallen from the summits of the mountains, affording us no room to pass. We were compelled to leave the bottom of the gorge, and with great caution, to find a path along the precipitous side of the mountains, so steep in many places that our mules were in constant danger of sliding over the precipices, and being thus destroyed.

The snows have recently disappeared. Their fertilizing irrigation has produced a verdant carpet of grass in the bottoms of the small hollows, bespangled with a variety of blooming plants and shrubs. The geranium, wild flax in bloom, and a purple phlox, have been the most conspicuous. In some places the blight of recent frosts is visible. I noticed several fir-trees in one place, while descending through the gorge, from 20 to 100 feet in height. Some of them were standing upon inaccessible projections from the mountain-side. The mountains on either side of us, during our march this afternoon, have raised their rocky and barren summits to a great height, presenting in places perpendicular walls and impending projections of red sandstone and conglomerate rock. Immense masses of many thousand tons' weight have fallen from the sides, and rolled from the summits into the trough of the gorge, where they lie imbedded deep in the earth, or shattered by the concussion of the fall. In other places, the soft red sandstone has been worn by the action of the atmosphere into many remarkable and some times fantastic shapes. Some of these are spiral and columnar, others present the grotesque forms of nondescript animals and birds. A very conspicuous object of this kind, of colossal magnitude, exhibited the profile of a rhinoceros or elephant. We named it the "Elephant's Statue."

The dislocated skeletons of buffaloes which perished here many years ago, have been frequently seen. Large flocks of antelope have been in sight during the day's march. We have seen as many as five hundred. A red fox, and an animal of a brown color, which I never saw described, approached within a short distance this afternoon.

13*

Just before sunset we reached a small opening between the mountain ranges, covered with a dense growth of willows, wild currants, and wild rose-bushes. The mountain-sides presented clumps of hawthorn, and a few diminutive and scattering cedars. Here we encamped in the small openings among the willows and other shrubbery, where we found grass and water sufficient for our animals. Distance 35 miles.

———◆———

CHAPTER XI.

More extreme cold weather—Ogden's Hole—Utah Indians—Weber River —Cañons—Indian visiters—Disgusting practice—Great fires in the mountains—First view of the great Salt Lake—Salmon-trout—Great Salt Lake—A sunset on the lake—Broke my thermometer—Indian chase—Warm sulphur springs—More Indian visiters—Indian fruit-cake—Grasshopper jam—Mode of taking grasshoppers by the Indians.

JULY 23.—Ice froze in our buckets and basins one-fourth of an inch in thickness. On the surface of the small shallow brook which runs through the valley, the congelation was of the thickness of window-glass. At home, in the low and humid regions of the Mississippi valley, at this stage of the thermometer we should suffer from sleeping in the open air. But here the atmosphere is so elastic, dry, and bracing, that we experience no inconvenience.

Continuing our march down the narrow defile in a southwest course, generally along the side of the mountain, (the bottom being choked up with willows, vines, briers, and rose-bushes,) we crossed the channels at their mouths, of two small streams emptying into the branch upon which we are travelling. These streams flow through narrow mountain defiles which, as far as we could discern, were timbered with cedars and poplars. One of these gorges presents a most savage and gloomy aspect. It is so narrow and deep that the rays of the sun never penetrate to its bottom. Mr. Hudspeth thinks this is what is called by the hunters, "Ogden's Hole." It derives this name from the circumstance that a trapper by the name of Ogden concealed himself here from a body of pursuing and hostile Indians, and perhaps perished. I am not sufficiently acquainted with the facts to relate them with accuracy. The romantic interest of the story is doubtless much enhanced by a view of the wild and forbidding spot where its incidents and catastrophe occurred.

The ranges of mountains, as we proceeded down the gorge, became more and more elevated, but less precipitous. I noticed, at a height of six or eight hundred feet above the level of the stream, numberless small white fossil shells, from half an inch to an inch in diameter. In places bare of vegetation, the ground was white with these crustaceous remains. About eleven o'clock, we passed through a grove of small poplars, at the upper end of a triangular valley. The stream down which we have been travelling, here runs through a perpendicular *cañon* of great elevation, and empties into the main Weber river, which flows into the Great Salt Lake, running in a nearly west course. Ascertaining by examination that we could not pass this *cañon*, without following a considerable distance the rocky channel of the stream, we crossed some low hills, or a gap in the mountains at the northeast corner of the valley. While marching over these hills, we were overtaken by five or six Indians mounted on horses. The Indians rode up and saluted us with much apparent friendship and cordiality. They were a small party encamped in the valley that we had just left, whose animals and lodges we had seen at a distance in the brush skirting the stream. After riding two miles, we entered a fertile valley several miles in length and breadth, covered with luxuriant grass, through which flows Weber river; but tracing the channel down to where it enters the mountains, we found a *cañon* more difficult to pass than the one we had just left. Observing at a distance a party of Indians, whose encampment was some two miles up the valley, coming towards us, we determined to halt for an hour or two, and gather from them such information as we could in reference to the route to the Salt Lake.

The first Indians that came up were two men and a small boy. One of the men called himself a Utah, the other a Soshonee or Snake. The Utah appeared to be overjoyed to see us. He was not satisfied with shaking hands, but he must embrace us, which, although not an agreeable ceremony, was submitted to by several of our party. This ceremony being over, he laughed merrily, and danced about as if in an ecstasy of delight in consequence of our appearance. He examined with great curiosity all of our baggage ; tried on, over his naked shoulders, several of our blankets, in which costume he seemed to regard himself with great satisfaction. He was, for an Indian, very comical in his deportment and very merry. The number of Indians about our camp soon accumulated to fifteen or twenty, all of whom were Utahs, except the one Snake mentioned, who had married a Utah squaw. A hasty dinner was prepared, and we distributed very sparingly among them (for our stock of provisions is becoming low) something from each dish, with which display of hospitality they appeared to be gratified. Most of these Indians were armed with bows and arrows. There were among them a miserable rifle and musket, which they had evidently procured from Mexican trappers or traders, as, when I inquired of the owner of one of them its name, he pronounced the word *carabina*. Those who had these guns were desirous that we should wait until they could ride some distance and bring dressed deer or elkskins, which they wished to trade for powder and balls. They were all miserably clothed, some wearing a filthy, ragged blanket, others a shirt and gaiters made of skins, and others simply a breech-cloth of skins. Their countenances, however, were sprightly and intelligent, and several of them were powerfully formed.

The result of our inquiries in reference to the route was not satisfactory. The merry old fellow we first met, advised us by signs to go southwest a distance until we struck water, and then go northwest. Another advised us to return to the small valley, and from thence to pass through the mountains parallel with Weber river. We determined on the latter route, it appearing to be the shortest.

Saddling up, we retraced our trail into the small valley, where we were overtaken by the Indians, desirous of trading skins for powder and balls. Several trades were made, generally at the rate of twelve charges of powder, and as many ounce-bullets, for a large elk or deer skin well dressed. We ascended from the valley through a winding and difficult ravine, to the summit of the range of mountains on the west, from which we could see nothing but mountain after mountain, one rising behind another, in the course we designed taking. A halt was called, and Mr. Hudspeth and myself, leaving our party, entered a ravine and followed it down steep declivities, (our mules frequently sliding ten or fifteen feet over bare and precipitous rocks,) with a view of ascertaining the practicability of passing along the bank of the river. Forcing our way, after our descent, through the thick brush and brambles, and over dead and fallen timber, we finally reached the stream and crossed it. The result of our observations was that the route was impracticable, without the aid of axes to clear away the brush and dead and fallen timber, unless we took the rocky bed of the river for a road, wading water generally three feet deep, and in places, probably of swimming depth to our animals. We returned after considerable difficulty to our party, and countermarching, encamped just as the sun was setting, in the small valley so often referred to.

There are two Indian lodges near our camp. We visited them, and made exchanges of small articles with the women for parched and pulverized sunflower and grass seeds. Its taste was much like that of parched corn, and agreeable. All the men, women, and children, some eight or ten in number, visited us during the preparation and discussion of our supper, watching with much curiosity and interest the culinary operations and other movements. They were good-natured and sociable, so far as there can be sociability between persons making known their thoughts by vague signs. Our supper to-night, with the exception of bread and coffee, consisted of a stew made of antelope flesh, which, as it happened, was very highly seasoned with pepper. I distributed several plates of this stew among the Indians. They tasted of it, and immediately made most ludcrous grimaces, blowing out and drawing in their breath, as if they had been burnt. They handed back the plates without eating their contents. To satisfy them that we were playing no tricks upon them, which they seemed to suspect, I ate from the same dishes; but they could not be prevailed upon to eat the stew. Coffee, bread, and a small lump of sugar to each was distributed among them, with which they seemed much pleased. The sugar delighted them beyond measure, and they evidently had never seen or tasted of it before. During the visit of these Indians, I noticed the females hunting for the vermin in the heads and on the bodies of their children; finding which, they ate the animals with an apparent relish. I had often heard of this disgusting practice, but this is the first instance of it I have seen. They retired to their lodges about nine o'clock, and so much confidence did we feel in their friendship, that no watch was set for the night. Distance from our last camp, seven miles.

July 24.—Crossing for the third time the low gap at the southeastern corner of the small valley, we entered the large, level, and fertile bottom, on the edge of which we had halted yesterday. Fording the river, we took a south course over this bottom, which is about three miles in breadth, covered with tall grass, the bloom upon which shows that, when ripe, it must be heavily seeded and nutritious. From the valley we ascended gradually five or six miles to the summit of a ridge of hills, from which, descending about the same distance in a southwest course, we struck another branch of Weber's river, flowing in a northwest course. Following the stream about a mile, much to our disappointment we found another impassable cañon. This cañon resembles a gate, about six or eight feet in width, the arch and superstructure of which have fallen in immense masses, rendering a passage by the channel of the stream impossible. The mountains on either side raise their perpendicular walls of red sandstone to a great elevation.

Looking up the side of the mountain on our right, we saw a small Indian trail winding under and over the projecting and impending cliffs. This evidence that the Indians had passed this way, satisfied us that we could do the same; although to the eye, when standing in the valley and looking upwards, it seemed impossible. We commenced the ascent, mules and men following each other along the narrow and dangerous path in single file. After much labor we reached the summit of the ascent. This first difficulty being over, we travelled about two miles along the side of the mountain, in a path so narrow that a slight jostle would have cast us over a precipice to the bottom of a gulf a thousand feet in depth. Continuing down the stream five miles, our progress being obstructed by many difficulties, we at length, much to our gratification, reached an opening between the mountains, displaying an extensive valley covered with grass, and the meanderings of the stream upon which we were travelling by the line of dark green shrubbery and herbage upon its banks. We reached the junction of this stream with Weber river between four and five o'clock, and encamped for the day.

A number of Utah Indians accompanied us several miles this morning. Among them was the pleasant and comical old fellow, who amused us so much yesterday. They all appeared to be much gratified by our visit, and were very pressing in their invitations to us to stop and trade with them. Near the last *cañon* there was a solitary lodge, from which the inhabitants, with the exception of an old man and woman, fled as soon as they saw us, driving before them their horses. The old man and woman, being unable to run, hid themselves under the bank of the stream. I noticed in one of the ravines to-day, the scrub-oak, or what is commonly called *black-jack*, also a few small maple-trees. The trunks of none of these are more than two inches in diameter. Distance 24 miles.

July 25.—We determined to remain encamped to-day, to rest and recruit our mules, the grass and water being good. The valley in which our camp is situated is about fifteen miles in length, and varies from one to three miles in breadth. The mountains on both sides rise in benches one above another, to an elevation of several thousand feet above the level of the valley. The summits of this range, on the west, exhibit snow. It is scarcely possible to imagine a landscape blending more variety, beauty, and sublimity, than is here presented. The quiet, secluded valley, with its luxuriant grass waving in the breeze; the gentle streamlet winding through it, skirted with clumps of willows and the wild rose in bloom; the wild currant, laden with ripe fruit; the aspen poplar, with its silvery, tremulous foliage; the low, sloping hills, rising at first by gentle ascents, and becoming gradually more and more elevated and rugged, until their barren and snowy summits seem almost to cleave the sky, compose a combination of scenery not often witnessed.

I noticed this morning, about ten o'clock, a column of smoke rising from the mountains to the west. The fire which produced it continued to increase with an almost frightful rapidity, and the wind, blowing from that quarter, has driven the smoke into the valley, darkening the sun, and imparting to every thing around a lurid and dismal coloring.

Jacob, Buchanan, and Brown started early this morning, with the intention of ascending one of the snowy mountain peaks. They returned about four o'clock, P. M., overcome with the fatigue of their walk, and without having accomplished their design, being prevented by distance, and the tangled brush in the hollows and ravines. Mr. Hudspeth rode down the valley to explore Weber's river to the Salt Lake. He returned in the afternoon, having passed through the next *cañon*. I noticed several magpies, and other small birds, in the valley during the day.

July 26.—The fires in the mountains were burning with great fury all night, threatening, although probably at a distance of twenty miles, to reach us before we decamped. Burnt leaves and ashes, driven by the winds, whirled through the atmosphere, and fell around us in the valley. Mr. Hudspeth and two of the men with him left us here, to explore the *cañon* above, and ascertain the practicability of wagons passing through it. Resuming our march, we proceeded down the valley about ten miles, passing through, at its lower end, a grove of poplars, in which a fire had been burning, and some of the fallen trees were yet blazing. Entering between the walls of the mountains forming the *cañon*, after laborious exertions for several hours, we passed through it without any serious accident. The *cañon* is four or five miles through, and we were compelled, as heretofore, to climb along the side of the precipitous mountains, frequently passing under, and sometimes scaling, immense overhanging masses and projections of rock. To be thus safely enlarged from this natural prison-house, locked at every point, was an agreeable, if not an important event in the history of our journey.

At four o'clock, P. M., we encamped on the bank of the Weber river, just below the *cañon*. The stream, at this point, is about thirty feet in breadth, with a limpid and rapid current, and a rocky channel. The grass along its margin is dry and dead, but well seeded, and consequently nutritious to our animals. A few small poplars, generally from two to three inches in diameter at the trunk, skirt the stream.

I ascended the range of hills bordering the valley of the river to the south, from which I had a most extensive and interesting view of the Great Salt Lake. My position was about ten miles distant from the lake, but my elevation was such that I could discern its surface from the north to the south, a distance which I estimated at sixty or eighty miles. The shore next to me, as far as I could see it, was white. Numerous mountainous islands, dark and apparently barren, sometimes in ranges of fifteen or twenty miles, sometimes in solitary peaks, rise to a considerable elevation above its surface; but the waters surrounding these insulations could be traced between them as far as the eye could reach. The evening was calm, and not a ripple disturbed the tranquil bosom of the lake. As the sun was sinking behind the far distant elevations to the west, the glassy surface of this vast inland ocean was illuminated by its red rays, and for a few minutes it appeared like a sea of molten fire. The plain or valley of the lake, to the right, is some eight or ten miles in width, and fertile. The Weber river winds through it, emptying into the lake some ten miles to the north of our camp. A few trees fringe its margin. I could smell a strong and offensive fetor wafted from the shore of the lake.

Returning to camp, Miller, who had employed his leisure in angling, exhibited a piscatory spectacle worthy the admiration

14

of the most epicurean ichthyophagist.   He had taken with his
hook about a dozen salmon-trout, from eight to eighteen inches
in length; and the longest weighing four or five pounds.   A
delicacy such as this, and so abundant, we determined to enjoy,
and from the results of Miller's sport we feasted this evening
upon a viand which epicures would give much to obtain; but
they nor my " Tonglythian" friends, Higgins and Frazer, would
scarcely undergo the fatigues and privations to which we had
been subjected for its acquisition.   Distance 16 miles.

July 27.—By an arrangement with Mr. Hudspeth, we remained encamped, awaiting his return from his exploring trip
through the upper *cañon* of Weber river.   Fishing apparatus
was in great demand this morning; and most of the party, as
soon as breakfast was over, were enjoying the Waltonian sport,
in angling for the delicious salmon-trout with which the stream
abounds.   Our bait is the large insect resembling the cricket,
heretofore described, myriads of which are creeping and hop-
ping among the grass, and other vegetation of the valley.
Every angler was more or less successful, according to his luck
or skill.   A quantity of fish, weighing each from two to five
pounds, was taken,—more than sufficient for our wants, although
our appetites at this time are not easily satisfied.   The fires
noticed day before yesterday, and yesterday, have continued to
burn ; and this afternoon they seemed to have found fresh fuel.
The wind changing to the southeast, and blowing a gale, just
before sunset, dense clouds of smoke and ashes were driven
down upon us.

July 28.—Some of the party went into the hills to gather
service-berries.   (I do not know that this orthography is correct.
It is in accordance with the orthoepy.)   The service-berry is
produced by a shrub, generally from four to six feet in height.
It is of a dark color, larger than the whortleberry, and not
very unlike it in flavor.   This fruit is abundant here.

July 29.—Mr. Hudspeth and two young men came into camp
early this morning, having bivouacked last night a short distance
from us, on the opposite side of the river.   They had forced
their way through the upper *cañon,* and proceeded six miles

further up Weber river, where they met a train of about forty emigrant wagons under the guidance of Mr. Hastings, which left Fort Bridger the same day that we did. The difficulties to be encountered by these emigrants by the new route will commence at that point ; and they will, I fear, be serious. Mr. Hudspeth thinks that the passage through the *cañon* is practicable, by making a road in the bed of the stream at short distances, and cutting out the timber and brush in other places.

Resuming our march, we took a south course over the low hills bordering the valley in which we have been encamped ; thence along the base of a range of elevated mountains which slope down to the marshy plain of the lake. This plain varies in width from fifteen to two miles, becoming narrower as we approach what is called the " Utah Outlet," the channel through which the Utah Lake empties its waters into the Salt Lake.

The Great Salt Lake has never been accurately surveyed. It is situated between 40 and 42 degrees of north latitude, and between 35 and 36 degrees of longitude west from Washington. Its length is variously stated by the hunters and trappers who have travelled along its shores, at from one hundred and fifty to one hundred and eighty miles. But in this estimate, the numerous large bays and other irregularities are included. Its extreme length in a straight line is probably one hundred miles, and its extreme breadth between forty and sixty miles. At this season the shore, as we pass along it, is white with a crust of the muriate and carbonate of soda combined. The muriate of soda predominates, but the alkali combined with it is sufficient to render the salt bitter and unfit for use in its natural state. When the wind blows from the lake, the stench arising from the stagnant water next to the shore is highly offensive to the smell. The surface of the lake does not present that rippling and sparkling appearance when the sudden breeze passes over it, so frequently seen on fresh-water lakes, and on the ocean. The waters undoubtedly are thoroughly saturated with saline matter, and hence, from their weight, when they move at all, it is with a lazy and sluggish undulatory motion. It is stated that

no fish exist in the lake. I have already mentioned that there
are numerous mountainous islands in the lake. There are also
several large bays indenting its shores. The plain or valley
along which we have travelled to-day is in some places argillaceous, in others sandy and gravelly. Where there is a soil, it
is covered with a growth of luxuriant vegetation,—grass, a
species of cane, rushes, and a variety of small shrubs and flower-
ing plants. A few scrub-oaksands tunted cedars can be seen
on the mountain-sides, and along the ravines. There are many
small streams of pure cold water flowing from the mountains.

The heat of the sun during our march this afternoon was
excessive. My bridle reins were frequently so hot that it was
painful to hold them in my hands. The road has been difficult,
and our progress slow. We encamped about three o'clock for
the day, on a small spring branch. The sunset scene this evening was splendid. The surface of the lake appeared like a sheet
of fire, varying in tint from crimson to a pale scarlet. This
flame-like ocean was bordered as far as we could see to the
north and south of us, with a field of salt, presenting all the
appearances of freshly fallen snow.

When I took out the thermometer this evening, much to my
regret I discovered that the bulb was broken. I hung the frame
and glass tube on a willow for the observation of the Indians.
It will be some time before they will venture to touch it. They
stand in great awe of the mysterious instruments which science
has invented, and never handle them except with due caution.
Distance 18 miles.

July 30.—At sunrise, clear and calm, with an agreeable temperature. The morning scene was beautifully grand. Our
camp being in the shadow of the mountains, the face of the
sun was invisible to us, long after his golden rays had tipped,
one after another, the summits of the far-distant islands in the
lake. By degrees the vast expanse of waters became illuminated, reflecting the bright beams of the god of day with
dazzling effulgence.

Our route to-day continued south, near the base of the range
of mountains on our left. We frequently crossed deep ravines

and piles of granite debris, with which the slope of the mountains in places is covered. Travelling about ten miles we reached the southern extremity of one of the bays of the Salt Lake. Beyond this there is a basin of water some three or four miles in circumference, surrounded by a smooth sandy beach. An immense number of ducks were walking and flying over this beach and playing in the basin. Approaching the shore of the pond, a solitary Indian rose from the weeds or grass near the water, and discovering us, he started immediately and ran with considerable speed towards a point of the mountains on our left. Several of us pursued and overtook him. He appeared much alarmed at first, but after shaking hands with us, and discovering that we had no hostile intentions, he soon forgot his fright. He carried in his hand a miserably lean duck, which he had just killed with an arrow. A quiver slung across his bare and tawny shoulders, was well supplied with this weapon. He was naked, with the exception of a small covering around his loins, and his skin was as dark as a dark mulatto. Learning from him that he was a Utah, we endeavored to make him comprehend that we wished to trade with his tribe for elk-meat. He shook his head, and appearing desirous of leaving us, we dismissed him. He was soon out of sight, hurrying away with long and rapid strides.

Proceeding about two miles and turning the point of the mountain, we came to seven warm springs, so strongly impregnated with sulphur as to have left a deposite of this mineral in some places several feet in depth. These springs gush out near the foot of a high precipice, composed of conglomerate rock and a bluish sandstone. The precipice seems to have been uplifted by some subterraneous convulsion. The temperature of the water in the basins was about 90°. The water of most of them was bitter and nauseous.

From these springs we crossed a level plain, on which we encamped at 11 o'clock, A. M., near a small stream of cold water flowing from the mountains, which is skirted with a few poplars and small willows. The grass immediately around our camp is fresh and green, but a short distance from us it is brown, dry, and crisp.

14*

After dinner we were visited by three Indians, one of whom was the man with the duck we saw this morning. The eldest of the three signified that he wished a friendly smoke and a "talk." A pipe was produced and filled with tobacco. Lighting it, I drew two or three puffs and handed it to the old man, and it passed from him to his comrades until the tobacco was consumed. They appeared to enjoy the fumes of the smoke highly. We informed them of our wish to trade for meat. They signified that they had none. Three females of middle age, miserably clad and ugly, soon made their appearance, bringing baskets containing a substance, which, upon examination, we ascertained to be service-berries, crushed to a *jam* and mixed with pulverized grasshoppers. This composition being dried in the sun until it becomes hard, is what may be called the "fruit-cake" of these poor children of the desert. No doubt these women regarded it as one of the most acceptable offerings they could make to us. We purchased all they brought with them, paying them in darning-needles and other small articles, with which they were much pleased. The prejudice against the grasshopper "fruit-cake" was strong at first, but it soon wore off, and none of the delicacy was thrown away or lost.

Two of our party mounted their mules and rode to the Indian encampment to ascertain if there were not more Indians, and some from whom meat could be obtained. As soon as the men and women in our camp saw them riding in the direction of their lodges, they hastened away with great speed and in much alarm. Returning from the Indian encampment, Jacob and Brookey reported that there were no more Indians, and that no meat could be obtained. They saw a large quantity of grasshoppers, or crickets, (the insect I have before described,) which were being prepared for pulverization.

The Indians of this region, in order to capture this insect with greater facility, dig a pit in the ground. They then make what hunters, for brevity of expression, call a *surround ;*—that is, they form a circle at a distance around this pit, and drive the grasshoppers or crickets into it, when they are easily secured and taken. After being killed, they are baked before the fire or dried in the sun, and then pulverized between smooth stones. Prejudice aside, I have tasted what are called delicacies, less agreeable to the palate. Although the Utahs are a powerful and warlike tribe, these Indians appeared to be wretchedly destitute.

A fire was raging on the mountain-side all night, and spread down into the valley, consuming the brown vegetation. The water of the small stream was made bitter with the ashes. Our camp-ground, we conjecture, is the same that was occupied by Captain Fremont last year. Distance 15 miles.

CHAPTER XII.

Utah Outlet and Lake—Enter the desert—Utah language—Col. Russell's nine-shooter—Digger Indians—Utter sterility.

JULY 31.—Morning clear, with a delightful temperature, and a light breeze blowing from the west. Our route to-day runs in a west course across the valley of the "Utah Outlet," about ten miles south from the bay or arm of the Salt Lake upon which we have been travelling. The waters of the Utah Lake are emptied into the Salt Lake through this channel. The Utah Lake is a body of fresh water between sixty and eighty miles in circumference, situated about twenty miles south of the Salt Lake. The shape of the extensive plain of this lake was made apparent to us by the mountains surrounding it. The plain of the lake is said to be fertile, but of the extent of its fertility I have no certain knowledge. The eastern side of the valley of the "Outlet" is well watered by small streams running from the mountains, and the grass and other herbage on the upland are abundant, but there is no timber visible from our position.*

Descending from the upland slope on which we encamped yesterday, we crossed a marsh about two miles in width, covered

---

* In 1847 the Mormons made a settlement between the Utah and the Salt Lake.

with grass so dense and matted that our animals could scarcely make their way through it. This grass is generally from five to eight feet in height. A species of rush called *tule* is produced on the marsh. It grows to the height of eight and ten feet. The ground is very soft and tremulous, and is covered for the most part with water to the depth of two or three inches. But our mules were prevented from sinking into it by the forest of herbage which they prostrated under their feet as they advanced. From the marsh we ascended a few feet upon hard, dry ground, producing a coarse grass with an ear resembling our small grains, wheat or barley, and some few flowers, with bunches of wild sage. The colors of the flowers were generally yellow and scarlet.

We reached the Utah Outlet after travelling four miles, and forded it without difficulty. The channel is about twenty yards in breadth, and the water in the deepest places about three feet. The bed of the channel is composed of compact bluish clay. The plain or valley, from the western bank of the " Outlet" to the base of the range of hills to the west, is level and smooth, and in places white with a saline deposite or efflorescence. There is but little vegetation upon it, and this is chiefly the wild sage, indicative of aridity, and poverty of soil. From this plain we struck the shore of another bay of the Salt Lake, bordered by a range of mountains running parallel with it. The shore, next to the white crust of salt, is covered with a debris precipitated from the rocky summits of the mountains.

Our route for several hours described nearly a semicircle, when there was a break in the range of mountains, and we entered upon another plain. About three o'clock, P. M., we passed several remarkable rocks rising in tower-like shapes from the plain, to the height of sixty or eighty feet. Beyond these we crossed two small streams bitter with saline and alkaline impregnation. The plain presents a sterile appearance, but little vegetation appearing upon it, and that stunted and withered. At seven o'clock, P. M., we reached a spring branch descending from a mountain ravine, and fringed with small willows, the water of which is comparatively fresh and cool.

Here we encamped after a march without halting, of twelve hours. There is a variety of vegetation along the stream—grass, weeds, some few flowers, briers, and rose-bushes.

Soon after we encamped, three Utah Indians visited us. They were mounted on horses, rather lean, and sore-backed from hard usage. The men appeared to be of a better class and more intelligent than those we had before met with. They were young and manifested much sprightliness, and an inquisitive curiosity, which they took no pains to conceal. We invited them to sup with us, and they partook of our simple viands with a high relish. A renewal of our overtures to trade for meat met with no better success than before. They had no meat to dispose of. They were dressed in buckskin shirts, gaiters, and moccasins ; and armed with bows and arrows. Two of these men, the most intelligent, concluded to encamp with us for the night. The principal of these, a young man of about twenty-five, with an amiable but sprightly expression of countenance, was so earnest and eager in his inquiries respecting every thing appertaining to us, and into our language, that I sat conversing with him until a late hour of the night. From him I learned the names of many things in the Utah dialect. I give some of these below. The orthography is in strict accordance with the sound.

ENGLISH.	UTAH.	ENGLISH.	UTAH.
Tobacco	Pah.	Water	Poh.
Fire	Coutouch.	Eye	Pooh.
Grass	Shawnip.	Ear	Nank.
Hair	Pamp.	Nose	Tamoucher
Sun	Tarp.	Hand	Moh.
Powder-horn	Naup.	Flint	Tuck.
Spur	Tannegan.	Wood	Schnip.
Mule	Moodah.	Blanket	Tochewanup.
Bullet	Navak.	Pipe	Toh.
Knife	Weitch.	Teeth	Tamp.
Horse	Punk.	Bear	Padewap.
Finger	Mushevan.	Rifle	Wokeat.
Foot	Mamp.	Powder	Noketouch.
Bear's Claw	Musheta.	Pantaloons	Wannacouch.
Saddle	Middenah.		

These are some of the words of the Utah language which I wrote down, from his pronunciation, by the light of our camp-fire. Furnishing him and his companion some skins, we requested them to retire for the night, which they seemed to do with reluctance. Distance 40 miles.

August 1.—Morning clear, with a delightfully soft breeze from the south. I purchased, this morning, of one of the Utahs, a dressed grisly bear-skin, for which I gave him twenty charges of powder and twenty bullets. Several other small trades were made with them by our party. Having determined to cross a range of mountains, instead of following to avoid it, the shore of another cove or bay of the Salt Lake,—by doing which we should lose in distance twenty-five or thirty miles,—we laid our course nearly west, towards the lowest gap we could discover in the range.

After we had proceeded two or three miles up the sloping plain, towards the base of the mountains, Colonel Russell recollected that he had left his rifle at the camp—a "nine-shooter." Accompanied by Miller, he returned back to recover it. I was very well satisfied that the Indians would have discovered it, and, considering it a valuable prize, would not wait for the return of the loser. According to their code of morals, it is not dishonest to take what is left in camp, and they never fail to do it. I halted for an hour, and long after our party had disappeared in a gorge of the mountains, for the return of Colonel Russell and Miller. I could see, from my elevated position, the dust raised by the horses of the retreating Indians on the plain, at a distance of six or eight miles from the camp. Becoming impatient, I commenced a countermarch, and while moving on, I saw, at a distance of a mile and a half, a solitary horseman, urging his animal with great speed towards me. There being but one instead of two, I felt considerable anxiety, not knowing but some disaster might have occurred. I moved faster towards the horseman, and, at the distance of a quarter of a mile, discovered that it was Colonel Russell. Riding towards him, I inquired what had become of Miller? He did not know. He had lost him in hunting through the willows and ravines. My anxiety was much increased at this report, and I started to return to the camp, when Miller, proceeding at a slow gait, appeared on one of the distant elevations. The result of the search for the "nine-shooting" rifle was fruitless. The Indians had carried it away with them. The only consolation I could offer to Colonel Russell for his loss was, that a more useless burden was never carried on the shoulders of man or mule. It was a weight upon the beast, and an incumbrance to the rider, and of no practical utility on this journey. This consolation, however, was not very soothing.

[I will state here, that this rifle was recovered by Mr. Hudspeth, brought into California, and returned to Colonel Russell. The Indian who took it from our camp, after he had returned to the village of his tribe, was much elated by his prize. But in discharging it, the ball, instead of making its passage through the barrel, took another direction, and wounded him in the leg. An instrument so mysterious and eccentric it was considered dangerous to retain, and the chief ordered its restoration to the emigrant parties following us. It was recognised by Mr. Hudspeth, and returned to its owner, as above stated.]

Following the trail of our party, we entered the narrow mountain-gorge, or valley, where I saw them disappear. Proceeding up this valley, we passed several temporary wigwams, erected by the Indians along the side of the small stream which flows through it from the summit of the mountain. These wigwams were all deserted; but fires were burning in front of them, dogs were barking, and willow-baskets, some of which contained service-berries, were standing about. A few poplar and pine trees, service-bushes, willows, and a variety of small shrubbery, with an occasional sunflower, ornament this narrow and romantic gorge. As we ascended, the sides of the mountain presented ledges of variegated marble, and a debris of the same was strewn in our path. We overtook our party when they were about halfway up the steep ascent to the crest of the range. Mules and men were strung out a mile, toiling and climbing up the almost insurmountable acclivity.

The inhabitants of the wigwams, who had fled and concealed

themselves until we had passed, now commenced whooping far below us, and we could see several of them following our trail. After much difficulty in urging our animals forward, and great fatigue to ourselves and them, we reached the summit of the ridge. Here we halted to take breath. Several of the Indians, whose whoops we had heard, came up to us. They were naked, and the most emaciated and wretched human objects I had ever seen. We shook hands, however, and greeted them kindly. The descent on the western side of the mountain, although steep, is not difficult, there being but few obstructions. Four miles from the summit brought us to a gentle slope, and to a faint stream which flows from the hills and sinks in the sands just below. Here we encamped for the day. Near us, on the slope, there is a grove of small cedars, the deep verdure of which is some relief to the brown and dead aspect of vegetable nature surrounding us. Distance 15 miles.

August 2.—Morning clear, with a soft breeze from the south. We were visited early by three miserable Digger Indians, calling themselves Soshonees. They were naked, with the exception of a few filthy, ragged skins, fastened around their loins. They brought with them a mixture composed of parched sunflower seed and grasshoppers, which they wished to exchange with us for some articles we possessed. We declined trading with them. One of them signified, that he knew where there was water over the next ridge of mountains. Water at the western base of the next range would diminish the long march without this necessary element, over the great Salt Plain, some ten or twelve miles. For a compensation in shirts and pantaloons, he consented to accompany and guide us to the water; but when we started, he declined his engagement.

Descending into the plain or valley before us, we took a northwest course across it, striking Capt. Fremont's trail of last year after we had commenced the ascent of the slope on the western side. The breadth of this valley at this point, from the base of one range of mountains to the other, is about twenty miles. Large portion sof it are covered with a saline efflorescence of a snowy whiteness. The only vegetation is the wild sage ; and this is parched and shrivelled by the extreme drought. Not a solitary flower or green plant has exhibited itself. In our march we crossed and passed several deep ravines and chasms, plowed by the waters from the mountains during the melting of the snows, or hollowed out by the action of the winds. Not a living object, animal, reptile, or insect, has been seen during our day's march.

We encamped at two o'clock, P. M. There are a few dwarf cedars in our vicinity, and scattered bunches of dead grass. In a ravine near us the sand is moist; and by making an excavation, we obtained a scant supply of water, impregnated with salt and sulphur. A dense smoky vapor fills the valley and conceals the summits of the distant mountains. The sun shining through this, dispenses a lurid light, coloring the brown and barren desert with a more dismal and gloomy hue. As soon as our afternoon meal had been prepared and discussed, we commenced preparations for the march over the Salt Desert to-morrow, which employment occupied us until a late hour of the night. Distance 20 miles.

CHAPTER XIII.

March over the great Salt Desert—Preparations—Singular illusion—Volcanic debris—Distant view of the great Salt Plain—Utter desolation—The mirage—Gigantic phantoms—Fata Morgana—Spectral army—Tempest on the Salt Plain—Clouds of salt—Instinct of mules—Mule-race—Excessive thirst—Arrival at oasis, and spring—Buchanan's well.

AUGUST 3.—I rose from my bivouac this morning at half-past one o'clock. The moon appearing like a ball of fire, and shining with a dim and baleful light, seemed struggling downwards through the thick bank of smoky vapor that overhung and curtained the high ridge of mountains to the west of us. This ridge, stretching far to the north and the south as the eye can reach, forms the western wall (if I may so call it) of the desert valley we had crossed yesterday, and is composed of rugged, barren peaks of dark basaltic rock, sometimes exhibiting misshapen outlines ; at others, towering upwards, and displaying a variety of architectural forms, representing domes, spires, and turreted fortifications.

Our encampment was on the slope of the mountain ; and the valley lay spread out at our feet, illuminated sufficiently by the red glare of the moon, and the more pallid effulgence of the stars, to display imperfectly its broken and frightful barrenness, and its solemn desolation.   No life, except in the little oasis occupied by our camp, and dampened by the sluggish spring, by excavating which with our hands we had obtained impure water sufficient to quench our own and our animals' thirst, existed as far as the eye could penetrate over mountain and plain. There was no voice of animal, no hum of insect, disturbing the tomb-like solemnity.   All was silence and death.   The atmosphere, chill and frosty, seemed to sympathize with this sepulchral stillness.   No wailing or whispering sounds sighed through the chasms of the mountains, or over the gulfy and waterless ravines of the valley.   No rustling zephyr swept over the scant dead grass, or disturbed the crumbling leaves of the gnarled and stunted cedars, which seemed to draw a precarious existence from the small patch of damp earth surrounding us.   Like the other elements sustaining animal and vegetable life, the winds seemed stagnant and paralyzed by the universal dearth around. I contemplated this scene of dismal and oppressive solitude until the moon sunk behind the mountain, and object after object became shrouded in its shadow.

Rousing Mr. Jacob, who slept soundly, and after him the other members of our small party, (nine in number,) we commenced our preparations for the long and much-dreaded march over the great Salt Desert.   Mr. Hudspeth, the gentleman who had kindly conducted us thus far from Fort Bridger as our pilot, was to leave us at this point, for the purpose of exploring a route for the emigrant wagons farther south.   He was accompanied by three gentlemen, Messrs. Ferguson, Kirkwood, and Minter.   Consequently, from this time forward we are without a guide, or any reliable index to our destination, except our course westward, until we strike Mary's river and the emigrant trail to California, which runs parallel with it, some two hundred miles distant. The march across the Salt Plain, without water or grass, was variously estimated by those with whom I conversed at Fort Bridger, at from sixty to eighty miles. Captain Walker, an old and experienced mountaineer, who had crossed it at this point as the guide of Captain Fremont and his party, estimated the distance at seventy-five miles, and we found the estimate to be nearly correct.

We gathered the dead limbs of the cedars which had been cut down by Captain Fremont's party when encamped here last autumn, and igniting them, they gave us a good light during the preparation and discussion of our frugal breakfast; which consisted to-day of bread and coffee, bacon being interdicted in consequence of its incitement to thirst—a sensation which at this time we desired to avoid, as we felt uncertain how long it might be before we should be able to gratify the unpleasant cravings it produces.

Each individual of the party busied himself around the blazing fires in making his various little but important arrangements, until the first gray of the dawn manifested itself above the vapory bank overhanging the eastern ridge of mountains, when the word to saddle up being given, the mules were brought to the camp-fires, and every arm and muscle of the party was actively employed in the business of saddling and packing "with care!"—with unusual care, as a short detention during the day's march to readjust the packs might result in an encampment upon the desert for the coming night, and all its consequent dangers, the death or loss by straying in search of water and grass of our mules, (next to death to us,) not taking into the account our own suffering from thirst, which for the next eighteen or twenty hours we had made up our minds to endure with philosophical fortitude and resignation. A small powder-keg, holding about three or four pints of coffee, which had been emptied of its original contents for the purpose, and filled with that beverage made from the brackish spring near our camp, was the only vessel we possessed in which we could transport water, and its contents composed our entire liquid refreshment for the march. Instructions were given to Miller, who had charge of this important and precious burden, to husband it with miserly care, and to make an equitable division whenever it should be called into use.

Every thing being ready, Mr. Hudspeth, who accompanied us to the summit of the mountain, led the way. We passed upwards through the *cañada* [pronounced kanyeada] or mountain-gorge, at the mouth of which we had encamped, and by a comparatively easy and smooth ascent reached the summit of the mountain after travelling about six miles. Most of us were shivering with cold, until the sun shone broadly upon us after emerging, by a steep acclivity, from the gorge through which we had passed to the top of the ridge. Here we should have had a view of the mountain at the foot of which our day's journey was to terminate, but for the dense smoke which hung over and filled the plain, shutting from the vision all distant objects.

Bidding farewell to Mr. Hudspeth and the gentleman with him, (Mr. Ferguson,) we commenced the descent of the mountain. We had scarcely parted from Mr. H. when, standing on one of the peaks, he stretched out his long arms, and with a voice and gesture as loud and impressive as he could make them, he called to us and exclaimed—"Now, boys, put spurs to your mules and ride like h—!" The hint was timely given and well meant, but scarcely necessary, as we all had a pretty just appreciation of the trials and hardships before us.

The descent from the mountain on the western side was more difficult than the ascent; but two or three miles, by a winding and precipitous path through some straggling, stunted, and tempest-bowed cedars, brought us to the foot and into the valley, where, after some search, we found a blind trail which we supposed to be that of Captain Fremont, made last year. Our course for the day was nearly due west; and following this trail where it was visible, and did not deviate from our course, and putting our mules into a brisk gait, we crossed a valley some eight or ten miles in width, sparsely covered with wild sage (artemisia) and grease-wood. These shrubs display themselves and maintain a dying existence, a brownish verdure, on the most arid and sterile plains and mountains of the desert, where no other vegetation shows itself. After crossing the valley, we rose a ridge of low volcanic hills, thickly strewn with sharp fragments of basaltes and a vitreous gravel resembling junk-bottle glass. We passed over this ridge through a narrow gap, the walls of which are perpendicular, and composed of the same dark scorious material as the debris strewn around. From the western terminus of this ominous-looking passage we had a view of the vast desert-plain before us, which, as far as the eye could penetrate, was of a snowy whiteness, and resembled a scene of wintry frosts and icy desolation. Not a shrub or object of any kind rose above the surface for the eye to rest upon. The hiatus in the animal and vegetable kingdoms was perfect. It was a scene which excited mingled emotions of admiration and apprehension.

Passing a little further on, we stood on the brow of a steep precipice, the descent from the ridge of hills, immediately below and beyond which a narrow valley or depression in the surface of the plain, about five miles in width, displayed so perfectly the wavy and frothy appearance of highly agitated water, that Colonel Russell and myself, who were riding together some distance in advance, both simultaneously exclaimed—"We must have taken a wrong course, and struck another arm or bay of the Great Salt Lake." With deep concern, we were looking around, surveying the face of the country to ascertain what remedy there might be for this formidable obstruction to our progress, when the remainder of our party came up. The difficulty was presented to them ; but soon, upon a more calm and scrutinizing inspection, we discovered that what represented so perfectly the "rushing waters" was moveless, and made no sound ! The illusion soon became manifest to all of us, and a hearty laugh at those who were the first to be deceived was the consequence ; denying to them the merit of being good pilots or pioneers, etc.

Descending the precipitous elevation upon which we stood,

15*

we entered upon the hard smooth plain we had just been surveying with so much doubt and interest, composed of bluish
clay, incrusted, in wavy lines, with a white saline substance, the
first representing the body of the water, and the last the crests
and froth of the mimic waves and surges. Beyond this we
crossed what appeared to have been the beds of several small
lakes, the waters of which have evaporated, thickly incrusted
with salt, and separated from each other by small mound-
shaped elevations of a white, sandy, or ashy earth, so imponderous that it has been driven by the action of the winds into these
heaps, which are constantly changing their positions and their
shapes. Our mules waded through these ashy undulations,
sometimes sinking to their knees, at others to their bellies, creating a dust that rose above and hung over us like a dense fog.

From this point on our right and left, diagonally in our front,
at an apparent distance of thirty or forty miles, high isolated
mountains rise abruptly from the surface of the plain. Those
on our left were as white as the snow-like face of the desert,
and may be of the same composition, but I am inclined to the
belief that they are composed of white clay, or clay and sand
intermingled.

The mirage, a beautiful phenomenon I have frequently mentioned as exhibiting itself upon our journey, here displayed its
wonderful illusions, in a perfection and with a magnificence surpassing any presentation of the kind I had previously seen.
Lakes, dotted with islands and bordered by groves of gently
waving timber, whose tranquil and limpid waves reflected their
sloping banks and the shady islets in their bosoms, lay spread
out before us, inviting us, by their illusory temptations, to stray
from our path and enjoy their cooling shades and refreshing
waters. These fading away as we advanced, beautiful villas,
adorned with edifices, decorated with all the ornaments of sub-
urban architecture, and surrounded by gardens, shaded walks,
parks, and stately avenues, would succeed them, renewing the
alluring invitation to repose, by enticing the vision with more
than Calypsan enjoyments or Elysian pleasures. These melting
from our view as those before, in another place a vast city, with

countless columned edifices of marble whiteness, and studded with domes, spires, and turreted towers, would rise upon the horizon of the plain, astonishing us with its stupendous grandeur and sublime magnificence. But it is in vain to attempt a description of these singular and extraordinary phenomena. Neither prose or poetry, nor the pencil of the artist, can adequately portray their beauties. The whole distant view around, at this point, seemed like the creations of a sublime and gorgeous dream, or the effect of enchantment. I observed that where these appearances were presented in their most varied forms, and with the most vivid distinctness, the surface of the plain was broken, either by chasms hollowed out from the action of the winds, or by undulations formed of the drifting sands.

About eleven o'clock we struck a vast white plain, uniformly level, and utterly destitute of vegetation or any sign that shrub or plant had ever existed above its snow-like surface. Pausing a few moments to rest our mules, and moisten our mouths and throats from the scant supply of beverage in our powder-keg, we entered upon this appalling field of sullen and hoary desolation. It was a scene so entirely new to us, so frightfully forbidding and unearthly in its aspects, that all of us, I believe, though impressed with its sublimity, felt a slight shudder of apprehension. Our mules seemed to sympathize with us in the pervading sentiment, and moved forward with reluctance, several of them stubbornly setting their faces for a countermarch.

For fifteen miles the surface of this plain is so compact, that the feet of our animals, as we hurried them along over it, left but little if any impression for the guidance of the future traveller. It is covered with a hard crust of saline and alkaline substances combined, from one-fourth to one-half of an inch in thickness, beneath which is a stratum of damp whitish sand and clay intermingled. Small fragments of white shelly rock, of an inch and a half in thickness, which appear as if they once composed a crust, but had been broken by the action of the atmosphere or the pressure of water rising from beneath, are strewn over the entire plain and imbedded in the salt and sand.

As we moved onward, a member of our party in the rear

called our attention to a gigantic moving object on our left, at
an apparent distance of six or eight miles.   It is very difficult
to determine distances accurately on these plains.   Your estimate is based upon the probable dimensions of the object, and
unless you know what the object is, and its probable size, you
are liable to great deception.   The atmosphere seems frequently to act as a magnifier ; so much so, that I have often seen a
raven perched upon a low shrub or an undulation of the plain,
answering to the outlines of a man on horseback.   But this
object was so enormously large, considering its apparent distance, and its movement forward, parallel with ours, so distinct,
that it greatly excited our wonder and curiosity.   Many and
various were the conjectures (serious and facetious) of the party,
as to what it might be, or portend.   Some thought it might be
Mr. Hudspeth, who had concluded to follow us ; others that it was
some cyclopean nondescript animal, lost upon the desert ; others
that it was the ghost of a mammoth or Megatherium wandering
on " this rendezvous of death ;" others that it was the d—l mounted on an Ibis, &c.   It was the general conclusion, however, that
no animal composed of flesh and blood, or even a healthy ghost,
could here inhabit.   A partner of equal size soon joined it, and
for an hour or more they moved along as before, parallel to us,
when they disappeared, apparently behind the horizon.

   As we proceeded, the plain gradually became softer, and our
mules sometimes sunk to their knees in the stiff composition of
salt, sand, and clay.   The travelling at length became so difficult and fatiguing to our animals that several of the party dismounted, (myself among the number,) and we consequently
slackened our hitherto brisk pace into a walk.   About two
o'clock, P. M., we discovered through the smoky vapor the dim
outlines of the mountains in front of us, at the foot of which
was to terminate our day's march, if we were so fortunate as to
reach it.   But still we were a long and weary distance from it,
and from the " grass and water" which we expected there to
find.   A cloud rose from the south soon afterwards, accompanied by several distant peals of thunder, and a furious wind,
rushing across the plain and filling the whole atmosphere

around us with the fine particles of salt, and drifting it in heaps like the newly fallen snow. Our eyes became nearly blinded and our throats choked with the saline matter, and the very air we breathed tasted of salt.

During the subsidence of this tempest, there appeared upon the plain one of the most extraordinary phenomena, I dare to assert, ever witnessed. As I have before stated, I had dismounted from my mule, and turning it in with the *caballada*, was walking several rods in front of the party, in order to lead in a direct course to the point of our destination. Diagonally in front, to the right, our course being west, there appeared the figures of a number of men and horses, some fifteen or twenty. Some of these figures were mounted and others dismounted, and appeared to be marching on foot. Their faces and the heads of the horses were turned towards us, and at first they appeared as if they were rushing down upon us. Their apparent distance, judging from the horizon, was from three to five miles. But their size was not correspondent, for they seemed nearly as large as our own bodies, and consequently were of gigantic stature. At the first view I supposed them to be a small party of Indians (probably the Utahs) marching from the opposite side of the plain. But this seemed to me scarcely probable, as no hunting or war party would be likely to take this route. I called to some of our party nearest to me to hasten forward, as there were men in front, coming towards us. Very soon the fifteen or twenty figures were multiplied into three or four hundred, and appeared to be marching forward with the greatest action and speed. I then conjectured that they might be Capt. Fremont and his party with others, from California, returning to the United States by this route, although they seemed to be too numerous even for this. I spoke to Brown, who was nearest to me, and asked him if he noticed the figures of men and horses in front? He answered that he did, and that he had observed the same appearances several times previously, but that they had disappeared, and he believed them to be optical illusions similar to the mirage. It was then, for the first time, so perfect was the deception, that I conjectured the probable fact that these figures were the reflection of our own images by the atmosphere, filled as it was with fine particles of crystallized matter, or by the distant horizon, covered by the same substance. This induced a more minute observation of the phenomenon, in order to detect the deception, if such it were. I noticed a single figure, apparently in front in advance of all the others, and was struck with its likeness to myself. Its motions, too, I thought, were the same as mine. To test the hypothesis above suggested, I wheeled suddenly around, at the same time stretching my arms out to their full length, and turning my face sidewise to notice the movements of this figure. It went through precisely the same motions. I then marched deliberately and with long strides several paces; the figure did the same. To test it more thoroughly, I repeated the experiment, and with the same result. The fact then was clear. But it was more fully verified still, for the whole array of this numerous shadowy host in the course of an hour melted entirely away, and was no more seen. The phenomenon, however, explained and gave the history of the gigantic spectres which appeared and disappeared so mysteriously at an earlier hour of the day. The figures were our own shadows, produced and reproduced by the mirror-like composition impregnating the atmosphere and covering the plain. I cannot here more particularly explain or refer to the subject. But this phantom population, springing out of the ground as it were, and arraying itself before us as we traversed this dreary and heaven-condemned waste, although we were entirely convinced of the cause of the apparition, excited those superstitious emotions so natural to all mankind.

About five o'clock, P. M., we reached and passed, leaving it to our left, a small *butte* rising solitary from the plain. Around this the ground is uneven, and a few scattering shrubs, leafless and without verdure, raised themselves above the white sand and saline matter, which seemed recently to have drifted so as nearly to conceal them. Eight miles brought us to the northern end of a short range of mountains, turning the point of which and bending our course to the left, we gradually came upon higher ground, composed of compact volcanic gravel. I was here considerably in the rear, having made a detour towards the base of the *butte* and thence towards the centre of the short range of mountains, to discover, if such existed, a spring of water. I saw no such joyful presentation nor any of the usual indications, and when I reached and turned the point, the whole party were several miles ahead of me, and out of sight. Congratulating myself that I stood once more on terra firma, I urged my tired mule forward with all the life and activity that spur and whip could inspire her with, passing down the range of mountains on my left some four or five miles, and then rising some rocky hills connecting this with a long and high range of mountains on my right. The distance across these hills is about seven or eight miles. When I had reached the most elevated point of this ridge the sun was setting, and I saw my fellow-travellers still far in advance of me, entering again upon a plain or valley of salt, some ten or twelve miles in breadth. On the opposite side of this valley rose abruptly and to a high elevation another mountain, at the foot of which we expected to find the spring of fresh water that was to quench our thirst, and revive and sustain the drooping energies of our faithful beasts.

About midway upwards, in a *cañada* of this mountain, I noticed the smoke of a fire, which apparently had just been kindled, as doubtless it had been, by Indians, who were then there, and had discovered our party on the white plain below; it being the custom of these Indians to make signals by fire and smoke, whenever they notice strange objects. Proceeding onward, I overtook an old and favorite pack-mule, which we familiarly called "Old Jenny." She carried our meat and flour—all that we possessed in fact—as a sustenance of life. Her pack had turned, and her burden, instead of being on her back was suspended under her belly. With that sagacity and discretion so characteristic of the Mexican pack-mule, being behind and following the party in advance, she had stopped short in the road until some one should come to re-arrange her cargo and place it on deck instead of under the keel. I dismounted and went through, by myself, the rather tedious and laborious process of unpacking and repacking. This done, "Old Jenny" set forward upon a fast gallop to overtake her companions ahead, and my own mule, as if not to be outdone in the race, followed in the same gait. "Old Jenny," however, maintained the honors of the race, keeping considerably ahead. Both of them, by that instinct or faculty which mules undoubtedly possess, had scented the water on the other side of the valley, and their pangs of extreme thirst urged them forward at this extraordinary speed, after the long and laborious march they had made, to obtain it.

As I advanced over the plain—which was covered with a thicker crust of salt than that previously described, breaking under the feet of the animals like a crust of frozen snow—the spreading of the fires in the *cañada* of the mountain appeared with great distinctness. The line of lights was regular like camp-fires, and I was more than half inclined to hope that we should meet and be welcomed by an encampment of civilized men—either hunters, or a party from the Pacific bound homewards. The moon shone out about nine o'clock, displaying and illuminating the unnatural, unearthly dreariness of the scenery.

"Old Jenny" for some time had so far beat me in the race as to be out of my sight, and I out of the sound of her footsteps. I was entirely alone, and enjoying, as well as a man could with a crust of salt in his nostrils and over his lips, and a husky mouth and throat, the singularity of my situation, when I observed, about a quarter of a mile in advance of me, a dark, stationary object standing in the midst of the hoary scenery. I supposed it to be "Old Jenny" in trouble once more about her pack. But coming up to a speaking distance, I was challenged in a loud voice with the usual guard-salutation, "Who comes there?" Having no countersign, I gave the common response in such cases, "A friend." This appeared to be satisfactory, for I heard no report of pistol or rifle, and no arrow took its soundless flight through my body. I rode up to the object and discovered it to be Buchanan sitting upon his mule, which had become so much exhausted that it occasionally refused to go along, notwithstanding his industrious application of the usual incentives to progress. He said that he had supposed himself to be the "last man," before "Old Jenny" passed, who had given him a surprise, and he was quite thunderstruck when an animal, mounted by a man, came charging upon him in his half-crippled condition. After a good laugh and some little delay and difficulty, we got his mule under way again, and rode slowly along together.

We left, to us, in our tired condition, the seemingly interminable plain of salt, and entered upon the sagey slope of the mountain about 10 o'clock. Hallooing as loudly as we could raise our voices, we obtained, by a response, the direction of our party who had preceded us, and after some difficulty in making our way through the sage, grass, and willows, (the last a certain indication of water in the desert,) we came to where they had discovered a faint stream of water, and made their camp. Men and mules, on their first arrival, as we learned, had madly rushed into the stream and drank together of its muddy waters,—made muddy by their own disturbance of its shallow channel and sluggish current.

Delay of gratification frequently gives a temporary relief to the cravings of hunger. The same remark is applicable to thirst. Some hours previously I had felt the pangs of thirst with an acuteness almost amounting to an agony. Now, when I had reached the spot where I could gratify my desires in this respect, they were greatly diminished. My first care was to unsaddle my mule and lead it to the stream, and my next to take a survey of the position of our encampment. I then procured a cup of muddy water, and drank it off with a good relish. The fires before noticed were still blazing brightly above us on the side of the mountain, but those who had lighted them, had given no other signal of their proximity. The moon shone brilliantly, and Jacob, Buchanan, McClary, and myself, concluded we would trace the small stream of water until we could find the fountain spring. After considerable search among the reeds, willow, and luxuriant grass, we discovered a spring. Buchanan was so eager to obtain a draught of cold, pure water, that

16

in dipping his cup for this purpose, the yielding weeds under him gave way, and he sank into the basin, from which he was drawn out after a good "*ducking,*" by one of those present. The next morning this basin was sounded to the depth of thirty-five feet, and no bottom found. We named this spring "Buchanan's well." We lighted no fires to-night, and prepared no evening meal. Worn down by the hard day's travel, after relieving our thirst we spread our blankets upon the ground, and laying our bodies upon them, slept soundly in the bright moonshine. Several of our party had been on the road upwards of seventeen hours, without water or refreshment of any kind, except a small draught of cold coffee from our powder-keg, made of the salt sulphur-water at our last encampment, and had travelled the distance of seventy-five miles. The Salt Plain has never at this place, so far as I could understand, been crossed but twice previously by civilized men, and in these instances two days were occupied in performing the journey. Distance 75 miles.

CHAPTER XIV.

The oasis—Anxiety respecting our animals—Prodigious tall grass—Deserted Indian huts—Old trail of lost wagons—Desert valley—Extinct volcanoes —Mountain spring—Elevated camp—Vast extent of the Salt Plain—Sublimity of scenery—Moonlight view—Sunrise—Indian picket or game-trap —Another oasis—Altercation—Extreme heat of the sun—Wells in the desert—More desert valleys—Stream of running water—View of Mary's River, and valley—Indian signal-fires.

AUGUST 4.—We did not rise from our grassy couches this morning until the sun shone broadly and bright upon us, above the distant mountain ridges to the east. The scene around, with the exception of the small but highly fertile oasis encircling our encampment, is a mixture of brown and hoary barrenness, aridity, and desolation, of which no adequate conception can be conveyed by language. The fires in the *cañada* of the mountain were still smoking, but no blaze was discernible. Last night they appeared as if not more than half a mile or a mile distant ; but considerably to our surprise this morning, by a day-light observation, we saw that the *cañada*, from whence the smoke was curling upwards in graceful wreaths, was some four or five miles from us.

Our first care was to look after and collect together the animals, which, upon our arrival last night, we had let loose to refresh themselves in the manner most agreeable to them. We found them busily employed in cropping the tall seeded grass of the oasis. The anxieties respecting the health, strength, and safety of our animals, constitute one of the most considerable drawbacks upon the pleasures of our trip,—pleasures, as the reader may suppose, derived almost exclusively from the sublime and singular novelties presented to the vision. The significance of the word is in no other respect applicable to this stage of our journey. To fathom the motives of an all-wise Providence, in creating so vast a field of desolation ; to determine in our minds whether the little oases we meet with are the beginnings of a system or process of fertilization which is to ramify and extend, and to render this hitherto abandoned and uninhabitable waste a garden of flowers, teeming with its millions of life ; or whether they are evidences of the last expiring struggles of nature to sustain animal and vegetable existence, which will leave this expansive region impenetrable to the curiosity of man, furnish a study for the thoughts, fruitful of interest and provocative of investigation.

For the purpose of resting and recruiting our over-labored mules, we had predetermined to remain encamped to-day. We cleared away with our hands and willow sticks the thickly-matted grass and weeds around " Buchanan's well," making a handsome basin, some five or six feet in diameter. The water is very cold and pure, and tasted to us more delicious than any of the invented beverages of the epicure to him. While engaged in this work, Brown brought forward a remarkable blade of grass which he had pulled up a short distance from us, to which he called my attention, and desired its measurement. It was measured, and found to be thirty-five feet in length. The diameter of the stalk was about half of an inch, and the distance between the joints about eighteen inches. It was heavily seeded at the top. With this prodigiously tall vegetable production, we endeavored to sound the depth of the spring; but after thrusting it down to its full length we could discover no bottom.

In the afternoon we saw two antelopes above us. Col. Russell and Miller saddled their mules and rode further up the slope of the mountain, for the purpose of hunting and to make other discoveries. During their absence a very dark cloud rose from the west, accompanied by distant thunder and a strong wind. The indications, judging as we would of the signs on the Atlantic side of the continent, were that we should have a heavy shower of rain; but our experience in this dry region had been such, that we felt but little dread of all the waters in the clouds. A few sprinkling drops of rain fell; just enough to leave a scarcely perceptible moisture upon the grass. Col. R. and M. returning, reported that they had killed no game. They found a small running stream of water from the *cañada* where the fires were burning, which sank in the sands and debris of the mountain before it reached the valley; and they also saw three Indian huts, constructed of cedars and grass, but unoccupied. The occupants of these huts, doubtless, after making their signal-fires upon discovering us, had all fled. Their probable motive for inhabiting temporarily this dismal region, was to trap for the few animals which roam in the neighborhood of the spring, and are compelled to approach it for water and grass.

During the course of our journey, nothing has contributed so largely to the depression of the spirits of our small party as inaction. I found to-day that the absence of our usual active employments, added to the desolate aspect of the scenery surrounding us, had produced much despondency in the minds of several of our company; and I felt a strong desire myself to be moving forward, to throw off those formidable mental incubi, ennui and melancholy.

August 5.—A most delightful, clear morning, with a light, soft breeze from the south fanning the parched and arid desert, playing over the waving grass, and sporting with the silvery leaves of the willows of the oasis.

Our mules, notwithstanding the day's rest we had allowed them after the long and laborious ride over the Salt Plain, evinced much stiffness and exhaustion. We took a southwest course along the slope of the range of mountains under which we had encamped. This slope is covered with a debris of gravel and sharp fragments of dark volcanic rock, and is furrowed from the base of the mountains down to the verge of the plain with deep and almost impassable ravines. The hoary and utterly desolate plain of salt on our left expands in breadth, and stretches, interminably to the eye, away to the southeast and the southwest. The brisk breeze having cleared the atmosphere of the smoke, our view is much more extensive than it was yesterday.

After travelling about ten miles we struck a wagon-trail, which evidently had been made several years. From the indentations of the wheels, where the earth was soft, five or six wagons had passed here. The appearance of this trail in this desolate region was at first inexplicable; but I soon recollected that some five or six years ago an emigrating expedition to California was fitted out by Colonel Bartlettson, Mr. J. Chiles, and others, of Missouri, who, under the guidance of Captain Walker, attempted to enter California by passing round the southern terminus of the Sierra Nevada; and that they were finally compelled to abandon their wagons and every thing they had, and did not reach their destination until they had suffered incredible hardships and privations. This, it appeared to me, was evidently their trail; and old as it was, and scarcely perceivable, it was nevertheless some gratification to us that civilized human beings had passed here before, and left their mark upon the barren earth behind them. My conjectures, above stated, have been subsequently confirmed by a conversation with Mr. Chiles.

Following this old trail some two or three miles, we left it on

16*

the right, and crossed some low and totally barren hills, which appear to have been thrown up by the action of volcanic fires at no very remote period of geological history.   They are composed of a white, imponderous earth, resembling ashes, intermingled with fragments of scoria, resembling the cinders from an iron-foundry, or a blacksmith's furnace.   A vitreous gravel, or glass, was also thickly strewn over the surface, and glittered brightly in the sunbeams.

From these hills, changing our course more to the west, we descended into a spacious and level valley, about fifteen miles in width, and stretching north and south as far as the vision could penetrate.   A continuous range of high mountains bounds this valley on the west, and a broken and irregular range on the east.   The only vegetation consists of patches of wild sage, and a shrub ornamented with a yellow flower, resembling the Scotch broom of our gardens.   A considerable portion of the plain is covered with salt, or composed of a white, barren clay, so compact that our horses' hoofs scarcely left an impression upon it. Crossing this valley, we entered the range of mountains on the west of it by a narrow gorge, and following its windings, we reached the foot of the steep dividing ridge about six o'clock, P. M.   Here we had expected to find water, but the ravine was entirely dry, and the grass bordering it was brown and dead. An elevated *butte* of red sandstone towered upwards on our right, like the dome of some Cyclopean cathedral.   On our left was a high but more sloping mountain ; and in front, the steep and apparently impassable crest of the Sierra.

After a fruitless search for water at the bottom of the gorge, among the rocks and crevices of the ravine, I accidentally discovered, near the top of the mountain on our left, a few straggling and stunted cedars, and immediately beneath them a small patch of green shrubs, which I conjectured were willows, a most welcome indication of water, after a ride of eleven hours without rest or refreshment of any kind.   Dismounting from my mule, and accompanied by McClary, I ascended the mountain as far up as the little green oasis, in the centre of which, much to our joy, we found a small spring.   No water flowed from its basin, although the ground immediately around was damp, and the grass green and luxuriant. Our party was soon apprized of the discovery, and following us up the mountain, we made our camp near the spring, which the mules soon completely exhausted of its scant supply of water, without obtaining sufficient to quench their thirst.

Ascending to the summit of the mountain, just as the sun was setting, I had a more extended view of the great Salt Plain than at any time previously. Far to the southeast, apparently from one hundred to one hundred and fifty miles, a solitary mountain of immense height rises from the white surface of the desert, and lifts its hoary summit so as almost to pierce the blue ceiling of the skies, reflecting back from its frozen pinnacle, and making frigid to the eye the warm and mellow rays of the evening sun. No words can describe the awfulness and grandeur of this sublime desolation. The only living object I saw to-day, and the only sign of animal existence separate from our party, was a small lizard.

About three o'clock, P. M., while we were on the march, a violent storm of wind, with some rain, raged in the valley to the south of us, raising a dense cloud of dust, which swept furiously up the eastern side of the valley in drifting masses that would have suffocated us, had we been travelling within its range. Fortunately, we were beyond the more disagreeable effects of the storm, although where we were the wind blew so violently as almost to dismount us from our horses.

We grazed our mules on the dry grass along the ravine below us, until nine o'clock, when they were brought up and picketed around the camp, as usual. The basin of the spring was enlarged so as to hold water enough, when filled, to satisfy the wants of our mules in the morning. These matters all being attended to, we bivouacked on the side of the mountain. Distance 30 miles.

August 6.—The knowledge that our mules had fared badly, and were in a position, on the steep side of the mountain, where they could neither obtain good rest nor food, kept me more wakeful than usual. The heaviest calamity that could befall us, at this time, would be the loss, by exhaustion or otherwise, of our animals.   Our condition in such an event would be deplorable.   I rose at two o'clock, and having first filled all our buckets and vessels with water from the spring, let the mules loose to satisfy their thirst.   One of them I found tangled in its rope, thrown down, and strangled nearly to suffocation.

The night was perfectly serene.   Not a cloud, or the slightest film of vapor, appeared on the face of the deep blue canopy of the heavens.   The moon and the countless starry host of the firmament exhibited their lustrous splendor in a perfection of brilliancy unknown to the night-watchers in the humid regions of the Atlantic; illuminating the numberless mountain peaks rising, one behind the other, to the east, and the illimitable desert of salt that spread its wintry drapery before me, far beyond the reach of the vision, like the vast winding-sheet of a dead world!   The night was cold, and kindling a fire of the small, dead willows around the spring, I watched until the rich, red hues of the morning displayed themselves above the eastern horizon, tinging slightly at first, and then deepening in color, the plain of salt, until it appeared like a measureless ocean of vermilion, with here and there a dark speck, the shadow of some solitary *buttes*, representing islands, rising from its glowing bosom.   The sublime splendors of these scenes cannot be conveyed to the reader by language.

As soon as it was light, I saddled my mule, and ascended to the crest of the ridge to observe the features of the country, and determine our route for the day.   I returned just as our morning meal was prepared, and at seven o'clock we were all in our saddles and on the march.   We passed around the side of the mountain on which we had encamped, and rose gradually to the summit of the range.   Here we were delayed for some time in finding a way to descend.   There are several gorges or ravines leading down, but they appeared to be choked up with rocks and brush so as to render them nearly impassable.

In searching to find a passage presenting the fewest difficulties, I discovered, at the entrance of one of these gorges, a remarkable picketing or fence, constructed of the dwarf cedars of the mountain, interlocked and bound together in some places by willow withes. It was about half a mile in length, extending along the ridge, and I supposed it at the time to have been constructed for defensive purposes, by some of the Indian tribes of this region, against the invasion of their enemies. At the foot of the mountain there was another picketing of much greater extent, being some four or five miles in length, made of the wild sage; and I have since learned from trappers that these are erected by the Indians for the purpose of intercepting the hares, and other small game of these regions, and assisting in their capture.

We descended the mountain through a very narrow gorge, the rocky walls of which, in many places, are perpendicular, leaving us barely room to pass. Emerging from this winding but not difficult passage, (compared with our former experience,) another spacious and level valley or plain spread itself before us. The breadth of this valley is about twenty miles, and its length, judging from the apparent distance of the mountains which exhibit their summits at either end, is about one hundred and fifty miles. The plain appears to be an almost perfect level, and is walled in by ranges of mountains on both sides, running nearly north and south. Wild sage, grease-wood, and a few shrubs of a smaller size, for the most part leafless, and apparently dead or dying, are the only vegetation of this valley. The earth is composed of the same white and light composition, heretofore described as resembling ashes, imbedded in and mixed with which is a scorious gravel. In some places it is so soft that the feet of our animals sink several inches; in others it is baked, and presents a smooth and sometimes a polished surface, so hard that the hoofs of our mules leave but a faint impression upon it. The snowy whiteness of the ground, reflecting back the bright and almost scorching rays of the sun, is extremely painful to the eyes, producing in some instances temporary blindness.

About two o'clock, P. M., after travelling three-fourths the distance across the valley, we struck an oasis of about fifty acres of green grass, reeds, and other herbage, surrounding a number of springs, some of cool fresh water, others of warm sulphur water. These waters rise here, and immedia:ely sink in the sands. Our information at Fort Bridger led us to expect a spring and grass at this point, and in order to make sure of it, we extended the flanks of our small party some three or four miles from the right to the left. The grass immediately around the springs, although not of the best quality, is very luxuriant, and on the whole, it being a favorable place for grazing our mules,—no apprehensions being entertained of their straying, or of Indian depredations,—we determined to encamp for the day.

In the course of our march to-day, we saw three hares, and near the spring; Miller saw an antelope. McClary and Brookey each killed a duck in one of the basins of the spring soon after our arrival, and later in the afternoon Brown killed a hawk. The signs of animals around the springs are numerous, and the wolves were howling near our camp until a late hour of the night. Distance 18 miles.

August 7.—A disagreeable altercation took place between two members of our party about a very trivial matter in dispute, but threatening fatal consequences. Under the excitement of angry emotions, rifles were levelled and the click of the locks, preparatory to discharging the death-dealing contents of the barrels, was heard. I rushed between the parties and ordered them to hold up their pieces, and cease their causeless hostility towards each other. I told them that the life of every individual of the party was, under the circumstances in which we were placed, the property of the whole party, and that he who raised a gun to take away a life, was, perhaps inconsiderately, worse than a common enemy or a traitor to all of us, and must be so considered in all future controversies of this nature, and be denied all further intercourse with us. It was truly a startling spectacle, to witness two men, in this remote desert, surrounded by innumerable dangers, to guard against which they were mutually dependent, so excited by their passions as to seek each other's destruction. The ebullition of insane anger was soon allayed, and we commenced our day's march about the usual hour of the morning.

Our course was due west, and after travelling some four or five miles, we commenced the ascent of the range of mountains in our front. We ascended and descended this range through winding *cañadas* such as I have previously described. Another spacious valley or plain opened to our view from the western side of this sierra, nearly as large in dimensions as that which we entered upon and partly crossed yesterday, and varying but little from it in its general characteristics. Crossing this valley, the sun pouring its scorching rays down upon us with such fervor as nearly to parch our bridle reins into a crisp, we found on the slope of the western side, near the foot of the mountain, another small oasis, of an acre or two of green vegetation, near the centre of which were one or two small springs or wells of cool fresh water. The waters of these springs rise to the surface and sink immediately, moistening only the small patch of fertile ground which I have described.

Refreshing ourselves and our animals with the most grateful beverage of this fountain of the desert, we pursued our wearisome journey over the next sierra, through a narrow gap, which brought us into another broad valley of an oval shape, walled in on all sides, apparently, by an elliptical circle of elevated mountains. The hue of the wild sage and grease-wood of this valley, is a shade greener than in the other valleys we have crossed since we entered the Desert Basin. The composition of the earth is nearly the same. A fine white sand, impalpable almost as ashes, mingled with which is a scorious gravel, in some places soft and yielding to the hoofs of our mules, in others baked and compact almost to the hardness of brick, are the leading characteristics of the *soil*, if soil it can be called.

Fifteen miles brought us to the slope of the mountain on the western side of this valley, where we found a bold spring gushing forth a volume of water sufficient to turn the most powerful mill-wheel, but like all the other springs of this desert which we have seen, after running a short distance, the water sinks and disappears in the thirsting sands. Around this spring there are a few small willows and a luxuriant growth of grass, with some handsome yellow flowers. Here we encamped at six o'clock, after a march of eleven hours, without rest to ourselves or our animals, which begin to manifest much fatigue and exhaustion.

The signs of game around our encampment are numerous, but nothing in the shape of bird or beast shows itself.   In the course of our day's journey we started three hares, which are all of animal life that has been seen.

Nothing can exceed the grandeur and sublimity of these magnificent valleys, walled in by the tall and spiral mountains, when lighted as they now are, by the brilliant and powerful rays of the moon, and the sparkling radiance of the starry host, suspended as it were, like chandeliers from the deep, soft, blue canopy of the heavens.   Their desolation is mellowed, and there is a purity, a holiness about them, which leads the imagination to picture them as vast saloons of nature, fashioned by the hand of the Almighty for the residence of uncontaminating and unsinful essences, and not for the doomed children of passion, want, sorrow, and care !   Should the economy of Providence, in the course of centuries, fertilize and adapt them to the residence of man, the fabled glories of Elysium would scarcely exceed their attractions.   Distance 35 miles.

August 8.—The morning was clear and cool.   A slight dew was perceptible on the grass and on our blankets.   Our course to-day was nearly the same as yesterday.   We passed over the range of mountains under which we had encamped, by ascending one of its most elevated peaks.   When we reached the summit of this peak, after repeatedly stopping on the side of the mountain to breathe our mules, they seemed nearly exhausted and scarcely able to proceed on the journey.   The descent on the western side was so steep and difficult, that our animals and ourselves (dismounted of course) slid or jumped down rather than walked.   At the foot, we entered a small valley, with comparatively strong signs of fertility.   A faint stream of water runs through it, from north to south, the margin of which is fringed with green grass ; and a few stunted cotton-wood trees and other shrubbery relieve the everlasting monotony of sage.   The sight of these trees and of a stream of running fresh water, was more agreeable to us than can be conceived by those who have never been deprived of such scenic objects.

Crossing this stream and the bottom opposite, we passed through a low gap of a range of hills, on the western side of which we struck another small stream of water, which flows through a fertile, grassy valley, in a northwestern course. After descending this valley some five or six miles, the stream *cañons* between high and precipitous hills, along the sides and over the tops of which we were compelled to select our way to the best advantage, until we emerged into the spacious valley of Mary's river, the sight of which gladdened our eyes about three o'clock, P. M.

At this point the valley is some twenty or thirty miles in breadth, and the lines of willows indicating the existence of streams of running water are so numerous and diverse, that we found it difficult to determine which was the main river and its exact course. After wandering about for some time, in compliance with the various opinions of the party, I determined to pursue a course due west, until we struck the river; and at sunset we encamped in the valley of the stream down which we had descended, in a bottom covered with most luxuriant and nutritious grass. Our mules fared most sumptuously both for food and water.

After dark, fires lighted by Indians were visible on the mountains through which we had passed, and in several places in the valley a few miles distant. Our watch, with which we had dispensed in crossing the desert, was set to-night, and it was fortunate for us that we were thus cautious, as an attempt was made by the Indians to steal our mules, which was frustrated by the man on duty at the time.

The mountains on either side of the valley of Mary's river, at this point, tower upwards to a great elevation, and are composed of dark basalt. I noticed near the summits of some of the peaks, small patches of snow. Distance 23 miles.

17

CHAPTER XV.

Mary's river Indians—Their fleetness—Mary's river—Unexpected and singular meeting—Applegate's exploring party from Oregon—Energy of the emigrant population on the Pacific—More Indian visiters—Large herds of antelopes—Flora of Mary's river—A merry Indian—Indian fish-trap—Extensive boiling springs—Rain in the desert—Large body of Indians—Indian foot-race with our mules.

AUGUST 9.—We had scarcely commenced our march when the Indian signal-fires were relighted, and we could discover far up and down the valley, many columns of smoke ascending from the most conspicuous positions on the sides of the mountains.

We took a west course down the grassy bottom of the stream on which we encamped last night, and after travelling some four or five miles, discovered at the distance of about a mile, six Indians running towards us with an apparent speed, greater than could be achieved by any of the animals we were riding. Notwithstanding we proceeded at our usual gait, they soon came up to us, and holding out their hands as we did to them, greeted us with much kindness and cordiality. By signs, we inquired of them their tribe, to which they answered that they were Soshonees, (Snakes.) All the Digger Indians of this valley claim to be Soshonees. The bodies of two or three of them were partially covered with the skins of hares sewn together. The others were entirely naked. Their skins are dark —nearly as dark as that of the negro. The distinguishing features between these Indians and the negro, are in the nose, which is aquiline, the long hair, and their handsome Arabian-shaped feet. Their average stature is about five feet six or seven inches in height. These Indians, doubtless, were the same that disturbed our camp and attempted to steal our mules last night.

One of them had a miserable gun, and was very desirous to

trade some roots prepared in a curious manner, for powder and balls. We declined all trades of this nature, but upon his earnest solicitations I presented him with a few charges of powder without the balls. Two or three of the others were armed with bows and well-filled quivers of iron-pointed arrows. These arrow-points they must have obtained at the northern trading-posts, or they have learned the art of smelting from trappers or emigrants passing down this valley, who have supplied them with iron. Some of them had small pouches or bags made of hare-skins, upon which they seemed to set a great value, and wished to trade them for blankets and other clothing. But our estimate of their wares did not equal their own appraisement, and we could effect no trades. We distributed among them a few pieces of bread and some fried bacon, the residuum of our breakfast, and bid them a very courteous and affectionate good-morning.

Continuing our course along the fertile bottom of the mountain branch, after travelling about two miles farther we struck and crossed Mary's river, which at this point, and at this season, is a very small stream. The channel is of considerable depth and about thirty or forty feet in width, with steep, perpendicular banks. In many places the channel is nearly dry; the water having been absorbed by the spongy earth, stands in stagnant pools with no flowing current to enliven its sluggishness and cool its offensive warmth, or to purge it of the saline, alkaline, and sulphurous substances with which the contiguous soil is strongly impregnated. Clumps of small willows, an inch in diameter, with here and there a few wild currant-bushes, fringe the margin of the river, and constitute the only "timber" that displays itself in this valley.

Just as I was crossing Mary's river, Colonel Russell being with me, considerably in advance of the main body of our party, I saw at the distance of about half a mile a party of some ten or fifteen men mounted on horses and mules, marching towards the north. Spurring our animals, we rode with as much speed as we could make, in a direction to intercept them. They soon discovered us, and halted until we approached them.

From their costume and color it was impossible, at a distance, to determine to which of the classes of the human race they belonged. But their demeanor was entirely pacific. Their rifles lay quietly on the pommels of their saddles, and they seemed to take advantage of the few moments of stoppage allowed them by our interruption of their progress, to rest in their saddles from the weariness of a long journey. I felt quite confident that they were a party from California, who, probably, had been compelled to leave the country in consequence of the war between the United States and Mexico, and were returning to the Atlantic side of the continent, their original homes.

We rode up to them, when they extended their hands and saluted us like brothers who had been long parted, and had met unexpectedly, and under difficult and trying circumstances. We spoke to them in our own language and they answered us in the same dialect, a sound not disagreeable to our ears. We soon learned that they were a party of men from the Wilhamette valley in Oregon, headed by the Messrs. Applegate, who had left their homes on the 10th of May, and since that time had been engaged in exploring a new and more feasible wagon-route to Oregon, by descending Mary's river some distance below this point, and from thence striking the head-waters of the Wilhamette river. Having completed their labors, they were now on their way to Fort Hall for the purpose of meeting the emigrant trains bound to Oregon, and guiding them by this route to their destination. Five members of their party had preceded them several days, having been supplied with their best animals, for the purpose of reaching Fort Hall, or meeting the emigrants this side as soon as possible, and returning immediately with supplies for the relief of the main party, they being nearly destitute of all provisions, and having been on very short allowance for several days. Such was their condition in regard to provisions, that they expected to be compelled to slaughter one of their horses for food, unless they met some of the emigrant trains within a day or two. They all manifested great interest in the "Oregon question," and with much cheerfulness we gave them such information in regard to it as we possessed before leaving our homes. They informed us that there were two emigrant wagons with ten or twelve men, about four or five days in advance of us.

It would be difficult to decide which of the two parties, when confronted, presented the most jaded, ragged, and travel-soiled aspect, but I think the Oregonese had a little the advantage of us in this respect. None of us, within the settlements of the United States, would have been recognised by our nearest kindred as civilized and christianized men. Both parties had been in the wilderness nearly three months, the Oregon party, as we learned, having started on the tenth of May, and our party on the fifth of the same month ; they from the shores of the Pacific travelling east, we from the waters of the Missouri travelling west. A singularity of the incident was, that after having travelled across a desert by a new route some three or four hundred miles, we should have met them just at the moment when they were passing the point of our junction with the old trail. Had we been ten minutes later, we should not have seen them. We met them with pleasure, and parted from them with regret, to pursue our long and toilsome journey, which seems to lengthen out as we proceed,—our point of destination, like the blue wall of the arch of the skies, receding from us as we advance.

I could not, however, but reflect upon and admire the public spirit and enterprise of the small band of men from whom we had just parted. Our government, doubtless, has been desirous of exploring and pointing out the most favorable routes to the Pacific, and has appropriated large sums of money for this purpose. But whatever has been accomplished in the way of explorations, which is of much practical utility, has resulted from the indomitable energy, the bold daring, and the unconquerable enterprise, in opposition to every discouragement, privation, and danger, of our hardy frontier men and pioneers, unaided directly or remotely by the patronage or even the approving smiles and commendations of the government. To them we are indebted for the originally discovered wagon-route to Oregon and Cali-

formia, and to them we are indebted for all the valuable improvements and *cut-offs* on this route.   To them we are indebted for
a good, well-beaten, and plain trail to the Pacific ocean, on the
shores of which, in the face of almost insurmountable difficulties,
unsupported, they have founded an empire.   Let us honor those
to whom honor is due.

Proceeding down the river about two miles, we encamped at
eleven o'clock for the day, in a handsome bottom of green nutritious grass, which the mules cropped with an apparent high
relish.   The varieties of grasses which I have seen since we
entered this valley are numerous, and although they are not as
fine and tender as the grasses of the Rocky Mountains, they are
all heavily seeded and must be highly sustaining.

Jacob and Miller, unknown to me, when we left our encampment this morning, returned back upon our trail to search for
a pocket-compass and some other small articles which Jacob
accidentally dropped on the march yesterday, and they had not
come up with us when we encamped.

Five more naked Indians, with which the valley and the
cañadas of the mountains seem to teem, judging from the numerous trails, footprints, and signal-fires, came into our camp
immediately after we halted.   They brought with them a small
quantity of dried meat and roots, with which they professed a
desire to make trades with us.   The meat I judged was that
of the ground-hog.   It did not present a very inviting or provocative aspect to the palate.   The roots, if roots they were,
were still more repulsive, but the Indians seemed to set an
extraordinary value both upon the meat and the roots.   We
could effect no trades with them, their demands being quite too
exorbitant.   The truth, without doubt was, that they came into
our camp for the purpose of discovering what chance there
might be for theft and plunder.   I requested such of our party
as were present, (only four in number,) to display as much as
possible their guns, pistols, and knives, in order to give them to
understand the consequences of any attempt at thieving or
depredation.   I set up a small mark and shot my pistols several times into the centre of it, which seemed to strike them

with much astonishment. At each report of the pistol, and the splintering of the small willow stick shot at, glances of surprise passed from one to another. They soon took their leave, much to my gratification. Nothing can be more troublesome than Indians about the camp. They compel us to keep a vigilant and constant watch upon every article we possess, to prevent and detect their thievish propensities. We gave each of them a small piece of bread when they were leaving. Buchanan and Brown killed an antelope soon after we encamped, on the opposite side of the river. It was one of a drove of about twenty, which they succeeded in approaching behind a clump of willows. It was brought to camp and cooked for dinner, and enjoyed with a *gusto* unknown to the epicure whose delicacies are prepared in the kitchens of civilization.

I began to feel considerable uneasiness respecting the non-appearance of Jacob and Miller, and was preparing to return back upon the trail to ascertain what delayed them, when about two o'clock, much to my relief, they appeared in sight, coming down the valley. They had mistaken the Oregon party which we met in the morning for us, and had travelled on after them, coming up to them when they halted at noon.

I noticed, during the day, several grouse or sage-hens, as they are commonly called, sand-hill cranes, and many other small birds, flying near the banks of the river. The day has been one of intense and scorching heat, mitigated occasionally by a few light clouds, shading us momentarily from the almost blistering rays of the sun. Distance 10 miles.

August 10.—A cloudy morning with a pleasant temperature. A sprinkle of rain fell in the course of the night, which dampened the grass and moistened our blankets. Some Indians were seen lurking in the willows near our camp about midnight; but discovering our watch, they made no further attempt to steal our animals. Our camp, around which the mules are picketed, is more than arrow-shot from the willows; and these Indians will not make any hostile demonstrations unless they are sheltered by ravines or bushes.

Having reached the wagon-trail to California, although in

many places it is blind and overgrown, yet we shall have less difficulty in searching out our road, and less anxiety respecting our course. The course of the river at this point is nearly south-west, and the trail runs through the bottom, occasionally crossing the low sand-hills, to cut off the bends and avoid the *cañons*. We passed around a *cañon* early this morning. The road being smooth, and generally hard and level, our mules travel off at a brisk trot, with comparative ease.

During the day's march we have seen not less than three or four hundred antelopes, with which the valley seems to teem. They are exceedingly timid and wild, discovering us usually by the scent, at the distance of a mile, and running almost with the fleetness of the wind into the hills and mountains.

The lupin is the only flower I have seen to-day. A coarse, heavily-seeded grass has been the prevailing vegetation of the river bottom. Benches of low hills, covered with sage and grease-wood, slope down to the fertile land, beyond which high mountains raise their rocky, totally barren, and inaccessible peaks. The river is now more a succession or chain of stagnant pools than a stream of running water,. and its banks are skirted, as heretofore, with small willows and wild currant-bushes. The soil of the bottom is highly fertile, wherever it is moistened by the waters of the river.

We encamped at three o'clock, P. M., as near the margin of the stream as safety would permit. The wind blew a gale from the south for two hours this afternoon ; and some sparks of fire catching in the dead grass around our camp, so rapid was the conflagration that we had great difficulty in saving our baggage from destruction. A panther approached within three hundred yards of our camp about sunset. We discharged a rifle at him, but he escaped. The heat of the afternoon has been intense. Distance 30 miles.

August 11.—At eight o'clock we resumed our march down the river, which, at the distance of ten miles from our last encampment, *cañons* between ranges of elevated mountains, composed of rugged, precipitous rocks, at the bottom of which is a coarse debris of sharp broken flint and sandstone. The trail here runs immediately upon the banks of the river, and crosses it in the course of five or six miles, as many times, in order to take advantage of the narrow bottoms made by the abrupt and worm-like windings of the stream. The small bottoms are highly fertile, and are covered with a luxuriant growth of grass and flowers. Among the flowers which ornamented these little *parterres,* I noticed the lupin, the sunflower, a small trumpet-shaped flower, the corol of which is blue and scarlet, a rare combination of colors, and a flower with a flaming, torch-like development of brilliant scarlet.

Emerging from this *cañon* we passed over another wide and fertile bottom, at the lower end of which a naked Indian, more bold than his hidden associates, made his appearance from the willows at some distance, and ran towards us with great speed. Approaching us, he extended his arm ; and when he came up, shook all of us by the hand with great cordiality. A grin, illustrative of a feeling of much delight, distorted his swarthy countenance, over which, and down his neck, the long, coarse, coal-black, and matted hair fell in neglected rankness and profusion. His delight at seeing and saluting us, was apparently so overwhelming, that he could not restrain his emotions, but laughed outright, (an unusual phenomenon in an Indian,) and shouted a gleeful shout.

We did not suspend our march on his account, but he trotted along by my side for a mile or more, his garrulous tongue rolling out with an oily fluency an eloquence quite as incomprehensible as that of many a member of congress. Three more of his brethren made their appearance from the distant willows, when our good-natured and nearly overjoyed friend left us and joined them. We gave him, as usual, a small piece of bread, which has become a scarce commodity with us.

The trail at this point, to avoid a *cañon,* leaves the river, turning abruptly from it to the right, and ascending over low gravelly hills, with the usual growth in such places, of wild sage, until it gradually mounts an elevated ridge, about a mile down the western slope of which we found a small spring of cold, pure water. There being a sufficiency of grass around this spring for our mules, we determined to encamp for the day and enjoy the luxury of good water. A large number of antelopes, as usual, were in sight of us to-day, and I saw several wild geese and sage-hens, but we have killed nothing. Distance 32 miles.

August 12.—Morning clear and cool, with a light breeze from the west. Continuing down the narrow valley or gorge, and passing within a mile or two of our camp several springs of cold, fresh water, we again, after travelling some eight or nine miles, came in sight of the river, winding through a spacious valley which stretches far to the south, with a range of high mountains bounding it on the west. The river here makes a long bend, turning to the north, in which course it runs about fifteen miles. We left this valley through a narrow gap, through which the river forces its way; and about one o'clock, p. m., turning the point of the mountain, we entered another large and level valley, which stretches to the north as far as the vision can penetrate through the smoky vapor. We travelled down this valley, in a southwest course, about ten miles, when we encamped for the day, at three o'clock.

There has been little or no variation in the general characteristics of the country and its productions. Sage, grease-wood, etc., cover the low hills and benches of the mountains, and grass and willows the margin of the river. The soil is extremely light and porous, resembling ashes ; and whenever it is disturbed by the feet of our mules, we are enveloped in clouds of dust. Our hair and beards look white and frosty, and our complexions are as cadaverous as so many corpses, until we perform our evening ablutions.

I saw to-day, while on our march, several Indians standing on a bluff at no great distance from the trail, but they did not venture to approach us. Near our encampment is the miserable dwelling of a Digger, but deserted. We discovered, on the bank of the river, a fish-trap, ingeniously constructed of willows interwoven. It was about ten or twelve feet in length, and shaped like the cornucopia. Multitudes of wolves serenade us every night with their harsh and discordant howlings. The day has been excessively hot, and the sky is of the color of copper, from the effects of the dense smoke with which the atmosphere of the valley is filled.   Distance 30 miles.

August 13.—About nine o'clock, A. M., the temperature became intensely hot, the wind changing to the south, and blowing a breeze that was almost scorching.   Nothing can be more oppressive than the currents of hot winds from the desert, whose fire-like fervency, sustained by the almost scorching rays of the sun, is sometimes nearly suffocating.

We travelled down the margin of the river about twelve miles, when we left the wagon-trail, turning to the right over some low hills, from which we descended into a wide valley, through which the river winds its serpentine channe. in a northwest direction.   Laying our course across this valley, after travelling about ten miles we again struck the river and the wagon-trail, and continued our course along the margin of the stream until we encamped, about two o'clock.

The low hills over which we passed are covered with a debris of sharp fragments of basalt.   The dark sides of the mountains beyond them indicate that they are composed of the same scorious substance.   The general features of the country and scenery are the same as heretofore described.   Several miles of our route, to-day, the ground was thickly incrusted with the carbonate of soda.   A few antelopes were seen at a distance, and occasionally a sage-hen was flushed.

During the afternoon some heavy, but dry-looking clouds obscured the sun, and I heard distant thunder in several directions, but no rain fell to moisten the parched ground.   The smoke in the valley continues very dense, and the coppery hue of the heavens increases—the atmosphere feeling as it looks, heated almost to blistering.   Distance 30 miles.

August 14.—The morning was hazy with thick, smoky vapor. About ten o'clock last night, a black cloud rose from the south, and continual and almost dazzling flashes of lightning were darting athwart its face in all directions, illuminating that portion of the heavens with a blaze of electrical light.   The wind blew with violence, and a few drops of rain fell, but not enough in this arid region, where all humidity seems almost instantly to be evaporated, to leave a perceptible moisture in the morning.

The channel of the river is very serpentine, winding abruptly to the right and left through the valley, to irrigate, in obedience to the economy of nature, and fertilize its ashy and spongy soil. Our general course to-day has been nearly west, bearing a little to the north of west, crossing two extensive valleys or plains, and passing through a narrow defile of the mountains, through which the river forces its way. The waters of the river appear to be decreasing, and the channel occasionally is quite dry, ex posing in some places a sandy, in others a soft, muddy bed. Extensive portions of the valleys through which we have passed have been incrusted with an alkaline efflorescence.

We encamped near the bank of the river at four o'clock, P. M About two miles from our camp, near the base of the moun tains, we discovered a circle of dark green herbage. A phe nomenon so unusual in such a position, excited my curiosity, and notwithstanding my fatigue, I determined to visit the spot, and ascertain its cause. Accompanied by Jacob and Nuttall, I walked to the place, and discovered that what produced the remarkable verdure was the water flowing from a number of boiling springs, which, cooling as it flowed down the slope of the valley, irrigated and fertilized the earth, producing luxuriant grass in the small circle dampened by it, before sinking and dis appearing in the sands. There are some ten or twelve of these springs, the basins of the largest of which are ten feet in diam eter. The temperature of the water is boiling heat. To test it by the best method within our power, (our thermometer having been broken,) we procured from camp a small piece of bacon, which, being placed on the end of a stick and thrust into the boiling basin, was well cooked in fifteen minutes. The water is slightly impregnated with salt and sulphur. Immediately around these basins, the ground is whitened with a crust of the carbonate of soda, beneath which is a stratum or shell of red dish rock, which appears to have been formed by a deposite from the springs.

Our observations and experiments detained us until it was

quite dark, and we had great difficulty, the fires being extinguished, in finding the camp. Distance 36 miles.

August 15.—A drizzling rain commenced falling this morning, about one o'clock, which did not cease until eight o'clock. Our blankets and skins were pretty thoroughly drenched with water; but the clouds clearing away, and the sun shining out before nine o'clock, such is the rapidity of evaporation here, that fifteen or twenty minutes sufficed to dry our baggage and the ground. Judging from appearances, no rains sufficient to penetrate the earth to any extent, have fallen in the valley since the wagons passed along last year. In those places over which the trail passes, where there is no vegetation except the sage, the marks of the wagon-tires, and the footprints of the oxen and horses, are quite distinct, and do not appear to have been made more than a month. The grass, except immediately on the margin of the river, is perfectly dry, and crumbles to powder under our feet.

Our course this morning run in a direction north of west for ten miles, when we turned the point of a range of mountains on our left, and the trail takes nearly a southwest course; sometimes through the bottom, near the banks of the river, at others over the elevated, barren portions of the valley, and through the wild sage.

About twelve o'clock, I saw on a bluff on the opposite side of the river, across a low bottom at the distance of two miles, a large body of Indians—some two or three hundred. Four of them left the main body, and running across the bottom with incredible celerity, soon overtook us, notwithstanding we were travelling at a brisk trot. They were naked, and armed with bows and arrows. When they came up to us, they held out their hands in token of friendship, and falling behind, I entered into such a conversation with them as my knowledge of their signs permitted. All I could learn was, that they wished us to make presents to them of shirts, and something to eat. This request, of course, we could not comply with, our stock of clothing and provisions being too scant. Two of them fell behind very soon; the other two travelled along with us, without

18

any apparent fatigue, for four hours, at the rate of five miles per hour. They have a great dread of a rifle when its muzzle is pointed towards them, and were always careful to keep out of the range of our pieces. About a mile before we encamped for the day, Buchanan and Brown being behind, killed a wolf, and a sand-hill crane. They were greatly astonished at the report of the rifle, and to them its mysterious and deadly effects. They looked in wonder, first at the muzzle of the gun, and then at the mortal wound made in the wolf, causing instant death. To them it was incomprehensible. The wolf and the crane were presented to them, with which they seemed to be delighted, and started to return to their fellows, with as much fleetness as if they had not travelled a mile during the day.

We encamped at half-past four o'clock, descending a steep bluff into a small low bottom of the river, where the grass was rank and green. Another cloud rose from the south-west just before sunset, and it rained enough before we retired for the night, to moisten the grass and the surface of the ground. The mountains bordering the valley of the river have exhibited every variety of rugged form, during the day's march. The rock of which they are composed is volcanic and of a dark hue ; they are entirely destitute of vegetation, and the scenery, consequently, is most gloomy and repulsive to the eye. Distance 30 miles.

CHAPTER XVI.

Refreshing rain—Dense smoky vapor—Scarcity of provisions—Horses giving out—Dismal journey—Soup of fresh-water shellfish—Agreeable meeting—Obtain a supply of provisions—Merry Digger Indian visitres An Indian coil—Petrifactions—Sink of Mary's river—Bitter waters —The desert between Mary's and Truckee river—Toilsome march— Unexpected refreshment—Remarkable boiling springs.

AUGUST 16.—When I woke this morning it was cloudy, and rain was falling copiously. From appearances, it had been raining several hours, and those of our party who had bivouacked were quite wet. Nothing could be more agreeable to us than this rain. By it the dust which in places is almost suffocating, has been laid for a short distance at least, and the sultry and dry atmosphere has been cooled and moistened.

Our course for the day has generally been southwest, and the trail which we have followed has sometimes passed through the grassy bottoms next to the river, and at others over the high and barren slopes of the valley, with a growth of leafless sage upon them.

We passed some places where water was standing in pools from the effects of last night's rain, a most unusual, but not unpleasing sight in this arid region. The atmosphere is so charged with smoke, upon which the rain of last night seems to have produced no effect, that distant objects are not discernible. The outlines of the nearest mountains, dimly seen through the thick vapor, present the same dark, rugged, and barren aspect as has heretofore been described.

I saw several Indians to-day at a distance, but they ran from us and concealed themselves in the willows bordering the river. The water of the river has become strongly impregnated with alkali, and being exposed to the sun, when taken from the pools is nearly blood heat. It is not, however, more distasteful than we expected to find it, and bad as it is, our excessive thirst renders it palatable.

This evening I made an inspection of the provisions of my mess, and found, owing to its increase of numbers from unavoidable circumstances since we left Fort Laramie, that there would be a deficiency, although we have been on short allowance for the last ten days, restricting ourselves to a single small slice of fried bacon and a very diminutive piece of bread, for each, twice a day, morning and evening. We estimate our journey to the settlements of California at fourteen days; and our provisions will not last us more than five or six days.

Brown's and Brookey's riding-horses nearly gave out to-day. This is a very great misfortune, as we have not a single animal whose services we can well dispense with. The sun sunk down behind the mountains this evening, appearing through the smoke like an immense ball of fire. Distance 30 miles.

August 17.—Turning our course considerably to the left, the trail following the winding and sluggish current of the river, and passing through a narrow gap of the mountains, we entered upon an extensive and level plain, upon which we saw large numbers of antelopes, frequently in droves of a hundred or more. Leaving this bottom, we again ascended upon high ground composed of ashy earth mixed with sharp volcanic gravel, with a growth of sage, over which we continued our monotonous march the remainder of the day. The river is crowded between steep sandy bluffs, for many miles, and the entire valley on both sides of it presents a most barren and desolate aspect. About five o'clock, P. M., we found an opening in the bluffs, and descended into a large circular basin covered with a growth of willows and other small brush, which I conjectured was the "*Sink*," but I was mistaken. We descended into this basin down a steep bank or precipice, and encamped in a small opening among the willows, under the bluff.

Brown's horse gave out entirely to-day, and was left on the road about six miles from our camp. Brookey did not reach our camp until dark. It has been a miserable and most fatiguing day's journey, the sun shining with such intense heat, that the perspiration rolled from my face in large drops.

After considerable labor, we cut a way through the thick brush and willows to the river, and got our mules down to the water. In the bed of the stream we found large quantities of muscles. Miller brought a bucketful of them to camp, and made of them a soup, which was not ungrateful to the palate. Distance 30 miles.

August 18.—We were in our saddles, and under way, as the sailors say, very early this morning, there being nothing in the features of our camp to entice delay a moment beyond the time necessary to prepare our coffee and fried bacon; the ast of which, by the way, has become very rancid, and is covered with a thick coating of the dust of the desert. The extreme heat of the sun during the day, has melted and wasted nearly all the unctuous qualities of our meat, leaving little else than the skin and cartilage, and these in a very bad condition.

Travelling usually in front of our party, I had watched with much interest and scrutiny the trail of the two emigrant wagons in advance of us when we struck Mary's river. I was fully satisfied from the freshness of the signs on the trail, and the number of their encampments, that we could not be more than a day in the rear at this point; and I determined, if possible, to overtake them this morning, and obtain from them, if they had it to spare, provision sufficient to carry us into the settlements of California. As soon, therefore, as our party were all fairly on the march, I urged my mule forward at a rapid pace, leaving my fellow-travellers, in a short time, far behind me, and out of sight.

After crossing a totally barren plain, ten miles wide, I saw at an apparent distance of five or six miles, two white specks upon a gentle swell of the plain, surrounded by verdant vegetation. These specks I instantly knew to be the wagons; and as I could perceive no motion, I was satisfied that they were encamped. Increasing the speed of my mule by a liberal application of spur and whip, it was not long before I approached the wagons.

I must remark here, by the way, that the sight of an emigrant wagon in these wildernesses and deserts, produces the same emotions of pleasure as are felt by the way-worn and benighted traveller, within the boundaries of civilization, when approaching some hospitable cottage or mansion on the roadside. More intense, perhaps, because the white tent-cloth of the wagon is a certain sign of welcome hospitality, in such form as can be afforded by the ever liberal proprietor, who without stint, even though he might have but a single meal, would cheerfully divide it among his stranger visiters. Civilization cannot always boast of such dispensers of hospitality ; but among the emigrants to the Pacific, it is nearly universal.

When the company of men belonging to the wagons discovered me at a distance, much apparent surprise was manifested.   A solitary individual in this abandoned region, was well calculated to excite curiosity.   I saw several of them mounted upon the tops of their wagons, to obtain, as I supposed, a correct idea of my nationality and purposes.   When I came up to the camp, I was greeted in the most cordial manner, with every mark of kindness that I should expect from my dearest friends. I soon explained to them the nature and purpose of my visit, and received such a response as was entirely satisfactory.

The proprietors of the two wagons were Messrs. Craig and Stanley, from Ray county, Missouri, accompanied by six or eight young men.   I learned from them that they left Fort Hall on the 23d day of July, and are some twelve or fifteen days in advance of all the other emigrant trains bound for California.   The intentions of Messrs. Craig and Stanley, are to visit California first ; and after travelling over it, to explore the fertile districts of Oregon ; and if upon an examination they are pleased with either of these countries, they design to dispose of their property in the United States, and settle on the Pacific. Messrs. C. and S. are highly intelligent and respectable gentlemen, and I derived from them much interesting and useful information in regard to the emigrant route, via Fort Hall.

Our party came up in about an hour and a half after my arrival ; and the grass being good, with a plentiful supply, in a reedy *slough,* of tolerable cool and fresh water, we determined to encamp for the day.   Messrs. Craig and Stanley are impressed with the belief, that we have reached the " *Sink*" of Mary's river ; that is, the place where the waters of the river cease to flow, and disappear in the dry and thirsting sands of the desert.   They informed me that some of the members of the party had made a reconnaissance of several miles to the south and southeast, and had not been able to discover any water beyond this point.   I nevertheless felt doubtful in regard to this supposition, as the place did not entirely correspond with the description I had received of the " *Sink.*"

Messrs. Craig and Stanley, in the course of the afternoon, although their supply of provisions was not more than equal to their probable consumption, before they would reach the settlements of California, generously furnished us with a quantity of flour and bacon, which I believed would be nearly or quite sufficient for our wants. They would accept of no compensation for this very great favor; and I consider myself, as well as every member of our party, under the highest obligations to them, for their most liberal manifestation of kindness and hospitality.

Two Digger Indians came into our camp about sunset. One of them mounted on a miserably lean and broken down horse; and the other walking by the side of the swarthy, and nearly naked savage *Caballero*. The mounted man was the spokesman; the other appearing to act in the capacity of a servant, or a personage of inferior consequence. After the first salutations, and shaking of hands, the principal desired a smoke. A pipe was produced, filled with tobacco, and lighted. Most of our party, as usual, declined a participation in this friendly ceremonial of the savages; but I took my turn at the pipe, and puffed with a *gusto* equalling that of our two sable and naked visiters.

The ceremony of smoking being concluded, the several members of the party commenced a conversation with our good-natured visiters. When one of the party spoke in English, the chief Indian would invariably imitate with great precision the sound of each word to the end of the sentence. The remarkable accuracy of this repetition or imitation, accompanied as it was with an indescribable comic action, was highly amusing, and produced peal upon peal of loud laughter. This sport continued around our willow fires long after dark.

A member of Messrs. Craig and Stanley's party, who for a number of years had been a trapper in the mountains, and was considerably skilled in the significance of Indian signs, afterwards held a conversation with the principal Indian, and learned from him, that a short day's journey would bring us to some pools of standing water, and that after this, we would find no water or grass for a long distance. The time was indicated by pointing to the course of the sun and its positions when the incidents respecting which we inquired would take place. Other matters were explained by a similar reference to objects connected with and illustrative of those inquired about. The information derived from this conversation was not sufficiently clear to solve the doubt, as to whether this was or was not the "Sink" of Mary's river.

Before our company retired to rest, I instructed the sentinel first on duty, to communicate to those who succeeded him, that the two Indians were not to be permitted to leave the principal camp-fire until morning, under any pretext. I did not know what designs upon our animals they might entertain themselves, or what concealed associates they might have to assist them. This order was communicated to the Indians in a manner which they could not misunderstand, and they submitted without the slightest opposition. One of them (the serving man, who was so obliging as several times during the evening to bring us water from the slough) had a small garment or shawl, made of hare-skins sewn together, about a yard in diameter. We gave the two a skin to spread on the ground for their bed, and coiling themselves up in an incredibly small space, the hare-skin shawl or blanket covered their bodies, heads and feet entirely. How they managed to compress their persons into so small a space, is a marvel. Distance 16 miles.

August 19.—I rose this morning before it was light, and approaching the embers of our watch-fire, which had been kept burning during the night by those on duty, the first object I discovered was the two Indians coiled up, and enveloped in the yard-square of rabbit-skins, as I had left them when I retired to my bivouac last night. They were in a profound slumber, evincing their perfect confidence in our good faith in regard to them. I touched this small round heap of human flesh gently with my foot, when they roused from their sleep, and rubbing their eyes, sat upright before the faint blaze made by the dry willow twigs I had placed upon the fire. The elder and more consequential of the two, ordered the other to go and collect some fuel, which service he performed with much promptitude, bringing in a large bundle of dead sage-bushes, which igniting upon the fire, burned with a brilliant blaze. During the absence of the junior or serving Indian, his *nakedness*, the seignior or master, gave many shrugs and shivers, showing conclusively that the cool morning atmosphere did not strike agreeably upon his bare skin, and he pointed with much meaning and earnestness to my coarse *palto*, as being an excellent protection against the chills of the morning.

Daylight dawning, our party was roused, and our morning meal prepared and discussed with all practicable dispatch,— as we felt certain that we had a long and dreary day's march before us. The two Indians were regaled with such food as we subsisted upon ourselves, and then dismissed, apparently well satisfied with our treatment and attention, parting from us with the most good-natured countenances and gesticulations.

Leaving the grassy oasis upon which we were encamped a little after sunrise, and travelling a few miles, we turned the point of a mountain, the slope of which juts into the plain on the right. From this point the trail takes a southwest course, and runs across a totally barren plain, with the exception of a few clumps of sage-bushes, a distance of twenty miles. No sign of the river or of the existence of water indicated itself within this distance. Some remarkable petrifactions displayed themselves near the trail early this morning. They had all the appearance of petrified fungi, and many of them were of large dimensions. The surface of the plain is generally soft and light. In places a dark scorious and vitreous gravel is mingled with the ashy and alkaline composition. This gravel is sharp and very severe upon the hoofs of our animals.

At the southern edge of this plain we came to some pools of standing water, as described by the Indians last night, covered with a yellowish slime, and emitting a most disagreeable fetor. The margins of these pools are whitened with an alkaline deposite, and green tufts of a coarse grass, and some reeds or flags, raise themselves above the snow-like soil. I procured from one of the pools a cup of the water, and found it so thoroughly saturated with alkali, that it would be dangerous for ourselves or our animals to make use of it. It was as acrid and bitter as the strongest lye filtered through ashes. Many of our animals being excessively thirsty, rushed to the pools immediately after we approached them, but upon tasting the water, they turned from it with disappointment and disgust.

A ridge of low sand-hills runs entirely across the plain or valley immediately below these pools, and from these features corresponding in some particulars with the description I had previously received of it, I was compelled to believe that this was the "*Sink of Mary's river*," instead of the place where we had encamped last night.

It was nearly two o'clock, P. M., when we reached these pools, and from them (supposing them, as was the fact, to be the "Sink") to the waters of Truckee, or Salmon Trout river, by the best information and estimate, it is forty-five miles. Some of our party were in favor of encamping here, forbidding as the place was in all its aspects. But I immediately came to the conclusion that to encamp at this place, would be not only useless to ourselves, so far as rest and comfort were concerned, but dangerous, in our thirsty state, both to us and our animals. In preference, therefore, I determined to proceed on our march, and encamp in the desert beyond, without grass or water. Adopting this plan, we would by diligence, before sunset, approach to within twenty or twenty-five miles of water and grass, and by starting early, after resting our animals six or eight hours, we could reach Truckee river before our own thirst and the thirst and hunger of our mules became unbearable.

We passed from the pools or "Sink" over the low ridge of sand-hills, in a south course. Our mules waded through these hills, or heaps of dry and ashy earth, rather than walked over them, sinking in many places nearly to their bellies, and manifesting the strongest signs of exhaustion. The dim outlines of mountains could be seen through the dense smoky vapor impregnating the atmosphere, about fifteen or twenty miles in front. The plain is utterly destitute of vegetation, with the exception of an occasional strip of sage on the swells, and a few patches of brown grass, and here and there a small clump of straggling flags or reeds, which seem to war for an existence with the parched and ungenerous soil.

We ascended the ridge of mountains just noticed, by an easy

inclined plain. Some miles before we commenced the ascent, I observed on the slope of the plain a line of perpendicular rocks, forming a wall, with occasional high elevations, representing watch-towers and turrets. A low gap afforded us an easy passage between the mountains, which are composed of nearly black basaltic rocks. The whole country in this vicinity, at no very remote period, has evidently been under the action of volcanic fires. The rocks are cinders, and the earthy substances with which they are mingled are ashes.

From the summit of the ridge, I had a view of the shadowy outlines of another range of mountains to the west of us, at an apparent distance of twenty miles. The smoke was so dense that I could determine nothing satisfactorily in regard to the valley between us and this range of mountains, but I entertained a strong hope that we should find a stream of water here. This hope, however, was disappointed. Just as the sun was sinking behind the spiral and dismal-looking summits of the western mountains, and before we had descended into the bottom, the trail turned abruptly to the left, keeping along the slope on the eastern side of the valley. I immediately gave up all expectations of water or grass to-night, as a more utterly barren prospect than that presented before us is not conceivable. It was impossible for us to proceed much further, as several of our party, whose mules were nearly exhausted, were at this point a long distance in the rear, and would find it difficult to urge their over-labored animals even a few miles.

A point in the valley, formed by the jutting of a low hill or bench of the mountain, about two miles before me, seemed to be a suitable position for our encampment, under the circumstances, for the night, or for the few hours necessary to rest our mules, before continuing our march. While marching towards this point, I noticed to the left, on the declivity of the mountain, a small patch of ground displaying a pale yellowish vegetation. A phenomenon so singular amidst the brown sterility of mountain and valley, excited my curiosity, and I thought it not *impossible* that we might find there a small quantity of water. Calling Miller, I requested him to ride up to the spot and ascertain what the yellowish growth might be. He was quickly at the place designated, and very soon afterwards, taking off his cap, swung it round and round, nearly overjoyed at the discovery he had made, which we all immediately knew to be a spring. Had he discovered a mine of solid gold, or a ton of diamonds, it would, in our thirsty condition, have produced no other sensations than those of extreme disappointment. Water was what we craved, and a universe of glittering wealth would not have weighed in the balance of our desires against it.

Turning short to the left, I rode up the slope to where Miller was still standing. Before I reached him, I could perceive a sensible moderation in his joyous manifestations. I asked him if he had found water? He answered that he had, but that his mule, in attempting to drink out of a hole, had nearly scalded its tongue off. I could see that the mule was suffering considerable pain from the effects of the boiling hot water which, incautiously, it had attempted to drink.

Passing a little further along, I found myself in the midst of a hundred or more holes or small basins, varying from two to ten feet in diameter, of boiling water. Searching about, I found in a ravine a small basin of water, that oozed sluggishly through a stratum of earth, which, although quite warm, was not burning hot. I drank copiously of this water, and the other members of our party, and our mules, coming up, one after another, drank likewise. But as soon as the stock in the basin was exhausted, the new supply that flowed in became too hot for use. We encamped here, after a ride of twelve hours, tying our mules closely to the wild sage-bushes, to prevent them from falling into the boiling holes by which they were surrounded.

These springs are a great curiosity, on account of their variety and the singularity of their action and deposites. The deposite from one had formed a hollow pyramid of reddish clay, about eight feet in height, and six feet in diameter at the base, tapering to a point. There were several air-holes near the top, and inside of it the waters were rumbling, and the steam puffing through the air-holes with great violence. Miller threw stones at the cap of this pyramid. It broke like brittle pottery, and the red and turbid waters ran down the sides of the frail structure which they had erected. Not far from this was a small basin, and a lively but diminutive stream running from it, of water as white as milk, which, indeed, it greatly resembled. I cooled some of it in my cup, and drinking, found it not unpalatable. It was impregnated with magnesia. In another basin, the water was thickened, almost to the consistence of slack mortar, with a blue clay. It was rolling and tumbling about with activity, and volumes of steam, accompanied with loud puffing reports, ascended from it. The water of the largest basin (about ten feet in diameter) was limpid, and impregnated with salt and sulphur. From this basin, when we encamped, a small stream ran down the slope. The rock surrounding these springs is a mere shell or crust, formed, doubtless, by a deposite from the overflowing waters from the basins or holes, which are so many ventilators for the escape of the steam from the heated and boiling mass of liquid beneath.

We made a dam across the stream flowing from the large basin, some distance below it, by raking together the slight covering of earth upon the rocks. We thus collected a considerable body of water, which, cooling, was more palatable to ourselves and our mules than any which we had before obtained. This dam was enlarged before we retired for the night, in order that we might have an abundant supply of cool water, brackish and bitter though it was, in the morning.

As we moved about our camp after dark, we were in constant danger of falling into the scalding and bottomless basins or holes by which we were surrounded. Fortunately no accident occurred. The ground under our blankets was quite warm, from the effects of the heated matter rolling, bubbling, and puffing in the bowels of the earth. Every thing around is sufficiently cheerless and desolate to depress the most buoyant temperament. The sable and utterly sterile mountains, the barren and arid plain, incapable of sustaining either insect or animal, present a dreariness of scenery that would be almost overpowering in its influences, but for the hope of more pleasing scenes beyond. Distance 45 miles.

CHAPTER XVII.

Mirage—Phantom cataract—Signs of water—Truckee river—Insanity produced by apprehension and excitement—Enter the California mountains—Mountain forests—Mountain valley—Truckee river Indians—
Cold nights—Mountain lake—Origin of the name of Truckee river and
lake—Scenery of the Sierra Nevada—Log-cabin erected by emigrants in
distress—Mountain raspberry—Pass of the Sierra—Uber valley—Spring
in August—An attack by hornets—Beautiful encampment—Human
skull.

AUGUST 20.—The disquiet of our animals, thirsting for water,
and famishing for food, kept me awake nearly the whole night.
As soon as the stars indicated the approach of the morning, I
woke my fellow-travellers, and a cup of coffee having been
made from the hot water of the springs, a little after daylight
we were ready to take leave of our dismal encampment.

Much to our astonishment and disappointment, when we
visited the dam and reservoir of water constructed last night, it
was entirely dry. Not a drop of water was contained in it.
The stream from the basin had ceased to flow. When I first
woke this morning, there was no sound of the agitation of water in any of the basins; but just as we were about to depart,
the rumbling and rolling, and the loud puffs, accompanied by
fog-like volumes of steam from the boiling liquid beneath us,
were resumed with an energy greatly increased from what I
observed on our first arrival. One of our party noticing this
display of infernal steam-power, exclaimed, " *Let us be off:—
h—ll is firing up ;*" and it did, indeed, seem as if the machinery
of the vast workshops in the subterranean recesses of nature,
had just been put in operation for the day, by the spirits and
powers of the middle earth.

About three miles from our encampment, I discovered in the
bank of a ravine, crossed by the trail, a faint spring. The water barely oozing from the earth, although cool, was bitter, and

the quantity was so small, that we could with difficulty obtain a cupful. A ride of several hours down the valley, brought us to a ridge of sandy hills running entirely across it.

In the course of the morning, I noticed the phenomenon of *mirage* in great perfection. A wide cascade or cataract of glittering, foaming, and tumbling waters was represented and perfectly well defined on the slope of the mountain to our left, at an apparent distance of five or six miles. Below this, was a limpid lake, so calm and mirror-like that it reflected with all the distinctness of reality, the tall, inverted shapes of the mountains and all the scenery beyond its tempting but illusory surface. Nature, in this desert region, if she does not furnish the reality, frequently presents the ghosts of beautiful objects and scenery.

The distance across the ridge, or rather elevated plain of sandy undulations, is about ten miles. Over this plain the travelling is very laborious. We were compelled to dismount from our animals, weakened as they were by thirst and hunger, in order to get them along through the deep sand. Soon after rising upon this plain, I noticed first the footprints on the sand of hares, afterwards of wolves, and presently of a variety of animals, all of which seemed to have travelled in the same direction that we were pursuing;—a certain indication that we were on the right course for water, and no great distance from it. We crossed an Indian foot-trail very deep, wide, and fresh, showing that Indians to the number of several hundred must have passed along within a short time. This trail leads to the Pyramid lake into which the waters of Truckee river debouche, and sink or evaporate. The Indians of this region take large quantities of salmon-trout from this lake.

At half-past 12 o'clock, we saw at the distance of about two miles, the course of Truckee river, indicated by a line of willows, grass, and other green herbage, and a number of *tall* trees,—the last a sight that has not saluted us for five hundred miles. Our animals, as if reinvigorated by the prospect of grass and the scent of water, rushed forward with great speed, and we were soon in the middle of the stream, from the clear current of which all drank copious draughts. We immediately crossed to the bottom on the opposite side and encamped, much fatigued, as the reader may imagine.

Truckee river at this point is about fifty feet in breadth, with a rapid current of clear water about two feet in depth and a gravelly bed. The bottom, or fertile land, is here about a mile in width, with a growth of small willows, hawthorns, and a few tall cotton-wood trees. In the openings, wild peas and a variety of grasses and other herbage, grow with luxuriance. The shade of the trees is most agreeable, and adds greatly to the pleasantness of our encampment, when contrasting our cool shelter from the sun, with its scorching fervor ·upon the surrounding desolation. We angled in the river, but contrary to our expectations, caught no fish. Some of our party killed a duck or two. Game sign is abundant, but the Indians, who have recently been here in large numbers, have driven off the game. Distance 20 miles.

August 21.—I was wakened from a profound slumber, this morning, by piercing shrieks and wailings. I was not quite certain when I woke, whether it was a dream or reality. Satisfying myself that I was not asleep, I listened attentively for a repetition of the strange and mournful sounds which had disturbed my repose. They were soon renewed with greater distinctness than before, and appeared to proceed from some animal, or person in distress or danger, on the opposite side of the river. They soon, however, ceased altogether, and it being quite dark, exhausted as I was, I concluded that I would lie down again, and when daylight dawned, ascertain the cause of these singular vocal performances in this desert region. I soon fell asleep again, however, and did not wake until after sunrise.

When I rose, Messrs. Craig and Stanley were riding towards our camp, and they informed us that their wagons had reached the opposite bank of the river just before daylight, having travelled all night, and that they were now crossing the stream for the purpose of encamping for the day. I was much gratified that these, our good friends, had crossed the desert in safety, and had reached a point where they could recruit their animals. I inquired of them, if they had heard the shrieks and wailings which had disturbed my slumbers early in the morning ?

Mr. Craig informed me that one of their party, soon after leaving the boiling springs, from some cause had become quite frantic, with, as he hoped, temporary insanity, brought on by the fatigues and hardships of the march, or from drinking the impure water of the desert. They had been compelled to place him inside of one of the wagons and confine him to it, in order to get him along. When, early this morning, they commenced the descent of the bluffs to the river, he leaped from the wagon, under the influence of a paroxysm of insanity with loud cries and shrieks, and after describing several times by his movements, a circle, he declared that the destiny of Providence, so far as regarded himself, was accomplished ; that nothing more was expected of him or could be demanded from him, and he was willing to submit to his fate and die on that spot, and be buried within that circle. It was some time, and the united strength of two or three men was required, before he could be got back again into the wagon.

By the request of Mr. Craig, after his camp was made, I visited the man so strangely attacked. His paroxysms had considerably abated in their strength, and he seemed to be returning to a more rational state of mind. He was continually endeavoring to vomit. Being a stout, vigorous young man, with an abundance of hard muscular flesh upon him, and having an excited pulse, but not one indicating physical disease, I inquired of him why he so frequently endeavored to vomit ? He answered, that soon after he left the boiling springs, strange sensations of pain and apprehension came over him, and he demanded some remedy for them ;—that a large vial containing camphor partially dissolved in alcohol was the only medicine they possessed, which was given to him ;—that he had first drank the liquid solution, and then, as he supposed, in an unconscious state, had swallowed a quantity of the undissolved gum, for he had already thrown up several pieces of the size of the end of his thumb, and still he believed there was a large quantity inside of him. I told him that I would prepare an emetic for him, by which he would be entirely relieved and restored to perfect health—that nothing was the matter with him but over-excitement. He said that he was willing to take the emetic to please me and Mr. Craig, but did not conceive it to be of any utility. He was not superstitious or given to superstitious freaks and notions. On the contrary, he was a cool, calm, calculating man, and he was fully satisfied that his appointed time under the dispensations of Providence had arrived, and he must die, and be buried near this place. It was in vain that I argued against this delusion, and told him that one so robust and healthy could not die even if he wished it, unless he took his own life. The response was the same,— Providence had ordered it—he had fulfilled his destiny, and here he must die and be buried.

I returned to my own camp, and procuring a quantity of ipecacuanka, it was administered to him. Under the operation of the emetic, he threw up nearly an ounce of the concrete gum of camphor. I could not wonder after this exhibition, that he imagined that his destiny was fulfilled! I visited him again in the afternoon, and although much more composed than in the morning, he was still laboring under his original delusion, and in this state of mind I left him.

The morning was clear, cool, and calm, but as usual, the sun's rays in the middle of the day were intensely hot. We remained encamped, to recruit the strength of our animals, which have become much exhausted by the rapid drives down Mary's river, and thence across the desert.

August 22.—We resumed our journey at seven o'clock. Our mules are considerably recruited by the rest we have allowed them, and by the nutritious grass and refreshing water at our last encampment.

The valley of the river for a few miles, as we travelled up it, is of nearly the same width as described at our encampment; but it soon contracts, and the river and narrow bottom are walled in on both sides by high ranges of barren mountains. Some of these mountains are composed of a reddish or brown sandstone, others, higher up, of basalt. A few tall cotton-wood trees occasionally skirt the margin of the river. These, with small willows, and a variety of diminutive shrubs and rank weeds, with an occasional opening of grass, make up the vegetation of the valley.

The river flows down, with a lively current of limpid water, over a rocky bed ; and the green vegetation along its banks contrasts finely with the brown sterility of the adjacent mountains. My sensations while travelling along its banks and in sight of its sparkling waters, are something like those experienced in a stormy and wintry day, when comfortably seated in a warm library or parlor, with a view from the window of the violent strife and bitter frigidity of the elements without. The water and grass are our comfort, and our security for the realization of our hopes, in regard to our destination.

We travelled at a rapid gait, the trail being good and our spirits buoyant ; and at three o'clock, coming to an excellent camping-ground, with fine grass, water, and wood, we halted, and encamped for the day. During the day's march we have forded the river about twenty times. This is necessary, in order to avoid the *cañones*, on one side or the other of the narrow valley. Among numerous footprints of Indians, to-day, I saw a plain and fresh shoe-track, showing that some person who has walked here has had communication with civilization.

I experimented with the hook and line in the river again, but without success. Not even a nibble compensated my patient perseverance. Along the banks of the river there are myriads of diminutive toads, or frogs, about an inch in length, which, when disturbed, leap into the water, furnishing abundant food for all the fish in the stream. The bait on the hook, therefore, has no temptations for these well-fed gentry of the clear mountain torrent. Distance 25 miles.

August 23.—When I rose this morning, just after the dawn of day, I discovered that the dew-drops condensed upon an India-rubber cloth lying by my side, were congealed, and that my buffalo-skins were hoary with frost. Ice as thick as window-glass, had also formed upon the water left in our buckets. The dawn was glorious, and the sun, when it rose above the mountain peaks, shone with unusual splendor through the clear atmosphere.

We commenced our day's march about eight o'clock, continuing up the river, the general course of which, as far as we have followed it, is nearly from the southwest to the northeast.   Of course, there are many turns and windings which vary from this usual direction of the current of the stream.   About twelve o'clock we emerged from the confined limits between the high ranges of mountains, affording us, in many places, room barely sufficient to pass, without leaving the bottom of the river, into a spacious and highly fertile valley, eight or ten miles in diameter. The grasses in this valley are very luxuriant, and their varieties numerous.   There is no timber, with the exception of the clumps of small willows belting the stream, and fringing the margin of a deep and miry *slough*, which runs entirely across it.   Pine timber, however, of stately dimensions, begins to exhibit itself on the sides and summits of the surrounding mountains.   In crossing the valley on the southern side, we passed through several miles of *tule*, a species of rush, or reed, which here grows to the height of eight feet, on the wet or swampy soil. We saw numbers of deer and antelope in the valley, and I noticed in several places fresh footprints of a horse.

After leaving the fertile land of the valley, the trail runs over an elevated and undulating barren plain, with a growth of stunted sage, and a soil mixed with sharp volcanic gravel, very injurious to the feet of our animals, some of which have become foot-sore and lame.   We gradually approached the river, which again becomes walled in by high mountains, leaving the channel and a narrow bottom alternating from one side to the other, for a road or passage.   During the afternoon we passed several yellow-pine trees in the bottom, of large dimensions, the trunk of one of them measuring eighteen feet in circumference.   A number of Indians were seen on the opposite bank of the river, one of whom had some fish.   We beckoned to them to come over and trade with us, but they were either alarmed or would not heed our signs, and soon disappeared.

We encamped at four o'clock, much fatigued with our day's

ride. The road has generally been rough and rocky, and very exhausting to our mules. In front of us, to the west, there is an elevated range of densely timbered mountains. Distance 20 miles.

August 24.—Our mules were greatly alarmed several times during the night, breaking their picket-ropes, and running in all directions. Indians were doubtless prowling about for the purposes of theft, but we saw none.

We resumed our march at the usual hour. Following the river between two and three miles farther up, we turned abruptly to the right, crossing its channel about the thirtieth time, and, through a ravine or gorge, ascended the range of mountains on our right. We reached the summit of the range by a comparatively easy and gradual ascent, passing over some rocky, but not difficult places.

The mountains are covered with a thick growth of tall and symmetrical timber. Among the varieties of trees I noticed the yellow and white-pine, the fir, the common red cedar, and the Chinese *arbor vitæ*. Many of the firs and cedars are two hundred feet in height, with a diameter at the trunk of six or eight feet, beautifully tapering to a point. Nothing could be more agreeable to us than the sight and the shade of these stately giants of the forest, piercing the sky with their tall and arrow-straight forms.

We reached the summit of the gap that afforded us a passage over the mountain, about eleven o'clock, and descended a long and very steep declivity on the other side, bringing us into a small, oval-shaped and grassy valley, with a faint spring branch of pure cold water running through it. This hollow is entirely surrounded by high mountains. The soil is rich, and the grass and other vegetation luxuriant. The impersonations of romance and solitude could scarcely find a more congenial abode than this beautiful and sequestered spot.

The trail here turns to the left again, taking a nearly south course, over a rolling country, heavily timbered with pines, firs, and cedars, with occasional grassy openings. At three o'clock, P. M., we struck a small stream, flowing in a southeast course, a tributary of Truckee river. We encamped in a small fertile bottom on this stream.

Soon after we crossed Truckee river this morning, and just as we were commencing the ascent of the mountain, several Indians made their appearance, about fifty yards from the trail. The leader and chief was an old man, with a deeply-furrowed face. I rode towards him, holding out my hand in token of friendship. He motioned me not to advance further, but to pass on and leave him, as he desired to have no communication with us. I insisted upon the reason of this unfriendly demonstration; assuring him, as well as I could by signs, that we desired to be at peace, and to do them no harm. His response was, if I understood it, that we, the whites, had slaughtered his men, taken his women and children into captivity, and driven him out of his country. I endeavored to assure him that we were not of those who had done him and his tribe these wrongs, and held out my hand a second time, and moved to approach him. With great energy of gesticulation, and the strongest signs of excited aversion and dread, he again motioned us not to come nearer to him, but to pass on and leave him. The other Indians, some six or eight in number, took no part in the dialogue, but were standing in a line, several yards from their chief, with their bows and arrows in their hands. Finding that it would be useless, perhaps dangerous, to press our friendship further, we continued our march. I have but little doubt, that these Indians are the remnant of some tribe that has been wantonly destroyed in some of the bloody Indian slaughters which have occurred in California. Distance 20 miles.

August 25.—The morning was clear and cold. Ice of the thickness of window-glass was congealed on the surface of the water left in our bucket and tin cups. The grass was white, and stiffened with frost. The extremities of my long hair had the hoary hue of old age. Notwithstanding this severity of the temperature, and our exposure to it, we felt little or no suffering or inconvenience from it.

Crossing the stream we travelled in a south course, over low hills and a rolling or undulating country, heavily timbered, principally with the yellow-pine, with some few firs and cedars. In the course of our day's march, we crossed a number of small branches, with green, grassy bottoms. About one o'clock, p. m., we descended a steep declivity, and struck a stream, which I at first conjectured might be one of the tributaries of the Sacramento ; but after an examination of its current, I discovered that it ran the wrong way, and was compelled, reluctantly, to believe that we had not yet reached the summit of the Sierra Nevada ; and that the stream was a tributary of, or the main Truckee river.

The trail runs along this stream a short distance, and then leaving it on the right hand, winds under a range of high mountainous elevations, until it strikes again the same water-course, in a distance of a few miles.

About two o'clock, p. m., we suddenly and unexpectedly came in sight of a small lake, some four or five miles in length, and about two miles in breadth. We approached this lake by ascending a small stream which runs through a flat bottom. On every side, except this outlet from it, the lake is surrounded by mountains of great elevation, heavily and darkly timbered with pines, firs, and cedars. The sheet of water just noticed, is the head of Truckee river, and is called by the emigrants who first discovered and named it, Truckee Lake.

[It may not be improper for me in this place to give the origin of this name. A small party of emigrants, with but little knowledge of the country, and the difficulties obstructing their progress, late in the autumn of 1844, were attempting to force their way through these mountains to California. They were lost, and nearly discouraged. The snows fell in the mountains before they had reached the Pass ; and death by starvation, frost, and fatigue, was staring them in the face. At the crisis of their distress, while forcing their way up the river, an Indian made his appearance, and in a most friendly manner volunteered his services to guide a portion of the party over the mountains. His appearance and eccentricities of manner resembled so much those of a man by the name of *Truckee*, who happened to have been an acquaintance of one of the party, that they gave the Indian the name of TRUCKEE; and called the river and lake, along which he conducted them, after this name. This same Indian (Truckee) was the principal of the two who encamped with us twenty-five miles above the " *Sink*" of Mary's river. He and his brother afterwards came over into California with a company of emigrants ; and accompanied the California battalion on its march from Monterey to the Ciudad de los Angelos.]

The Alps, so celebrated in history and by all travellers and admirers of mountain landscape, cannot, I am satisfied, present scenery more wild, more rugged, more grand, more romantic, and more enchantingly picturesque and beautiful, than that which surrounds this lake, of which the lake itself composes a part.

Just before we struck the shore of the lake at its lower or eastern end, we came to a tolerably well-constructed log-house,* with one room, which evidently had been erected and occupied by civilized men. The floor inside of this house was covered with feathers, and strewn around it on the outside, were pieces of ragged cloth, torn newspapers, and manuscript letters, the writing in most of which was nearly obliterated. The title of one of the newspapers, was that of a religious publication in Philadelphia. It had, from its date, been printed several years. One of the letters which I picked up and examined, bore the frank of some member of congress, and was addressed to " Dr. John Townsend, Bloomfield, Ind." Another letter was dated at Morristown, N. J., but by whom it was written, or to whom addressed, I could not decipher. The emigrant party which erected this cabin is the same to which I have alluded above. They were belated in the mountains, and suffered almost incredible hardships, before they reached the settlements of California.

We experienced considerable difficulty in making our way round the northeastern side of the lake, the steep side of the

---

* This is the place where the horrible disasters to the emigrants of 1846 took place.

mountain being in many places so boggy that our mules sunk to their bellies in the mire.   We reached the upper end of the lake at four o'clock, and encamped on the left of the trail, in a small grassy opening surrounded by tall and dense timber. The forest in the narrow but fertile bottom of the lake, and on the sides of the mountains, where there is any soil for its sustenance, is dense, and the trees are of immense size.   A brilliantly green and highly ornamental moss covers the limbs of many of the trees.   The rock composing the mountains here, is chiefly granite.

Just beyond us, and overlooking the gap where we expect to-morrow to pass the crest of the Sierra Nevada, is a high mountain with a natural fortification upon its extreme summit, which but for its cyclopean magnitude, the wild and desolate country in which it is situated, and its unapproachable height, the observer would at once say was the work of human hands, so apparently regular and perfect is the construction of its walls, turrets, and bastions.

While travelling along the side of the mountain near the shore of the lake, we found a most delicious variety of the raspberry, ripe and in full perfection.   Its flavor is, I think, fully equal, if not superior to any raspberry I have before tasted. Were it cultivated in our gardens, I cannot doubt that it would supersede the varieties which they produce, and which we so much prize.

After we encamped, Jacob and McClary ascended one of the rocky peaks of the mountain, the base of which rested near us.   When they returned, which they did not until it was nearly dark, they informed us that they saw on the mountain a female grisly bear with cubs.   Brown killed a fat deer just before sunset, on the densely-timbered bottom of the lake near our camp, the meat of which in our nearly destitute condition was highly acceptable.   Nothing can exceed the almost awful profoundness of the solitude by which we are surrounded. Distance 24 miles.

August 26.—We did not leave our encampment until the sun, rising above the lofty mountains to the east, dispensed its

20

warm and cheerful rays throug: the openings of the magnificent forest, by which we had been sheltered for the night. It
is quite impossible to convey by language an adequate conception of the symmetrical beauty and stateliness of the forest-
trees surrounding the lake, and covering the sides of the adjacent mountains. A skilful artist with his pencil and his brush,
alone, can do justice to this contrast of Alpine and Elysian
scenery. The sublime altitude of the mountains, their granite
and barren heads piercing the sky ; the umbrageous foliage of
the tall pines and cedars, deepening in verdure and density as
the forest approaches the more gentle and grassy slopes along
the banks of the lake, the limpid and tranquil surface of which
daguerreotypes distinctly every object, from the moss-covered
rocks laved by its waves to the bald and inaccessible summits
of the Sierra—these scenic objects, with the fresh incense of
the forest, and the fragrant odor of the wild rose, constituted
a landscape that, from associations, melted the sensibilities,
blunted as they were by long exposure and privation, and
brought back to our memories the endearments of home and the
pleasures of civilization.

The trail leaves the shore of the lake on the right hand,
ascending over some rocky hills, and after crossing some difficult ravines and swampy ground densely timbered, we reached
the base of the crest of the Sierra Nevada. To mount this was
our next great difficulty. Standing at the bottom and looking
upwards at the perpendicular, and in some places, impending
granite cliffs, the observer, without any further knowledge on
the subject, would doubt if man or beast had ever made good a
passage over them. But we knew that man and horse, oxen
and wagon, women and children, had crossed this formidable
and apparently impassable barrier erected by Nature between
the desert and the fertile districts on the coast of the Pacific.
What their energy had accomplished, impelled though it had been
by an invincible desperation, we knew could be achieved by us.

In good heart, therefore, we commenced the steep ascent,
leaping our animals from crag to crag, and climbing in places
nearly perpendicular precipices of smooth granite rocks. One

of our mules in this ascent, heavily packed, fell backwards twice, and rolled downwards, until her descent was interrupted by a projecting rock. We thought, each time, that her career of duty and usefulness had terminated ; and that her bones would bleach among the barren rocks of the mountain. But she revived from the stunning and bruising effects of her backward somersets ; and with great exertions on our own part in assisting her, she reached with us the summit of the Pass.

The view from the crest of the Sierra to the east, is inexpressibly comprehensive, grand, and picturesque. After congratulating ourselves upon the safe achievement of our morning feat, and breathing our mules a few minutes, we proceeded on our journey. A mile brought us to a small dimple on the top of the mountain, in the centre of which is a miniature lake, surrounded by green grass.

It was some time before we could determine our course down the Sierra on the western side. The emigrant wagon-trail was here entirely effaced. Around the small lake we saw the traces of encampments ; but beyond it, in no direction, could we discover any signs that man had ever passed. Accompanied by Col. Russell, I rode several miles down the left side of the ravine. We experienced great difficulty in making our way through the rocks, and over fallen timber. After an hour or more spent in this exploration, we returned to the lake, and found that our party had all left it. We could hear faintly, however, at a long distance, an occasional whoop, which was echoed by the caverns and the rocks of the mountain. Searching about, we ascertained, by the fresh trail of our party, that they had left the lake on the right hand, over a small rocky elevation ; on the other side of which, we could discover the indentations of wagon-wheels made last year. Following the fresh trail, which it was difficult to do, over the rocky surface of the ground, and the sound of the whoops of our party, we came up to them after an hour's hard and difficult riding.

Descending the rocky ravine a few miles, we emerged from it and entered a beautiful level valley, some four or five miles in length from east to west, and about two miles in breadth. A narrow, sluggish stream runs through this valley, the waters of which are of considerable depth, and the banks steep and miry. A luxuriant growth of grasses, of an excellent quality, covered the entire valley with the richest verdure. Flowers were in bloom; and although late in August, the vegetation presented all the tenderness and freshness of May. This valley has been named by the emigrants " Uber Valley ;" and the stream which runs through it, and is a tributary of the Rio de los Plumas, or Feather river, has the same name. It is sometimes pronounced *Juba;* but I think Uber is the correct etymology. How the name was derived, I never could learn.

We found, after some search, a place where we could ford the stream without stalling our animals in its soft and spongy banks and bed. But it was some time before we could discover at what point the wagon-trail left the valley.

Leaving the valley we crossed a high undulating country, timbered with pines, firs, and cedars, whose symmetrical proportions and rich foliage, with the bright green moss clothing their branches, would baffle the skill and coloring of the most artistical painter, to represent them faithfully on canvass. This country is watered by a connected chain of seven small lakes, between which, and surrounded by the beautiful and fairy-like groves I have mentioned, there are several green grassy lawns and openings, which lend to the scenery a charm and a fascination more like that which the imagination ascribes to the effect of enchantment, or the creations of a beautiful dream, than the presentations of reality. The soil of this rolling country is rich and highly fertile, where there is any moisture to sustain vegetation.

Our course continued nearly south, until we reached and entered another deep ravine or gorge, down which runs a small stream of water, in a direction nearly west. After proceeding down this ravine a few miles, the elevated mountain walls on both sides of the stream, at the foot of which immense granite rocks raise their impassable forms, approach each other so nearly as to form a *cañon,* to avoid which the trail winds up and down the side of the mountain, over and under steep precipices and impending cliffs.

Our progress during the entire day, owing to the obstructions in our route, has been slow. A little before five o'clock, P. M., after having labored up to the summit of the mountain, we commenced its descent again. I left our party here, riding on as rapidly as I could, or rather plunging down the steep side of the mountain, in order to find and select an encampment for the night. About a mile, after I had reached the foot of the mountain, I found a small opening in the timber, with an easy access to the stream, but deficient in grass, and here, there being no better spot in view, I concluded to encamp for the night.

I had not remained long in this place before two or three of the pack-mules came rushing towards me, with their packs much disarranged, snorting with excitement, and smoking with perspiration. Others soon came following after them, in the same condition. Not being able to account for this singular excitement of the mules, after waiting a few moments, I started back to meet the party, and ascertain what had occurred since I left them to produce so much irregularity in our usual order of march. I met one of them near the foot of the mountain. In response to my inquiries, he said that in descending the mountain they had been attacked by a numerous swarm of yellow hornets, which, stinging the mules, they became frantic with pain and uncontrollable; and rushing down the mountain and through timber and brush, in order to force their venomous assailants to leave them, some of their riders had been thrown, and the baggage had been so much scattered that considerable time had been required to recover it. The party, with most of the baggage, soon came up, and we moved on to our camp. Some of them had their clothes much torn, by the mules, on which they were mounted, rushing into the thick brush.

After we had encamped I crossed the stream, which has a very rocky bed, to ascertain if there was any convenient spot where the grazing would be better for our mules. I found, about a mile distant, two openings in the timber of the bottom, in which the grass was green and rank. Returning to camp, and assisted by McClary, (no other member of the party volunteering,) we drove the mules across the stream, and after picketing them in the tall grass, and kindling a good fire from some dead logs of fallen timber, for their protection, we bivouacked among them in the opening for the night. The timber surrounding the circular space which we occupied is very tall. The bright blaze of our fire defined indistinctly the columnar shapes of the pines, and their overarching branches. Fancy soon pictured our residence for the night a spacious gothic temple, whose walls had mouldered away, leaving the pillars and the skeleton roof, through which the bright stars were twinkling, standing, in defiance of the assaults of time and the fury of the elements. The temperature of the evening is delightful, and the sky serene and cloudless.

One of our party this morning picked up a human skull near the trail. Some unfortunate emigrant, probably, had been interred near the spot, and, being exhumed by the Indians or wolves, this was a portion of his skeleton. I saw large numbers of pheasants during our march to-day, and shot one with my pistol while riding along. Raspberries, and a small, bitter cherry, have been quite abundant in places. Distance 25 miles.

CHAPTER XVIII.

Bear Valley—Provisions exhausted—California quail—Manzanita—The pine-nut—Deep hollow—Evergreen oak—First view of the Sacramento Valley—A body of California Indians—Live-oak acorns—Arrive at Johnson's—Indian dandy—Cheering and astonishing news from Mexico—Obtain food—A Californian newspaper.

AUGUST 27.—A slight frost was perceptible on the grass this morning. We descended the stream, on which we were encamped, several miles, keeping generally in sight of it, and passing around several *cañones* by climbing, with much difficulty, the steep sides of the mountains. We reached at last a *cañon* of several miles in length, around which it was impossible to pass without ascending to the summit of the steep and rocky ridge. Passing from this ridge, in a southwest course, we crossed a valley in which there is a small lake. From this lake we returned back to the ridge again, along which we travelled over a very rocky and difficult road, through tall and dense timber, until three o'clock, P. M., when we reached a narrow place, so steep on both sides and so sharp on the top that our mules could with difficulty stand upon it.

The emigrant wagons of last year were let down this precipice, on the northern side, with ropes. With considerable difficulty we got our mules down it. A descent of two miles brought us into a handsome, fertile valley, five or six miles in length, and varying from one to two in breadth. This is called "Bear Valley." Vegetation is very luxuriant and fresh. In addition to the usual variety of grasses and some flowers, I noticed large patches of wild peas. We found a small stream winding through it, bordered by clumps of willows. We encamped near this rivulet of the lonely mountain-vale, under some tall pines.

Here was cooked the last of our flour. A pint of rice, a skin or scrap of rancid bacon, weighing a half-pound, and some coffee, (our sugar having been exhausted for two weeks,) compose our stock of provisions for the residue of our journey. The truly impoverished condition of our larder produced a slight sensation of uneasiness and regret. But a hope that we were not far from the settlements; a huge, blazing fire, made of the dry pine logs, flashing its cheerful light over our camp; the peaceful and holy serenity of the scenery, illuminated by the rays of the waxing moon shining with brilliant splendor from the vaporless blue arch of the heavens, soon dispelled all unpleasant forebodings in regard to the future.

We flushed, in the course of the day's march, several flocks of the California quail or partridge. It is not so large as the quail of the Atlantic. Its plumage is dark and glossy, and it has a small tuft or crown of feathers on its head. It is a most graceful and beautiful bird. There has been but little variation in the growth of timber. A few oaks have exhibited themselves among the pines, firs, and cedars. We have met occasionally with a reddish berry called by the Californians, *manza-nita*, (little apple.) The berry is produced by small trees which stand in clumps, about ten or twelve feet in height, shedding their bark annually, leaving a smooth red surface. The flavor of the fruit is an agreeable acid, something like that of our apple. The burrs of the pine, which have fallen to the ground, are sometimes twelve inches in length, and contain a nut, (*piñon*,) which, although it is said to be nutritious, is not agreeable to the taste. A shrub, which growing in our gardens is called the wax-berry, I saw in several places to-day. The signs of the grisly bear and of the deer have been numerous since we crossed the Pass of the Sierra Nevada, but not one of these animals has been seen on this side. Distance 24 miles.

August 28.—A cup of coffee without sugar constituted our breakfast. Our march to-day has been one of great fatigue, and almost wholly without incident or interest. During the forenoon we were constantly engaged in rising and descending the sides of the high mountain ranges, on either hand of the stream, to avoid the *cañones*, deep chasms and ravines, and immense ledges of granite rocks, with which the narrow valley is choked. In the afternoon we travelled along a high ridge, sometimes over elevated peaks, with deep and frightful abysses yawning their darkened and hideous depths beneath us. About five o'clock, P. M., by a descent so steep for a mile and a half, that ourselves and our animals slid rather than walked down it, we entered a small hollow or ravine, which we named "Steep Hollow." A gurgling brook of pure cold water runs through it over a rocky bed. In the hollow there was about a quarter of an acre of pretty good grass, and our mules soon fed this down to its roots, without leaving a blade standing.

Having nothing else to do, we made large fires of the dead oak timber that had been cut down by the emigrants of previous years, for the purpose of subsisting their animals upon its foliage. A cup of coffee without sugar, was our supper.

The oak timber has been more plentiful to-day than yesterday. The pines, firs, and cedars maintain their majestic dimensions. Our animals are much exhausted. The road has been exceedingly difficult, and consequently our progress has been slow. Distance 20 miles.

August 29.—The morning was clear and severely cold. The keen atmosphere, as soon as I threw off my blankets, just before daylight, produced an aguish sensation that I have not previously felt on the journey. The depth and consequent dampness of our encampment, probably, was one cause of this affection. Our physical exhaustion from incessant labor, and the want of adequate nourishment, was another.

Nuttall, a young gentleman of our mess, of fine intelligence and many interesting and amiable qualities of mind and heart, feeling, as we all did, the faintness, if not the pangs of hunger, insisted that if we would delay the commencement of our day's march a short time, he would prepare a soup from the rancid bacon-skins remaining in our provision-sack. In compliance with his request, the camp-kettle was placed on the fire, and the scraps placed in it, and in about fifteen minutes the soup was declared to be made. We gathered around it, with high expectations of a repast, under the circumstances, of great richness, and a high, if not a delicate flavor. But a single spoonful to each seemed to satisfy the desires of the whole party for this kind of food, if it did not their appetites. It produced a nausea that neither hunger nor philosophy could curb or resist.

We rose from the deep hollow of our encampment by a very steep ascent, and mounting the high ridges once more, continued along them nearly the whole day, in a general southwest course. The mountains have not been so rugged or so elevated to-day, but have approximated nearer the dimensions and features of hills, and we have found less difficulty in our progress over them. This change in the physical formation of the surface of the country, cheered us with the hope that we should obtain a view of the valley of the Sacramento before night. But as we ascended elevation after elevation, with anticipations of a prospect so gratifying, our hopes were as often disappointed by a succession of hills or mountains rising one after another beyond us.

We crossed, near the close of our day's march, one or two

small valleys or bottoms timbered with evergreen oaks, (*Quercus Ilex*,) giving them the appearance of old apple-orchards. The shape and foliage of this oak, previous to minute examination, presents an exact resemblance of the apple-tree. The channels of the water-courses running through these valleys were dry, and the grass parched and dead. A plant having a yellow flower, dispensing a strong and agreeable aromatic odor, perfumed the atmosphere in many places. Some berries, but not very abundant or pleasant to the taste, were observed. We saw in a number of places, ladders erected by the Indians, for climbing the pine-trees to gather the nuts, and the poles used for the same purpose. An Indian was seen, but he ran from us with great speed, disappearing behind the forest-trees. Some hares and a fox were started, and a hare was killed by one of the party.

One of our pack-mules became so exhausted this afternoon, that she refused to proceed. After stripping and vainly trying various expedients to urge her along, I haltered her with a tight noose around the nose, and fastening the end of the rope to the horn of my saddle, dragged her into camp. She had performed such faithful service, that I could not leave her to perish of hunger and thirst, or to be devoured by the wolves of the wilderness. The feet of all our mules are very tender, and they move with much apparent pain. We encamped at five o'clock in a ravine, half a mile to the left of the trail, where we found some small pools of water and a little dead grass in their vicinity. A soup of the hare killed on our march to-day, constituted our supper and only meal for two days. Distance 25 miles.

August 30.—The temperature this morning was pleasant, and the atmosphere perfectly clear and calm. We commenced our march early, determined, if possible, to force our way out of the mountains and to reach Johnson's, the nearest settlement in the valley of Sacramento, about 40 miles, above or north of Sutter's Fort, before we encamped.

After travelling some three or four miles rising and descending a number of hills, from the summit of one more elevated

than the others surrounding it, the spacious valley of the Sacra
mento suddenly burst upon my view, at an apparent distance
of fifteen miles. A broad line of timber running through the
centre of the valley indicated the course of the main river, and
smaller and fainter lines on either side of this, winding through
the brown and flat plain, marked the channels of its tributaries.
I contemplated this most welcome scene with such emotions of
pleasure as may be imagined by those who have ever crossed
the desert plains and mountains of western America, until Jacob,
who was in advance of the remainder of the party, came within
the reach of my voice. I shouted to him that we were "out
of the woods"—to pull off his hat and give three cheers, so
loud that those in the rear could hear them. Very soon the
huzzas of those behind were ringing and echoing through the
hills, valleys, and forests, and the whole party came up with
an exuberance of joy in their motions and depicted upon their
countenances. It was a moment of cordial and heartfelt con-
gratulations.

Taking a direct course west, in order to reach the valley at
the nearest point, we soon struck a small horse-trail, which we
followed over low gravelly hills with grassy hollows between,
timbered with the evergreen oak, forming in many places a
most inviting landscape. About one o'clock we discovered
at the distance of half a mile, a number of men, apparently
twenty or thirty. Some of them were dressed in white shirts
and pantaloons, with the Mexican sombrero, or broad-brim hat,
others were nearly naked and resembled the Indians we had
frequently seen on the eastern side of the Sierra. They had
evidently discovered us before we saw them, for they seemed
to be in great commotion, shouting and running in various
directions. Some of our party suggested that they might be a
body of Mexican soldiers stationed here for the purpose of opposing the entrance of the emigrants into California, a conjecture that seemed reasonable, under the probable existing relations
between Mexico and the United States. However, upon a
careful examination I could not discover that they had any arms,
and felt pretty well assured from their movements, that they

were not an organized body of soldiers. But halting until the whole party came up, I requested them to see that all their pieces were charged and capped, which being done, we moved forward to the point (a small grove of oaks on a gentle elevation) where the most numerous body of the strange men were concentrated. We rode up to them, at the same time holding out our hands in token of friendship, a signal which they reciprocated immediately.

They were evidently very much rejoiced to find that we had no hostile designs upon them. With the exception of two half-breed Spaniards, they were Indians, and several of them conversed in Spanish, and were or had been the servants of settlers in the valley. One of the half-breeds, of a pleasing and intelligant countenance and good address, introduced us to their chief, (El Capitan,) and wished to know if we had not some tobacco to give him. I had a small quantity of tobacco, about half of which I gave to the chief, and distributed the residue among the party as far as it would go. I saw, however, that the chief divided his portion among those who received none. *El Capitan* was a man of about forty-five, of large frame and great apparent muscular power, but his countenance was heavy, dull, and melancholy, manifesting neither good humor nor intelligence. His long, coarse, and matted hair fell down upon his shoulders in a most neglected condition. A faded cotton handkerchief was tied around his head. I could see none of the ornaments of royalty upon him, but his clothing was much inferior to that of many of his party, who I presume had obtained theirs by laboring for the white settlers. Many of them were in a state of nudity.

We soon learned from them that they were a party engaged in gathering acorns, which to these poor Indians are what wheat and maize are to us. They showed us large quantities in their baskets under the trees. When dried and pulverized, the flour of the acorn is made into bread or mush, and is their "staff of life." It is their chief article of subsistence in this section of California. Their luxuries, such as bull-beef and horse-meat, they obtain by theft, or pay for in labor at exorbitant rates. The acorn of California, from the evergreen oak, (*Quercus Ilex,*) is much larger, more oily, and less bitter than on the Atlantic side of the continent. In fruitful seasons the ground beneath the trees is covered with the nuts, and the Indians have the providence, when the produce of the oak is thus plentiful, to provide against a short crop and the famine which must necessarily result to them from it, by laying up a supply greater than they will consume in one year.

We inquired the distance to the residence of Mr. Johnson. They made signs indicating that it was but a short distance. After some little delay we prevailed upon one of them who was naked, by promising him a reward, to accompany us as our guide. He conducted us safely, in about an hour and a half, to the house of Mr. Johnson, situated on Bear creek, a tributary of the Rio de los Plumas, near the edge of the valley of the Sacramento. The house of Mr. Johnson is a small building of two rooms, one-half constructed of logs, the other of adobes or sun-dried bricks. Several pens made of poles and pickets surround the house. A building of any kind, inhabited by civilized beings, was almost a curiosity to us. Some of our party, when about a mile distant, fancied from something white which they saw in the door, resembling at a distance the shape of a woman clad in light garments, that it was Mrs. Johnson, who would be there to welcome them with all the hospitality of an American lady. Great was their disappointment, however, when they came in front of the door, to find it closed. A light frame with a raw-hide nailed upon it, was the construction of the door. The central portion of the raw-hide was white, the natural color of the animal from which it had been taken, and into this melted the graceful figure, and the welcome countenance of the white woman in white. Mr. Johnson was not at home, and the house was shut up. This we learned from a little Indian, the only human object we could find about the premises; he intimated by signs, however, that Mr. Johnson would return when the sun set.

We encamped under some trees in front of the house, resolved to do as well as we could, in our half-famished condi-

21

tion, until Mr. J. returned. In looking around the place, we saw where a quantity of wheat had been threshed, consequently there should be flour in the house. In one of the pens there were several young calves, showing conclusively that there must be milk. There was a small attempt at gardening, but no vegetables visible. We tried to prevail upon the Indian to bring us some flour, but the little heathen shook his head, either not understanding us or signifying that he could not get at it. We then made him comprehend that we wanted milk, and after showing him a bright-colored cotton handkerchief, he demanded our bucket and started with it after the cows. They were brought to the pen where the calves were confined, and one of them being fastened by the horns with a raw-hide rope, the calf was admitted to her to keep her gentle during the process of milking. Our bucket was nearly filled with rich milk, and this, with a cup of coffee, took off the edge of our hunger.

In the mean time we performed our ablutions in the creek, and having shed our much-worn clothing, we presented most of it to the naked Indian who acted as our guide. He was soon clad in a complete suit from head to feet, and strutted about with a most dandified and self-satisfied air. A small pocket looking-glass completed his happiness. He left us with a bundle of rags under his arms, nearly overjoyed at his good luck.

At sunset the dogs about the house began to bark most vociferously, and ran off over a gentle rise of ground to the north. Two men on horseback soon made their appearance on the rising ground, and, seeing us, rode to our camp. They were two Franco-Americans, originally from Canada or St. Louis, who had wandered to California in some trapping expedition, and had remained in the country. They were arranging to build houses and settle permanently in this neighborhood. From them we learned the gratifying intelligence, that the whole of Upper California was in possession of the United States. Intelligence, they further stated, had been received, that General Taylor, after having met and defeated the Mexican forces in four pitched battles, killing an incredible number, some forty or fifty thousand, had triumphantly marched into the city of Mexico. The last part of this news, of course, judging from the situation of General Taylor when we left the United States, (war not having then been declared,) was impossible; but sifting the news and comparing one statement with another, the result to our minds was, that General T. had been eminently successful, defeating the Mexicans, whenever he had met them, with considerable slaughter. This, of course, produced much exultation and enthusiasm among us.

We informed the two gentlemen, that we were and had been for some time entirely destitute of provisions, and were in a state bordering upon starvation. One of them immediately started off at a gallop to his cabin not far distant, and soon returned with a pan of unbolted flour and some tallow to cook it with. This, he said, was all he had, and if such had not been the case, he would have brought us something more. But we could not comprehend the use of tallow in cooking. We, however, afterwards learned that beef-tallow in California is used for culinary purposes in the same manner that hog's-lard is with us; and, on the whole, the prejudice against it being done away with by habit, I do not know that the former is not preferable to the latter—so much does habit and prejudice enter into the account and make up the sum of our likes and dislikes. We felt very grateful to this gentleman for his opportune present, for he would receive no compensation for it; and the fires were immediately blazing to render his generous donation of practical benefit.

Mr. Johnson returned home about nine o'clock. He was originally a New England sailor, and cast upon this remote coast by some of the vicissitudes common to those of his calling, had finally turned farmer or ranchero. He is a bachelor, with Indian servants, and stated that he had no food prepared for us, but such as was in the house was at our service. A pile of small cheeses, and numerous pans of milk with thick cream upon them, were exhibited on the table, and they disappeared with a rapidity dangerous to the health of those who consumed them.

Mr. J. gave us the first number of the first newspaper ever

published in California, entitled "THE CALIFORNIAN," and published and edited at Monterey by Dr. ROBERT SEMPLE, a native Kentuckian. It was dated about two weeks back. From the columns of this small sheet we gleaned some farther items of general intelligence from the United States, all of great interest to us. The leading paragraph, under the editorial head, was, in substance, a call upon the people of California to set about the organization of a territorial government, with a view to immediate annexation to the United States. This seemed and sounded very odd. We had been travelling in as straight a line as we could, crossing rivers, mountains, and deserts, nearly four months beyond the bounds of civilization, and for the greater distance beyond the boundaries of territory claimed by our government; but here, on the remotest confines of the world as it were, where we expected to visit and explore a foreign country, we found ourselves under American authority, and about to be "annexed" to the American Union. Events such as this are very remarkable, and are well calculated to excite the pride and vanity, if they do not always tally with the reason and judgment, of American citizens and republicans. Distance 17 miles.

CHAPTER XIX.

Soil of Johnson's rancho—His crops—Price of flour—Soil of the Sacramento valley—Sinclair's rancho—A white woman—Sutter's Fort—New Helvetia—Interview with Captain Sutter—Reflections upon our journey—Table of distances from Independence to San Francisco.

AUGUST 31.—The soil of the bottom-land of Mr. Johnson's rancho appears to be fertile and productive of good crops. He settled here last October. A small wheat-field, although the season was not regarded as a good one, produced him 300 bushels, an average of 25 or 30 bushels to the acre. In addition to this he raised a crop of barley, the kernel of which is the largest I have ever previously seen. I saw corn standing in the field, but it did not look promising,—the ground was evidently too dry for it.

We procured of Mr. Johnson a quantity of unbolted flour at the rate of $8 per 100 lbs. ; also some fresh beef, cheese, and butter, (the last three luxuries, which we had not for a long time tasted.) At 1 o'clock we marched south seven miles, and encamped on the bank of a chain of small ponds of water. The grass around the ponds was rank and green, and we were protected from the hot rays of the afternoon sun by the shade of evergreen oaks. This oak, which is the prevailing timber in the valleys of Upper California, although it much resembles the live-oak of Florida, is not precisely the same species. It is much more porous and brittle. We saw on the plain several flocks of antelope, one of which numbered at least two hundred. A species of the jackal, called here the *coyote*, frequently approached within a few rods of us. Large numbers of wild ducks were flying about and swimming in the ponds. We shot several of these. Distance 7 miles.

September 1.—A clear, pleasant morning. We took a south course down the valley, and at 4 o'clock, P. M., reached the residence of JOHN SINCLAIR, Esq., on the Rio de los Americanos, about two miles east of Sutter's Fort. The valley of the Sacramento, as far as we have travelled down it, is from 30 to 40 miles in width, from the foot of the low benches of the Sierra Nevada, to the elevated range of hills on the western side. The composition of the soil appears to be such as to render it highly productive, with proper cultivation, of the small grains. The ground is trodden up by immense herds of cattle and horses which grazed here early in the spring, when it was wet and apparently miry. We passed through large evergreen oak groves, some of them miles in width. Game is very abundant. We frequently saw deer feeding quietly one or two hundred yards from us, and large flocks of antelopes.

Mr. Sinclair, with a number of horses and Indians, was engaged in threshing wheat. His crop this year, he informed me, would be about three thousand bushels. The soil of his

21*

rancho, situated in the bottom of the Rio de los Americanos, just above its junction with the Sacramento, is highly fertile. His wheat-fields are secured against the numerous herds of cattle and horses, which constitute the largest item in the husbandry of this country, by ditches about five feet in depth, and four or five feet over at the surface. The dwelling-house and out-houses of Mr. Sinclair, are all constructed after American models, and present a most comfortable and neat appearance. It was a pleasant scene, after having travelled many months in the wilderness, to survey this abode of apparent thrift and enjoyment, resembling so nearly those we had left in the far-off country behind us.

In searching for the ford over the Rio de los Americanos, in order to proceed on to Sutter's Fort, I saw a lady of a graceful though fragile figure, dressed in the costume of our own countrywomen. She was giving some directions to her female servants, and did not discover me until I spoke to her and inquired the position of the ford. Her pale and delicate, but handsome and expressive countenance, indicated much surprise, produced by my sudden and unexpected salutation. But collecting herself, she replied to my inquiry in vernacular English, and the sounds of her voice, speaking our own language, and her civilized appearance, were highly pleasing. This lady, I presume, was Mrs. Sinclair, but I never saw her afterwards.

Crossing the Rio de los Americanos, the waters of which, at this season, are quite shallow at the ford, we proceeded over a well-beaten road to Sutter's Fort, arriving there when the sun was about an hour and a half high. Riding up to the front gate I saw two Indian sentinels pacing to and fro before it, and several Americans, or *foreigners*, (as all who are not Californians by birth are here called,) sitting in the gateway, dressed in buckskin pantaloons and blue sailors' shirts with white stars worked on the collars. I inquired if Captain Sutter was in the fort? A very small man, with a peculiarly sharp red face and a most voluble tongue, gave the response. He was probably a corporal. He said in substance, that perhaps I was not aware of the great changes which had recently taken place in California;—that the fort now belonged to the United States, and that Captain Sutter, although he was in the fort, had no control over it. He was going into a minute history of the complicated circumstances and events which had produced this result, when I reminded him that we were too much fatigued to listen to a long discourse, but if Captain Sutter was inside the walls, and could conveniently step to the gate a moment, I would be glad to see him. A lazy-looking Indian with a ruminating countenance, after some time spent in parleying, was dispatched with my message to Captain Sutter.

Capt. S. soon came to the gate, and saluted us with much gentlemanly courtesy, and friendly cordiality. He said that events had transpired in the country, which, to his deep regret, had so far deprived him of the control of his own property, that he did not feel authorized to invite us inside of the walls to remain. The fort, he said, was occupied by soldiers, under the pay of the U. S., and commanded by Mr. Kern. I replied to him, that although it would be something of a novelty to sleep under a roof, after our late nomadic life, it was a matter of small consideration. If he would supply us with some meat, a little salt, and such vegetables as he might have, we neither asked nor desired more from his hospitality, which we all knew was liberal, to the highest degree of generosity.

A servant was immediately dispatched with orders to furnish us with a supply of beef, salt, melons, onions, and tomatoes, for which no compensation would be received. We proceeded immediately to a grove of live-oak timber, about two miles west of the fort, and encamped within a half a mile of the Sacramento river. Our fires were soon blazing brightly, added to the light of which was the brilliant effulgence of the moon, now near its full, clothing the tree-tops, and the far-stretching landscape, with a silvery light; and rendering our encampment far more agreeable to me than the confined walls of any edifice erected by human hands.

With sincere and devout thankfulness I laid myself on my hard bed, to sleep once more within the boundaries of civilization. Since we left our homes none of our party have met with any serious accidents or disasters. With the small number of only nine men, we have travelled from Fort Laramie to Sutter's Fort, a distance of nearly 1700 miles, over trackless and barren deserts, and almost impassable mountains; through tribes of savage Indians, encountering necessarily many difficulties, and enduring great hardships and privations; and here we all are, in good health, with the loss of nothing materially valuable belonging to us, except a single animal, which gave out from fatigue, and was left on the road. We have had no quarrels with Indians, rendering it necessary in self-defence to take their lives; but on the contrary, whenever we have met them on our journey, by our deportment towards them, their friendship has been conciliated, or their hostility softened and disarmed, without striking a blow. We uniformly respected their feelings and their rights, and they respected us. Results so favorable as these, to expeditions constituted as was ours, and acting under such circumstances, are not often recorded. Distance 28 miles.

TABLE *of distances from Independence, Missouri, to Sutter's Fort, on the Sacramento river, Upper California.*

The following is a table of distances from Independence to Sutter's Fort, in California, by the route which I travelled, according to the daily estimate of our marches.

From Independence, Mo., to Fort Laramie,	672	miles.
From Fort Laramie to " Pacific Springs," (South Pass,)	311	"
From the " South Pass," (Pacific Springs,) to Fort Bridger,	133	"
From Fort Bridger to Salt Lake,	106	"
From Salt Lake to Mary's river,	315	"
Down Mary's river to the " Sink,"	274	"
From the " Sink" to Truckee Lake,	134	"
From Truckee Lake to Johnson's,	111	"
From Johnson's to Sutter's Fort,	35	"

Total distance from Independence, Mo., to Sutter's Fort, in California,	2091	
The distance from Sutter's Fort by land, to the town of San Francisco, (via the Puebla of San Jose,) near the mouth of the Bay of S. F., and five miles from the Pacific Ocean, is	200	"

Total,	2291	miles.

CHAPTER XX.

Account of the disasters to the emigrating parties of 1846—The Oregon emigrants—Causes of delay which resulted in fatal consequences—Generosity
of the people of San Francisco, and Capt. Sutter—John Sinclair's statement—Dreadful sufferings of the first party who crossed on the snows—
George McKinstry's statement—Journal of one of the sufferers—List of
those who perished—Particulars of the death of George Donner and wife
—Keysburgh's cannibalism—Interment of the bones by Gen. Kearney's
party in June, 1847.

HAVING accomplished the journey from the United States to
the civilized districts of Upper California, it is proper that I
should give some account of those with whom I started and
travelled a portion of the distance.

The great bulk of the emigration of 1846 both to California
and Oregon took the old routes of former emigrating parties.
The company of Capt. West on Mary's river had a difficulty
and a fight with a large party of Digger Indians. In this encounter a Mr. Sallee lost his life from a wound by a poisoned
arrow. Mr. Lippincott was wounded in the knee, but he recovered. With this exception all of these, I believe, reached
their destination in safety and in good season.

A party consisting of some sixty or eighty wagons bound for
Oregon, among whom were the Messrs. Putnam of Lexington,
Ky., took the new route to the Wilhamette valley, explored by
Mr. Applegate and his party, whom we met on Mary's river.
This company became entangled in the Umpqua mountains,
(not very distant from the settlements of Oregon,) and after
suffering great hardships, were compelled to abandon all their
wagons and baggage. With the aid of parties sent for their
relief from the Wilhamette valley, nearly all of them, however,
reached their destination. Mr. Newton, whom I have previously
mentioned, was murdered by some Indians. They professed
to be friendly and loitered about Mr. N.'s camp. He suspected

them of hostile intentions and ordered them away. They however managed to secure some powder and balls, and availing themselves of a moment when Mr. N., being worn out with watching, had fallen asleep outside of his tent, they shot three balls into him. He sprang into the tent to secure his rifle, but was seized by one of his assailants, who with an axe nearly severed one of his legs. He died of his wounds the next day. Mrs. N. escaped. The Indians robbed the tent of all its portable contents.

The number of wagons which took the new route from Fort Bridger via the south end of the Great Salt Lake, intersecting with the old wagon-trail on Mary's river 250 miles above the Sink, was about eighty. The advance company of these was Mr. Harlan's. The pioneers, and those following their trail, succeeded by energetic exertions in opening a road through the difficult mountain passes near the Salt Lake, and reached the settlements of California in good season. The rear party, known as Messrs. Reed and Donner's company, did not follow the trail of those who had preceded them, but explored for a portion of the distance, another route, and opened a new road through the Desert Basin. In making these explorations and from other causes, they lost a month's time, the consequence of which was, that they did not reach the Pass of the Sierra Nevada until the 31st of October, when they should have been there by the 1st of October.

The snow commenced falling on the Sierra, two or three weeks earlier in 1846 than is usual, and when this party arrived at the foot of the Pass they found it impossible to proceed from its depth. The people of the town of San Francisco, as soon as they received intelligence of the dangerous situation of these emigrants, held a public meeting, and with a liberality that reflects the highest credit upon them, subscribed fifteen hundred dollars for the organization of a party that would penetrate the mountains for their relief. This party started, and soon afterwards other parties under the direction of the naval commandant at the Port of San Francisco, were organized for the same object. Capt. J. A. SUTTER, a philanthropist in its most expressive and least ostentatious sense, displayed his characteristic generosity and benevolence on this occasion. At his own expense and hazard, before other exertions were made, he furnished men and mules laden with provisions for the relief of the perishing sufferers. The result of these exertions in behalf of the unfortunate emigrants, and the melancholy and in some respects horrible details of their sufferings, will be best understood by a perusal of the following extracts from authentic papers in my possession. They compose a chapter of human misery, for which there are but few parallels in fact or fiction.

STATEMENT OF JOHN SINCLAIR ESQ., ALCALDE. DISTRICT OF SACRAMENTO.

RANCHO DEL PASO, February, 1847.

DEAR SIR,—

The following brief sketch of the sufferings of the emigrants who endeavored at different times to reach this valley from the mountains, where they had been caught by the snow in October, is drawn up at the request of the survivors, with whom I have held several conversations on the subject, and from a few short notes handed me by W. H. Eddy, one of the party. Such as they are, and hastily thrown together, I place them at your disposal.

On the first of November, Patrick Brin, Patrick Dolan, —— Keysburg, and W. H. Eddy, left their cabins, and attempted to cross the dividing ridge of the mountains; but owing to the softness and depth of the snow, they were obliged to return. On the third they tried it again, taking with them Mrs. Reed and family, Mr. Stanton, and two Indians, who were in the employ of J. A. Sutter; but after being out one day and night, they returned to their cabins. On the twelfth, Mr. Graves, and two daughters, Messrs. Fosdick, Foster, Eddy, Stanton, Sheumacher, with two New Mexicans, and the two Indians, started on another trial, but met with no better success. Not discouraged, and impelled by the increasing scarcity of provisions at the cabins, on the twentieth they tried it again, and succeeded in crossing the divide; but found it was impossible for them to proceed for the want of a pilot, Mr. Stanton having refused to allow the Indians to accompany them on account of not being able to bring the mules out with them, which Mr. Stanton had taken there with provisions from J. A. Sutter's, previous to the falling of the snow. Here again were their warmest hopes blighted; and they again turned with heavy hearts towards their miserable cabins. Mrs. Murphy, daughter, and two sons were of this party. During the interval between this last attempt and the next, there came on a storm, and the snow fell to the depth of eight feet. In the midst of the storm, two young men started to go to another party of emigrants, (twenty-four in number,) distant about eight miles, who it was known at the commencement of the storm had no cabins built, neither had they killed their cattle, as they still had hopes of being able to cross the mountains. As the two young men never returned, it is supposed they perished in the storm ; and it is the opinion of those who have arrived here, that the party to whom they were going must have all perished. On the sixteenth of December, expecting that they would be able to reach the settlements in ten days, Messrs. Graves, Fosdick, Dolan, Foster, Eddy, Stanton, L. Murphy, (aged thirteen,) Antonio, a New Mexican ; with Mrs. Fosdick, Mrs. Foster, Mrs. Pike, Mrs. McCutcheon, and Miss M. Graves, and the two Indians before mentioned, having prepared themselves with snow-shoes, again started on their perilous undertaking, determined to succeed or perish.

Those who have ever made an attempt to walk with snow-shoes will be able to realize the difficulty they experienced. On first starting, the snow being so light and loose, even with their snow-shoes, they sank twelve inches at every step; however, they succeeded in travelling about four miles that day. On the seventeenth they crossed the divide, with considerable difficulty and fatigue, making about five miles, the snow on the divide being twelve feet deep. The next day they made six miles, and, on the nineteenth five, it having snowed all day. On the twentieth the sun rose clear and beautiful, and cheered by its sparkling rays, they pursued their weary way. From the first day, Mr. Stanton, it appears, could not keep up with them, but had always reached their camp by the time they got their fire built, and preparations made for passing the night. This day they had travelled eight miles, and encamped early ; and as the shades of evening gathered round them, many an anxious glance was cast back through the deepening gloom for Stanton ; but he came not. Before morning the weather became stormy, and at daylight they started and went about four miles, when they encamped, and agreed to wait and see if Stanton would come up ; but that night his place was again vacant by their cheerless fire, while he, I suppose, had escaped from all further suffering, and lay wrapped in his " winding sheet of snow"—

" His weary wand'rings and his travels o'er.'

On the twenty-second the storm still continued, and they remained in camp until the twenty-third, when they again started, although the storm still continued, and travelled eight miles. They encamped in a deep valley. Here the appearance of the country was so different from what it had been represented to them, (probably by Mr. Stanton,) that they came to the conclusion that they were lost ; and the tr. ʒ Indians on whom they had placed all their confidence, were bewildered. In this melancholy situation they consulted together, and concluded they would go on, trusting in Providence, rather than return to their miserable cabins. They were, also, at this time, out of provisions, and partly agreed, with the exception of Mr. Foster, that in case of necessity, they would cast lots who should die to preserve the remainder. During the whole of the night it rained and snowed very heavily, and by morning the snow had so increased that they could not travel ; while, to add to their sufferings, their fire had been put out by the rain, and all their endeavors to light another proved abortive.

How heart-rending must have been their situation at this time, as they gazed upon each other, shivering and shrinking from the pitiless storm ! Oh ! how they must have thought of those happy, happy homes, which but a few short months before they had left with buoyant hopes and fond anticipations ! Where, oh where were the green and flowery plains which they had heard of, dreamt, and anticipated beholding, in the month of January, in California ? Alas ! many of that little party were destined never to behold them. Already was death in the midst of them. Antonio died about nine, A. M. ; and at eleven o'clock, P. M., Mr. Graves. The feelings of the rest may be imagined, on seeing two of their small party removed by death in a few hours from among them, while the thought must have struck home to every bosom, that they too would shortly follow.

In this critical situation, the presence of mind of Mr. Eddy suggested a plan for keeping themselves warm, which is common amongst the trappers of the Rocky Mountains, when caught in the snow without fire. It is simply to spread a blanket on the snow, when the party, (if small,) with the exception of one, sit down upon it in a circle, closely as possible, their feet piled over one another in the centre, room being left for the person who has to complete the arrangement. As many blankets as necessary are then spread over the heads of the party, the ends being kept down by billets of wood or snow. After every thing is completed, the person outside takes his place in the circle. As the snow falls it closes up the pores of the blankets, while the breath from the party underneath soon causes a comfortable warmth. It was with a great deal of difficulty that Mr. Eddy succeeded in getting them to adopt this simple plan, which undoubtedly was the means of saving their lives at this time. In this situation they remained thirty-six hours.

On the twenty-fifth, about four o'clock, P. M., Patrick Dolan died ; he had been for some hours delirious, and escaped from under their shelter, when he stripped off his coat, hat, and boots, and exposed himself to the storm. Mr. Eddy tried to force him back, but his strength was unequal to the task. He, however, afterwards returned of his own accord, and laid down outside of their shelter, when they succeeded in dragging him inside. On the twenty-sixth, L. Murphy died, he likewise being delirious ; and was only kept under their shelter by the united strength of the party.

In the afternoon of this day they succeeded in getting fire into a dry pine-tree. Having been four entire days without food, and since the month of October on short allowance, there was now but two alternatives left them—either to die, or preserve life by eating the bodies of the dead : slowly and reluctantly they adopted the latter alternative. On the twenty-seventh they took the flesh from the bodies of the dead; and on that, and the two following days they remained in camp drying the meat, and preparing to pursue their journey. On the thirtieth they left this melancholy spot, where so many of their friends and relatives had perished; and with heavy hearts and dark forebodings of the future, pursued their pathless course through the new-fallen snow, and made about five miles: next day about six miles. January first was one of the most fatiguing day's journeys which they had. They were compelled to climb a mountain, which they represent as nearly perpendicular; to accomplish which, they were obliged to take advantage of every cleft of rock, and pull themselves up by shrubs growing in the crevices. On the second they found they could go without snow-shoes, which, however, gave them but little relief; their feet being so badly frozen by this time, that every step was marked with blood, and the toes of one of the Indians had dropped off at the first joint. They were also again out of provisions. On the third they travelled seven miles, and at night fared on the strings of their snow-shoes.

Some time during the night of the fourth, the Indians left them; no doubt fearful to remain, lest they might be sacrificed for food. Poor fellows, they stood the pangs of hunger two days longer than their white fellow-travellers before they tasted of the human flesh. On the morning of the fifth, the party took the trail of the Indians, following it by the blood which marked their steps. After having travelled about a mile, they discovered fresh footprints of deer in the snow, when Mr. Eddy, who had a rifle, started with Miss Graves, in advance, hoping to fall in with them, which they fortunately did, and succeeded in killing one, after travelling about eight miles, at the foot of a mountain. That night Mr. Foster and wife, Mrs. Pike, and Mrs. McCutcheon, encamped on the top of the mountain, not being able to get to where Eddy was with the deer. Mr. Fosdick having given out, remained with his wife about a mile back from them. On the next day they got what remained of the deer to the top of the mountain, and two of them went back to look for Fosdick; but he was at that time " where the weary are at rest," having died about eleven o'clock, P. M.; and his wife had lain by his side that lonesome night, and prayed that death might release her from suffering, but in vain.

The flesh was taken from the bones of poor Fosdick, and brought into camp; but there was one there who tasted not of it. On the seventh and eighth they only made about two and a half miles, going down one mountain and over another. On the ninth, after travelling four miles, they fell in with the two Indians, who had then got out of the snow. Salvador was dead. Lewis had crawled to a small stream of water, and lain down to drink. They raised him up, and offered him some food; he tried to eat, but could not; and only lived about an hour. Being nearly out of provisions, and knowing not how far they might be from the settlements, they took their flesh likewise.

On the tenth and eleventh they made about seventeen miles, when falling in with an Indian trail, they concluded they would follow it, which they accordingly did; and on the twelfth, fell in with some of the Indians, who treated them kindly, gave them some acorns, and put them on to another trail the next day, which they took, and after travelling four miles in a heavy rain-storm, they came to more Indians, with whom they stopped the remainder of that day and the next. The two next days they made about seventeen miles. The seventeenth, after walking two or three miles, with an Indian for a pilot, Mr. Foster and the women gave out, their feet being swollen to such a degree that they could go no further.

Mr. Eddy, who it appears stood the fatigues of the journey better than any of them, here left them; and assisted by two Indians, that evening reached the settlement on Bear Creek. The inhabitants, on being informed of the situation of the party behind, immediately started with provisions on foot, and reached them that night about twelve o'clock. On the morning of the eighteenth, others started with horses, and brought them to the settlement, where they were treated with every mark of kindness by the inhabitants.

I remain, very respectfully,

Your obd't servant,

JOHN SINCLAIR.

EXTRACT OF A LETTER FROM MR. GEO. M'KINSTRY.

Captain E. Kern informed you of the men sent up from this place to the assistance of the sufferers, when we were first informed of their situation. I will again give you a list of their names, as I think they ought to be recorded in letters of gold. Aquila Glover, R. S. Montrey, Daniel Rhodes, John Rhodes, Daniel Tucker, Joseph Sel, and Edward Copymier. Mr. Glover, who was put in charge of this little, brave band of men, returns to me his journal, from which I extract as follows:—" On the 13th of February, 1847, our party arrived at the Bear River Valley. 14th, remained in camp, preparing packs and provisions. 15th, left Bear River Valley, and travelled fifteen miles, and encamped on Yuba river. 16th, travelled three miles, and stopped to make snow-shoes. 17th, travelled five miles, and camped on Yuba river —snow fifteen feet deep, dry and soft. 18th, travelled eight miles, and encamped on the head of Yuba river. 19th, travelled nine miles, crossed the summit of the California mountains, and reached part of the suffering company about sundown, in camp near Truckee Lake." Mr. Glover informs me that he found them in a most deplorable condition, entirely beyond description. Ten of their number had already died from starvation; and he thinks several others will die in camp, as they are too low to resuscitate. The whole party had been living on bullock-hides four weeks. On the morning of the 20th, the party went down to the camp of Geo. Donner, eight miles below the first camp, and found them with but one hide left. They had come to the conclusion, that when that was consumed, to dig up the bodies of those who had died from starvation, and use them as food. When the party arrived at the camp, they were obliged to guard the little stock of provision that they had carried over the mountains on their backs on foot, for the relief of the poor beings, as they were in such a starving condition that they would have immediately used up the small store. They even stole the buckskin strings from their snow-shoes, and ate them. This little, brave band of men immediately left with twenty-one persons, principally women and children, for the settlements. They left all the food they could spare with those (twenty-nine in number) that they were obliged to leave behind, and promised them that they would immediately return to their assistance. They were successful in bringing all safe over the mountains. Four of the children they were obliged to carry on their backs, the balance walked. On their arrival at the Bear River Valley they met a small party with provisions, that Captain Kern, of this fort, had sent for their relief. The same day they met Mr. Reed with fifteen men, on foot, packed with provisions, who ere this have reached the sufferers. Lieutenant Woodworth was going ahead with a full force, and will himself visit them in their mountain camp, and see that every person is brought out. Mr. Greenwood was three days behind Mr. Reed, with the horses. Captain Kern will remain in camp, with the Indian soldiers, to guard the provisions and horses, and will send the sufferers down to this post as soon as possible, where they will be received by Captain J. A. Sutter with all the hospitality for which he is so celebrated. And in the mean time Captain Sutter will keep up a communication with Captain Kern's camp, so as to be in readiness to assist him on all occasions. Mr. Glover informed me that the wagons belonging to the emigrants are buried some fifteen feet under the snow. He thinks that it will be some three weeks from this date before Lieutenant Woodworth can arrive at this fort. Mr. Glover left the party at Bear River Valley on express, as I had written to him, by the second party, of the death of one member of his family, and the severe illness of his wife. The balance of the party will reach here in some four or five days. The weather is very fine, and we have no doubt but that Lieutenant Woodworth will be able to bring all left on the mountains.

———

Copy of a Journal kept by a suffering Emigrant on the California mountains, from Oct. 31st, 1846, to March 1st, 1847.

TRUCKEE LAKE, Nov. 20, 1846.—Came to this place on the 31st of last month ; went into the Pass, the snow so deep we were unable to find the road, and when within three miles from the summit, turned back to this shanty on Truckee Lake. Stanton came up one day after we arrived here ; we again took our teams and wagons and made another unsuccessful attempt to cross in company with Stanton ; we returned to the shanty, it continuing to snow all the time. We now have killed most part of our cattle, having to remain here until next spring, and live on lean beef without bread or salt. It snowed during the space of eight days with little intermission, after our arrival here, though now clear and pleasant, freezing at night, the snow nearly gone from the valleys.—21. Fine morning, wind N. W. ; twenty-two of our company about starting to cross the mountains this day, including Stanton and his Indians.—22. Froze hard last night ; fine and clear to-day ; no account from those on the mountains.—23. Same weather, wind w. ; the expedition across the mountains returned after an unsuccessful attempt.—25. Cloudy, looks like the eve of a snow-storm ; our mountaineers are to make another trial to-morrow, if fair;— froze hard last night.—26. Began to snow last evening, now rains or sleets ; the party does not start to-day.—29. Still snowing, now about three feet deep ; wind w. ; killed my last oxen to-day ; gave another yoke to Foster ; wood hard to be got.—30. Snowing fast, looks as likely to continue as when it commenced ; no living thing without wings can get about.

Dec. 1.—Still snowing, wind w. ; snow about six or six and a half feet deep ; very difficult to get wood, and we are completely housed up ; our cattle all killed but two or three, and these, with the horses and Stanton's mules, all supposed to be lost in the snow ; no hopes of finding them alive. —3. Ceased snowing ; cloudy all day ; warm enough to thaw.—5. Beautiful sunshine, thawing a little ; looks delightful after the long storm ; snow seven or eight feet deep.—6. The morning fine and clear ; Stanton and Graves manufacturing snow-shoes for another mountain scrabble ; no account of mules.—8. Fine weather, froze hard last night ; wind s. w. ; hard work to find wood sufficient to keep us warm or cook our beef.—9. Commenced snowing about 11 o'clock, wind N. W. ; took in Spitzer yesterday so weak, that he cannot rise without help, caused by starvation. Some have a scant supply of beef ; Stanton trying to get some for himself and Indians ; not likely to get much.—10. Snowed fast all night with heavy squalls of wind ; continues to snow, now about seven feet in depth.—13. Snows faster than any previous day ; Stanton and Graves, with several others, making preparations to cross the mountains on snow-shoes. Snow eight feet deep on a level.—16. Fair and pleasant, froze hard last night ; the company started on snow-shoes to cross the mountains, wind s. E.—17. Pleasant. Wm. Murphy returned from the mountain party last evening ; Balis Williams died night before last ; Milton and Noah started for Donner's eight days ago ; not returned yet ; think they are lost in the snow.—19. Snowed last night, thawing to-day, wind N. W. ; a little singular for a thaw.—20. Clear and pleasant ; Mrs. Reed here ; no account from Milton yet ; Charles Berger set out for Donner's ; turned back, unable to proceed ; tough times, but not

22*

discouraged; our hopes are in God, Amen.—21. Milton got back last night from Donner's camp; sad news, Jacob Donner, Samuel Shoemaker, Rhinehart, and Smith, are dead the rest of them in a low situation; snowed all night with a strong s. w. wind.—23. Clear to-day; Milton took some of his meat away; all well at their camp. Began this day to read the " Thirty days' prayers." Almighty God grant the requests of unworthy sinners!—24. Rained all night and still continues; poor prospect for any kind of comfort, spiritual or temporal.—25. Began to snow yesterday, snowed all night, and snows yet rapidly; extremely difficult to find wood; offered our prayers to God this Christmas morning; the prospect is appalling, but we trust in Him.—27. Cleared off yesterday, continues clear, snow nine feet deep; wood growing scarce; a tree when felled sinks into the snow and hard to be got at.—30. Fine clear morning, froze hard last night; Charles Berger died last evening about 10 o'clock.—31. Last of the year; may we, with the help of God, spend the coming year better than we have the past, which we propose to do if it is the will of the Almighty to deliver us from our present dreadful situation, Amen. Morning fair but cloudy, wind E. by s.; looks like another snow-storm—snow-storms are dreadful to us; the snow at present very deep.

Jan. 1, 1847.—We pray the God of mercy to deliver us from our present calamity, if it be His holy will. Commenced snowing last night and snows a little yet; provisions getting very scant; dug up a hide from under the snow yesterday—have not commenced on it yet.—3. Fair during the day, freezing at night; Mrs. Reed talks of crossing the mountains with her children.—4. Fine morning, looks like spring; Mrs. Reed and Virginia, Milton Elliot, and Eliza Williams, started a short time ago with the hope of crossing the mountains; left the children here—it was difficult for Mrs. Reed to part with them.—6. Eliza came back from the mountains yesterday evening, not able to proceed, the others kept ahead.—8. Very cold this morning; Mrs. Reed and the others came back; could not find the way on the other side of the mountains; they have nothing but hides to live on.—10. Began to snow last night, still continues; wind w. N. w.—13. Snowing fast—snow higher than the shanty; it must be 13 feet deep; cannot get wood this morning; it is a dreadful sight for us to look upon.—14. Cleared off yesterday; the sun shining brilliantly renovates our spirits, praises be to the God of heaven.—15. Clear day again, wind N. w.; Mrs. Murphy blind; Lantron not able to get wood, has but one axe between him and Keysburg; it looks like another storm—expecting some account from Sutter's soon.—17. Eliza Williams came here this morning; Lantron crazy last night; provisions scarce, hides our main subsistence. May the Almighty send us help.—21. Fine morning; John Battise and Mr Denton came this morning with Eliza; she will not eat hides. Mrs. —— sent her back to live or die on them.—22. Began to snow after sunrise; likely to continue; wind w.—23. Blew hard and snowed all night, the most severe storm we have experienced this winter; wind w.—26. Cleared up yesterday; to-day fine and pleasant, wind s.; in hopes we are done with snow-storms; those who went to Sutter's not yet returned; provisions getting scant; people growing weak living on small allowance of hides.—27. Commenced snowing yesterday; still continues to-day; Lewis (Sutter's Indian) died three days ago; wood getting scarce; don't have fire enough to cook our hides.—30. Fair and pleasant, wind w., thawing in the sun; John and Edward Breen went to Graves' this morning; the ———— seized on Mrs. ———— goods, until they should be paid; they also took the hides which she and her family subsisted upon. She regained two pieces only, the balance they have taken. You may judge from this what our fare is in camp; there is nothing to be had by hunting, yet perhaps there soon will be.—31. The sun does not shine out brilliant this morning; froze hard last night, wind N. W. Lantron Murphy died last night about 1 o'clock. Mrs. Reed went to Graves' this morning to look after goods.

February 5.—Snowed hard until two o'clock last night; many uneasy for fear we shall all perish with hunger; we have but a little meat left and only three hides; Mrs. Reed has nothing but one hide and that is on Graves' house; Milton lives there and likely will keep that—Eddy's child died last night.—6. It snowed faster last night and to-day than it has done this winter before, still continues without intermission, wind s. w.; Murphy's folks and Keysburg say they cannot eat hides; I wish we had enough of them. Mrs. Eddy is very weak.—7. Ceased to snow at last, to-day it is quite pleasant. McCutcheon's child died on the second of this month.—8. Fine clear morning, Spitzer died last night, we shall bury him in the snow. Mrs. Eddy died on the night of the seventh.—9. Mr. Pike's child all but dead. Milton is at Murphy's not able to get out of bed; Keysburg never gets up, says he is not able. Mrs. Eddy and child were buried to-day, wind s. E.—10. Beautiful morning, thawing in the sun. Milton Elliot died last night at Murphy's shanty. Mrs. Reed went there this morning to see after his effects. J. Denton trying to borrow meat for Graves; had none to give; they had nothing but hides. All are entirely out of meat but a little we have. Our hides are nearly all eat up, but with God's help spring will soon smile upon us.—12. Warm, thawing morning.—14. Fine morning, but cold; buried Milton in the snow. John Denton not well.—15. Morning cloudy until nine o'clock, then cleared off warm. Mrs. ———— refused to give Mrs. ———— any hides; put Sutter's pack-hides on her shanty and would not let her have them.—16. Commenced to rain last evening and turned to snow during the night and continued until morning; weather changeable, sunshine then light showers of hail and wind at times. We all feel very unwell; the snow is not getting much less at present.—19. Froze hard last night, seven men arrived from California yesterday evening with provisions, but left the greater part on the way; to-day it is clear and warm for this region. Some of the men have gone to Donner's camp; they will start back on

Monday.—22. The Californians started this morning, twenty-four in number, some in a very weak state. Mrs. Keysburg started with them and left Keysburg here unable to go ; buried Pike's child this morning in the snow, it died two days ago.—23. Froze hard last night, to-day pleasant and thawy ; has the appearance of spring, all but the deep snow ; wind s. s. e. ; shot a dog to-day and dressed his flesh.—25. To-day Mrs. Murphy says the wolves are about to dig up the dead bodies around her shanty, and the nights are too cold to watch them, but we hear them howl.—26. Hungry times in camp ; plenty of hides, but the folks will not eat them ; we eat them with tolerable good appetite, thanks be to the Almighty God. Mrs. Murphy said here yesterday that she thought she would commence on Milton and eat him ; I do not think she has done so yet—it is distressing ; the Donner's told the California folks four days ago that they would commence on the dead people if they did not succeed that day or next in finding their cattle, then ten or twelve feet under the snow, and did not know the spot or near it ; they have done it ere this.—28. One solitary Indian passed by yesterday, came from the Lake, had a heavy pack on his back, gave me five or six roots resembling onions in shape, tasted some like a sweet potato full of tough little fibres.

March 1. Ten men arrived this morning from Bear Valley with provisions; we are to start in two or three days and shall *cache* our goods here. They say the snow will remain until June.

The above mentioned ten men started for the valley with seventeen of the sufferers ; they travelled fifteen miles and a severe snow-storm came on ; they left fourteen of the emigrants, the writer of the above journal and his family, and succeeded in getting in but three children. Lieut. Woodworth immediately went to their assistance, but before he reached them they had eaten three of their number, who had died from hunger and fatigue ; the remainder Lieut. Woodworth's party brought in. On the 29th of April, 1847, the last member of that party was brought to Capt. Sutter's Fort: it is utterly impossible to give any description of the sufferings of the company. Your readers can form some idea of them by perusing the above diary.

Yours, &c.

GEORGE MCKINSTRY, Jr.

Fort Sacramento, April 29, 1847.

Names of the late Emigration from the United States, who were prevented by the snow from crossing the California mountains, October 31st, 1846.

ARRIVED IN CALIFORNIA.

William Graves, Sarah Fosdick, Mary Graves, Ellen Graves, Viney Graves, Nancy Graves, Jonathan Graves, Elizabeth Graves, Loithy Donner, Lean Donner, Francis Donner, Georgiana Donner, Eliza Donner, John Battiste, Solomon Hook, George Donner, Jr., Mary Donner, Mrs. Wool—finger, Lewis Keysburg, Mrs. Keysburg, William Foster, Sarah Foster, Simon Murphy, Mary Murphy, Harriet Pike, Miomin Pike, Wm. Eddy, Patrick Breen, Margaret Breen, John Breen, Edward Breen, Patrick Breen, Jr., Simon Breen, James Breen, Peter Breen, Isabella Breen, Eliza Williams, James F. Reed, Mrs. Reed, Virginia Reed, Martha Reed, James Reed, Thomas Reed, Noah James.

PERISHED IN THE MOUNTAINS.

C. T. STANTON, Mr. Graves, Mrs. Graves, Mr. J. Fosdick, Franklin Graves, John Denton, Geo. Donner, Sen., Mrs. Donner, Charles Berger, Joseph Rhinehart, Jacob Donner, Betsey Donner, Wm. Johnson, Isaac Donner, Lewis Donner, Samuel Donner, Samuel Shoemaker, James Smith, Balis Williams, Bertha Keysburg, (child,) Lewis Keysburg, Mrs. Murphy, Lemuel Murphy, George Foster, Catharine Pike, Ellen Eddy, Margaret Eddy, James Eddy, Patrick Dolan, Augustus Spitzer, Milton Elliot, Lantron Murphy, Mr. Pike, Antonio, (New Mexican,) Lewis, (Sutter's Indian,) Salvadore, do.

At the time the occurrences above related took place, 1 was marching with the California battalion, under the command of Col. Fremont, to Ciudad de los Angelos, to assist in suppressing a rebellion which had its origin in that quarter. After my return from that expedition, I saw and conversed with several of the survivors in the above list. The oral statements made to me by them in regard to their sufferings, far exceed in horror the descriptions given in the extracts. Mr. Fallon, who conducted the last relief party over the mountains, made a statement, in regard to what he saw upon his arrival at the "cabins," so revolting that I hesitate before alluding to it. The parties which had preceded him had brought into the settlements all the living sufferers except three. These were Mr. and Mrs. George Donner, and —— Keysburg. At the time the others left, Mr. George Donner was unable to travel from debility, and Mrs. D. refused to leave him. Why Keysburg remained, there is no satisfactory explanation. Mrs. Donner offered a reward of five hundred dollars to any party that would return and rescue them. I knew the Donners well. Their means in money and merchandise, which they had brought with

them, were abundant.   Mr. Donner was a man of about sixty,
and was at the time of his leaving the United States a highly
respectable citizen of Illinois—a farmer of independent circumstances.   Mrs. D. was considerably younger than her husband,
and an active, energetic woman of refined education.

Mr. Fallon and his party reached the "cabins" some time in
April.   The snow in the valley, on the eastern side of the Pass,
had melted so as in spots to expose the ground.   He found the
main cabin empty, but evidences that it had not been long deserted.   He and his party commenced a search, and soon
discovered fresh tracks in the snow leading from it.   These
they followed some miles, and by pursuing them they returned
again to the cabin.   Here they now found Keysburg.   He was
reclining upon the floor of the cabin, smoking his pipe.   Near
his head a fire was blazing, upon which was a camp kettle filled
with human flesh.   His feet were resting upon skulls and dislocated limbs denuded of their flesh.   A bucket partly filled
with blood was standing near, and pieces of human flesh, fresh
and bloody, were strewn around.   The appearance of Keysburg was haggard and revolting.   His beard was of great
length ; his finger-nails had grown out until they resembled the
claws of beasts.   He was ragged and filthy, and the expression
of his countenance ferocious.   He stated that the Donners were
both dead.   That Mrs. Donner was the last to die, and had expired some two days previously.   That she had left her
husband's camp, some eight miles distant, and came to this
cabin.   She attempted to return in the evening to the camp,
but becoming bewildered she came back to the cabin, and died
in the course of the night.   He was accused of having murdered her, for her flesh and the money the Donners were known
to possess, but denied it.   When questioned in regard to the
money of the Donners, he denied all knowledge respecting it.
He was informed that if he did not disclose where he had
secreted the money, he would immediately be hung to a tree.
Still persisting in his denial, a rope, after much resistance from
him, was placed around his neck, and Mr. Fallon commenced
drawing him up to the limb of a tree, when he stated that if

they would desist from this summary execution, he would disclose all he knew about the money. Being released, he produced $517 in gold. He was then notified that he must accompany the party to the settlements. To this he was disinclined, and he did not consent until the order was so peremptory that he was compelled to obey it. The body of George Donner was found dead in his tent. He had been carefully laid out by his wife, and a sheet was wrapped around the corpse. This sad office was probably the last act she performed before visiting the cabin of Keysburg. This is briefly a statement of particulars as detailed to me by Mr. Fallon, who accompanied Gen. Kearny on his return to the United States in the capacity of guide.

When the return party of Gen. KEARNY (which I accompanied) reached the scene of these horrible and tragical occurrences, on the 22d of June, 1847, a halt was ordered, for the purpose of collecting and interring the remains. Near the principal cabins, I saw two bodies, entire with the exception that the abdomens had been cut open and the entrails extracted. Their flesh had been either wasted by famine or evaporated by exposure to the dry atmosphere, and they presented the appearance of mummies. Strewn around the cabins were dislocated and broken bones—skulls, (in some instances sawed asunder with care for the purpose of extracting the brains,)—human skeletons, in short, in every variety of mutilation. A more revolting and appalling spectacle I never witnessed. The remains were, by an order of Gen. Kearny, collected and buried under the superintendence of Major Swords. They were interred in a pit which had been dug in the centre of one of the cabins for a *cache*. These melancholy duties to the dead being performed, the cabins, by order of Major Swords, were fired, and with every thing surrounding them connected with this horrid and melancholy tragedy, were consumed. The body of George Donner was found at his camp, about eight or ten miles distant, wrapped in a sheet. He was buried by a party of men detailed for that purpose.

I subjoin the following description of the sufferings of these unfortunate emigrants, and the horrid and revolting extremities to which some of them were reduced to sustain life, from the " California Star" of April 10th, 1847 :—

" A more shocking scene cannot be imagined, than that witnessed by the party of men who went to the relief of the unfortunate emigrants in the California mountains. The bones of those who had died and been devoured by the miserable ones that still survived, were lying around their tents and cabins. Bodies of men, women, and children, with half the flesh torn from them, lay on every side. A woman sat by the side of the body of her husband, who had just died, cutting out his tongue ; the heart she had already taken out, broiled, and ate! The daughter was seen eating the flesh of the father—the mother that of her children—children that of father and mother. The emaciated, wild, and ghastly appearance of the survivors added to the horror of the scene. Language cannot describe the awful change that a few weeks of dire suffering had wrought in the minds of these wretched and pitiable beings. Those who but one month before would have shuddered and sickened at the thought of eating human flesh, or of killing their companions and relatives to preserve their own lives, now looked upon the opportunity these acts afforded them of escaping the most dreadful of deaths, as a providential interference in their behalf. Calculations were coldly made, as they sat around their gloomy camp-fires, for the next and succeeding meals. Various expedients were devised to prevent the dreadful crime of murder, but they finally resolved to kill those who had the least claims to longer existence. Just at this moment, however, as if by Divine interposition, some of them died, which afforded the rest temporary relief. Some sunk into the arms of death cursing God for their miserable fate, while the last whisperings of others were prayers and songs of praise to the Almighty.

" After the first few deaths, but the one all-absorbing thought of individual self-preservation prevailed. The fountains of natural affection were dried up. The cords that once vibrated with connubial, parental, and filial affection, were rent asunder, and each one seemed resolved, without regard to the fate of others, to escape from the impending calamity.   Even the wild, hostile mountain Indians, who once visited their camps, pitied them, and instead of pursuing the natural impulse of their hostile feelings to the whites, and destroying them, as they could easily have done, divided their own scanty supply of food with them.

"So changed had the emigrants become, that when the party sent out arrived with food, some of them cast it aside, and seemed to prefer the putrid human flesh that still remained. The day before the party arrived, one of the emigrants took a child of about four years of age in bed with him, and devoured the whole before morning ; and the next day ate another about the same age before noon."

CHAPTER XXI.

California Indians—Captain Sutter—Difficulties in making his first settlement in California—Laboring Indians—Propensity for gambling—Captain Sutter's coin—Account of their games—Food of the Indians—Captain Sutter's wheat crops in 1846—Scarcity of flouring-mills—Waterpower—Hemp—Dine with Captain Sutter ; description of the dinner—Oppressive impost-duties of the Mexican government—Indian rancherias—Indian orgies—Sacramento river—Salmon—New Helvetia—Indian sweat-house—Reported Indian invasion by the Waila-Wallas—Description of the Walla-Wallas

Sept. 3.—We remained encamped near Sutter's Fort, or Fort Sacramento, as subsequently it has been named.   This morning we were visited by numerous Indians from the neighboring *rancherias,* who brought with them watermelons, muskmelons, and strings of pan-fish, taken from a small pond about half a mile distant, with a sort of hand-trap.   The Indians wade into the pond with their traps in hand, and take with them the fish, sometimes by dozens at a haul.   These they wished to trade for such small articles as we possessed, and the cast-off clothing of the members of our party.   Some of these Indians were partially clothed, others were entirely naked, and a portion of them spoke the Spanish language. They exhibited considerable sharpness in making a bargain, holding their wares at a high valuation, and although their desire to trade appeared to be strong, they would make no sacrifices to obtain the articles offered in exchange for them. But such was the desire of our men to obtain vegetables, of which they had been for so long a time deprived, that there was scarcely any article which they possessed, which they would refuse to barter for them.

The Indians generally are well made and of good stature, varying from five feet four inches to five feet ten and eleven inches in height, with strong muscular developments. Their hair is long, black, and coarse, and their skin is a shade lighter than that of a mulatto. They appear to be indolent and averse from labor of every kind, unless combined with their sports and amusements, when they are as reckless of fatigue and danger as any class of men I have seen.

By invitation of Captain Sutter, addressed to myself and Mr. Jacob, we visited and dined at the fort. The fort is situated near the confluence of the Rio de los Americanos and the Rio Sacramento. The valley of the Sacramento is here of great width, and consequently the fort is surrounded by an extensive plain, bounded by distant mountains on the east and on the west. This plain exhibits every evidence of a most fertile soil. The grasses, although they are now brown and crisp from the periodical drought, still stand with their ripened seeds upon them, showing their natural luxuriance. Groves or parks of the evergreen oak relieve the monotony of the landscape, and dot the level plain as far as the eye can reach.

Captain Sutter received us with manifestations of cordial hospitality. He is a gentleman between forty-five and fifty years of age, and in manners, dress, and general deportment, he approaches so near what we call the "old school gentleman," as to present a gulfy contrast from the rude society by which he is surrounded. Captain Sutter is a native of Switzerland, and was at one time an officer in the French army. He emigrated to the United States, and was naturalized. From thence, after a series of most extraordinary and romantic incidents, to relate which would furnish matter for a volume, he planted himself on the spot where his fort now stands, then a savage wilderness, and in the midst of numerous and hostile tribes of Indians. With the small party of men which he originally brought with him, he succeeded in defending himself against the Indians, until he constructed his first defensive building. He told me, that several times, being hemmed in by his assailants, he had subsisted for many days upon grass alone. There is a grass in this valley which the Indians eat, that is pleasant to the taste and nutritious. He succeeded by degrees in reducing the Indians to obedience, and by means of their labor erected the spacious fortification which now belongs to him.

The fort is a parallelogram, about five hundred feet in length and one hundred and fifty in breadth. The walls are constructed of adobes, or sun-dried bricks. The main building, or residence, stands near the centre of the area, or court, enclosed by the walls. A row of shops, store-rooms, and barracks, are enclosed within, and line the walls on every side. Bastions project from the angles, the ordnance mounted in which sweep the walls. The principal gates on the east and the south are also defended by heavy artillery, through portholes pierced in the walls. At this time the fort is manned by about fifty well-disciplined Indians, and ten or twelve white men, all under the pay of the United States. These Indians are well clothed and fed. The garrison is under the command of Mr. Kern, the artist of Captain Fremont's exploring expedition.

The number of laboring Indians employed by Captain Sutter during the seasons of sowing and harvest, is from two to three hundred. Some of these are clothed in shirts and blankets, but a large portion of them are entirely naked. They are paid so much per day for their labor, in such articles of merchandise as they may select from the store. Cotton cloth and handkerchiefs are what they most freely purchase. Common brown cotton cloth sells at one dollar per yard. A tin coin issued by Captain Sutter circulates among them, upon which is stamped the number of days that the holder has labored. These stamps indicate the value in merchandise to which the laborer or holder is entitled.

They are inveterate gamblers, and those who have been so fortunate as to obtain clothing, frequently stake and part with every rag upon their backs. The game which they most generally play is carried on as follows. Any number which may be concerned in it seat themselves cross-legged on the ground, in a circle. They are then divided into two parties, each of which has two champions or players. A ball, or some small article, is placed in the hands of the players on one side, which they transfer from hand to hand with such sleight and dexterity that it is nearly impossible to detect the changes. When the players holding the balls make a particular motion with their hands, the antagonist players guess in which hand the balls are at the time. If the guess is wrong it counts one in favor of the playing party. If the guess is right, then it counts one in favor of the guessing party, and the balls are transferred to them. The count of the game is kept with sticks. During the progress of the game, all concerned keep up a continual monotonous grunting, with a movement of their bodies to keep time with their grunts. The articles which are staked on the game are placed in the centre of the ring.

The laboring or field Indians about the fort are fed upon the offal of slaughtered animals, and upon the bran sifted from the ground wheat. This is boiled in large iron kettles. It is then placed in wooden troughs standing in the court, around which the several messes seat themselves and scoop out with their hands this poor fodder. Bad as it is, they eat it with an apparent high relish; and no doubt it is more palatable and more healthy than the acorn, mush, or *atóle*, which constitutes the principal food of these Indians in their wild state.

The wheat crop of Captain Sutter, the present year, (1846,) is about eight thousand bushels. The season has not been a favorable one. The average yield to the acre Captain S. estimates at twenty-five bushels. In favorable seasons this yield is doubled; and if we can believe the statements often made upon respectable authority, it is sometimes quadrupled. There is no doubt that in favorable seasons, that is when the rains fall abundantly during the winter, the yield of wheat, and all small grains in California, is much greater per acre of land than in any part of the United States. The wheat-fields of Captain S. are secured against the cattle and horses by ditches. Agriculture, among the native Californians, is in a very primitive state, and although Captain S. has introduced some American implements, still his ground is but imperfectly cultivated. With good cultivation the crops would be more certain and much more abundant. The crop from the same ground the second and third years, without sowing, is frequently very good.

Wheat is selling at the fort at two dollars and fifty cents per fanega, rather more than two bushels English measure. It brings the same price when delivered at San Francisco, near the mouth of the Bay of San Francisco. It is transported from the Sacramento valley to a market in launches of about fifty tons burden. Unbolted flour sells at eight dollars per one hundred pounds. The reason of this high price is the scarcity of flouring-mills in the country. The mills which are now going up in various places will reduce the price of flour, and probably they will soon be able to grind all the wheat raised in the country. The streams of California afford excellent water-power, but the flour consumed by Captain Sutter is ground by a very ordinary horse-mill.

I saw near the fort a small patch of hemp, which had been sown as an experiment, in the spring, and had not been irrigated. I never saw a ranker growth of hemp in Kentucky. Vegetables of several kinds appeared to be abundant and in perfection, but I shall speak more particularly of the agricultural productions of California in another place, when my knowledge of the country and its resources becomes, from observation, more general and perfect.

Captain Sutter's dining-room and his table furniture do not present a very luxurious appearance. The room is unfurnished, with the exception of a common deal table standing in the centre, and some benches, which are substitutes for chairs. The table, when spread, presented a correspondingly primitive simplicity of aspect and of viands. The first course consisted of good soup, served to each guest in a china bowl with silver spoons. The bowls, after they had been used for this purpose, were taken away and cleansed by the Indian servant, and were afterwards used as tumblers or goblets, from which we drank our water. The next course consisted of two dishes of meat, one roasted and one fried, and both highly seasoned with onions. Bread, cheese, butter, and melons, constituted the desert. I am thus particular because I wish to convey as accurately as I can the style and mode of living in California of intelligent gentlemen of foreign birth, who have been accustomed to all the luxuries of the most refined civilization.

It is not for the purpose of criticising, but to show how destitute the people of this naturally favored country have been of many of the most common comforts of domestic life, owing to the wretched system of government which has heretofore existed. Such has been the extortion of the government in the way of impost-duties, that few supplies which are included among even the most ordinary elegancies of life, have ever reached the inhabitants, and for these they have been compelled to pay prices that would be astonishing to a citizen of the United States or of Europe, and such as have impoverished the population. As a general fact, they cannot be obtained at any price, and hence those who have the ability to purchase are compelled to forego their use from necessity.

With our appetites, however, we enjoyed the dinner as much as if it had been served up in the most sumptuously-furnished dining-saloon, with all the table appurtenances of polished silver, sparkling crystal, and snow-like porcelain. By our long journey we had learned to estimate the value of a thing for its actual utility and the amount of enjoyment it confers. The day is not distant when American enterprise and American ingenuity will furnish those adjuncts of civilization of which California is now so destitute, and render a residence in this country one of the most luxurious upon the globe. The conversation at dinner turned upon the events which have recently occurred in the country, and which I shall narrate in another place.

From the 3d to the 7th of September we remained encamped. Our camp is near an Indian *rancheria*. These *rancherias* consist of a number of huts constructed of a rib-work or frame of small poles or saplings in a conical shape, covered with straw, grass, or *tule*, a species of rush, which grows to the height of five or six feet. The huts are sometimes fifteen feet in diameter at their bases, and the number of them grouped together vary according to the number of the tribe which inhabits them. A different language in many respects is spoken at the different *rancherias*. In this remark I refer to the gentile Indians, as they are here called, and not to the christianized, the last of whom speak the Spanish. There was a large gathering at the *rancheria* on the night of the 6th to celebrate some event. Dancing, singing, loud shouting, and howling, were continued without intermission the whole night. One of their orgies consisted in fixing a scalp upon a pole and dancing around it, accompanying the dance with, at first, a low melancholy howl, then with loud shrieks and groans, until the performers appeared to become frantic with excitement of some kind, it would be difficult to tell what. The noise made by them was such as to prevent sleep, although a quarter of a mile distant from our camp.

The Sacramento river, at this point, is a stream nearly half a mile in width. The tide rises and falls some two or three feet. The water is perfectly limpid and fresh. The river is said to be navigable for craft of one hundred tons burden, at all seasons, a hundred miles above this place. In the season of high waters, from January to July, it is navigable a much greater distance. The Sacramento rises above latitude 42° north, and runs from north to south nearly parallel with the coast of the Pacific, until it empties into the Bay of San Francisco by several mouths in latitude 38½° north. It is fringed with timber, chiefly oak and sycamore. Grape-vines and a variety of shrubbery ornament its banks, and give a most charming effect when sailing upon its placid and limpid current. I never saw a more beautiful stream. In the rainy season, and in the spring, when the snows on the mountains are melting, it overflows its banks in many places. It abounds in fish, the most valuable of which is the salmon. These salmon are the largest and the fattest I have ever seen. I have seen salmon taken from the Sacramento five feet in length. All of its tributaries are equally rich in the finny tribe. American enterprise will soon develop the wealth contained in these streams, which hitherto has been entirely neglected.

The site of the town of Nueva Helvetia, which has been laid out by Captain Sutter, is about a mile and a half from the Sacramento. It is on an elevation of the plain, and not subject to overflow when the waters of the river are at their highest known point. There are now but three or four small houses in this town, but I have little doubt that it will soon become a place of importance.

Near the *embarcadero* of New Helvetia is a large Indian "sweat-house," or *Temascál*, an appendage of most of the *rancherias*. The "sweat-house" is the most important medical agent employed by these Indians. It has, I do not doubt, the effect of consigning many of them to their graves, long before their appointed time. A "sweat-house" is an excavation in the earth, to the depth of six or eight feet, arched over with slabs split from logs. There is a single small aperture or skylight in the roof. These slabs are covered to the depth of several feet with earth. There is a narrow entrance, with steps leading down and into this subterraneous apartment. Rude shelves are erected around the walls, upon which the invalids repose their bodies. The door is closed and no air is admitted except from the small aperture in the roof, through which escapes the smoke of a fire kindled in the centre of the dungeon. This fire heats the apartment until the perspiration rolls from the naked bodies of the invalids in streams. I incautiously entered one of these caverns during the operation above described, and was in a few moments so nearly suffocated with the heat, smoke, and impure air, that I found it difficult to make my way out.

In the afternoon of the 7th, we received a note from Captain Sutter, stating that he had succeeded in obtaining a room in the fort for our accommodation, and inviting us to accept of it. He sent two servants to assist in packing our baggage; and accepting the invitation, we took up our lodgings in the fort. By this change we were relieved from the annoyance of mosquitoes, which have troubled us much during the night at our encampment. But with this exception, so long have we been accustomed to sleeping in the open air, with no shelter but our blankets and the canopy of the heavens, that our encampment was preferable to our quarters within the confined walls of the fort.

It is scarcely possible to imagine a more delightful temperature, or a climate which is more agreeable and uniform. The sky is cloudless, without the slightest film of vapor apparent in all the vast azure vault. In the middle of the day the sun shines with great power, but in the shade it is nowhere uncomfortable. At night, so pure is the atmosphere, that the moon gives a light sufficiently powerful for the purposes of the reader or student who has good eyesight. There is no necessity of burning the "midnight oil." Nature here, lights the candle for the bookworm.

On the 9th, we commenced preparations for leaving the fort, for San Francisco, a journey by land of about two hundred miles. Our intention was to leave early the next morning. While thus engaged, some couriers arrived from the settlements on the Sacramento, about one hundred miles north, with the startling information that one thousand Walla-Walla Indians, from Oregon, had made their appearance in the valley, for hostile purposes. The couriers, who were themselves settlers, appeared to be in great alarm, and stated that they had seen the advance party of the Walla-Wallas, and that their object was to assault the fort for a murder which they alleged had been committed one or two years since, by an American upon a chief of their tribe, and for some indebtedness of Captain Sutter to them, in cattle, &c. In the event of a failure in their assault upon the fort, then they intended to drive off all the cattle belonging to the settlers in the valley. This was the substance of their information. It was so alarming, that we postponed at once our departure for San Francisco, and volunteered such assistance as we could render in defending the fort against this formidable invasion.

The Walla-Wallas are a powerful and warlike tribe of Indians, inhabiting a district of country on the Columbia river. They are reported to be good marksmen and fight with great bravery and desperation. Their warriors are armed with good rifles and an abundance of ammunition, which they procure from the Hudson's Bay Company. They are rapidly advancing in civilization, and many of them have good farms under cultivation, with numerous herds of cattle and horses.

Couriers were immediately dispatched in every direction to apprize the settlers in the valley of the invasion, and to the nearest military posts, for such assistance as they could rende under the circumstances. The twelve pieces of artillery by which the fort is defended were put in order, and all inside were busily employed in preparing for the expected combat. Indian spies were also dispatched to reconnoitre and discover the position and actual number of the invaders.

The spies returned to the fort on the 11th without having seen the Walla-Walla invaders. A small party of some forty or fifty only, are supposed to be about twenty-five or thirty miles distant, on the opposite side of the Sacramento. On the twelfth, Lieut. Revere of the Navy, with a party of twenty-five men, arrived at the fort from Sonoma, to reinforce the garrison ; and on the morning of the thirteenth, it having been pretty well ascertained that the reported 1000 hostile Walla-Wallas were a small party only of men, women, and children, whose disposition was entirely pacific, we determined to proceed immediately on our journey to San Francisco.

CHAPTER XXII.

Geographical sketch of California—Its political and social institutions—Colorado river—Valley and river of San Joaquin—Former government—Presidios—Missions—Ports and commerce.

BEFORE proceeding farther in my travels througn Upper California, for the general information of the reader, it will be proper to give a brief geographical sketch of the country, and some account of its political and social institutions, as they have heretofore existed.

The district of country known, geographically, as Upper California, is bounded on the north by Oregon, the forty-second degree of north latitude being the boundary line between the two territories; on the east by the Rocky Mountains and the Sierra de los Mimbres, a continuation of the same range; on the south by Sonora and Old or Lower California, and on the west by the Pacific Ocean. Its extent from north to south is about 700 miles, and from east to west from 600 to 800 miles, with an area of about 400,000 square miles. A small portion only of this extensive territory is fertile or inhabitable by civilized man, and this portion consists chiefly in the strip of country along the Pacific Ocean, about 700 miles in length, and from 100 to 150 in breadth, bounded on the east by the Sierra Nevada and on the west by the Pacific. In speaking of Upper California, this strip of country is what is generally referred to.

The largest river of Upper California is the Colorado or Red, which has a course of about 1000 miles, and empties into the Gulf of California in latitude about 32° north. But little is known of the region through which this stream flows. The report of trappers, however, is that the river is *cañoned* between high mountains and precipices a large portion of its course, and that its banks and the country generally through which it flows are arid, sandy, and barren. Green and Grand rivers are its principal upper tributaries, both of which rise in the Rocky Mountains and within the territories of the United States. The Gila is its lowest and largest branch, emptying into the Colorado, just above its mouth. Sevier and Virgin rivers are also tributaries of the Colorado. Mary's river, which I have previously described, rises near latitude 42° north, and has a course of about 400 miles, when its waters sink in the sands of the desert. This river is not laid down on any map which I have seen. The Sacramento and San Joaquin rivers, have each a course of from 300 to 400 miles, the first flowing from the north and the last from the south, and both emptying into the Bay of San Francisco at the same point. They water the large and fertile valley lying between the Sierra Nevada and the coast range of mountains. I subjoin a description of the valley and river San Joaquin, from the pen of a gentleman (Dr. Marsh) who has explored the river from its source to its mouth.

"This noble valley is the first undoubtedly in California, and one of the most magnificent in the world. It is about 500 miles long, with an average width of about fifty miles. It is bounded on the east by the great Snowy Mountains, and on the west by the low range, which in many places dwindles into insignificant hills, and has its northern terminus at the strait of Carquines, on the Bay of San Francisco, and its southern near the Colorado river.

"The river of San Joaquin flows through the middle of the valley for about half of its extent, and thence diverges towards the eastern mountain, in which it has its source. About sixty miles further south is the northern end of the Buena Vista lake, which is about one hundred miles long, and from ten to twenty wide. Still farther south, and near the western side of the valley, is another and much smaller lake.

"The great lake receives about a dozen tributaries on its eastern side, which all rise in the great range of the Snowy Mountains. Some of these streams flow through broad and fertile valleys within the mountain's range, and from thence emerging, irrigate the plains of the great valley for the distance of twenty or thirty miles. The largest of these rivers is called by the Spanish inhabitants the River Reyes, and falls into the lake near its northern end ; it is a well-timbered stream, and flows through a country of great fertility and beauty. The tributaries of the San Joaquin are all on the east side.

" On ascending the stream we first meet with the Stanislaus, a clear, rapid mountain stream, some forty or fifty yards wide, with a considerable depth of water in its lower portion. The Mormons have commenced a settlement, called New Hope, and built some two or three houses near the mouth.

" There are considerable bodies of fertile land along the river, and the higher plains afford good pasturage.

" Ten miles higher up is the river of the Tawalomes ; it is about the size of the Stanislaus, which it greatly resembles, except that the soil is somewhat better, and that it particularly abounds with salmon.

" Some thirty miles farther comes in the Merced, much the largest of the tributaries of the San Joaquin. The lands along and between the tributaries of the San Joaquin and the lake of Buena Vista form a fine pastoral region, with a good proportion of arable land, and a very inviting field for emigration. The whole of this region has been but imperfectly explored ; enough, however, is known, to make it certain that it is one of the most desirable regions on the continent.

" In the valleys of the rivers which come down from the great Snowy Mountains, are vast bodies of pine, and red-wood, or cedar timber, and the streams afford water-power to any desirable amount.

" The whole country east of the San Joaquin and the water communication which connects it with the lakes, is considered, by the best judges, to be particularly adapted to the culture of the vine, which must necessarily become one of the principal agricultural resources of California."

The Salinas river empties into the Pacific, about twelve miles above Monterey. Bear river empties into the Great Salt Lake. The other streams of California are all small.

The Great Salt Lake and the Utah Lake I have already described.   There are numerous small lakes in the Sierra Nevada. The San Joaquin is connected with Tule lake, or lake Buena Vista, a sheet of water about eighty miles in length and fifteen in breadth.   A lake, not laid down in any map, and known as the *Laguna* among the Californians, is situated about sixty miles north of the Bay of San Francisco.   It is between forty and sixty miles in length.   The valleys in its vicinity are highly fertile, and romantically beautiful.   In the vicinity of this lake there is a mountain of pure sulphur.   There are also soda springs, and a great variety of other mineral waters, and minerals.

The principal mountains west of the eastern boundary of California, (the Rocky Mountains,) are the Bear River, Wahsatch, Utah, the Sierra Nevada, and the Coast range.   The Wahsatch mountains form the eastern rim of the "great interior basin."   There are numerous ranges in this desert basin, all of which run north and south, and are separated from each other by spacious and barren valleys and plains.   The Sierra Nevada range is of greater elevation than the Rocky Mountains.   The summits of the most elevated peaks are covered with perpetual snow.   This and the Coast range run nearly parallel with the shore of the Pacific.   The first is from 100 to 200 miles from the Pacific, and the last from forty to sixty miles.   The valley between them is the most fertile portion of California.

Upper California was discovered in 1548, by Cabrillo, a Spanish navigator.   In 1578, the northern portion of it was visited by Sir Francis Drake, who called it New Albion.   It was first colonized by the Spaniards, in 1768, and formed a province of Mexico until after the revolution in that country. There have been numerous revolutions and civil wars in California within the last twenty years, but up to the conquest of the country by the United States in 1846, Mexican authority has generally been exercised over it.

The following description of the political and social condition of Upper California in 1822, is extracted and translated from a Spanish writer of that date.   I have thought that the extract would not be uninteresting :—

"*Government.*—Upper California, on account of its small

population, not being able to become a state of the great Mexican republic, takes the character of territory, the government of which is under the charge of a commandant-general, who exercises the charge of a superior political chief, whose attributes depend entirely upon the president of the republic and the general congress. But to amplify the legislation of its centre, it has a deputation made up of seven vocals, the half of these individuals being removed every two years. The superior political chief presides at their sessions. The inhabitants of the territory are divided amongst the presidios, missions, and towns.

"*Presidios.*—The necessity of protecting the apostolic predication was the obligatory reason for forming the presidios, which were established according to circumstances. That of San Diego was the first; Santa Barbara, Monterey, and San Francisco, were built afterwards. The form of all of them is nearly the same, and this is a square, containing about two hundred yards in each front, formed of a weak wall made of mud-bricks. Its height may be four yards in the interior of the square, and built on to the same wall. In its entire circumference are a chapel, storehouses, and houses for the commandant; officers and troops having at the entrance of the presidio quarters for a *corps de garde.*

"These buildings in the presidios, at the first idea, appear to have been sufficient; the only object having been for a defence against a surprise from the gentiles, or wild Indians in the immediate vicinity. But this cause having ceased, I believe they ought to be demolished, as they are daily threatening a complete ruin, and from the very limited spaces of habitation, must be very incommodious to those who inhabit them. As to the exterior of the presidios, several private individuals have built some very decent houses, and having evinced great emulation in this branch of business, I have no doubt but in a short time we shall see very considerable towns in California.

"At the distance of one, or at the most two miles from the presidio, and near to the anchoring-ground, is a fort, which has a few pieces of artillery of small calibre. The situation of most of them is very advantageous for the defence of the port, though the form of the walls, esplanades, and other imperfections, which may be seen, make them very insignificant.

"The battalion of each presidio is made up of eighty or more horse-soldiers, called *cuera*; besides these, it has a number of auxiliary troops and a detachment of artillery. The commandant of each presidio is the captain of its respective company, and besides the intervention, military and political, he has charge of all things relating to the marine department.

"*Missions.*—The missions contained in the territory are twenty-one. They were built at different epochs: that of San Diego, being the first, was built in 1769; its distance from the presidio of the same name is two leagues. The rest were built successively, according to circumstances and necessity. The last one was founded in the year 1822, under the name of San Francisco Dolores, and is the most northern of all.

"The edifices in some of those missions are more extensive than in others, but in form they are all nearly equal. They are all fabricated of mud-bricks, and the divisions are according to necessity. In all of them may be found commodious habitations for the ministers, storehouses to keep their goods in, proportional granaries, offices for soap-makers, weavers, blacksmiths, and large parterres, and horse and cattle pens, independent apartments for Indian youths of each sex, and all such offices as were necessary at the time of its institution. Contiguous to and communicating with the former, is a church, forming a part of the edifices of each mission; they are all very proportionable, and are adorned with profusion.

"The Indians reside about two hundred yards distant from the above-mentioned edifice. This place is called the rancheria. Most of the missions are made up of very reduced quarters, built with mud-bricks, forming streets, while in others the Indians have been allowed to follow their primitive customs; their dwellings being a sort of huts, in a conical shape, which at the most do not exceed four yards in diameter, and the top of the cone may be elevated three yards. They are built of rough sticks, covered with bulrushes or grass, in such a manner as to completely protect the inhabitants from all the inclemencies of the weather. In my opinion, these rancherias are the most adequate to the natural uncleanliness of the Indians, as the families often renew them, burning the old ones, and immediately building others with the greatest facility. Opposite the rancherias and near to the mission, is to be found a small garrison, with proportionate rooms, for a corporal and five soldiers with their families. This small garrison is quite sufficient to prevent any attempt of the Indians from taking effect, there having been some examples made, which causes the Indians to respect this small force. One of these pickets in a mission has a double object; besides keeping the Indians in subjection, they run post with a monthly correspondence, or with any extraordinaries that may be necessary for government.

" All the missions in this California are under the charge of religious men of the order of San Francisco. At the present time their number is twenty-seven, most of them of an advanced age. Each mission has one of these fathers for its administrator, and he holds absolute authority. The tilling of the ground, the gathering of the harvest, the slaughtering of cattle, the weaving, and every thing that concerns the mission, is under the direction of the fathers, without any other person interfering in any way whatever, so that if any one mission has the good fortune to be superintended by an industrious and discreet padre, the Indians disfrute in abundance all the real necessaries of life ; at the same time the nakedness and misery of any one mission, are a palpable proof of the inactivity of its director. The missions extend their possession from one extremity of the territory to the other, and have made the limits of one mission from those of another. Though they do not require all this land for their agriculture and the maintenance of their stock, they have appropriated the whole; always strongly opposing any individual who may wish to settle himself or his family on any piece of land between them. But it is to be hoped that the new system of illustration, and the necessity of augmenting private property, and the people of reason, will cause the government to take such adequate measures as will conciliate the interests of all. Amongst all the missions there are from twenty-one to twenty-two thousand Catholic Indians; but each mission has not an equal or a proportionate part in its congregation. Some have three or four thousand, whilst others have scarcely four hundred; and at this difference may be computed the riches of the missions in proportion. Besides the number of Indians already spoken of, each mission has a considerable number of gentiles, who live chiefly on farms annexed to the missions. The number of these is undetermined.

"The Indians are naturally filthy and careless, and their understanding is very limited. In the small arts they are not deficient in ideas of imitation, but they never will be inventors. Their true character is that of being revengeful and timid, consequently they are very much addicted to treachery. They have no knowledge of benefits received, and ingratitude is common amongst them. The education they receive in their infancy is not the proper one to develop their reason, and if it were, I do not believe them capable of any good impression. All these Indians, whether from the continual use of the sweat-house, or from their filthiness, or the little ventilation in their habitations, are weak and unvigorous; spasms and rheumatics, to which they are so much subject, are the consequences of their customs. But what most injures them, and prevents propagation, is the venereal disease, which most of them have very strongly; clearly proving that their humors are analogous to receiving the impressions of this contagion. From this reason may be deduced the enormous differences between the births and deaths, which, without doubt, is one-tenth per year in favor of the latter; but the missionaries do all in their power to prevent this, with respect to the catechumens situated near them.

"The general production of the missions are, the breed of the larger class of cattle, and sheep, horses, wheat, maize or Indian corn, beans, peas, and other vegetables; though the productions of the missions situated more to the southward are more extensive, these producing the grape and olive in abundance. Of all these articles of production, the most lucrative is the large cattle; their hides and tallow affording an active commerce with foreign vessels on this coast. This being the only means the inhabitants, missionaries, or private individuals have of supplying their actual necessities, for this reason they give this branch all the impulse they possibly can, and on it generally place all their attention.

"It is now six years since they began to gather in hides and tallow for commerce. Formerly they merely took care of as many or as much as they required for their own private use, and the rest was thrown away as useless; but at this time, the actual number of hides sold annually on board of foreign vessels amount to thirty or forty thousand, and about the same amount of arrobas (twenty-five pounds) of tallow; and in pursuing their present method, there is no doubt but in three or four years the amount of the exportation of each of these articles will be doubled. Flax, linen, wine, olive oil, grain, and other agricultural productions, would be very extensive if there were stimulants to excite industry; but this not being the case, there is just grain enough sown and reaped for the consumption of the inhabitants in the territory.

"The towns contained in this district are three; the most populous being that of Angeles, which has about twelve hundred souls, that of St. Joseph's of Guadaloupe may contain six hundred, and the village of Branciforte two hundred: they are all formed imperfectly and without order, each person having built his own house on the spot he thought most convenient for himself. The first of these pueblos is governed by its corresponding body of magistrates, composed of an alcalde or judge, four regidores or municipal officers, a syndic and secretary; the second, of an alcalde, two regidores, a syndic and secretary; and the third, on account of the smallness of its population, is subject to the commandancia of Monterey.

"The inhabitants of the towns are white, and to distinguish them from the Indians are vulgarly called *people of reason*. The number of these contained in the territory may be nearly five thousand. These families are divided amongst the pueblos and presidios. They are nearly all the descendants of a small number of individuals who came from the Mexican country, some as settlers, others in the service of the army, and accompanied by their wives. In the limited space of little more than fifty years the present generation has been formed.

"The whites are in general robust, healthy, and well made. Some of them are occupied in breeding and raising cattle, and cultivating small quantities of wheat and beans; but for want of sufficient land, for which they cannot obtain a rightful ownership, their labors are very limited. Others dedicate themselves to the service of arms. All the presidial companies are composed of the natives of the country, but the most of them are entirely indolent, it being very rare for any individual to strive to augment his fortune. Dancing, horse-riding, and gambling, occupy all their time. The arts are entirely unknown, and I am doubtful if there is one individual who exercises any trade; very few who understand the first rudiments of letters, and the other sciences are unknown amongst them.

" The fecundity of the *people of reason* is extreme. It is very rare to find a married couple with less than five or six children, while there are hundreds who have from twelve to fifteen. Very few of them die in their youth, and in reaching the age of puberty are sure to see their grand-children. The age of eighty and one hundred has always been common in this climate; most infirmities are unknown here, and the freshness and robustness of the people show the beneficial influence of the climate; the women in particular, have always the roses stamped on their cheeks. This beautiful species is without doubt the most active and laborious, all their vigilance in duties of the house, the cleanliness of their children, and attention to their husbands, dedicating all their leisure moments to some kind of occupation that may be useful towards their maintenance. Their clothing is always clean and decent, nakedness being entirely unknown in either sex.

" *Ports and Commerce.*—There are four ports, principal bays, in this territory, which take the names of the corresponding presidios. The best guarded is that of San Diego. That of San Francisco has many advantages. Santa Barbara is but middling in the best part of the season; at other times always bad. Besides the above-mentioned places, vessels sometimes anchor at Santa Cruz, San Luis Obispo, El Refugio, San Pedro, and San Juan, that they may obtain the productions of the missions nearest these last-mentioned places ; but from an order sent by the minister of war, and circulated by the commandante-general, we are given to understand that no foreign vessel is permitted to anchor at any of these places, Monterey only excepted, notwithstanding the commandante-general has allowed the first three principal ports to remain open provisionally. Were it not so, there would undoubtedly be an end to all commerce with California, as I will quickly show.

"The only motive that induces foreign vessels to visit this coast, is for the hides and tallow which they barter for in the territory. It is well known, that at any of these parts there is no possibility of realizing any money, for here it does not circulate. The goods imported by foreign vessels are intended to facilitate the purchase of the aforesaid articles, well knowing that the missions have no interest in money, but rather such goods as are necessary for the Indians, so that several persons who have brought goods to sell for nothing but money, have not been able to sell them. It will appear very extraordinary that money should not be appreciated in a country where its value is so well known ; but the reason may be easily perceived by attending to the circumstances of the territory.

"The quantity of hides gathered yearly is about thirty or forty thousand ; and the arrobas of tallow, with very little difference, will be about the same. Averaging the price of each article at two dollars, we shall see that the intrinsic value in annual circulation in California, is $140,000. This sum divided between 21 missions, will give each one $6,666. Supposing the only production of the country converted into money, with what would the Indians be clothed, and by what means would they be able to cover a thousand other necessaries ? Money is useful in amplifying speculations; but in California, as yet, there are no speculations, and its productions are barely sufficient for the absolute necessary consumption. The same comparison may be made with respect to private individuals, who are able to gather a few hides and a few arrobas of tallow, these being in small quantities."

CHAPTER XXIII.

Sketch of the Bear revolution, and first conquest of California by the American troops—Capture of Lieut. De Arcé—Capture of Sonoma, by Capt. Merritt and party, on the 14th of July—Proclamation of William B. Ide—Barbarous and brutal murder of Cowie and Fowler—Four-fingered Jack—Capt. Ford's engagement with the Californians ; defeat of the latter—Flight of De la Torre—Proclamations of Castro—Capt. Fremont joins the revolutionists at Sonoma, on the 25th of July—Commodore Sloat's arrival in California—Raising of the U. S. flag at Monterey, San Francisco, Sonoma, and other places—Proclamation of Com. Sloat —Capt. Fremont occupies San Juan—Castro retreats to the south—Los Angeles captured by Com. Stockton—Com. Stockton's proclamation.

I DEEM it proper to record here the events which occurred in California immediately preceding my arrival, and which finally resulted in the conquest of the country by the United States naval and military forces. For some of the facts stated, in reference to the revolutionary movement, I am indebted to ROBERT SEMPLE, Esq., who has been a resident of California for a number of years, and was himself an eye-witness to, and a participator in, many of the transactions described.

The population of California, in the spring of 1846, was estimated at about 10,000, exclusive of Indians. Two thousand of these were supposed to be foreigners, chiefly from the United States. The latter class had been rapidly increasing for several years ; and it became apparent to the more intelligent of the Californians, that this population, if suffered to increase in the same ratio, would, in a few years, change the government and institutions of the country. A natural jealousy prompted a course of measures on the part of the government, founded upon apprehensions such as has been stated, which resulted in precipitating the event they were intended to guard against.

In 1845 a revolutionary movement, headed by Don José Castro, Alvarado, Pio Pico, and others, in which the foreigners participated, resulted in deposing Gen. Micheltorena, governor of California under the appointment of the government of Mexico. After the deposition of Micheltorena, the gubernatorial office was assumed by Pico. Gen. Castro, at the same time, assumed the command of the military. Gen. Castro, soon after he came into power, adopted a policy towards the foreigners highly offensive. Among his acts was the promulgation of a proclamation, requiring all Americans to leave the country. This was its *interpretation* by the latter. No immediate steps were taken to enforce this order, and but little attention was paid to it by those to whom it was addressed. Their intention from the first, however, was, doubtless, to resist any force that should attempt their expulsion from the country.

About the 1st of June, 1846, an order was issued by Gen. Castro to Lieut. Francisco de Arcé, commandant of the garrison at Sonoma, to remove a number of horses, the property of the government, from the Mission of San Rafael, to his headquarters, then at Santa Clara. This officer was accompanied by a guard of fourteen men. In the execution of the order, he was compelled to cross the Sacramento river at New Helvetia, the nearest point at which the horses could swim the stream. While travelling in that direction, he was seen by an Indian, who reported to the American settlers on the Sacramento, that he had seen two or three hundred armed men advancing up the Sacramento valley. At this time Captain Fremont, with his exploring party, was encamped at "the *Buttes*," near the confluence of the Rio de las Plumas and the Sacramento, and about sixty or seventy miles above Sutter's Fort. This officer had previously had some difficulties with Gen. Castro, and the inference from the information given by the Indian was, that Castro, at the head of a considerable force, was marching to attack Captain Fremont. The alarm was spread throughout the valley with as much celerity as the swiftest horses could convey it, and most of the settlers joined Captain Fremont at his camp, to assist in his defence against the supposed meditated attack of Castro. They were met here, however, by a person (Mr. Knight) who stated that he had seen the party of Californians in charge of the horses, and conversed with the officer commanding it.   Mr. Knight stated that the officer told him, that Gen. Castro had sent for the horses for the purpose of mounting a battalion of 200 men, with which he designed to march against the Americans settled in the Sacramento valley, and to expel them from the country.   This being accomplished, he intended to fortify the Bear River Pass in the California mountains, and prevent the ingress of the emigrants from the United States to California.   The recent proclamations of Castro gave strong probability to this report, and the American settlers determined at once to take measures for their own protection.

After some consultation, it was resolved that a force of sufficient strength for the purpose should pursue the Californians, and capture the horses.   This measure would weaken Castro, and for the present frustrate his supposed designs.   Twelve men immediately volunteered for the expedition, and Mr. Merritt, being the eldest of the party, was chosen captain.   At daylight on the morning of the 10th of June, they surprised the party of Californians under the command of Lieut. De Arcé, who, without resistance, gave up their arms and the government horses.   An individual travelling with this party claimed six horses as belonging to himself, which he was allowed to take and depart with, the leader of the Americans declaring that they would not seize upon or disturb private property.

The Californians, after they had delivered their arms and horses, were dismissed with a horse for each to ride, and a message to Gen. Castro, that if he wished his horses again *he must come and get them.*   The revolutionary movement on the part of the American foreigners was now fairly commenced, and it became necessary, in self-defence, for them to prosecute what they had begun, with vigor.   The party being increased to thirty-three men, still under the command of Mr. Merritt, marched directly to Sonoma, and on the morning of the 14th of June captured and took possession of that town and military post.   They made prisoners here of Gen. Gaudaloupe, M. Valléjo, Lieut.-Col. Prudon, and Capt. Don Salvador Valléjo.

The writer from whom the foregoing facts are chiefly compiled, who was a member of the party, proceeds to say : that " Sonoma was taken without a struggle, in which place were nine pieces of artillery, about two hundred stand of small-arms, (public property.) There was also a large amount of private property and considerable money. A single man cried out, ' Let us divide the spoils,' but a unanimous indignant frown made him shrink from the presence of honest men ; and from that time forward no man dared to hint any thing like violating the sanctity of a private house or private property. So far did they carry this principle, that they were unwilling to take the beef which was offered by the prisoners. General Valléjo sent for his *caballada* and offered them fresh horses, which were accepted, but with the determination of remunerating him as soon as the new government should be established. The party was composed mostly of hunters, and such men as could leave home at the shortest notice. They had not time to dress, even if they had had fine clothes, so that most of them were dressed in leather hunting-shirts. Taking the whole party together, they were about as rough-looking a set of men as could be imagined. It is not to be wondered at that one should feel some dread of falling into their hands, but the prisoners, instead of being dragged away with rough hands and harsh treatment, met with nothing but the kindest of treatment and the most polite attentions from the whole party ; and in fact, before five hours' ride from their homes they seemed to feel all confidence, and conversed freely on the subject of the establishment of a better government, giving their opinions and their plans without any apparent restraint.

" The writer cannot leave this part of the subject without telling an anecdote, which will illustrate the character of one of the actors in this scene. A year or two previous, one of the prisoners, (Salvador Valléjo,) in an official capacity, had fallen in with Mr. Merritt, the leader of the revolutionary party, and under the pretence that Mr. Merritt had harbored a runaway man-of-war's man, beat him severely with his sword. With all the keen resentment of a brave man, Mr. Merritt suddenly found this same man in his power. The blood rushed to his cheeks, and

25

his eyes sparkled; he leaned forward like a mad tiger in the act of springing upon his prey, and in an energetic but manly tone, said : ' When I was your prisoner, you struck me; now you are my prisoner, I will NOT STRIKE YOU.' The motives which had prompted him to act in the present contest, were too high, too holy to permit him for a moment to suffer his private feelings to bias him in his public duties. However able may be the pen which shall record these events, none but those who have witnessed the moderation and discreet deportment of the little garrison left at Sonoma, can do them justice; for there has been no time in the history of the world, where men without law, without officers, without' the scratch of a pen, as to the object had in view, have acted with that degree of moderation and strict observance of the rights of persons and property as was witnessed on this occasion. Their children, in generations yet to come, will look back with pleasure upon the commencement of a revolution carried on by their fathers, upon principles high and holy as the laws of eternal justice."

A small garrison was left at Sonoma, consisting of about eighteen men, under command of William B. Ide, which in the course of a few days was increased to about forty. On the 18th of June, Mr. Ide, by the consent of the garrison, published a proclamation, setting forth the objects for which the party had gathered, and the principles which would be adhered to in the event of their success.

———

" *A Proclamation to all persons and citizens of the district of Sonoma, requesting them to remain at peace, and follow their rightful occupations without fear of molestation.*

" The Commander-in-chief of the troops assembled at the fortress of Sonoma, gives his inviolable pledge to all persons in California, not found under arms, that they shall not be disturbed in their persons, their property, or social relations, one with another, by men under his command.

" He also solemnly declares his object to be, first, to defend himself and companions in arms, who were invited to this country by a promise of lands on which to settle themselves and families ; who were also promised a Republican Government, when having arrived in California they were denied the privilege of buying or renting lands of their friends ; who, instead of being allowed to participate in or being protected by a Republican Government, were oppressed by a military despotism ; who were even threatened by proclamation, by the chief officers of the aforesaid despotism, with extermination if they should not depart out of the country, leaving all their property, arms, and beasts of burden ; and thus deprived of their means of flight or defence, we were to be driven through deserts inhabited by hostile Indians, to certain destruction.

" To overthrow a government which has seized upon the property of the missions for its individual aggrandizement ; which has ruined and shamefully oppressed the laboring people of California, by their enormous exactions on goods imported into the country, is the determined purpose of the brave men who are associated under my command.

" I also solemnly declare my object, in the second place, to be to invite all peaceable and good citizens of California, who are friendly to the maintenance of good order and equal rights, and I do hereby invite them to repair to my camp at Sonoma, without delay, to assist us in establishing and perpetuating a Republican Government, which shall secure to all civil and religious liberty ; which shall encourage virtue and literature ; which shall leave unshackled by fetters, agriculture, commerce, and manufactures.

" I further declare that I rely upon the rectitude of our intentions, the favor of Heaven, and the bravery of those who are bound and associated with me, by the principles of self-preservation, by the love of truth, and the hatred of tyranny, for my hopes of success.

" I furthermore declare, that I believe that a government to be prosperous and happy, must originate with the people who are friendly to its existence ; that the citizens are its guardians, the officers its servants, its glory its reward.

(Signed,)   WILLIAM B. IDE.

" Headquarters, Sonoma, June 18th, 1846."

" About the time the foregoing proclamation was issued, two young men, Mr. T. Cowie and Mr. Fowler, who lived in the neighborhood of Sonoma, started to go to the Bodega. On their way they were discovered by a small party of Californians, under the command of one Padilla, and taken prisoners. They were kept as prisoners for a day and a half, and then tied to trees and cut to pieces in the most brutal manner. A Californian, known as Four-fingered Jack, was subsequently captured, and gave the following account of that horrid scene :—The party, after keeping the prisoners a day or two, tied them to trees, and stoned them. One of them had his jaw broken. A *riata* (rope) was then made fast to the broken bone, and the jaw dragged out. They were then cut up by piecemeal, and the pieces thrown at them, or crammed into their throats. They were finally dispatched by cutting out their bowels!

"Fortunately for humanity, these cold-blooded, savage murders were soon put to an end, by the very active measures taken by the garrison at Sonoma. Having heard nothing of the arrival of Cowie and Fowler at their place of destination, it was suspected that they had been taken and probably killed; and hearing that three others were prisoners in Padilla's camp, Captain Ford (then 1st lieutenant at Sonoma) headed a party of twenty-two men, officers included, and took the road for the enemy's camp, which had been reinforced by Captain Joaquin de la Torre, with seventy men. It was reported that their headquarters were at Santa Rosa Plains, to which point Ford proceeded. Finding that they had left, he followed them in the direction of San Rafael; and after travelling all night, making about sixty miles in sixteen hours, came up with the enemy twelve miles from San Rafael, where they had stopped to breakfast.

"The enemy occupied a position at a house on the edge of the plains, about sixty yards from a small grove of brushwood. Captain Ford, having several prisoners, left four men to guard them, and with the remainder advanced upon the enemy. Reaching the brushwood, he directed his party to tie their horses, and take such positions as would cut off the Californians, but by no means to fire until they could kill their man; which order was so well obeyed, that out of twenty or twenty-five shots fired by the Americans, eleven took effect. Eight of the enemy were killed, two wounded, and one horse shot through the neck. One party of the Californians, led by a sergeant, charged up handsomely; but the deadly fire of Ford's riflemen forced them to retire, with the loss of the sergeant and several of his men. The fall of the sergeant seemed to be the signal for retreat. The whole party retired to a high hill, about a mile from the field of battle. Ford and his gallant followers waited a short time, and finding that the enemy showed no disposition to return to the fight, released the prisoners who had been taken by them, and then went to a corral, where they found a large *caballada* of horses, and exchanged their tired horses for fresh ones. They then returned to Sonoma. The Californians, on this occasion, did not sustain the reputation they had previously gained. They were eighty-six strong, while Captain Ford had but eighteen men engaged."

Captain Fremont having heard that Don Jose Castro was crossing the bay with 200 men, marched and joined the garrison at Sonoma, on the 25th of June. Several days were spent in active pursuit of the party under Captain De la Torre, but they succeeded in crossing the bay before they could be overtaken. With the retreat of De la Torre, ended all opposition on the north side of the bay of San Francisco.

On the 17th June, after the receipt of the news of the taking of Sonoma, Don Jose Castro issued two proclamations, one addressed to the old citizens, and the other to the new citizens and foreigners. The following are translations of these proclamations :

The citizen Jose Castro, lieutenant-colonel of cavalry in the Mexican army, and acting general-commander of the department of California.

Fellow-citizens :—The contemptible policy of the agents of the United States of North America, in this department, has induced a portion of adventurers, who, regardless of the rights of men, have daringly commenced an invasion, possessing themselves of the town of Sonoma, taking by surprise all that place, the military commander of that border, Colonel Don Mariano Guadaloupe Valléjo, Lieutenant-colonel Don Victor Prudon, Captain Don Salvador Valléjo, and Mr. Jacob P. Leese.

Fellow-countrymen—The defence of our liberty, the true religion which our fathers possessed, and our independence, calls upon us to sacrifice ourselves, rather than lose these inestimable blessings ; banish from your hearts all petty resentments, turn you, and behold yourselves, these families, these innocent little ones, which have unfortunately fallen into the hands of our enemies, dragged from the bosoms of their fathers, who are prisoners among foreigners, and are calling upon us to succor them. There is still time for us to rise " en masse," as irresistible as retributive. You need not doubt but that divine providence will direct us in the way to glory. You should not vacillate because of the smallness of the garrison of the general headquarters, for he who first will sacrifice himself will be your friend and fellow-citizen. **JOSE CASTRO.**

HEADQUARTERS, SANTA CLARA, June 17th, 1846.

———

Citizen Jose Castro, lieutenant-colonel of artillery in the Mexican army, and acting general-commander of the department of Upper California.

25*

All foreigners residing among us, occupied with their business, may rest assured of the protection of all the authorities of the department, whilst they refrain entirely from all revolutionary movements.

The general commandancia under my charge will never proceed with vigor against any persons, neither will its authority result in mere words, wanting proof to support it ; declaration shall be taken, proofs executed, and the liberty and rights of the laborious, which is ever commendable, shall be protected.

Let the fortune of war take its chance with those ungrateful men, who, with arms in their hands, have attacked the country, without recollecting they were treated by the undersigned with all the indulgence of which he is so characteristic. The imparative inhabitants of the department are witnesses to the truth of this. I have nothing to fear—my duty leads me to death or to victory. I am a Mexican soldier, and I will be free and independent, or I will gladly die for these inestimable blessings.

JOSE CASTRO.

HEADQUARTERS, SANTA CLARA, June 17th, 1846.

Captain Fremont, with about 170 men, after the retreat of De la Torre, returned, via Sonoma, to the mouth of the Rio de los Americanos, near Sutter's Fort, for the purpose of crossing his horses and baggage at that point, and then marching to Santa Clara, understood to be the headquarters of General Castro.

A small party of ten men commanded by R. Semple was ordered to cross the Bay of San Francisco to the town of San Francisco, and if practicable to make prisoner the captain of the Port, Mr. R. T. Ridley. This service was performed, and Mr. Ridley was conveyed to New Helvetia, where the other prisoners were confined. The party reached New Helvetia on the eighth of July.

Commodore Sloat arrived at Monterey in the United States Frigate Savannah, on the second of July. He had heard of the first difficulties between the Mexican and the United States forces on the Rio Grande, at Mazatlan, but had not heard of the declaration of Congress that war existed. On the seventh of July he determined to hoist the American flag in Monterey, which act was performed by Capt. Mervine, commanding 250 marines and seamen. After the raising of the flag, amidst the cheers of the troops and foreigners present, a salute of twenty-one guns was fired by all the ships in the harbor, and the following proclamation was read and posted in English and Spanish:

TO THE INHABITANTS OF CALIFORNIA.

The central government of Mexico having commenced hostilities against the United States of America, by invading its territory, and attacking the troops of the United States stationed on the north side of the Rio Grande, and with a force of 7000 men under the command of Gen. Arista, which army was totally destroyed, and all their artillery, baggage, &c., captured on the eighth and ninth of May last, by a force of 2300 men, under the command of Gen. Taylor, and the city of Matamoras taken and occupied by the forces of the United States, and the two nations being actually at war by this transaction, I shall hoist the standard of the United States at Monterey immediately, and shall carry it throughout California.

I declare to the inhabitants of California, that, although I come in arms with a powerful force, I do not come among them as an enemy to California: on the contrary, I come as their best freind, as henceforth California will be a portion of the United States, and its peaceable inhabitants will enjoy the same rights and privileges they now enjoy, together with the privilege of choosing their own magistrates, and other officers for the administration of justice among themselves, and the same protection will be extended to them as to any other State in the Union. They will also enjoy a permanent government, under which life, property, and the constitutional right and lawful security to worship the Creator in the way most congenial to each one's sense of duty, will be secured, which, unfortunately, the central government of Mexico cannot afford them, destroyed as her resources are by internal factions and corrupt officers, who create constant revolutions to promote their own interests and oppress the people. Under the flag of the United States, California will be free from all such troubles and expenses; consequently, the country will rapidly advance and improve both in agriculture and commerce, as, of course, the revenue laws will be the same in California as in all other parts of the United States, affording them all manufactures and produce of the United States, free of any duty, and all foreign goods at one quarter of the duty they now pay. A great increase in the value of real estate and the products of California may also be anticipated.

With the great interest and kind feelings I know the government and people of the United States possess towards the citizens of California, the country cannot but improve more rapidly than any other on the continent of America.

Such of the inhabitants of California, whether native or foreigners, as may not be disposed to accept the high privileges of citizenship, and to live peaceably under the government of the United States, will be allowed time to dispose of their property, and to remove out of the country, if they choose, without any restriction ; or remain in it, observing strict neutrality.

With full confidence in the honor and integrity of the inhabitants of the country, I invite the judges, alcaldes, and other civil officers, to execute their functions as heretofore, that the public tranquillity may not be disturbed ; at least until the government of the territory can be more definitely arranged.

All persons holding titles to real estate, or in quiet possession of lands under color of right, shall have those titles guarantied to them.

All churches and the property they contain in possession of the clergy of California, shall continue in the same rights and possession they now enjoy.

All provisions and supplies of every kind furnished by the inhabitants for the use of the United States ships and soldiers, will be paid for at fair rates ; and no private property will be taken for public use without just compensation at the moment.

JOHN D. SLOAT,
Commander-in-chief of the U. S. Naval force in the Pacific Ocean.

On the sixth of July, Commodore Sloat dispatched a courier to Commander Montgomery of the sloop-of-war Portsmouth, lying at San Francisco, notifying him of his intention to hoist the American flag at Monterey, and requiring him, if his force was sufficient, to do the same at San Francisco and elsewhere in the upper portion of the territory. On the morning of the eighth, Com. Montgomery at the head of seventy sailors and marines landed and hoisted the American flag in the public square, under a salute of twenty-one guns from the Portsmouth. A volunteer corps of American foreigners was immediately organized for the defence of the place.

On the tenth, a flag dispatched by Com. Montgomery to Sonoma was received and raised there with shouts of satisfaction from the revolutionary garrison. The United States flag was soon after unfurled, without serious opposition, at every principal place in the northern part of California.

On the eighth, the next day after the raising of the United States flag at Monterey, Purser Fauntleroy, of the Savannah, was ordered to organize a company of dragoons, volunteers from the ships and citizens on shore, to reconnoitre the country and keep the communication open between Monterey and the more northern posts, in possession of the Americans. On the seventeenth, this corps marched to the Mission of San Juan, about thirty miles east of Monterey, for the purpose of raising at that place the United States flag, and of taking possession of guns and other munitions said to have been concealed there.

Capt. Fremont having left his position on the Sacramento on the twelfth, had reached San Juan about an hour before Purser Fauntleroy, and taken possession of the Mission without opposition. There were found here 9 pieces of cannon, 200 old muskets, 20 kegs of powder, and 60,000 pounds of cannon-shot. Both parties marched into Monterey the next day.

The fortification of Monterey was commenced immediately after the raising of the United States flag. On the twenty-third, Com. Sloat sailed in the Levant for the United States, via Panama, leaving Com. Stockton, who had arrived at Monterey in the Congress on the fifteenth, in command of the Pacific squadron. Immediately after, the Cyane, Com. Dupont, with Capt. Fremont and volunteers on board, sailed for San Diego, and the frigate Congress, Com. Stockton, sailed for San Pedro, the port of Los Angeles, the then capital of California. The frigate Savannah remained at Monterey, and the sloop Portsmouth at San Francisco.

Gen. Castro in the mean time had formed a junction at Santa Barbara with Gov. Pio Pico, their joint forces numbering about 600. From Santa Barbara they marched to Los Angeles, arriving at that place early in August. Capt. Fremont with the volunteers landed at San Diego about the same time. San Diego is 130 miles south of Los Angeles, and Com. Stockton landed his force of marines and sailors from the Congress at San Pedro. Com. Stockton marched immediately towards Los Angeles, hauling his artillery with oxen. As he approached the camp of the enemy on the Mesa, they fled with precipitation and without making any resistance. The Commodore marched into the city of Angels and took possession of it and the public property without opposition. Capt. Fremont, owing to the difficulty of procuring horses, did not arrive at Los Angeles until several days after the occupation of the town by Com. Stockton. Castro with a few followers fled to Sonora.

On the 17th of August Commodore Stockton issued the following proclamation, declaring California in the full and peaceable possession of the United States, and authorizing and requesting the election of civil officers throughout the country.

TO THE PEOPLE OF CALIFORNIA.

On my approach to this place with the forces under my command, José Castro, the commandant-general of California, buried his artillery and abandoned his fortified camp " of the Mesa," and fled, it is believed, towards Mexico.

With the sailors, the marines, and the California battalion of mounted riflemen, we entered the " City of the Angeles," the capital of California, on the 13th of August, and hoisted the North American flag.

The flag of the United States is now flying from every commanding position in the territory, and California is entirely free from Mexican dominion.

The territory of California now belongs to the United States, and will be governed, as soon as circumstances may permit, by officers and laws similar to those by which the other territories of the United States are regulated and protected.

But, until the governor, the secretary, and council are appointed, and the various civil departments of the government are arranged, military law will prevail, and the commander-in-chief will be the governor and protector of the territory.

In the mean time the people will be permitted, and are now requested, to meet in their several towns and departments, at such time and place as they may see fit, to elect civil officers to fill the places of those who decline to continue in office, and to administer the laws according to the former usages of the territory.

In all cases where the people fail to elect, the commander-in-chief and governor will make the appointments himself.

All persons, of whatever religion or nation, who faithfully adhere to the new government, will be considered as citizens of the territory, and will be zealously and thoroughly protected in the liberty of conscience, their persons, and property.

No persons will be permitted to remain in the territory who do not agree to support the existing government; and all military men who desire to remain, are required to take an oath that they will not take up arms against it, or do or say any thing to disturb its peace.

Nor will any persons, come from where they may, be permitted to settle in the territory, who do not pledge themselves to be, in all respects, obedient to the laws which may be from time to time enacted by the proper authorities of the territory.

All persons who, without special permission, are found with arms, outside of their own houses, will be considered as enemies, and will be shipped out of the country.

All thieves will be put to hard labor on the public works, and there kept, until compensation is made for the property stolen.

The California battalion of mounted riflemen will be kept in the service of the territory, and constantly on duty, to prevent and punish any aggressions by the Indians, or any other persons, upon the property of individuals, or the peace of the territory; and California shall hereafter be so governed and defended as to give security to the inhabitants, and to defy the power of Mexico.

All persons are required, as long as the territory is under martial law, to be within their houses from ten o'clock at night until sunrise in the morning.

R. F. STOCKTON,

Commander-in-Chief, and Governor

of the Territory of California.

CIUDAD DE LOS ANGELES, }
August 17*th*, 1846.   }

CHAPTER XXIV.

Resume my travels—Leave New Helvetia for San Francisco—Cosçumne river—Mickélemes river—Ford of the San Joaquin—Extensive plain—Tule marshes—Large droves of wild horses and elk—Arrive at Dr. Marsh's—Vineyard—Californian grape—Californian wine—Aguardiénte—Mormon settlements on the San Joaquin—Californian beef—Cattle—Grasses of California—Horses—Breakfast—Leave Dr. Marsh's—Arrive at Mr. Livermore's—Comforts of his dwelling—Large herds of cattle—Sheep—Swine—Californian señora—Slaughtering of a bullock—Fossil oyster-shells—Skeleton of a whale on a high mountain—Arrive at mission of San José—Ruinous and desolate appearance of the mission—Pedlers—Landlady—Filth—Gardens of the mission—Fruit orchards—Empty warehouses and workshops—Foul lodgings.

SEPTEMBER 13th.—We commenced to-day our journey from New Helvetia to San Francisco. Our party consisted, including myself, of Colonel Russell, Dr. McKee of Monterey, Mr. Pickett, a traveller in the country, recently from Oregon, and an Indian servant, who had been furnished us by Captain

Sutter. Starting about three o'clock, P. M., we travelled in a south course over a flat plain until sunset, and encamped near a small lake on the rancho of Mr. Murphy, near the Cosçumne river, a tributary of the Sacramento, which heads near the foot of the Sierra Nevada. The stream is small, but the bottom-lands are extensive and rich. Mr. Murphy has been settled in California about two years, and, with his wife and several children, has resided at this place sixteen months, during which time he has erected a comfortable dwelling-house, and other necessary buildings and conveniences. His wheat crop was abundant this year; and he presented us with as much milk and fresh butter as we desired. The grass on the upland plain over which we have travelled, is brown and crisp from the annual drought. In the low bottom it is still green. Distance 18 miles.

September 14.—We crossed the Cosçumne river about a mile from our camp, and travelled over a level plain covered with luxuriant grass and timbered with the evergreen oak, until three o'clock, when we crossed the Mickelemes river, another tributary of the Sacramento, and encamped on its southern bank in a beautiful grove of live-oaks. The Mickelemes, where we crossed it, is considerably larger than the Cosçumnes. The soil of the bottom appears to be very rich, and produces the finest qualities of grasses. The grass on the upland is also abundant, but at this time it is brown and dead. We passed through large tracts of wild oats during the day; the stalks are generally from three to five feet in length.

Our Indian servant, or vaquero, feigned sickness this morning, and we discharged him. As soon as he obtained his discharge, he was entirely relieved from the excruciating agonies under which he had affected to be suffering for several hours. Eating his breakfast, and mounting his horse, he galloped off in the direction of the fort. We overtook this afternoon an English sailor, named Jack, who was travelling towards Monterey; and we employed him as cook and hostler for the remainder of the journey.

A variety of autumnal flowers, generally of a brilliant yellow, are in bloom along the beautiful and romantic banks of the rivulet. Distance 25 miles.

September 15.—Our horses were frightened last night by bears, and this morning, with the exception of those which were picketed, had strayed so far that we did not recover them until ten o'clock. Our route has continued over a flat plain, generally covered with luxuriant grass, wild oats, and a variety of sparkling flowers. The soil is composed of a rich argillaceous loam. Large tracts of the land are evidently subject to annual inundations. About noon we reached a small lake surrounded by *tule*. There being no trail for our guidance, we experienced some difficulty in shaping our course so as to strike the San Joaquin river at the usual fording-place. Our man Jack, by some neglect or mistake of his own, lost sight of us, and we were compelled to proceed without him. This afternoon we saw several large droves of antelope and deer. Game of all kinds appears to be very abundant in this rich valley. Passing through large tracts of *tule* we reached the San Joaquin river at dark, and encamped on the eastern bank. Here we immediately made large fires and discharged pistols as signals to our man Jack, but he did not come into camp. Distance 35 miles.

September 16.—Jack came into camp while we were breakfasting, leading his tired horse. He had bivouacked on the plain, and fearful that his horse would break loose if he tied him, he held the animal by the bridle all night.

The ford of the San Joaquin is about forty or fifty miles from its mouth. At this season the water is at its lowest stage. The stream at the ford is probably one hundred yards in breadth, and our animals crossed it without much difficulty, the water reaching about midway of their bodies. Oak and small willows are the principal growth of wood skirting the river. Soon after we crossed the San Joaquin this morning we met two men, couriers, bearing dispatches from Commodore Stockton, the governor and commander-in-chief in California, to Sutter's Fort. Entering upon the broad plain we passed, in about three miles, a small lake, the water of which was so much impregnated with alkali as to be undrinkable. The grass is brown and crisp, but the seed upon it is evidence that it had fully matured before the drought affected it. The plain is furrowed with numerous deep trails, made by the droves of wild horses, elk, deer, and antelope, which roam over and graze upon it. The hunting sportsman can here enjoy his favorite pleasure to its fullest extent.

Having determined to deviate from our direct course, in order to visit the rancho of Dr. Marsh, we parted from Messrs. McRee and Pickett about noon. We passed during the afternoon several *tule* marshes, with which the plain of the San Joaquin is dotted. At a distance, the tule of these marshes presents the appearance of immense fields of ripened corn. The marshes are now nearly dry, and to shorten our journey we crossed several of them without difficulty. A month earlier, this would not have been practicable. I have but little doubt that these marshes would make fine rice plantations, and perhaps, if properly drained, they might produce the sugar-cane.

While pursuing our journey we frequently saw large droves of wild horses and elk grazing quietly upon the plain. No spectacle of moving life can present a more animated and beautiful appearance than a herd of wild horses. They were divided into droves of some one or two hundred. When they noticed us, attracted by curiosity to discover what we were, they would start and run almost with the fleetness of the wind in the direction towards us. But arriving within a distance of two hundred yards, they would suddenly halt, and after bowing their necks into graceful curves, and looking steadily at us a few moments, with loud snortings they would wheel about and bound away with the same lightning speed. These evolutions they would repeat several times, until having satisfied their curiosity, they would bid us a final adieu, and disappear behind the undulations of the plain.

The herds of elk were much nore numerous. Some of them numbered at least two thousand, and with their immense antlers presented, when running, a very singular and picturesque appearance. We approached some of these herds within fifty yards before they took the alarm. Beef in California is so abundant, and of so fine a quality, that game is but little hunted, and not much prized. Hence the elk, deer, and even antelope, are comparatively very tame, and rarely run from the traveller, unless he rides very near them. Some of these elk are as large as a medium-sized Mexican mule.

We arrived at the rancho of Dr. Marsh about 5 o'clock, P. M., greatly fatigued with the day's ride. The residence of Dr. M. is romantically situated, near the foot of one of the most elevated mountains in the range separating the valley of the San Joaquin from the plain surrounding the Bay of San Francisco. It is called "Mount Diablo," and may be seen in clear weather a great distance. The dwelling of Dr. M. is a small one-story house, rudely constructed of adobes, and divided into two or three apartments. The flooring is of earth, like the walls. A table or two, and some benches and a bed, are all the furniture it contains. Such are the privations to which those who settle in new countries must submit. Dr. M. is a native of New England, a graduate of Harvard University, and a gentleman of fine natural abilities and extensive scientific and literary acquirements. He emigrated to California some seven or eight years since, after having travelled through most of the Mexican States. He speaks the Spanish language fluently and correctly, and his accurate knowledge of Mexican institutions, laws and customs, was fully displayed in his conversation in regard to them. He obtained the grant of land upon which he now resides, some ten or twelve miles square, four or five years ago; and although he has been constantly harassed by the wild Indians, who have several times stolen all his horses, and sometimes numbers of his cattle, he has succeeded in permanently establishing himself. The present number of cattle on his rancho is about two thousand, and the increase of the present year he estimates at five hundred.

I noticed near the house a vegetable garden, with the usual variety of vegetables. In another enclosure was the commencement of an extensive vineyard, the fruit of which (now ripe) exceeds in delicacy of flavor any grapes which I have ever tasted. This grape is not indigenous, but was introduced by the *padres*, when they first established themselves in the country. The soil and climate of California have probably improved it. Many of the clusters are eight and ten inches in length, and weigh several pounds. The fruit is of medium size, and in color a dark purple. The rind is very thin, and when broken the pulp dissolves in the mouth immediately. Although Dr. M. has just commenced his vineyard, he has made several casks of wine this year, which is now in a state of fermentation. I tasted here, for the first time, *aguardiénte*, or brandy distilled from the Californian grape. Its flavor is not unpleasant, and age, I do not doubt, would render it equal to the brandies of France. Large quantities of wine and *aguardiénte* are made from the extensive vineyards farther south. Dr. M. informed me that his lands had produced a hundredfold of ˉwheat without irrigation. This yield seems almost incredible ; but if we can believe the statements of men of unimpeached veracity, there have been numerous instances of reproduction of wheat in California equalling and even exceeding this.

Some time in July, a vessel arrived at San Francisco from New York, which had been chartered and freighted principally by a party of Mormon emigrants, numbering between two and three hundred, women and children included. These Mormons are about making a settlement for agricultural purposes, on the San Joaquin river, above the rancho of Dr. Marsh. Two of the women and one of the men are now here, waiting for the return of the main party, which has gone up the river to explore and select a suitable site for the settlement. The women are young, neatly dressed, and one of them may be called good-looking. Captain Gant, formerly of the U. S. army, in very bad health, is also residing here. He has crossed the Rocky Mountains eight times, and, in various trapping excursions, has explored nearly every river between the settlements of the United States and the Pacific ocean.

The house of Dr. Marsh being fully occupied, we made our beds in a shed, a short distance from it. Suspended from one of the poles forming the frame of this shed, was a portion of the carcass of a recently slaughtered beef. The meat was very fat, the muscular portions of it presenting that marbled appearance, produced by a mixture of the fat and lean, so agreeable to the sight and palate of the epicure. The horned cattle of California which I have thus far seen, are the largest and the handsomest in shape which I ever saw. There is certainly no breed in the United States equalling them in size. They, as well as the horses, subsist entirely upon the indigenous grasses, at all seasons of the year ; and such are the nutritious qualities of the herbage, that the former are always in condition for slaughtering, and the latter have as much flesh upon them as is desirable, unless (which is often the case) they are kept up at hard work and denied the privilege of eating, or are broken down by hard riding. The varieties of grass are very numerous, and nearly all of them are heavily seeded when ripe, and are equal if not superior, as food for animals, to corn and oats. The horses are not as large as the breeds of the United States, but in point of symmetrical proportions and in capacity for endurance, they are fully equal to our best breeds. The distance we have travelled to-day I estimate at thirty-five miles.

Sept. 17.—The temperature of the mornings is most agreeable, and every other phenomenon accompanying it is correspondingly delightful to the senses. Our breakfast consisted of warm bread, made of unbolted flour, stewed beef, seasoned with *chile colorado*, a species of red pepper, and *frijoles*, a dark-colored bean, with coffee. After breakfast I walked with Dr. Marsh to the summit of a conical hill, about a mile distant from his house, from which the view of the plain on the north, south, and east, and the more broken and mountainous country on the west, is very extensive and highly picturesque. The hills and the plain are ornamented with the evergreen oak, sometimes in clumps or groves, at others standing solitary. On the summits, and in the gorges of the mountains, the cedar, pine, and fir, display their tall, symmetrical shapes ; and the San Joaquin, at a distance of about ten miles, is belted by a dense forest of oak, sycamore, and smaller timber and shrubbery. The herds of cattle are scattered over the plain,—some of them grazing upon the brown, but nutritious grass ; others sheltering themselves from the sun, under the wide-spreading branches of the oaks. The *toute ensemble* of the landscape is charming.

Leaving Dr. Marsh's about three o'clock, P. M., we travelled fifteen miles, over a rolling and well-watered country, covered generally with wild oats, and arrived at the residence of Mr. Robert Livermore just before dark. We were most kindly and hospitably received, and entertained by Mr. L., and his interesting family. After our mules and baggage had been cared for, we were introduced to the principal room in the house, which consisted of a number of small adobe buildings, erected apparently at different times, and connected together. Here we found chairs, and for the first time in California, saw a sideboard set out with glass tumblers, and chinaware. A decanter of *aguardiénte*, a bowl of loaf-sugar, and a pitcher of cold water from the spring, were set before us ; and being duly honored, had a most reviving influence upon our spirits as well as our corporeal energies. Suspended from the walls of the room were numerous coarse engravings, highly colored with green, blue, and crimson paints, representing the Virgin Mary, and many of the saints. These engravings are held in great veneration by the devout Catholics of this country. In the corners of the room were two comfortable-looking beds, with clean white sheets and pillow-cases, a sight with which my eyes have not been greeted for many months.

The table was soon set out, and covered with a linen cloth of snowy whiteness, upon which were placed dishes of stewed beef, seasoned with *chile colorado*, *frijoles*, and a plentiful supply of *tortillas*, with an excellent cup of tea, to the merits of which we did ample justice. Never were men blessed with better appetites than we are at the present time.

Mr. Livermore has been a resident of California nearly thirty years ; and having married into one of the wealthy families of the country, is the proprietor of some of the best lands for tillage and grazing. An *arroyo*, or small rivulet fed by springs, runs through his rancho, in such a course that, if expedient, he could, without much expense, irrigate one or two thousand acres. Irrigation in this part of California, however, seems to be entirely unnecessary for the production of wheat or any of the small grains. To produce maize, potatoes, and garden vegetables, irrigation is indispensable. Mr. Livermore has on his rancho about 3500 head of cattle. His horses, during the late disturbances, have nearly all been driven off or stolen by the Indians. I saw in his corral a flock of sheep numbering several hundred. They are of good size, and the mutton is said to be of an excellent quality, but the wool is coarse. It is, however, well adapted to the only manufacture of wool that is carried on in the country,—coarse blankets and *serápes*. But little attention is paid to hogs here, although the breeds are as fine as I have ever seen elsewhere. Beef being so abundant, and of a quality so superior, pork is not prized by the native Californians.

The Señora L. is the first Hispano-American lady I have seen since arriving in the country. She was dressed in a white cambric robe, loosely banded round the waist, and without ornament of any kind, except several rings on her small delicate fingers. Her complexion is that of a dark brunette, but lighter and more clear than the skin of most Californian women. The dark lustrous eye, the long black and glossy hair, the natural ease, grace, and vivacity of manners and conversation, characteristic of Spanish ladies, were fully displayed by her from the moment of our introduction. The children, especially two or three little *señoritas*, were very beautiful, and manifested a remarkable degree of sprightliness and intelligence. One of them presented me with a small basket wrought from a species of tough grass, and ornamented with the plumage of birds of a variety of brilliant colors. It was a beautiful specimen of Indian ingenuity.

Retiring to bed about ten o'clock, I enjoyed, the first time for four months, the luxury of clean sheets, with a mattress and a soft pillow. My enjoyment, however, was not unmixed with regret, for I noticed that several members of the family, to accommodate us with lodgings in the house, slept in the piazza outside. To have objected to sleeping in the house, however, would have been considered discourteous and offensive.

September 18.—Early this morning a bullock was brought up and slaughtered in front of the house. The process of slaughtering a beef is as follows : A *vaquero*, mounted on a trained horse, and provided with a lasso, proceeds to the place where the herd is grazing. Selecting an animal, he soon secures it by throwing the noose of the lasso over the horns, and fastening the other end around the pommel of the saddle. During the first struggles of the animal for liberty, which usually are very violent, the vaquero sits firmly in his seat, and keeps his horse in such a position that the fury and strength of the beast are wasted without producing any other result than his own exhaustion. The animal, soon ascertaining that he cannot release himself from the rope, submits to be pulled along to the place of execution. Arriving here, the vaquero winds the lasso around the legs of the doomed beast and throws him to the ground, where he lies perfectly helpless and motionless. Dismounting from his horse, he then takes from his leggin the butcher-knife that he always carries with him, and sticks the animal in the throat. He soon bleeds to death, when, in an incredibly short space of time for such a performance, the carcass is flayed and quartered, and the meat is either roasting before the fire or simmering in the stewpan. The *lassoing* and slaughter of a bullock is one of the most exciting sports of the Californians ; and the daring horsemanship and dexterous use of the lariat usually displayed on these occasions are worthy of admiration. I could not but notice the Golgotha-like aspect of the grounds surrounding the house. The bones of cattle were thickly strewn in all directions, showing a terrible slaughter of the four-footed tribe and a prodigious consumption of flesh.

A *carretada* of fossil oyster-shells was shown me by Mr. Livermore, which had been hauled for the purpose of being manufactured into lime. Some of these shells were eight inches in length, and of corresponding breadth and thickness. They were dug from a hill two or three miles distant, which is composed almost entirely of this fossil. Several bones belonging to the skeleton of a whale, discovered by Mr. L. on the summit of one of the highest elevations in the vicinity of his residence, were shown to me. The skeleton when discovered was nearly perfect and entirely exposed, and its elevation above the level of the sea between one and two thousand feet. How the huge aquatic monster, of which this skeleton is the remains, managed to make his dry bed on the summit of an elevated mountain, more experienced geologists than myself will hereafter determine. I have an opinion on the subject, however, but it is so contrary in some respects to the received geological theories, that I will not now hazard it.

Leaving Mr. Livermore's about nine o'clock, A. M., we travelled three or four miles over a level plain, upon which immense herds of cattle were grazing. When we approached they fled from us, with as much alarm as herds of deer and elk. From this plain we entered a hilly country, covered to the summits of the elevations with wild oats and tufts or bunches of a species of grass, which remains green through the whole season. Cattle were scattered through these hills, and more sumptuous grazing they could not desire. Small streams of water, fed by springs, flow through the hollows and ravines, which, as well as the hill-sides, are timbered with the evergreen oak and a variety of smaller trees. About two o'clock, P. M., we crossed an *arroyo* which runs through a narrow gorge of the hills, and struck an artificial wagon-road, excavated and embanked so as to afford a passage for wheeled vehicles along the steep hill-side. A little farther on we crossed a very rudely-constructed bridge. These are the first signs of road-making I have seen in the country. Emerging from the hills, the southern arm of the Bay of San Francisco came in view, separated from us by a broad and fertile plain some ten or twelve miles in width, sloping gradually down to the shore of the bay, and watered by several small creeks and estuaries.

We soon entered through a narrow street the mission of San José, or St. Joseph. Passing the squares of one-story adobe buildings, once inhabited by thousands of busy Indians, but now deserted, roofless, and crumbling into ruins, we reached the plaza in front of the church and the massive two-story edifices occupied by the *padres* during the flourishing epoch of the establishment. These were in good repair, but the doors and windows with the exception of one were closed, and nothing of moving life was visible except a donkey or two, standing near a fountain which gushed its waters into a capacious stone trough. Dismounting from our mules, we entered the open door, and here we found two Frenchmen dressed in sailor costume, with a quantity of coarse shirts, pantaloons, stockings, and other small articles, together with *aguardiénte*, which they designed retailing to such of the natives in the vicinity as chose to become their customers. They were itinerant merchants, or pedlers, and had opened their wares here for a day or two only, or so long as they could find purchasers.

Having determined to remain here the residue of the day, and the night, we inquired of the Frenchmen if there was any family in the place that could furnish us with food. They directed us to a house on the opposite side of the plaza, to which we immediately repaired. The señora, a dark-skinned and rather shrivelled and filthy specimen of the fair sex, but with a black, sparkling, and intelligent eye, met us at the door of the miserable hovel and invited us in. In one corner of this wretched and foul abode was a pile of raw hides, and in another a heap of wheat. The only furniture it contained were two small benches, or stools, one of which, being higher than the other, appeared to have been constructed for a table. We informed the señora that we were travellers, and wished refreshment and lodgings for the night. "*Está bueno, señores, está bueno,*" was her reply; and she immediately left us, and opening the door of the kitchen, commenced the preparation of our dinner. The interior of the kitchen, of which I had a good view through the door, was more revolting in its filthiness than the room in which we were seated. In a short time, so industrious was our hostess, our dinner, consisting of two plates of jerked beef, stewed, and seasoned with *chile colorado*, a plate of *tortillas*, and a bowl of coffee, was set out upon the most elevated stool. There were no knives, forks, or spoons,

on the table. Our amiable landlady apologized for this deficiency of table furniture, saying that she was "*muy pobre*,"
(very poor,) and possessed none of these table implements.
"Fingers were made before forks," and in our recent travels
we had learned to use them as substitutes, so that we found no
difficulty in conveying the meat from the plates to our mouths.

Belonging to the mission are two gardens, enclosed by high
adobe walls. After dinner we visited one of these. The area
of the enclosure contains fifteen or twenty acres of ground, the
whole of which is planted with fruit-trees and grape-vines.
There are about six hundred pear-trees, and a large number of
apple and peach trees, all bearing fruit in great abundance and
in full perfection. The quality of the pears is excellent, but
the apples and peaches are indifferent. The grapes have been
gathered, as I suppose, for I saw none upon the vines, which
appeared healthy and vigorous. The gardens are irrigated
with very little trouble, from large springs which flow from the
hills a short distance above them. Numerous aqueducts, formerly conveying and distributing water over an extensive tract
of land surrounding the mission, are still visible, but as the
land is not now cultivated, they at present contain no water.

The mission buildings cover fifty acres of ground, perhaps
more, and are all constructed of adobes with tile roofs. Those
houses or barracks which were occupied by the Indian families, are
built in compact squares, one story in height. They are generally
partitioned into two rooms, one fronting on the street, the other
upon a court or corral in the rear. The main buildings of the
mission are two stories in height, with wide corridors in front
and rear. The walls are massive, and if protected from the
winter rains, will stand for ages. But if exposed to the storms
by the decay of the projecting roofs, or by leaks in the main
roof, they will soon crumble, or sink into shapeless heaps of
mud. I passed through extensive warehouses and immense
rooms, once occupied for the manufacture of woollen blankets
and other articles, with the rude machinery still standing in
them, but unemployed. Filth and desolation have taken the
place of cleanliness and busy life. The granary was very ca-

pacious, and its dimensions were an evidence of the exuberant fertility of the soil, when properly cultivated under the superintendence of the *padres*. The calaboose is a miserable dark room of two apartments, one with a small loophole in the wall, the other a dungeon without light or ventilation. The stocks, and several other inventions for the punishment of offenders, are still standing in this prison. I requested permission to examine the interior of the church, but it was locked up, and no person in the mission was in possession of the key. Its length I should suppose is from one hundred to one hundred and twenty feet, and its breadth between thirty and forty, with small exterior pretensions to architectural ornament or symmetry of proportions.

Returning from our rambles about the mission, we found that our landlady had been reinforced by an elderly woman, whom she introduced as "*mi madre*," and two or three Indian *muchachas*, or girls, clad in a costume not differing much from that of our mother Eve. The latter were obese in their figures, and the mingled perspiration and filth standing upon their skins were any thing but agreeable to the eye. The two señoras, with these handmaids near them, were sitting in front of the house, busily engaged in executing some needlework.

Supper being prepared and discussed, our landlady informed us that she had a husband, who was absent, but would return in the course of the night, and if he found strange men in the house, he would be much offended with her. She had therefore directed her *muchachas* to sweep out one of the deserted and half-ruined rooms on the opposite square, to which we could remove our baggage, and in which we could lodge during the night; and as soon as the necessary preparations were made, we retired to our dismal apartment. The "compound of villanous smells" which saluted our nostrils when we entered our dormitory for the night, augured unfavorably for repose. The place had evidently been the abode of horses, cattle, pigs, and foul vermin of every description. But with the aid of a dark-colored tallow-candle, which gave just light enough to display the murkiness and filth surrounding us, we spread our beds in the cleanest places, and laid down to rest. Distance travelled, 18 miles.

CHAPTER XXV.

Armies of fleas—Leave the mission—Clover—Wild mustard—A carreta—
Family travelling—Arrive at Pueblo de San José—Capt. Fisher—Description of the Pueblo—The embarcadero—Beautiful and fertile valley
of the Pueblo—Absence of architectural taste in California—Town squirrels—Fruit garden—Grapes—Tropical fruits—Gaming rooms—Contrast
between Californian and American gamesters—Leave San José—
Beautiful avenue—Mission of Santa Clara—Rich but neglected lands—
Effects of a bad government—A señora on the road-side—Kindness of
Californian women—Fast riding—Cruel treatment of horses—Arrive at
the mission of San Francisco— A poor but hospitable family—Arrive at
the town of San Francisco—W. A. Leidesdorff, Esq., American vice-
consul—First view of the Bay of San Francisco—Muchachos and Mu-
chacas—Capt. Montgomery—U. S. sloop-of-war Portsmouth—Town of
San Francisco ; its situation, appearance, population—Commerce of
California—Extortion of the government and traders.

SEPT. 19.—Several Californians came into the mission during the night or early this morning ; among them the husband of our hostess, who was very kind and cordial in his greetings.

While our man Jack was saddling and packing the mules, they gathered around us to the number of a dozen or more, and were desirous of trading their horses for articles of clothing ; articles which many of them appeared to stand greatly in need of, but which we had not to part from. Their pertinacity exceeded the bounds of civility, as I thought ; but I was not in a good humor, for the fleas, bugs, and other vermin, which in- fested our miserable lodgings, had caused me a sleepless night, by goring my body until the blood oozed from the skin in count- less places. These ruinous missions are prolific generators, and the nurseries of vermin of all kinds, as the hapless traveller who tarries in them a few hours will learn to his sorrow. When

27

these bloodthirsty assailants once make a lodgment in the clothing or bedding of the unfortunate victim of their attacks, such are their courage and perseverance, that they never capitulate. " Blood or death" is their motto ;—the war against them, to be successful, must be a war of extermination.

Poor as our hostess was, she nevertheless was reluctant to receive any compensation for her hospitality. We, however, insisted upon her receiving a dollar from each of us, (*dos pesos,*) which she finally accepted ; and after shaking us cordially by the hand she bade us an affectionate *adios*, and we proceeded on our journey.

From the Mission of San José to the Pueblo of San José, the distance is fifteen miles, for the most part over a level and highly fertile plain, producing a variety of indigenous grasses, among which I noticed several species of clover, and mustard, large tracts of which we rode through, the stalks varying from six to ten feet in height. The plain is watered by several *arroyos*, skirted with timber, generally the evergreen oak.

We met this morning a Californian *carreta*, or travelling-cart, freighted with women and children, bound on a pleasure excursion. The *carreta* is the rudest specimen of the wheeled vehicle I have seen. The wheels are transverse sections of a log, and are usually about $2\frac{1}{2}$ feet in diameter, and varying in thickness from the centre to the rim. These wheels are coupled together by an axletree, into which a tongue is inserted. On the axletree and tongue rests a frame, constructed of square pieces of timber, six or eight feet in length, and four or five in breadth, into which are inserted a number of stakes about four feet in length. This frame-work being covered and floored with raw hides, the carriage is complete. The *carreta* which we met was drawn by two yokes of oxen, driven by an Indian vaquero, mounted on a horse. In the rear were two *caballeros*, riding fine spirited horses, with gaudy trappings. They were dressed in steeple-crowned, glazed *sombreros*, *serapes* of fiery colors, velvet (cotton) *calzoneros*, white cambric *calzoncillos*, and leggins and shoes of undressed leather. Their spurs were of immense size.

The party halted as soon as we met them, the men touching their heavy *sombreros*, and uttering the usual salutation of the morning, " *Buenos dias señores*," and shaking hands with us very cordially. The same salutation was repeated by all the señoras and señoritas in the *carreta*. In dress and personal appearance the women of this party were much inferior to the men. Their skins were dark, sallow, and shrivelled, and their costume, a loose gown and *reboso*, were made of very common materials. The children, however, were all handsome, with sparkling eyes and ruddy complexions. Women and children were seated, *à la Turque*, on the bottom of the *carreta*, there being no raised seats in the vehicle.

We arrived at the Pueblo de San José about 12 o'clock. There being no hotels in California, we were much at loss where to apply for refreshments and lodgings for the night. Soon, however, we were met by Captain Fisher, a native of Massachusetts, but a resident of this country for twenty years or more, who invited us to his house. We were most civilly received by Señora F., who, although she did not speak English, seemed to understand it very well. She is a native of the southern Pacific coast of Mexico, and a lady of fine manners and personal appearance. Her eldest daughter, about thirteen years of age, is very beautiful. An excellent dinner was soon set out, with a variety of the native wines of California and other liquors. We could not have felt ourselves more happy and more at home, even at our own firesides and in the midst of our own families.

The Pueblo de San José is a village containing some six or eight hundred inhabitants. It is situated in what is called the "Pueblo valley," about fifteen miles south of the southern shore of the Bay of San Francisco. Through a navigable creek vessels of considerable burden can approach the town within a distance of five or six miles. The *embarcadero*, or landing, I think, is six miles from the Pueblo. The fertile plain between this and the town, at certain seasons of the year, is sometimes inundated. The "Pueblo valley," which is eighty or one hundred miles in length, varying from ten to twenty in breadth, is well watered by the Rio Santa Clara and numerous *arroyos*, and is one of the most fertile and picturesque plains in California. For pastoral charms, fertility of soil, variety of productions, and delicious voluptuousness of climate and scenery, it cannot be surpassed. This valley, if properly cultivated, would alone produce breadstuffs enough to supply millions of population. The buildings of the Pueblo, with few exceptions, are constructed of adobes, and none of them have even the smallest pretensions to architectural taste or beauty. The church, which is situated near the centre of the town, exteriorly resembles a huge Dutch barn. The streets are irregular, every man having erected his house in a position most convenient to him. Aqueducts convey water from the Santa Clara river to all parts of the town. In the main plaza hundreds, perhaps thousands, of squirrels, whose abodes are under ground, have their residences. They are of a brownish color, and about the size of our common gray squirrel. Emerging from their subterraneous abodes, they skip and leap about over the plaza without the least concern, no one molesting them.

The population of the place is composed chiefly of native Californian land-proprietors. Their ranchos are in the valley, but their residences and gardens are in the town. We visited this afternoon the garden of Señor Don Antonio Suñol. He received us with much politeness, and conducted us through his garden. Apples, pears, peaches, figs, oranges, and grapes, with other fruits which I do not now recollect, were growing and ripening. The grape-vines were bowed to the ground with the luxuriance and weight of the yield; and more delicious fruit I never tasted. From the garden we crossed over to a flouring-mill recently erected by a son-in-law of Don Antonio, a Frenchman by birth. The mill is a creditable enterprise to the proprietor, and he will coin money from its operations.

The Pueblo de San José is one of the oldest settlements in Alta California. Captain Fisher pointed out to me a house built of adobes, which has been standing between 80 and 90 years, and no house in the place appeared to be more substantial or in better repair. A garrison, composed of marines from the United States ships and volunteers enlisted from the American settlers in the country, is now stationed here. The post is under the command of Purser Watmough, of the United States sloop-of-war Portsmouth, commanded by Captain Montgomery. During the evening I visited several public places, (bar-rooms,) where I saw men and women engaged promiscuously at the game of *monte*. Gambling is a universal vice in California. All classes and both sexes participate in its excitements to some extent. The games, however, while I was present, were conducted with great propriety and decorum so far as the native Californians were concerned. The loud swearing and other turbulent demonstrations generally proceeded from the unsuccessful foreigners. I could not but observe the contrast between the two races in this respect. The one bore their losses with stoical composure and indifference; the other announced each unsuccessful bet with profane imprecations and maledictions. Excitement prompted the hazards of the former, avarice the latter.

September 20.—The morning was cloudy and cool; but the clouds broke away about nine o'clock, and the sun shone from a vaporless sky, as usual. We met, at the Pueblo, Mr. Grove Cook, a native of Gerrard county, Ky., but for many years a resident of California. He is the proprietor of a rancho in the vicinity. We determined to leave our mules in charge of Mr. Cook's vaquero, and proceed to San Francisco on hired horses. The distance from the Pueblo de San José to San Francisco is called sixty miles. The time occupied in performing the journey, on Californian horses at Californian speed, is generally six or seven hours. Procuring horses for the journey, and leaving our baggage, with the exception of a change of clothing, we left the Pueblo about eleven o'clock, A. M.

The mission of Santa Clara is situated about two and a half miles from the town. A broad *alameda*, shaded by stately trees, (elms and willows,) planted by the *padres*, extends nearly the entire distance, forming a most beautiful drive or walk for equestrians or pedestrians. The motive of the *padres* in planting this avenue, was to afford the devout señoras and señoritas

27*

a shade from the sun, when walking from the Pueblo to the church at the mission to attend mass. A few minutes over the smooth, level road, at the rapid speed of our fresh Californian horses, brought us to the mission, where we halted to make our observations. This mission is not so extensive in its buildings as that of San José, but the houses are generally in better repair. They are constructed of adobes. The church was open, and entering the interior, I found the walls hung with coarse paintings and engravings of the saints, etc., etc. The chancel is decorated with numerous images, and symbolical ornaments used by the priests in their worship. Gold-paper, and tinsel, in barbaric taste, are plastered without stint upon nearly every object that meets the eye, so that when on festive occasions the church is lighted, it must present a very glittering appearance.

The rich lands surrounding the mission are entirely neglected. I did not notice a foot of ground under cultivation, except the garden enclosure, which contained a variety of fruits and plants of the temperate and tropical climates. From want of care these are fast decaying. Some excellent pears were furnished us by Mrs. Bennett, an American lady, of amazonian proportions, who, with her family of sons, has taken up her residence in one of the buildings of the mission. The picture of decay and ruin presented by this once flourishing establishment, surrounded by a country so fertile and scenery so enchantiug, is a most melancholy spectacle to the passing traveller, and speaks a language of loud condemnation against the government.

Proceeding on our journey, we travelled fifteen miles over a flat plain, timbered with groves and parks of evergreen oaks, and covered with a great variety of grasses, wild oats, and mustard. So rank is the growth of mustard in many places, that it is with difficulty that a horse can penetrate through it. Numerous birds flitted from tree to tree, making the groves musical with their harmonious notes. The black-tailed deer bounded frequently across our path, and the lurking and stealthy *coyotes* were continually in view. We halted at a small cabin, with a *corral* near it, in order to breathe our horses, and refresh ourselves. Captain Fisher had kindly filled a small sack with bread, cheese, roasted beef, and a small jug of excellent schiedam. Entering the cabin, the interior of which was cleanly, we found a solitary woman, young, neatly dressed, and displaying many personal charms. With the characteristic ease and grace of a Spanish woman, she gave the usual salutation for the hour of the day, "*Buenas tardes señores caballeros ;*" to which we responded by a suitable salutation. We requested of our hostess some water, which she furnished us immediately, in an earthen bowl. Opening our sack of provisions, we spread them upon the table, and invited the señora to partake of them with us, which invitation she accepted without the slightest hesitation, and with much good-nature, vivacity, and even thankfulness for our politeness. There are no women in the world for whose manners nature has done so much, and for whom art and education, in this respect, have done so little, as these Hispano-American females on the coast of the Pacific. In their deportment towards strangers they are queens, when, in costume, they are peasants. None of them, according to our tastes, can be called beautiful ; but what they want in complexion and regularity of feature, is fully supplied by their kindliness, the soul and sympathy which beam from their dark eyes, and their grace and warmth of manners and expression.

While enjoying the *pic-nic* with our agreeable hostess, a *caballada* was driven into the *corral* by two *vaqueros,* and two gentlemen soon after came into the house. They were Messrs. Lightson and Murphy, from the Pueblo, bound for San Francisco, and·had stopped to change their horses. We immediately made ready to accompany them, and were soon on the road again, travelling at racehorse speed ; these gentlemen having furnished us with a change of horses, in order that we might be able to keep up with them.

To account for the fast travelling in California on horseback, it is necessary to explain the mode by which it is accomplished. A gentleman who starts upon a journey of one hundred miles, and wishes to perform the trip in a day, will take with him ten fresh horses and a *vaquero.* The eight loose horses are placed under the charge of the *vaquero,* and are driven in front, at the rate of ten or twelve miles an hour, according to the speed that is required for the journey. At the end of twenty miles, the horses which have been rode are discharged and turned into the *caballada,* and horses which have not been rode, but driven along without weight, are saddled and mounted and rode at the same speed, and so on to the end of the journey. If a horse gives out from inability to proceed at this gait, he is left on the road. The owner's brand is on him, and if of any value, he can be recovered without difficulty. But in California, no one thinks of stopping on the road, on account of the loss of a horse, or his inability to travel at the rate of ten or twelve miles an hour. Horseflesh is cheap, and the animal must go as long as he can, and when he cannot travel longer he is left, and another horse is substituted.

Twenty-five miles, at a rapid gait over a level and fertile plain, brought us to the rancho of Don Francisco Sanchez, where we halted to change horses. Breathing our animals a short time, we resumed our journey, and reached the mission of San Francisco Dolores, three miles from the town of San Francisco, just after sunset. Between the mission and the town the road is very sandy, and we determined to remain here for the night, *corraling* the loose animals and picketing those we rode. It was some time, however, before we could find a house to lodge in. The foreign occupants of the mission buildings, to whom we applied for accommodations for the night, gave us no satisfaction. After several applications, we were at last accommodated by an old and very poor Californian Spaniard, who inhabited a small house in one of the ruinous squares, formerly occupied by the operative Indians. All that he had (and it was but little) was at our disposal. A more miserable supper I never sat down to ; but the spirit of genuine hospitality in which it was given, imparted to the poor viands a flavor that rendered the entertainment almost sumptuous—in my imagination. A cup of water cheerfully given to the weary and thirsty traveller, by him who has no more to part with, is worth a cask of wine grudgingly bestowed by the stingy or the ostentatious churl. Notwithstanding we preferred sleeping on our own blankets, these poor people would not suffer us to do it, but spread their own pallets on the earth floor of their miserable hut, and insisted so strongly upon our occupying them, that we could not refuse.

September 21.—We rose at daylight. The morning was clear, and our horses were shivering with the cold. The mission of San Francisco is situated at the northern terminus of the fertile plain over which we travelled yesterday, and at the foot, on the eastern side, of the coast range of mountains. These mountains are of considerable elevation. The shore of the Bay of San Francisco is about two miles distant from the mission. An *arroyo* waters the mission lands and empties into the bay. The church of the mission, and the main buildings contiguous, are in tolerable repair. In the latter, several Mormon families, which arrived in the ship Brooklyn from New York, are quartered. As in the other missions I have passed through, the Indian quarters are crumbling into shapeless heaps of mud.

Our aged host, notwithstanding he is a pious Catholic and considers us as heretics and heathens, gave us his benediction in a very impressive manner when we were about to start. Mounting our horses at sunrise, we travelled three miles over low ridges of sand-hills, with sufficient soil, however, to produce a thick growth of scrubby evergreen oak, and brambles of hawthorn, wild currant and gooseberry bushes, rose-bushes, briers, etc. We reached the residence of Wm. A. Leidesdorff, Esq., late American vice-consul at San Francisco, when the sun was about an hour high. The morning was calm and beautiful. Not a ripple disturbed the placid and glassy surface of the magnificent bay and harbor, upon which rested at anchor thirty large vessels, consisting of whalemen, merchantmen, and the U. S. sloop-of-war Portsmouth, Captain Montgomery. Besides these, there were numerous small craft, giving to the harbor a commercial air, of which some of the large cities on the Atlantic coast would feel vain. The bay, from the town of San Francisco due east, is about twelve miles in breadth. An elevated range of hills bounds the view on the opposite side. These slope gradually down, and between them and the shore there is a broad and fertile plain, which is called the *Contra Costa*. There are several small islands in the bay, but they do not present a fertile appearance to the eye.

We were received with every mark of respectful attention and cordial hospitality by Mr. Leidesdorff. Mr. L. is a native of Denmark; was for some years a resident of the United States; but subsequently the captain of a merchant vessel, and has been established at this place as a merchant some five or six years. The house in which he resides, now under the process of completion, is the largest private building in the town. Being shown to a well-furnished room, we changed our travel-soiled clothing for a more civilized costume, by which time breakfast was announced, and we were ushered into a large dining-hall. In the centre stood a table, upon which was spread a substantial breakfast of stewed and fried beef, fried onions, and potatoes, bread, butter, and coffee. Our appetites were very sharp, and we did full justice to the merits of the fare before us. The servants waiting upon the table were an Indian *muchachito* and *muchachita*, about ten or twelve years of age. They had not been long from their wild *rancherias*, and knew but little of civilized life. Our host, however, who speaks, I believe, nearly every living language, whether of Christian, barbarian, or savage nations, seemed determined to impress upon their dull intellects the forms and customs of civilization. He scolded them with great vivacity, sometimes in their own tongue, sometimes in French, Spanish, Portuguese, Danish, German, and English, in accordance with the language in which he was thinking at the moment. It seemed to me that the little fat Indians were more confused than enlightened by his emphatic instructions. At the table, besides ourselves and host, was Lieutenant W. A. Bartlett, of the U. S. sloop-of-war Portsmouth, now acting as alcalde of the town and district of San Francisco.

The Portsmouth, Commander Montgomery, is the only United States vessel of war now lying in the harbor. She is regarded as the finest vessel of her class belonging to our navy.

By invitation of Lieutenant Bartlett, I went on board of her between ten and eleven o'clock. The crew and officers were assembled on deck to attend Divine service. They were all dressed with great neatness, and seemed to listen with deep attention to the Episcopal service and a sermon, which were read by Commander Montgomery, who is a member of the church.

In the afternoon I walked to the summit of one of the elevated hills in the vicinity of the town, from which I had a view of the entrance to the Bay of San Francisco, and of the Pacific ocean. A thick fog hung over the ocean outside of the bay. The deep roar of the eternally restless waves, as they broke one after another upon the beach, or dashed against the rock-bound shore, could be heard with great distinctness, although some five or six miles distant. The entrance from the ocean into the bay is about a mile and a half in breadth. The waters of the bay appear to have forced a passage through the elevated ridge of hills next to the shore of the Pacific. These rise abruptly on either side of the entrance. The water at the entrance and inside is of sufficient depth to admit the largest ship that was ever constructed; and so completely land-locked and protected from the winds is the harbor, that vessels can ride at anchor in perfect safety in all kinds of weather. The capacity of the harbor is sufficient for the accommodation of all the navies of the world.

The town of San Francisco is situated on the south side of the entrance, fronting on the bay, and about six miles from the ocean. The flow and ebb of the tide are sufficient to bring a vessel to the anchorage in front of the town and to carry it outside, without the aid of wind, or even against an unfavorable wind. A more approachable harbor, or one of greater security, is unknown to navigators. The permanent population of the town is at this time between one and two hundred,* and is composed almost exclusively of foreigners. There are

---

* This was in September, 1846. In June, 1847, when I left San Francisco, on my return to the United States, the population had increased to about twelve hundred, and houses were rising in all directions.

but two or three native Californian families in the place. The transient population, and at present it is quite numerous, consists of the garrison of marines stationed here, and the officers and crews attached to the merchant and whale ships lying in the harbor. The houses, with a few exceptions, are small adobes and frames, constructed without regard to architectural taste, convenience, or comfort. Very few of them have either chimneys or fireplaces. The inhabitants contrive to live the year round without fires, except for cooking. The position of San Francisco for commerce is, without doubt, superior to any other port on the Pacific coast of North America. The country contiguous and tributary to it cannot be surpassed in fertility, healthfulness of climate, and beauty of scenery. It is capable of producing whatever is necessary to the sustenance of man, and many of the luxuries of tropical climates, not taking into the account the mineral wealth of the surrounding hills and mountains, which there is reason to believe is very great. This place is, doubtless, destined to become one of the largest and most opulent commercial cities in the world, and under American authority it will rise with astonishing rapidity. The principal merchants now established here are Messrs. Leidesdorff, Grimes & Davis, and Frank Ward, a young gentleman recently from New York. These houses carry on an extensive and profitable commerce with the interior, the Sandwich Islands, Oregon, and the southern coast of the Pacific. The produce of Oregon for exportation is flour, lumber, salmon, and cheese ; of the Sandwich Islands, sugar, coffee, and preserved tropical fruits.

California, until recently, has had no commerce in the broad signification of the term. A few commercial houses of Boston and New York have monopolized all the trade on this coast for a number of years. These houses have sent out ships freighted with cargoes of dry goods and a variety of *knick-knacks* saleable in the country. The ships are fitted up for the retail sale of these articles, and trade from port to port, vending their wares on board to the rancheros at prices that would be astonishing at home. For instance, the price of common brown cotton cloth is one dollar per yard, and other articles in this and even greater proportion of advance upon home prices. They receive in payment for their wares, hides and tallow. The price of a dry hide is ordinarily one dollar and fifty cents. The price of tallow I do not know. When the ship has disposed of her cargo she is loaded with hides, and returns to Boston, where the hides bring about four or five dollars, according to the fluctuations of the market. Immense fortunes have been made by this trade; and between the government of Mexico and the traders on the coast, California has been literally *skinned*, annually for the last thirty years. Of natural wealth the population of California possesses a superabundance, and are immensely rich; still, such have been the extortionate prices that they have been compelled to pay for their commonest artificial luxuries and wearing apparel, that generally they are but indifferently provided with the ordinary necessaries of civilized life. For a suit of clothes, which in New York or Boston would cost seventy-five dollars, the Californian has been compelled to pay five times that sum in hides at one dollar and fifty cents; so that a *caballero*, to clothe himself genteelly, has been obliged, as often as he renewed his dress, to sacrifice about two hundred of the cattle on his rancho. No people, whether males or females, are more fond of display; no people have paid more dearly to gratify this vanity; and yet no civilized people I have seen are so deficient in what they most covet.

CHAPTER XXVI.

Climate of San Francisco—Periodical winds—Dine on the Portsmouth—A supper party on shore—Arrival of Commodore Stockton at San Francisco—Rumors of rebellion from the south—Californian court—Trial by jury—Fandango—Californian belles—American pioneers of the Pacific—Reception of Commodore Stockton—Sitga—Captain Fremont leaves San Francisco for the south—Offer our services as volunteers.

From the 21st of September to the 13th of October I remained at San Francisco. The weather during this period was uniformly clear.   The clim ite of San Francisco is peculiar and local, from its position.   During the summer and autumnal months, the wind on this coast blows from the west and north-west, directly from the ocean.   The mornings here are usually calm and pleasantly warm.   About twelve o'clock, M., the wind blows strong from the ocean, through the entrance of the bay, rendering the temperature cool enough for woollen cloth-ing in midsummer.   About sunset the wind dies away, and the evenings and nights are comparatively calm.   In the winter months the wind blows in soft and gentle breezes from the southeast, and the temperature is agreeable, the thermometer rarely sinking below 50°.   When the winds blow from the ocean, it never rains ; when they blow from the land, as they do during the winter and spring months, the weather is showery, and resembles that of the month of May in the same latitude on the Atlantic coast.   The coolness of the climate and briskness of the air above described, are confined to par-ticular positions on the coast, and the description in this re-spect is not applicable to the interior of the country, nor even to other localities immediately on the coast.

On the 21st, by invitation of Captain Montgomery, I dined on board of the sloop-of-war Portsmouth.   The party, in-cluding myself, consisted of Colonel Russell, Mr. Jacob, Lieu-tenant Bartlett, and a son of Captain M.   There are few if any officers in our navy more highly and universally esteemed, for their moral qualities and professional merits, than Captain M.   He is a sincere Christian, a brave officer, and an accomplished gentleman.   Under the orders of Commodore Sloat, he first raised the American flag in San Francisco.   We spent the afternoon most agreeably, and the refined hospitality, courteous manners, and intelligent and interesting conversation of our host, made us regret the rapidly fleeting moments.   The wines on the table were the produce of the vine of California, and having attained age, were of an excellent quality in substance and flavor.

I attended a supper-party given this evening by Mr. Frank Ward.   The party was composed of citizens of the town, and officers of the navy and the merchant and whale ships in the harbor. In such a company as was here assembled, it was very difficult for me to realize that I was many thousand miles from home, in a strange and foreign country. All the faces about me were American, and there was nothing in scene or sentiment to remind the guests of their remoteness from their native shores. Indeed, it seems to be a settled opinion, that California is henceforth to compose a part of the United States, and every American who is now here considers himself as treading upon his own soil, as much as if he were in one of the old thirteen revolutionary states. Song, sentiment, story, and wit, heightened the enjoyments of the excellent entertainment of our host, and the jovial party did not separate until a late hour of the night. The guests, as may be supposed, were composed chiefly of gentlemen who had, from their pursuits, travelled over most of the world,—had seen developments of human character under every variety of circumstance, and observed society, civilized, barbarous, and savage, in all its phases. Their conversation, therefore, when around the convivial board, possessed an unhackneyed freshness and raciness highly entertaining and instructive.

On the 27th of September, the U. S. frigate Congress, Captain Livingston, bearing the broad pennant of Commodore Stockton, and the U. S. frigate Savannah, Captain Mervine, anchored in the harbor, having sailed from Monterey a day or two previously. The arrival of these large men-of-war produced an increase of the bustle in the small town. Blue coats and bright buttons (the naval uniform) became the prevailing costume at the billiard-rooms and other public places, and the plain dress of a private citizen might be regarded as a badge of distinction.

On the 1st of October a courier arrived from the south with intelligence that the Californians at Los Angeles had organized a force and rebelled against the authority of the Americans,—that they had also captured an American merchant-vessel lying at San Pedro, the port of the city of Angels, about thirty miles distant, and robbed it of a quantity of merchandise and specie.

Whether this latter report was or was not true, I do not know
—the former was correct. The frigate Savannah sailed for
Los Angeles immediately.

Among those American naval officers whose agreeable acquaintance I made at San Francisco, was Mr. James F. Schenck,
first-lieutenant of the frigate Congress, brother of the distinguished member of congress from Ohio of that name,—a native
of Dayton, Ohio,—a gentleman of intelligence, keen wit, and a
most accomplished officer. The officers of our navy are our
representatives in foreign countries, and they are generally such
representatives as their constituents have reason to feel proud
of. Their chivalry, patriotism, gentlemanlike deportment, and
professional skill, cannot be too much admired and applauded
by their countrymen. I shall ever feel grateful to the naval
officers of the Pacific squadron, for their numerous civilities
during my sojourn on the Pacific coast.

Among the novelties presented while at San Francisco, was
a trial by jury—the second tribunal of this kind which had
been organized in California. The trial took place before
Judge Bartlett, and the litigants were two Mormons. Counsel
was employed on both sides. Some of the forms of American
judicial proceedings were observed, and many of the legal
technicalities and nice flaws, so often urged in common-law
courts, were here argued by the learned counsel of the parties,
with a vehemence of language and gesticulation with which I
thought the legal learning and acumen displayed did not correspond. The proceedings were a mixture, made up of common law, equity, and a sprinkling of military despotism—which
last ingredient the court was compelled to employ, when entangled in the intricate meshes woven by the counsel for the
litigants, in order to extricate itself. The jury, after the case
was referred to them, were what is called "hung;" they could
not agree, and the matters in issue, therefore, remained exactly
where they were before the proceedings were commenced.

I attended one evening a *fandango* given by Mr. Ridley, an
English gentleman, whose wife is a Californian lady. Several
of the señoras and señoritas from the ranchos of the vicinity

were present. The Californian ladies dance with much ease and grace. The waltz appears to be a favorite with them. Smoking is not prohibited in these assemblies, nor is it confined to the gentlemen. The *cigarita* is freely used by the señoras and señoritas, and they puff it with much gusto while threading the mazes of the cotillon or swinging in the waltz.

I had the pleasure of being introduced, at the residence of Mr. Leidesdorff, to two young ladies, sisters and belles in Alta California. They are members of an old and numerous family on the Contra Costa. Their names are singular indeed, for if I heard them correctly, one of them was called Donna Maria Jesus and the other Donna Maria Conception. They were interesting and graceful young ladies, with regular features, symmetrical figures, and their dark eyes flashed with all the intelligence and passion characteristic of Spanish women.

Among the gentlemen with whom I met soon after my arrival at San Francisco, and whose acquaintance I afterwards cultivated, were Mr. E. Grimes and Mr. N. Spear, both natives of Massachusetts, but residents of this coast and of the Pacific Islands, for many years. They may be called the patriarchs of American pioneers on the Pacific. After forming an acquaintance with Mr. G., if any one were to say to me that

" Old Grimes is dead, that good old man,"

I should not hesitate to contradict him with emphasis ; for he is still living, and possesses all the charities and virtues which can adorn human nature, with some of the eccentricities of his namesake in the song. By leading a life of peril and adventure on the Pacific ocean for fifty years he has accumulated a large fortune, and is a man now proverbial for his integrity, candor, and charities. Both of these gentlemen have been largely engaged in the local commerce of the Pacific. Mr. S., some twenty-five or thirty years ago, colonized one of the Cannibal Islands, and remained upon it with the colony for nearly two years. The attempt to introduce agriculture into the island was a failure, and the enterprise was afterwards abandoned.

28*

On the evening of the third of October, it having been announced that Commodore Stockton would land on the fifth, a public meeting of the citizens was called by the alcalde, for the purpose of adopting suitable arrangements for his reception, in his civic capacity as governor. The meeting was convened in the *plaza*, (Portsmouth-square.)   Col. Russell was appointed chairman, and on motion of E. Bryant a committee was appointed to make all necessary and suitable arrangements for the reception of his excellency, Governor Stockton. The following account of this pageant I extract from the " Californian" newspaper of October 24th, 1846.

" Agreeable to public notice, a large number of the citizens of San Francisco and vicinity, assembled in Portsmouth-square for the purpose of meeting His Excellency Robert F. Stockton, to welcome his arrival, and offer him the hospitalities of the city.   At ten o'clock, a procession was formed, led by the Chief Marshal of the day, supported on either hand by two aids, followed by an excellent band of music—a military escort, under command of Captain J. Zeilen, U. S. M. C.—Captain John B. Montgomery and suite—Magistracy of the District, and the Orator of the day—Foreign Consuls—Captain John Paty, Senior Captain of the Hawanian Navy—Lieutenant-Commanding Ruducoff, Russian Navy, and Lieutenant-Commanding Bonnett, French Navy.   The procession was closed by the Committee of Arrangements, Captains of ships in port, and a long line of citizens.

" General Mariano Guadaloupe Valléjo, with several others who had held office under the late government, took their appropriate place in the line.

" The procession moved in fine style down Portsmouth-street to the landing, and formed a line in Water-street.   The Governor-General landed from his barge, and was met on the wharf by Captain John B. Montgomery, U. S. N., Judge W. A. Bartlett, and Marshal of the day, (Frank Ward,) who conducted him to the front of the line, and presented him to the procession, through the orator of the day, Colonel Russell, who addressed the Commodore."

When the governor and commander-in-chief had closed his reply, the procession moved through the principal streets and halted in front of Captain Leidesdorff's residence, where the governor and suite entered, and was presented to a number of ladies, who welcomed him to the shores of California. After which a large portion of the procession accompanied the governor, on horseback, to the mission of San Francisco Dolores, several miles in the country, and returned to an excellent collation prepared by the committee of arrangements, at the house of Captain Leidesdorff. After the cloth was removed, the usual number of regular toasts prepared by the committee of arrangements, and numerous volunteer sentiments by the members of the company, were drank with many demonstrations of enthusiasm, and several speeches were made. In response to a complimentary toast, Commodore Stockton made an eloquent address of an hour's length. The toasts given in English were translated into Spanish, and those given in Spanish were translated into English. A ball in honor of the occasion was given by the committee of arrangements in the evening, which was attended by all the ladies native and foreign in the town and vicinity, the naval officers attached to the three ships of war, and the captains of the merchant vessels lying in the harbor. So seductive were the festivities of the day and the pleasures of the dance, that they were not closed until a late hour of the night, or rather until an early hour in the morning.

Among the numerous vessels of many nations at anchor in the harbor, is a Russian brig from Sitca, the central port of the Russian-American Fur Company, on the northwestern coast of this continent. She is commanded by Lieutenant Ruducoff of the Russian navy, and is here to be freighted with wheat to supply that settlement with breadstuff. Sitca is situated in a high northern latitude, and has a population of some four or five thousand inhabitants. A large portion of these, I conjecture, are christianized natives or Indians. Many of the crew of this vessel are the aborigines of the country to which she belongs, and from which she last sailed. I noticed, however, from an inscription, that the brig was built at Newbury-

port, Massachusetts, showing that the autocrat of all the
Russias is tributary, to some extent, to the free Yankees of
New England for his naval equipment. On the 11th of October, by invitation of Lieutenant Ruducoff, in company of Mr.
Jacob and Captain Leidesdorff, I dined on board this vessel. The
Russian customs are in some respects peculiar. Soon after
we reached the vessel and were shown into the cabin, a lunch
was served up. This consisted of a variety of dried and smoked
fish, pickled fish-roe, and other hyperborean pickles, the nature
of which, whether animal cr vegetable, I could not determine.
Various wines and liquors accompanied this lunch, the discussion of which lasted until an Indian servant, a native of the
north-pole, or thereabouts, announced dinner. We were then
shown into a handsomely-furnished dining cabin, where the table was spread.   The dinner consisted of several courses, some
of which were peculiarly Russian or Sitcan, and I regret that my
culinary knowledge is not equal to the task of describing them,
for the benefit of epicures of a more southern region than the
place of their invention.   They were certainly very delightful to
the palate.   The afternoon glided away most agreeably.

On the 12th of October, Captain Fremont, with a number
of volunteers destined for the south, to co-operate with Commodore Stockton in the suppression of the reported rebellion at
Los Angeles, arrived at San Francisco from the Sacramento. I
had previously offered my services, and Mr. Jacob had done the
same, to Commodore Stockton, as volunteers in this expedition,
if they were necessary or desirable.   They were now repeated.
Although travellers in the country, we were American citizens,
and felt under obligations to assist in defending the flag of our
country wherever it had teen planted by proper authority.
At this time we were given to understand that a larger force
than was already organized, was not considered necessary for
the expedition.

CHAPTER XXVII.

OCTOBER 13.—This morning the United States frigate Congress, Commodore Stockton, and the merchant-ship Sterling, employed to transport the volunteers under the command of Captain Fremont, (one hundred and eighty in number,) sailed for the south. The destination of these vessels was understood to be San Pedro or San Diego. While these vessels were leaving the harbor, accompanied by Mr. Jacob, I took passage for Sonoma in a cutter belonging to the sloop-of-war Portsmouth. Sonoma is situated on the northern side of the Bay of San Francisco, about 15 miles from the shore, and about 45 miles from the town of San Francisco. Sonoma creek is navigable for vessels of considerable burden to within four miles of the town.

Among the passengers in the boat, were Mr. Ide, who acted so conspicuous a part in what is called the "Bear Revolution," and Messrs. Nash and Grigsby, who were likewise prominent in this movement. The boat was manned by six sailors and a cockswain. We passed Yerba Buena, Bird, and several other small islands in the bay. Some of these are white, as if covered with snow, from the deposite upon them of bird-manure. Tens of thousands of wild geese, ducks, gulls, and other water-fowls were perched upon them, or sporting in the waters of the bay, making a prodigious cackling and clatter with their voices and wings. By the aid of oars and sails we reached the mouth of Sonoma creek about 9 o'clock at night, where we landed and encamped on the low marsh which borders the bay on this side. The marshes contiguous to the Bay of San Francisco are extensive, and with little trouble I believe they could be reclaimed and transformed into valuable and productive rice plantations. Having made our supper on raw salt-pork and bread generously furnished by the sailors, as soon as we landed, we spread our blankets on the damp and rank vegetation, and slept soundly until morning.

October 14.—Wind and tide being favorable, at daylight we proceeded up the serpentine creek, which winds through a flat and fertile plain, sometimes marshy, at others more elevated and dry, to the *embarcadero*, ten or twelve miles from the bay. We landed here between nine and ten o'clock, A. M. All the passengers, except ourselves, proceeded immediately to the town. By them we sent for a cart to transport our saddles, bridles, blankets, and other baggage, which we had brought with us. While some of the sailors were preparing breakfast, others, with their muskets, shot wild geese, with which the plain was covered. An excellent breakfast was prepared in a short time by our sailor companions, of which we partook with them. No benevolent old gentleman provides more bountifully for his servants than " Uncle Sam." These sailors, from the regular rations served out to them from their ship, gave an excellent breakfast, of bread, butter, coffee, tea, fresh beefsteaks, fried salt-pork, cheese, pickles, and a variety of other delicacies, to which we had been unaccustomed for several months, and which cannot be obtained at present in this country. They all said that their rations were more than ample in quantity, and excellent in quality, and that no government was so generous in supplying its sailors as the government of the United States. They appeared to be happy, and contented with their condition and service ; and animated with a patriotic pride for the honor of their country, and the flag under which they sailed. The open frankness, and honest patriotism of these single-hearted and weather-beaten tars, gave a spice and flavor to our entertainment which I shall not soon forget.

From the *embarcadero* we walked, under the influence of the rays of an almost broiling sun, four miles to the town of Sonoma.

The plain which lies between the landing and Sonoma, is timbered sparsely with evergreen oaks. The luxuriant grass is now
brown and crisp. The hills surrounding this beautiful valley or
plain, are gentle, sloping, highly picturesque, and covered to
their tops with wild oats. Reaching Sonoma, we procured
lodgings in a large and half-finished adobe house, erected by
Don Salvador Valléjo, but now occupied by Mr. Griffith, an
American emigrant, originally from North Carolina. Sonoma
is one of the old mission establishments of California; but there
is now scarcely a mission building standing, most of them having
fallen into shapeless masses of mud; and a few years will prostrate the roofless walls which are now standing. The principal
houses in the place are the residences of Gen. Don Mariano
Guadaloupe Valléjo, his brother-in-law, Mr. J. P. Leese, an
American, and his brother, Don Salvador Valléjo. The quartel,
a barn-like adobe house, faces the public square. The town
presents a most dull and ruinous appearance; but the country
surrounding it is exuberantly fertile, and romantically picturesque,
and Sonoma, under American authority, and with an American
population, will very soon become a secondary commercial point,
and a delightful residence. Most of the buildings are erected
around a *plaza*, about two hundred yards square. The only
ornaments in this square are numerous skulls and dislocated
skeletons of slaughtered beeves, with which hideous remains the
ground is strewn. Cold and warm springs gush from the hills
near the town, and supply, at all seasons, a sufficiency of water
to irrigate any required extent of ground on the plain below. I
noticed outside of the square several groves of peach, and other
fruit-trees, and vineyards, which were planted here by the
padres; but the walls and fences that once surrounded them
are now fallen, or have been consumed for fuel; and they are
exposed to the *mercies* of the immense herds of cattle which
roam over and graze upon the plain.

October 15.—I do not like to trouble the reader with a frequent reference to the myriads of fleas and other vermin which
infest the rancherias and old mission establishments in California;
but if any sinning soul ever suffered the punishments of purga-

tory before leaving its tenement of clay, those torments were endured by myself last night. When I rose from my blankets this morning, after a sleepless night, I do not think there was an inch-square of my body that did not exhibit the inflammation consequent upon a puncture by a flea, or some other equally rabid and poisonous insect. Smallpox, erysipelas, measles, and scarlet-fever combined, could not have imparted to my skin a more inflamed and sanguineous appearance. The multitudes of these insects, however, have been generated by Indian filthiness. They do not disturb the inmates of those *casas* where cleanliness prevails.

Having letters of introduction to General Valléjo and Mr. Leese, I delivered them this morning. General Valléjo is a native Californian, and a gentleman of intelligence and taste far superior to most of his countrymen. The interior of his house presented a different appearance from any house occupied by native Californians which I have entered since I have been in the country. Every apartment, even the main entrance-hall and corridors, were scrupulously clean, and presented an air of comfort which I have not elsewhere seen in California. The parlor was furnished with handsome chairs, sofas, mirrors, and tables, of mahogany framework, and a fine piano, the first I have seen in the country. Several paintings and some superior engravings ornamented the walls. Señora Valléjo is a lady of charming personal appearance, and possesses in the highest degree that natural grace, ease, and warmth of manners which render Spanish ladies so attractive and fascinating to the stranger. The children, some five or six in number, were all beautiful and interesting. General V. is, I believe, strongly desirous that the United States shall retain and annex California. He is thoroughly disgusted with Mexican sway, which is fast sending his country backwards, instead of forwards, in the scale of civilization, and for years he has been desirous of the change which has now taken place.

In the afternoon we visited the house of Mr. Leese, which is also furnished in American style. Mr. L. is the proprietor of a vineyard in the vicinity of the town, and we were regaled upon grapes, as luscious, I dare say, as the forbidden fruit that provoked the first transgression. Nothing of the fruit kind can exceed the delicious richness and flavor of the California grape.

This evening Thomas O. Larkin, Esq., late United States Consul for California, arrived here, having left San Francisco on the same morning that we did, travelling by land. Mr. L. resides in Monterey, but I had the pleasure of an introduction to him at San Francisco several days previous to my leaving that place. Mr. L. is a native of Boston, and has been a resident in California for about fifteen years, during which time he has amassed a large fortune, and from the changes now taking place he is rapidly increasing it. He will probably be the first American millionaire of California.

October 17.—The last two mornings have been cloudy and cool. The rainy season, it is thought by the weather-wise in this climate, will set in earlier this year than usual. The periodical rains ordinarily commence about the middle of November. It is now a month earlier, and the meteorological phenomena portend "falling weather." The rains during the winter, in California, are not continuous, as is generally supposed. It sometimes rains during an entire day, without cessation; but most generally the weather is showery, with intervals of bright sunshine and a delightful temperature. The first rains of the year fall usually in November, and the last about the middle of May. As soon as the ground becomes moistened, the grass, and other hardy vegetation, springs up, and by the middle of December the landscape is arrayed in a robe of fresh verdure. The grasses grow through the entire winter, and most of them mature by the first of May. The season for sowing wheat commences as soon as the ground is sufficiently softened by moisture to admit of plowing, and continues until March or April.

We had made preparations this morning to visit a rancho belonging to General Valléjo, in company with the general and Mr. Larkin. This rancho contains about eleven leagues of land, bordering upon a portion of the Bay of San Francisco, twenty-five or thirty miles distant from Sonoma. Just as we were

29

about mounting our horses, however, a courier arrived from San Francisco with dispatches from Captain Montgomery, addressed to Lieutenant Revere, the military commandant at this post, giving such intelligence in regard to the insurrection at the south, that we determined to return to San Francisco forthwith. Procuring horses, and accompanied by Mr. Larkin, we left Sonoma about two o'clock in the afternoon, riding at the usual California speed. After leaving Sonoma plain we crossed a ridge of hills, and entered the fertile and picturesque valley of Petaluma creek, which empties into the bay. General Valléjo has an extensive rancho in this valley, upon which he has recently erected, at great expense, a very large house. Architecture, however, in this country is in its infancy. The money expended in erecting this house, which presents to the eye no tasteful architectural attractions, would in the United States have raised a palace of symmetrical proportions, and adorned it with every requisite ornament. Large herds of cattle were grazing in this valley.

From Petaluma valley we crossed a high rolling country, and reached the mission of San Rafael (forty-five miles) between seven and eight o'clock in the evening. San Rafael is situated two or three miles from the shore of the bay, and commands an extensive view of the bay and its islands. The mission buildings are generally in the same ruinous condition I have before described. We put up at the house of a Mr. Murphy, a scholastic Irish bachelor, who has been a resident of California for a number of years. His *casa*, when we arrived, was closed, and it was with some difficulty that we could gain admission. When the occupant of the house had ascertained, from one of the loopholes of the building, who we were, however, the doors were soon unbarred and we were admitted, but not without many sallies of Irish wit, sometimes good-natured, and sometimes keenly caustic and ironical. We found a table spread with cold mutton and cold beef upon it. A cup of coffee was soon prepared by the Indian muchachos and muchachas, and our host brought out some scheidam and *aguardiénte*. A draught or two of these liquids seemed to correct the acidity of his humor, and he entertained us with his jokes and conversation several hours.

October 18.—From San Rafael to Sausolito, opposite San Francisco on the north side of the entrance to the bay, it is five leagues, (fifteen miles,) generally over elevated hills and through deep hollows, the ascents and descents being frequently steep and laborious to our animals. Starting at half-past seven o'clock, we reached the residence of Captain Richardson, the proprietor of Sausolito, about nine o'clock in the morning. In travelling this distance we passed some temporary houses, erected by American emigrants on the mission lands, and the rancho of Mrs. Reed, a widow. We immediately hired a whale-boat from one of the ships lying here, at two dollars for each passenger, and between ten and eleven o'clock we landed in San Francisco.

I met, soon after my arrival, Mr. Lippincott, heretofore mentioned, who accompanied us a portion of the distance over the mountains; and Mr. Hastings, who, with Mr. Hudspeth, conducted a party of the emigrants from Fort Bridger by the new route, *via* the south end of the Salt lake, to Mary's river. From Mr. Lippincott I learned the particulars of an engagement between a party of the emigrants (Captain West's company) and the Indians on Mary's river, which resulted, as has before been stated, in the death of Mr. Sallee and a dangerous arrow wound to Mr. L. He had now, however, recovered from the effects of the wound. The emigrants which accompanied Messrs. Hastings and Hudspeth, or followed their trail, had all reached the valley of the Sacramento without any material loss or disaster.

I remained at San Francisco from the 18th to the 22d of October. The weather during this time was sufficiently cool to render fires necessary to comfort in the houses; but fireplaces or stoves are luxuries which but few of the San Franciscans have any knowledge of, except in their kitchens. This deficiency, however, will soon be remedied. American settlers here will not build houses without chimneys. They would as soon plan a house without a door, or with the entrance upon its roof, in imitation of the architecture of the Pueblo Indians of New Mexico.

CHAPTER XXVIII.

Boat trip up the bay and the Sacramento to New Helvetia—An appeal to the alcalde—Kanackas—Straits of San Pueblo and Pedro—Straits of Carquinez—Town of Francisca—Feather-beds furnished by nature—Mouth of the Sacramento—Islands—Delaware Tom—A man who has forgotten his mother tongue—Salmon of the Sacramento—Indian fishermen—Arrive at New Helvetia.

OCTOBER 22.—Having determined to make a trip to Nueva Helvetia by water, for the purpose of examining more particularly the upper portion of the bay and the Sacramento river, in conjunction with Mr. Larkin, we chartered a small open sail-boat for the excursion. The charter, to avoid disputes, was regularly drawn and signed, with all conditions specified. The price to be paid for a certain number of passengers was thirty-two dollars, and demurrage at the rate of twenty-five cents per hour for all delays ordered by the charter-party, on the trip upwards to Nueva Helvetia. The boat was to be ready at the most convenient landing at seven o'clock this morning, but when I called at the place appointed, with our baggage, the boat was not there. In an hour or two the skipper was found, but refused to comply with his contract. We immediately laid our grievance before the alcalde, who, after reading the papers and hearing the statements on both sides, ordered the skipper to perform what he had agreed to perform, to which decision he reluctantly assented. In order to facilitate matters, I paid the costs of the action myself, although the successful litigant in the suit.

We left San Francisco about two o'clock, P. M., and crossing the mouth of the bay, boarded a Mexican schooner, a prize captured by the U. S. sloop-of-war Cyane, Captain Dupont, which had entered the bay this morning and anchored in front of Sausolito. The prize is commanded by Lieutenant Renshaw, a gallant officer of our navy. Our object in boarding the schooner was to learn the latest news, but she did not bring much. We met on board the schooner Lieutenant Hunter of the Portsmouth, a chivalrous officer, and Lieutenant Ruducoff, commanding the Russian brig previously mentioned, whose vessel, preparatory to sailing, was taking in water at Sausolito. Accepting of his pressing invitation, we visited the brig, and took a parting glass of wine with her gallant and gentlemanly commander.

About five o'clock, P. M., we proceeded on our voyage. At eight o'clock a dense fog hung over the bay, and the ebb-tide being adverse to our progress, we were compelled to find a landing for our small and frail craft. This was not an easy matter, in the almost impenetrable darkness. As good luck would have it, however, after we had groped about for some time, a light was discovered by our skipper. He rowed the boat towards it, but grounded. Hauling off, he made another attempt with better success, reaching within hailing distance of the shore. The light proceeded from a camp-fire of three Kanacka (Sandwich island) runaway sailors. As soon as they ascertained who we were and what we wanted, they stripped themselves naked, and wading through the mud and water to the boat, took us on their shoulders, and carried us high and dry to the land. The boat being thus lightened of her burden, was rowed farther up and landed.

The natives of the Sandwich islands (Kanackas, as they are called) are, without doubt, the most expert watermen in the world. Their performances in swimming and diving are so extraordinary, that they may almost be considered amphibious in their natures and instincts. Water appears to be as much their natural element as the land. They have straight black hair, good features, and an amiable and intelligent expression of countenance. Their complexion resembles that of a bright mulatto; and in symmetrical proportions and muscular developments, they will advantageously compare with any race of men I have seen. The crews of many of the whale and merchant ships on this coast are partly composed of Kanackas, and they are justly esteemed as most valuable sailors.

October 23.—The damp, raw weather, auguring the near approach of the autumnal rains, continues. A drizzling mist fell on us during the night, and the clouds were not dissipated when we resumed our voyage this morning. Passing through the straits of San Pablo and San Pedro, we entered a division of the bay called the Bay of San Pablo. Wind and tide being in our favor, we crossed this sheet of water, and afterwards entered and passed through the straits of *Carquinez*. At these straits the waters of the bay are compressed within the breadth of a mile, for the distance of about two leagues. On the southern side the shore is hilly, and *cañoned* in some places. The northern shore is gentle, the hills and table-land sloping gradually down to the water. We landed at the bend of the straits of *Carquinez*, and spent several hours in examining the country and soundings on the northern side. There is no timber here. The soil is covered with a growth of grass and wild oats. The bend of the straits of Carquinez, on the northern side, has been thought to be a favorable position for a commercial town. It has some advantages and some disadvantages, which it would be tedious for me now to detail.

[Subsequently to this my first visit here, a town of extensive dimensions has been laid off by Gen. Valléjo and Mr. Semple, the proprietors, under the name of "FRANCISCA." It fronts for two or three miles on the "*Soeson*," the upper division of the Bay of San Francisco, and the straits of Carquinez. A ferry has also been established, which crosses regularly from shore to shore, conveying travellers over the bay. I crossed, myself and horses, here in June, 1847, when on my return to the United States. Lots had then been offered to settlers on favorable conditions, and preparations, I understood, were making for the erection of a number of houses.]

About sunset, we resumed our voyage. The wind having lulled, we attempted to stem the adverse tide by the use of oars, but the ebb of the tide was stronger than the propelling force of our oars. Soon, in spite of all our exertions, we found ourselves drifting rapidly backwards, and after two or three hours of hard labor in the dark, we were, at last, so fortunate as to effect a landing in a cove on the southern side of the straits, having retrograded several miles. In the cove there is a small sandy beach, upon which the waves have drifted and deposited a large quantity of oat-straw, and feathers shed by the millions of water-fowls which sport upon the bay. On this downy deposite furnished by nature, we spread our blankets, and slept soundly.

October 24.—We proceeded on our voyage at daylight, coasting along the southern shore of the *Soeson.* About nine o'clock we landed on a marshy plain, and cooked breakfast. A range of mountains bounds this plain, the base of which is several miles from the shore of the bay. These mountains, although of considerable elevation, exhibit signs of fertility to their summits. On the plain, numerous herds of wild cattle were grazing. About two o'clock, P. M., we entered the mouth of the Sacramento. The Sacramento and San Joaquin rivers empty into the Bay of San Francisco at the same point, about sixty miles from the Pacific, and by numerous mouths, or *sloughs* as they are here called. These sloughs wind through an immense timbered swamp, and constitute a terraqueous labyrinth of such intricacy, that unskilful and inexperienced navigators have been lost for many days in it, and some, I have been told, have perished, never finding their way out. A range of low sloping hills approach the Sacramento a short distance above its mouth, on the left-hand side as you ascend, and run parallel with the stream several miles. The banks of the river, and several large islands which we passed during the day, are timbered with sycamore, oak, and a variety of smaller trees and shrubbery. Numerous grape-vines, climbing over the trees, and loaded down with a small and very acid fruit, give to the forest a tangled appearance. The islands of the Sacramento are all low, and subject to overflow in the spring of the year. The soil of the river bottom, including the islands, is covered with rank vegetation, a certain evidence of its fertility. The water, at this season, is perfectly limpid, and although the tide ebbs and flows more than a hundred miles above the mouth of the river, it is fresh and sweet. The channel of the Sacramento is remarkably free from snags and other obstructions to navigation. A more beautiful and placid stream of water I never saw.

At twelve o'clock at night, the ebb tide being so strong that we found ourselves drifting backwards, with some difficulty we effected a landing on one of the islands, clearing a way through the tangled brush and vines with our hatchets and knives. Lighting a fire, we bivouacked until daylight.

October 25.—Continuing our voyage, we landed about nine o'clock, A. M., at an Indian *rancheria*, situated on the bank of the river. An old Indian, his wife, and two or three children, were all the present occupants of this *rancheria*. The woman was the most miserable and emaciated object I ever beheld. She was probably a victim of the " sweat-house." Surrounding the *rancheria* were two or three acres of ground, planted with maize, beans, and melons. Purchasing a quantity of water and muskmelons, we re-embarked and pursued our voyage. As we ascended the stream the banks became more elevated, the country on both sides opening into vast savannas, dotted occasionally with parks of evergreen oak.

The tide turning against us again about eleven or twelve o'clock, we landed at an encampment of Walla-Walla Indians, a portion of the party previously referred to, and reported to have visited California for hostile purposes. Among them was a Delaware Indian, known as " Delaware Tom," who speaks English as fluently as any Anglo-Saxon, and is a most gallant and honorable Indian. Several of the party, a majority of whom were women and children, were sick with chills and fever. The men were engaged in hunting and jerking deer and elk meat. Throwing our hooks, baited with fresh meat, into the river, we soon drew out small fish enough for dinner.

The specimens of Walla-Wallas at this encampment are far superior to the Indians of California in features, figure, and intelligence. Their complexion is much lighter, and their features more regular, expressive, and pleasing. Men and women were clothed in dressed skins. The men were armed with rifles.

At sunset we put our little craft in motion again, and at one o'clock at night landed near the cabin of a German emigrant named Schwartz, six miles below the *embarcadero* of New Helvetia. The cabin is about twenty feet in length by twelve in breadth, constructed of a light, rude frame, shingled with *tule*. After gaining admission, we found a fire blazing in the centre of the dwelling on the earth-floor, and suspended over us were as many salmon, taken from the Sacramento, as could be placed in position to imbibe the preservative qualities of the smoke.

Our host, Mr. Schwartz, is one of those eccentric human phenomena rarely met with, who, wandering from their own nation into foreign countries, forget their own language without acquiring any other. He speaks a tongue (language it cannot be called) peculiar to himself, and scarcely intelligible. It is a mixture, in about equal parts, of German, English, French, Spanish, and *rancheria* Indian, a compounded polyglot or lingual *pi*—each syllable of a word sometimes being derived from a different language. Stretching ourselves on the benches surrounding the fire, so as to avoid the drippings from the pendent salmon, we slept until morning.

October 26.—Mr. Schwartz provided us with a breakfast of fried salmon and some fresh milk. Coffee, sugar, and bread we brought with us, so that we enjoyed a luxurious repast.

Near the house was a shed containing some forty or fifty barrels of pickled salmon, but the fish, from their having been badly put up, were spoiled. Mr. Schwartz attempted to explain the particular causes of this, but I could not understand him. The salmon are taken with seines dragged across the channel of the river by Indians in canoes. On the bank of the river the Indians were eating their breakfast, which consisted of a large fresh salmon, roasted in the ashes or embers, and a kettle of *atóle*, made of acorn-meal. The salmon was four or five feet in length, and when taken out of the fire and cut open, presented a most tempting appearance. The Indians were all nearly naked, and most of them having been wading in the water at daylight to set their seines, were shivering with the cold whilst greedily devouring their morning meal.

We reached the *embarcadero* of New Helvetia about eleven o'clock, A. M., and finding there a wagon, we placed our baggage in it and walked to the fort, about two and a half miles.

CHAPTER XXIX.

Disastrous news from the south—Return of Colonel Fremont to Monterey— Call for volunteers—Volunteer our services—Leave New Helvetia— Swimming the Sacramento—First fall of rain—Beautiful and romantic valley—Precipitous mountains—Deserted house—Arable land of California—Fattening qualities of the acorn—Lost in the Coast Mountains— Strange Indians—Indian women gathering grass-seed for bread—Indian guide—Laguna—Rough dialogue—Hunters' camp—" Old Greenwood"— Grisly bear meat—Greenwood's account of himself—His opinion of the Indians and Spaniards—Retrace our steps—Severe storm—Nappa valley —Arrive at Sonoma—More rain—Arrive at San Francisco—Return to New Helvetia.

I REMAINED at the fort from the 27th to the 30th of October. On the 28th, Mr. Reed, whom I have before mentioned as belonging to the rear emigrating party, arrived here. He left his party on Mary's river, and in company with one man crossed the desert and the mountains. He was several days without provisions, and when he arrived at Johnson's, was so much emaciated and exhausted by fatigue and famine, that he could scarcely walk. His object was to procure provisions immediately, and to transport them with pack-mules over the mountains for the relief of the suffering emigrants behind. He had lost all of his cattle, and had been compelled to *cache* two of his wagons and most of his property. Captain Sutter generously furnished the requisite quantity of mules and horses, with Indian vaqueros, and jerked meat, and flour. This is the second expedition for the relief of the emigrants he has fitted out since our arrival in the country. Ex-governor Boggs and family reached Sutter's Fort to-day.

On the evening of the 28th, a courier arrived with letters from Colonel Fremont, now at Monterey. The substance of the intelligence received by the courier was, that a large force of Californians (varying, according to different reports, from five to fifteen hundred strong) had met the marines and sailors, four hundred strong, under the command of Captain Mervine, of the U. S. frigate Savannah, who had landed at San Pedro for the purpose of marching to Los Angeles, and had driven Captain Mervine and his force back to the ship, with the loss, in killed, of six men. That the towns of Angeles and Santa Barbara had been taken by the insurgents, and the American garrisons there had either been captured or had made their escape by retreating. What had become of them was unknown.* Colonel Fremont, who I before mentioned had sailed with a party of one hundred and eighty volunteers from San Francisco to San Pedro, or San Diego, for the purpose of co-operating with Commodore Stockton, after having been some time at sea, had put into Monterey and landed his men, and his purpose now was to increase his force and mount them, and to proceed by land to Los Angeles.

On the receipt of this intelligence, I immediately drew up a paper which was signed by myself, Messrs. Reed, Jacob, Lippincott, and Grayson, offering our services as volunteers, and our exertions to raise a force of emigrants and Indians which would be a sufficient reinforcement to Colonel Fremont. This paper was addressed to Mr. Kern, the commandant of Fort Sacramento, and required his sanction. The next morning (29th) he accepted of our proposal, and the labor of raising the volunteers and of procuring the necessary clothing and supplies for them and the Indians was apportioned.

It commenced raining on the night of the twenty-eighth, and

* The garrison under Captain Gillespie, at Los Angeles, capitulated. The garrison at Santa Barbara, under Lieutenant Talbot, marched out in defiance of the enemy, and after suffering many hardships arrived in safety at Monterey.

the rain fell heavily and steadily until twelve o'clock, M., on the twenty-ninth. This is the first fall of rain since March last. About one o'clock, P. M., the clouds cleared away and the weather and temperature were delightful.

About twelve o'clock, on the 30th, accompanied by Mr. Grayson, I left New Helvetia. We crossed the Sacramento at the *embarcadero,* swimming our horses, and passing ourselves over in a small canoe. The method of swimming horses over so broad a stream as the Sacramento is as follows. A light canoe, or " dug-out," is manned by three persons, one at the bow, one at the stern, and one in the centre; those at the bow and stern have paddles, and propel and steer the craft. The man in the centre holds the horses one on each side, keeping their heads out of water. When the horses are first forced into the deep water they struggle prodigiously, and sometimes upset the canoe; but when the canoe gets fairly under way, they cease their resistance, but snort loudly at every breath to clear their mouths and nostrils of the water.

Proceeding ten miles over a level plain, we overtook a company of emigrants bound for Nappa valley, and encamped with them for the night on Puta creek, a tributary of the Sacramento. Five of the seven or eight men belonging to the company enrolled their names as volunteers. The grass on the western side of the Sacramento is very rank and of an excellent quality.

It commenced raining about two o'clock on the morning of the 31st, and continued to rain and mist all day. We crossed from Puta to Cache creek, reaching the residence of Mr. Gordon (25 miles) about three o'clock, P. M. Here we enrolled several additional emigrants in our list of volunteers, and then travelled fifteen miles up the creek to a small log-house, occupied temporarily by some of the younger members of the family of Mr. Gordon, who emigrated from Jackson county, Mo., this year, and by Mrs. Grayson. Here we remained during the night, glad to find a shelter and a fire, for we were drenched to our skins.

On the morning of the 1st of November the sun shone out

warm and pleasant. The birds were singing, chattering, and flitting from tree to tree, through the romantic and picturesque valley where we had slept during the night. The scenery and its adjuncts were so charming and enticing that I recommenced my travels with reluctance. No scenery can be more beautiful than that of the small valleys of California. Ascending the range of elevated mountains which border the Cache creek, we had a most extensive view of the broad plain of the Sacramento, stretching with islands and belts of timber far away to the south as the eye could penetrate. The gorges and summits of these mountains are timbered with large pines, firs, and cedars, with a smaller growth of magnolias, manzanitas, hawthorns, etc., etc. Travelling several miles over a level plateau, we descended into a beautiful valley, richly carpeted with grass and timbered with evergreen oak. Proceeding across this three or four miles, we rose another range of mountains, and travelling a league along the summit ridge, we descended through a crevice in a steep rocky precipice, just sufficient in breadth to admit the passage of our animals. Our horses were frequently compelled to slide or leap down nearly perpendicular rocks or stairs, until we finally, just after sunset, reached the bottom of the mountain, and found ourselves in another level and most fertile and picturesque valley.

We knew that in this valley, of considerable extent, there was a house known as "Barnett's," where we expected to find quarters for the night. There were numerous trails of cattle, horses, deer, and other wild animals, crossing each other in every direction through the live-oak timber. We followed one of the largest of the cattle trails until it became so blind that we could not see it. Taking another, we did the same, and the result was the same : another and another, with no better success. We then shouted so loud that our voices were echoed and re-echoed by the surrounding mountains, hoping if there were any inhabitants in the valley, that they would respond to us. There was no response,—all was silent when the sound of our voices died away in the gorges and ravines ; and at ten o'clock at night we encamped under the wide-spreading branches of an oak, having travelled about 40 miles. Striking a fire and heaping upon it a large quantity of wood, which blazed brightly, displaying the gothic shapes of the surrounding oaks, we picketed our animals, spread our blankets, and slept soundly.

It rained several hours during the night, and in the morning a dense fog filled the valley. Saddling our animals, we searched along the foot of the next range of mountains for a trail, but could find none. Returning to our camp, we proceeded up the valley, and struck a trail, by following which two miles, we came to the house, (Barnett's.) The door was ajar, and entering the dwelling we found it tenantless. The hearth was cold, and the ashes in the·jambs of the large fireplace were baked. In the corners of the building there were some frames, upon which beds had been once spread. The house evidently had been abandoned by its former occupants for some time. The prolific mothers of several families of the swinish species, with their squealing progenies, gathered around us, in full expectation, doubtless, of the dispensation of an extra ration, which we had not to give. Having eaten nothing but a crust of bread for 24 hours, the inclination of our appetites was strong to draw upon them for a ration; but for old acquaintance sake, and because they were the foreshadowing of the "manifest destiny," they were permitted to pass without molestation. There were two or three small enclosures near the house, where corn and wheat had been planted and harvested this year; but none of the product of the harvest could be found in the empty house, or on the place. Dismounting from our horses at a limpid spring-branch near the house, we slaked our thirst, and made our hydropathical breakfast from its cool and delicious water.

Although the trail of the valley did not run in our course, still, under the expectation that it would soon take another direction, we followed it, passing over a fertile soil, sufficiently timbered and watered by several small streams. The quantity of arable land in California, I believe, is much greater than has generally been supposed from the accounts of the country given by travellers who have visited only the parts on the Pacific, and some few of the missions. Most of the mountain valleys between the Sierra Nevada and the coast are exuberantly fertile, and finely watered, and will produce crops of all kinds, while the hills are covered with oats and grass of the most nutritious qualities, for the sustenance of cattle, horses, and hogs. The acorns which fall from the oaks are, of themselves, a rich annual product for the fattening of hogs ; and during the period of transition (four or five weeks after the rains commence falling) from the dry grass to the fresh growth, horses, mules, and even horned cattle, mostly subsist and fatten upon these large and oleaginous nuts.

We left the valley in a warm and genial sunshine, about 11 o'clock, and commenced ascending another high mountain, timbered as those I have previously described. When we reached the summit we were enveloped in clouds, and the rain was falling copiously, and a wintry blast drove the cold element to our skins. Crossing this mountain three or four miles, we descended its steep sides, and entered another beautiful and romantic hollow, divided as it were into various apartments by short ranges of low conical hills, covered to their summits with grass and wild oats. The grass and other vegetation on the level bottom are very rank, indicating a soil of the most prolific qualities. In winding through this valley, we met four Indians on foot, armed with long bows, and arrows of corresponding weight and length, weapons that I have not previously seen among the Indians. Their complexions were lighter than those of the *rancheria* Indians of California. They evidently belonged to some more northern tribe. We stopped them to make inquiries, but they seemed to know nothing of the country, nor could we learn from them from whence they came or where they were going. They were clothed in dressed skins, and two of them were highly rouged.

Ascending and descending gradually over some low hills, we entered another circular valley, through which flows a stream, the waters of which, judging from its channel, at certain seasons are broad and deep. The ground, from the rains that have recently fallen and are now falling, is very soft, and we had difficulty in urging our tired animals across this valley. We soon discovered fresh cattle signs, and afterwards a large herd grazing near the stream.   Farther on, we saw five old and miserably emaciated Indian women, gathering grass-seed for bread.   This process is performed with two baskets, one shaped like a round shield, and the other having a basin and handle. With the shield the top of the grass is brushed, and the seed by the motion is thrown into the deep basket held in the other hand.   The five women appeared at a distance like so many mowers cutting down the grass of a meadow.   These women could give us no satisfaction in response to inquiries, but pointed over the river, indicating that we should there find the *casa* and *rancheria*.   They then continued their work with as much zeal and industry as if their lives were dependent upon the proceeds of their labor, and I suppose they were.

Crossing the river, we struck a trail which led us to the *casa* and *rancheria*, about two miles distant.   The *casa* was a small adobe building, about twelve feet square, and was locked up. Finding that admission was not to be gained here, we hailed at the *rancheria*, and presently some dozen squalid and naked men, women, and children made their appearance.   We inquired for the *mayor domo*, or overseer.   The chief speaker signified that he was absent, and that he did not expect him to return until several suns rose and set.   We then signified that we were hungry, and very soon a loaf made of pulverized acorns, mingled with wild fruit of some kind, was brought to us with a basket of water.   These Indians manufacture small baskets which are impervious to water, and they are used as basins to drink from, and for other purposes.

I knew that we had been travelling out of our course all day, and it was now three o'clock, P. M.   Rain and mist had succeeded each other, and the sun was hidden from us by dark and threatening masses of clouds.   We had no compass with us, and could not determine the course to Nappa valley or Sonoma.   Believing that the Indian would have some knowledge of the latter place, we made him comprehend that we wished to go there, and inquired the route.   He pointed in a direction which he signified would take us to Sonoma.   We pointed in another course, which it seemed to us was the right one. But he persisted in asserting that he was right. After some further talk, for the shirt on my back he promised to guide us, and placing a ragged skin on one of our horses, he mounted the animal and led the way over the next range of hills. The rain soon poured down so hard upon the poor fellow's bare skin, that he begged permission to return, to which we would not consent; but out of compassion to him, I took off my overcoat, with which he covered his swarthy hide, and seemed highly delighted with the shelter from the pitiless storm it afforded him, or with the supposition that I intended to present it to him.

Crossing several elevated and rocky hills, just before sunset, we had a view of a large timbered valley and a sheet of water, the extent of which we could not compass with the eye, on account of the thickness of the atmosphere. When we came in sight of the water, the Indian uttered various exclamations of pleasure; and although I had felt but little faith in him as a pilot from the first, I began now to think that we were approaching the Bay of San Francisco. Descending into the valley, we travelled along a small stream two or three miles, and were continuing on in the twilight, when we heard the tinkling of a cow-bell on the opposite side of the stream. Certain, from this sound, that there must be an encampment near, I halted and hallooed at the top of my voice. The halloo called forth a similar response, with an interrogation in English, "Who the d—l are you—Spaniards or Americans?" "Americans." "Show yourself, then, d—n you, and let us see the color of your hide," was the answer.

"Tell us where we can cross the stream and you shall soon see us," was our reply.

"Ride back and follow the sound of my voice, and be d—d to you, and you can cross the stream with a deer's jump."

Accordingly, following the sound of the voice of this rough colloquist, who shouted repeatedly, we rode back in the dark several hundred yards, and plunging into the stream, the channel of which was deep, we gained the other side, where we

30*

found three men standing ready to receive us. We soon dis-covered them to be a party of professional hunters or trappers, at the head of which was Mr. Greenwood, a famed mountaineer, commonly known as "Old Greenwood." They invited us to their camp, situated across a small opening in the timber about half a mile distant. Having unsaddled our tired animals and turned them loose to graze for the night, we placed our bag-gage under the cover of a small tent, and taking our seats by the huge camp-fire, made known as far as was expedient our business. We soon ascertained that we had ridden the entire day (about 40 miles) directly out of our course to Nappa val-ley and Sonoma, and that the Indian's information was all wrong. We were now near the shore of a large lake, called the *Laguna* by Californians, some fifty or sixty miles in length, which lake is situated about sixty or seventy miles north of the Bay of San Francisco; consequently, to-morrow we shall be com-pelled to retrace our steps and find the trail that leads from Barnett's house to Nappa, which escaped us this morning. We received such directions, however, from Mr. Greenwood, that we could not fail to find it.

We found in the camp, much to our gratification after a long fast, an abundance of fat, grisly bear-meat, and the most deli-cious and tender deer-meat. The camp looked like a butcher's stall. The pot filled with bear-flesh was boiled again and again, and the choice pieces of the tender venison were roasting, and disappearing with singular rapidity for a long time. Bread there was none of course. Such a delicacy is unknown to the mountain trappers, nor is it much desired by them.

The hunting party consisted of Mr. Greenwood, Mr. Turner, Mr. Adams, and three sons of Mr. G., one grown, and the other two boys 10 or 12 years of age, half-breed Indians, the mother being a Crow. One of these boys is named "Governor Boggs," after ex-governor Boggs of Missouri, an old friend of the fa-ther. Mr. Greenwood, or "Old Greenwood," as he is famil-iarly called, according to his own statement, is 83 years of age, and has been a mountain trapper between 40 and 50 years. He lived among the Crow Indians, where he married his wife, between thirty and forty years. He is about six feet in height, raw-boned and spare in flesh, but muscular, and notwithstanding his old age, walks with all the erectness and elasticity of youth. His dress was of tanned buckskin, and from its appearance one would suppose its antiquity to be nearly equal to the age of its wearer. It had probably never been off his body since he first put it on. " I am," said he, " an old man—eighty-three years— it is a long time to live;—eighty-three years last ——. I have seen all the Injun varmints of the Rocky Mountains,—have fout them—lived with them. I have many children—I don't know how many, they are scattered ; but my wife was a Crow. The Crows are a brave nation,—the bravest of all the Injuns ; they fight like the white man ; they don't kill you in the dark like the Black-foot varmint, and then take your scalp and run, the cowardly reptiles. Eighty-three years last —— ; and yet old Greenwood could handle the rifle as well as the best on 'em, but for this infernal humor in my eyes, caught three years ago in bringing the emigrators over the *de*-sart." (A circle of scarlet surrounded his weeping eyeballs.) " I can't see jist now as well as I did fifty years ago, but I can always bring the game or the slinking and skulking Injun. I have jist come over the mountains from Sweetwater with the emigrators as pilot, living upon bacon, bread, milk, and sich like mushy stuff. It don't agree with me; it never will agree with a man of my age, eighty-three last —— ; that is a long time to live. I thought I would take a small hunt to get a little exercise for my old bones, and some good fresh meat. The grisly bear, fat deer, and poultry, and fish—them are such things as a man should eat. I came up here where I knew there was plenty. I was here twenty years ago, before any white man see this lake and the rich land about it. It's filled with big fish. Thar's beer-springs here, better than them in the Rocky Mountains ; thar's a mountain of solid brimstone, and thar's mines of gold and silver, all of which I know'd many years ago, and I can show them to you if you will go with me in the morning. These black-skinned Spaniards have rebel'd again. Wall, they can make a fuss, d——m 'em, and have revolutions every year, but they can't fight. It's no use to go arter 'em, unless when you ketch 'em you kill 'em. They won't stand an' fight like men, an' when they can't fight longer give up; but the skared varmints run away and then make another fuss, d—m 'em." Such was the discourse of our host.

The camp consisted of two small tents, which had probably been obtained from the emigrants. They were pitched so as to face each other, and between them there was a large pile of blazing logs. On the trees surrounding the camp were stretched the skins of various animals which had been killed in the hunt; some preserved for their hides, others for the fur. Bear-meat and venison enough for a winter's supply were hanging from the limbs. The swearing of Turner, a man of immense frame and muscular power, during our evening's conversation, was almost terrific. I had heard mountain swearing before, but his went far beyond all former examples. He could do all the swearing for our army in Mexico, and then have a surplus.

The next morning, (Nov. 3d,) after partaking of a hearty breakfast, and suspending from our saddles a sufficient supply of venison and bear-meat for two day's journey, we started back on our own trail. We left our miserable Indian pilot at his *rancheria.* I gave him the shirt from my back, out of compassion for his sufferings,—he well deserved a *dressing* of another kind. It rained all day, and when we reached Barnett's (the empty house) about four o'clock, p. m., the black masses of clouds which hung over the valley portended a storm so furious, that we thought it prudent to take shelter under a roof for the night. Securing our animals in one of the enclosures, we encamped in the deserted dwelling. The storm soon commenced, and raged and roared with a fierceness and strength rarely witnessed. The hogs and pigs came squealing about the door for admission; and the cattle and horses in the valley, terrified by the violence of elemental battle, ran backwards and forwards, bellowing and snorting. In comfortable quarters, we roasted and enjoyed our bear-meat and venison, and left the wind, rain, lightning, and thunder to play their pranks as best suited them, which they did all night.

On the morning of the fourth, we found the trail described to us by Mr. Greenwood, and crossing a ridge of mountains, descended into the valley of Nappa creek, which empties into the Bay of San Francisco just below the straits of Carquinez. This is a most beautiful and fertile valley, and is already occupied by several American settlers. Among the first who established themselves here is Mr. Yount, who soon after erected a flouring-mill and saw-mill. These have been in operation several years. Before reaching Mr. Yount's settlement we passed a saw-mill more recently erected, by Dr. Bale. There seems to be an abundance of pine and red-wood (a species of fir) in the *cañadas*. No lumber can be superior for building purposes than that sawed from the red-wood. The trees are of immense size, straight, free from knots and twists, and the wood is soft, and easily cut with plane and saw. Arriving at the residence of Dr. Bale, in Nappa valley, we were hospitably entertained by him, with a late breakfast of coffee, boiled eggs, steaks, and *tortillas*, served up in American style. Leaving Nappa, after travelling down it some ten or twelve miles, we crossed another range of hills or mountains, and reached Sonoma after dark, our clothing thoroughly drenched with the rain, which, with intermissions, had fallen the whole day. I put up at the same quarters as when here before. The house was covered with a dilapidated thatch, and the rain dripped through it, not leaving a dry spot on the floor of the room where we slept. But there was an advantage in this,—the inundation of water had completely discomfited the army of fleas that infested the building when we were here before.

It rained incessantly on the fifth. Col. Russell arrived at Sonoma early in the morning, having arrived from San Francisco last night. Procuring a boat belonging to Messrs. Howard & Mellus, lying at the *embarcadero*, I left for San Francisco, but owing to the storm, and contrary winds, did not arrive there until the morning of the seventh, being two nights and a day in the creek, and *churning* on the bay. Purchasing a quantity of clothing, and other supplies for volunteers, I sailed early on the morning of the eighth for New Helvetia, in a boat belonging to the sloop-of-war Portsmouth, manned by U. S. sailors, under the command of Midshipman Byres, a native of Maysville, Ky. We encamped that night at the head of "Seeson," having sailed about fifty miles in a severe storm of wind and rain. The waves frequently dashed entirely over our little craft. The rain continued during the ninth, and we encamped at night above the mouth of the Sacramento. On the night of the tenth we encamped at "Merritt's camp," the rain still falling, and the river rising rapidly, rendering navigation up-stream impossible, except with the aid of the tide. On the night of the eleventh we encamped fifteen miles below New Helvetia, still raining. On the morning of the twelfth the clouds cleared away, and the sun burst out warm and spring-like. After having been exposed to the rain for ten or twelve days, without having the clothing upon me once dry, the sight of the sun, and the influence of his beams, were cheering and most agreeable. We arrived at New Helvetia about twelve o'clock.

CHAPTER XXX.

Leave New Helvetia—Pleasant weather—Meet Indian volunteers—Tuleboats—Engagement between a party of Americans and Californians—Death of Capt. Burroughs and Capt. Foster—Capture of Thomas O. Larkin—Reconnaissance—San Juan Bautista—Neglect of the dead—Large herds of cattle—Join Col. Fremont.

On my arrival at New Helvetia, I found there Mr. Jacob. Mr. Reed had not yet returned from the mountains. Nothing had been heard from Mr. Lippincott, or Mr. Grayson, since I left the latter at Sonoma. An authorized agent of Col. Fremont had arrived at the fort the day that I left it, with power to take the *caballada* of public horses, and to enroll volunteers for the expedition to the south. He had left two or three days before my arrival, taking with him all the horses and trappings suitable for service, and all the men who had previously *rendezvoused* at the fort, numbering about sixty, as I understood. At my request messengers were sent by Mr. Kern, commandant of the fort, and by Captain Sutter, to the Indian chiefs on the San Joaquin river and its tributaries, to meet me at the most convenient points on the trail, with such warriors of their tribes as chose to volunteer as soldiers of the United States, and perform military service during the campaign. I believed that they would be useful as scouts and spies. On the 14th and 15th eight men (emigrants who had just arrived in the country, and had been enrolled at Johnson's settlement by Messrs. Reed and Jacob) arrived at the fort; and on the morning of the 16th, with these, we started to join Colonel Fremont, supposed to be at Monterey; and we encamped at night on the Cosçumne river.

The weather is now pleasant. We are occasionally drenched with a shower of rain, after which the sun shines warm and bright; the fresh grass is springing up, and the birds sing and chatter in the groves and thickets as we pass through them. I rode forward, on the morning of the 17th, to the Michelemes river, (twenty-five miles from the Cosçumne,) where I met Antonio, an Indian chief, with twelve warriors, who had assembled here for the purpose of joining us. The names of the warriors were as follows :—Santiago, Masua, Kiubu, Tocoso, Nonelo, Michael, Weala, Arkell, Nicolas, Heel, Kasheano, Estephen. Our party coming up in the afternoon, we encamped here for the day, in order to give the Indians time to make further preparations for the march. On the 18th we met, at the ford of the San Joaquin river, another party of eighteen Indians, including their chiefs. Their names were—José Jesus, Filipe, Raymundo, and Carlos, chiefs; Huligario, Bonefasio, Francisco, Nicolas, Pablo, Feliciano, San Antonio, Polinario, Manuel, Graviano, Salinordio, Romero, and Merikeeldo, warriors. The chiefs and some of the warriors of these parties were partially clothed, but most of them were naked, except a small garment around the loins. They were armed with bows and arrows. We encamped with our sable companions on the east bank of the San Joaquin.

The next morning (Nov. 19) the river being too high to ford, we constructed, by the aid of the Indians, tule-boats, upon which our baggage was ferried over the stream. The tule-boat consists of bundles of tule firmly bound together with willow withes. When completed, in shape it is not unlike a small keel-boat. The buoyancy of one of these craft is surprising. Six men, as many as could sit upon the deck, were passed over, in the largest of our three boats, at a time. The boats were towed backwards and forwards by Indian swimmers—one at the bow, and one at the stern as steersman, and two on each side as propellers. The poor fellows, when they came out of the cold water, trembled as if attacked with an ague. We encamped near the house of Mr. Livermore, (previously described,) where, after considerable difficulty, I obtained sufficient beef for supper, Mr. L. being absent. Most of the Indians did not get into camp until a late hour of the night, and some of them not until morning. They complained very much of sore feet, and wanted horses to ride, which I promised them as soon as they reached the Pueblo de San José.

About ten o'clock on the morning of the 20th, we slaughtered a beef in the hills between Mr. Livermore's and the mission of San José; and leaving the hungry party to regale themselves upon it and then follow on, I proceeded immediately to the Pueblo de San José to make further arrangements, reaching that place just after sunset. On the 21st I procured clothing for the Indians, which, when they arrived with Mr. Jacob in the afternoon, was distributed among them.

On my arrival at the Pueblo, I found the American population there much excited by intelligence just received of the capture on the 15th, between Monterey and the mission of San Juan, of Thos. O. Larkin, Esq., late U. S. consul in California, by a party of Californians, and of an engagement between the same Californians and a party of Americans escorting a *caballada* of 400 horses to Colonel Fremont's camp in Monterey. In this affair three Americans were killed, viz. : Capt. Burroughs, Capt. Foster, and Mr. Eames, late of St. Louis, Mo. The mission of San Juan lies on the road between the Pueblo de San José and Monterey, about fifty miles from the former place, and thirty from the latter. The skirmish took place ten miles south of San Juan, near the Monterey road. I extract the following account of this affair from a journal of his captivity published by Mr. Larkin:—

"On the 15th of November, from information received of the sickness of my family in San Francisco, where they had gone to escape the expected revolutionary troubles in Monterey, and from letters from Captain Montgomery requesting my presence respecting some stores for the Portsmouth, I, with one servant, left Monterey for San Francisco, knowing that for one month no Californian forces had been within 100 miles of us. That night I put up at the house of Don Joaquin Gomez, sending my servant to San Juan, six miles beyond, to request Mr. J. Thompson to wait for me, as he was on the road for San Francisco. About midnight I was aroused from my bed by the noise made by ten Californians (unshaved and unwashed for months, being in the mountains) rushing into my chamber with guns, swords, pistols, and torches in their hands. I needed but a moment to be fully awake and know my exact situation; the first cry was, 'Como estamos Señor Consul.' 'Vamos Señor Larkin.' At my bedside were several letters that I had re-read before going to bed. On dressing myself, while my captors were saddling my horse, I assorted these letters, and put them into different pockets. After taking my own time to dress and arrange my valise, we started, and rode to a camp of seventy or eighty men on the banks of the Monterey river; there each officer and principal person passed the time of night with me, and a remark or two. The commandante took me on one side, and informed me that his people demanded that I should write to San Juan, to the American captain of volunteers, saying that I had left Monterey to visit the distressed families of the river, and request or demand that twenty men should meet me before daylight, that I could station them, before my return to town, in a manner to protect these families. The natives, he said, were determined on the act being accomplished. I at first endeavored to reason with him on the infamy and the impossibility of the deed, but to no avail: he said my life depended on the letter; that he was willing, nay, anxious to preserve my life as an old acquaintance, but could not control his people in this affair. From argument I came to a refusal: he advised, urged, and demanded. At this period an officer called out * * * * (Come here, those who are named.) I then said, 'In this manner you may act and threaten night by night; my life on such condition is of no value or pleasure to me. I am by accident your prisoner—make the most of me—write, I will not: shoot as you see fit, and I am done talking on the subject.' I left him, and went to the camp-fire. For a half-hour or more there was some commotion around me, when all disturbance subsided.

"At daylight we started, with a flag flying and a drum beating, and travelled eight or ten miles, when we camped in a low valley or hollow. There they caught with the lasso three or four head of cattle belonging to the nearest rancho, and breakfasted. The whole day their outriders rode in every direction, on the look-out, to see if the American company left the mission of San Juan, or Lieutenant-colonel Fremont left Monterey: they also rode to all the neighboring ranchos, and forced the rancheros to join them. At one o'clock, they began their march with one hundred and thirty men, (and two or three hundred extra horses;) they marched in four single files, occupying four positions, myself under charge of an officer and five or six men in the centre. Their plan of operation for the night was, to rush into San Juan ten or fifteen men, who were to retreat, under the expectation that the Americans would follow them, in which case the whole party outside was to cut them off. I was to be retained in the centre of the party. Ten miles south of the mission, they encountered eight or ten Americans, a part of whom retreated into a low ground covered with oaks, the others returned to the house of Señor Gomez, to alarm their companions. For over one hour the hundred and thirty Californians surrounded the six or eight Americans, occasionally giving and receiving shots. During this period, I was several times requested, then commanded, to go among the oaks and bring out my countrymen, and offer them their lives on giving up their rifles and persons. I at last offered to go and call them out, on condition that they should return to

San Juan or go to Monterey, with their arms; this being refused, I told the commandante to go in and bring them out
himself. While they were consulting how this could be done,
fifty Americans came down on them, which caused an action of
about twenty or thirty minutes. Thirty or forty of the natives
leaving the field at the first fire, they remained drawn off by
fives and tens until the Americans had the field to themselves.
Both parties remained within a mile of each other until dark.
Our countrymen lost Captain Burroughs, of St. Louis, Missouri,
Captain Foster, and two others, with two or three wounded.
The Californians lost two of their countrymen, and José Garcia,
of Val., Chili, with seven wounded."

The following additional particulars I extract from the
"Californian" newspaper of November 21, 1846, published at
Monterey: "Burroughs and Foster were killed at the first onset.
The Americans fired, and then charged on the enemy with
their empty rifles, and ran them off. However, they still
kept rallying, and firing now and then a musket at the Americans, until about eleven o'clock at night, when one of the
Walla-Walla Indians offered his services to come into Monterey and give Colonel Fremont notice of what was passing
Soon after he started he was pursued by a party of the
enemy. The foremost in pursuit drove a lance at the Indian,
who, trying to parry it, received the lance through his hand;
he immediately, with the other hand, seized his tomahawk,
and struck a blow at his opponent, which split his head from
the crown to the mouth. By this time the others had come
up, and with the most extraordinary dexterity and bravery,
the Indian vanquished two more; and the rest ran away. He
rode on towards this town as far as his horse was able to carry
him, and then left his horse and saddle, and came in on foot.
He arrived here about eight o'clock on Tuesday morning, December 17th."

The Americans engaged in this affair were principally the
volunteer emigrants just arrived in the country, and who had
left New Helvetia a few days in advance of me.

Colonel Fremont marched from Monterey as soon as he

heard of this skirmish, in pursuit of the Californians, but did not meet with them. He then encamped at the mission of San Juan, waiting there the arrival of the remaining volunteers from above.

Leaving the Pueblo on the afternoon of the 25th, in conjunction with a small force commanded by Captain Weber, we made an excursion into the hills, near a rancho owned by Captain W., where were herded some two or three hundred public horses. It had been rumored that a party of Californians were hovering about here, intending to capture and drive off these horses. The next day, (November 26th,) without having met any hostile force, driving these horses before us, we encamped at Murphy's rancho. Mr. Murphy is the father of a large and respectable family, who emigrated to this country some three or four years since from the United States, being originally from Canada. His daughter, Miss Helen, who did the honors of the rude cabin, in manners, conversation, and personal charms, would grace any drawing-room. On the 28th, we proceeded down the Pueblo valley, passing Gilroy's rancho, and reaching the mission of San Juan just before dark. The hills and valleys are becoming verdant with the fresh grass and wild oats, the latter being, in places, two or three inches high. So tender is it, however, that it affords but little nourishment to our horses.

The mission of San Juan Bautista has been one of the most extensive of these establishments. The principal buildings are more durably constructed than those of other missions I have visited, and they are in better condition. Square bricks are used in paving the corridors and the ground floors. During the twilight, I strayed accidentally through a half-opened gate into a cemetery, enclosed by a high wall in the rear of the church. The spectacle was ghastly enough. The exhumed skeletons of those who had been deposited here, lay thickly strewn around, showing but little respect for the sanctity of the grave or the rights of the dead, from the living. The cool, damp night-breeze sighed and moaned through the shrubbery and ruinous arches and corridors, planted and reared by those whose neglected bones were now exposed to the rude insults of man and beast. I could not but imagine that the voices of complaining spirits mingled with these dismal and mournful tones; and plucking a cluster of roses, the fragrance of which was delicious, I left the spot, to drive away the sadness and melancholy produced by the scene.

The valley contiguous to the mission is extensive, well watered by a large *arroyo*, and highly fertile. The gardens and other lands for tillage, are enclosed by willow hedges. Elevated hills, or mountains, bound this valley on the east and the west. Large herds of cattle were scattered over the valley, greedily cropping the fresh green herbage, which now carpets mountain and plain.

Colonel Fremont marched from San Juan this morning, and encamped, as we learned on our arrival, ten miles south. Proceeding up the *arroyo* on the 29th, we reached the camp of Colonel F. about noon. I immediately reported, and delivered over to him the men and horses under my charge. The men were afterwards organized into a separate corps, of which Mr. R. T. Jacob, my travelling-companion, was appointed the captain by Colonel Fremont.

CHAPTER XXXI.

California battalion—Their appearance, and costume—List of the officers —Commence our march to Los Angeles—Appearance of the country in the vicinity of San Juan—Slaughter of beeves—Astonishing consumption of beef by the men—Beautiful morning—Ice—Salinas river and valley —Californian prisoners—Horses giving out from fatigue—Mission of San Miguel—Sheep—Mutton—March on foot—More prisoners taken—Death of Mr. Stanley—An execution—Dark night—Capture of the mission or San Luis Obispo—Orderly conduct and good deportment of the California battalion.

NOVEMBER 30.—The battalion of mounted riflemen under the command of Lieutenant-colonel Fremont, numbers, rank and file, including Indians and servants, 428. With the exception of the exploring party, which left the United States with Colonel F., they are composed of volunteers from the American settlers, and the emigrants which have arrived in the country within a few weeks. The latter have generally furnished their own ammunition and other equipments for the expedition. Most of these are practiced riflemen, men of undoubted courage, and capable of bearing any fatigue and privations endurable by veteran troops. The Indians are composed of a party of Walla-Wallas from Oregon, and a party of native Californians. Attached to the battalion are two pieces of artillery, under the command of Lieutenant McLane, of the navy. In the appearance of our small army there is presented but little of "the pomp and circumstance of glorious war." There are no plumes nodding over brazen helmets, nor coats of broadcloth spangled with lace and buttons. A broad-brimmed, low-crowned hat, a shirt of blue flannel, or buckskin, with pantaloons and moccasins of the same, all generally much the worse for wear, and smeared with mud and dust, make up the costume of the party, officers as well as men. A leathern girdle surrounds the waist, from which are suspended a bowie and a hunter's knife, and sometimes a brace of pistols. These, with the rifle and holster-pistols, are the arms carried by officers and privates. A single bugle (and a sorry one it is) composes the band. Many an embryo Napoleon, in his own conceit, whose martial spirit has been excited to flaming intensity of heat by the peacock-plumage and gaudy trappings of our militia companies, when marching through the streets to the sound of drum, fife, and brass band, if he could have looked upon us, and then consulted the state of the military thermometer within him, would probably have discovered that the mercury of his heroism had fallen several degrees below zero. He might even have desired that we should not come

"Between the wind and his nobility."

War, stripped of its pageantry, possesses but few of the attractions with which poetry and painting have embellished it. The following is a list of the officers :—

List of Officers composing the California Battalion.

Lieutenant-colonel J. C. Fremont, commanding ; A. H. Gillespie, major ; P. B. Reading, paymaster ; Henry King, commissary ; J. R. Snyder, quartermaster, since appointed a land-surveyor by Colonel Mason ; Wm. H. Russell, ordnance officer ; T. Talbot, lieutenant and adjutant ; J. J. Myers, sergeant-major, appointed lieutenant in January, 1847.

Company A.—Richard Owens, captain ; Wm. N. Loker, 1st lieutenant, appointed adjutant Feb. 10th, 1847 ; B. M. Hudspeth, 2d lieutenant, appointed captain Feb. 1847 ; Wm. Findlay, 2d lieutenant, appointed captain Feb. 1847.

Company B.—Henry Ford, captain ; Andrew Copeland, 1st lieutenant.

Company C.—Granville P. Swift, captain ; Wm. Baldridge, 1st lieutenant ; Wm. Hartgrove, 2d do.

Company D.—John Sears, captain ; Wm. Bradshaw, 1st lieutenant.

Company E.—John Grigsby, captain ; Archibald Jesse, 1st lieutenant.

Company F.—L. W. Hastings, captain, (author of a work on California;) Wornbough, 1st lieutenant ; J. M. Hudspeth, 2d do.

Company G.—Thompson, captain ; Davis, 1st lieutenant ; Rock, 2d do.

Company H.—R. T. Jacobs, captain ; Edwin Bryant, 1st lieutenant, (afterwards alcalde at San Francisco;) Geo. M. Lippincott, 2d do., of New York.

Artillery Company.—Louis McLane, captain, (afterwards major;) John K. Wilson, 1st lieutenant, appointed captain in January, 1847 ; Wm. Blackburn, 2d do., (now alcalde of Santa Cruz.)

Officers on detached service and doing duty at the South.

S. Hensley, captain ; S. Gibson, do., (lanced through the body at San Pascual;) Miguel Pedrorena, do., Spaniard, (appointed by Stockton;) Stgo. Arguello, do., Californian, (appointed by do.;) Bell, do., (appointed by do.,) old resident of California, (Los Angeles;) H. Rhenshaw, 1st lieutenant, (appointed by do.;) A. Godey, do., (appointed by do.;) Jas. Barton, do., (appointed by do.;) L. Arguello, do., Californian, (appointed by do.)

After a march of six or eight hours, up the valley of the *arroyo*, through a heavy rain, and mud so deep that several of our horses gave out from exhaustion, we encamped in a circular bottom, near a deserted adobe house. A *caballada* of some 500 or 600 loose horses and mules is driven along with us, but many of them are miserable, sore-backed skeletons, having been exhausted with hard usage and bad fare during the summer campaign. Besides these, we have a large number of pack-mules, upon which all our baggage and provisions are transported. Distance 10 miles.

We did not move on the 1st and 2d of December. There being no cattle in the vicinity of our camp, a party was sent back to the mission, on the morning of the 1st, who in the afternoon returned, driving before them about 100 head, most of them in good condition. After a sufficient number were slaughtered to supply the camp with meat for the day, the remainder were confined in a *corral* prepared for the purpose, to be driven along with us, and slaughtered from day to day. The rain has continued, with short intermissions, since we commenced our march on the 30th of November. The ground has become saturated with water, and the small branches are swollen into large streams. Notwithstanding these discomforts, the men are in good spirits, and enjoy themselves in singing, telling stories, and playing *monte*.

December 3.—The rain ceased falling about 8 o'clock this morning ; and the clouds breaking away, the sun cheered us once more with his pleasant beams. The battalion was formed into a hollow square, and the order of the day being read, we resumed our march. Our progress, through the deep mud, was very slow. The horses were constantly giving out, and many were left behind. The young and tender grass upon which they feed affords but little nourishment, and hard labor soon exhausts them. We encamped on a low bluff, near the *arroyo*, timbered with evergreen oak. Distance eight miles.

December 4.—I was ordered with a small party in advance this morning. Proceeding up the valley a few miles, we left it, crossing several steep hills sparsely timbered with oak, from which we descended into another small valley, down which we continued to the point of its termination, near some narrow and difficult mountain gorges. In exploring the gorges, we discovered the trail of a party of Californians, which had passed south several days before us, and found a horse which they had left in their march. This, doubtless, was a portion of the party which captured Mr. Larkin, and had the engagement between Monterey and St. Juan, on the 17th ult. The main body coming up, we encamped at 3 o'clock. The old grass around our camp is abundant; but having been so much washed by the rains, and consequently exhausted of its nutritious qualities, the animals refuse to eat it. The country over which we have travelled to-day, and as far as I can see, is mountainous and broken, little of it being adapted to other agricultural purposes than grazing.

Thirteen beeves are slaughtered every afternoon for the consumption of the battalion. These beeves are generally of good size, and in fair condition. Other provisions being entirely exhausted, beef constitutes the only subsistence for the men, and most of the officers. Under these circumstances, the consumption of beef is astonishing. I do not know that I shall be believed when I state a fact, derived from observation and calculation, that the average consumption per man of fresh beef is at least ten pounds per day. Many of them, I believe, consume much more, and some of them less. Nor does this quantity appear to be injurious to health, or fully to satisfy the appetite. I have seen some of the men roast their meat and devour it by the fire from the hour of encamping until late bedtime. They would then sleep until one or two o'clock in the morning, when the cravings of hunger being greater than the desire for repose, the same occupation would be resumed and continued until the order was given to march. The Californian beef is generally fat, juicy, and tender, and surpasses in flavor any which I ever tasted elsewhere. Distance 10 miles.

December 5.—I rose before daylight. The moon shone brightly. The temperature was cold. The vapor in the atmosphere had congealed and fallen upon the ground in feathery flakes, covering it with a white semi-transparent veil, or crystal sheen, sparkling in the moonbeams. The smoke from the numerous camp-fires soon began to curl languidly up in graceful wreaths, settling upon the mountain summits. The scene was one for the pencil and brush of the artist ; but when the envious sun rose, he soon stripped Madam Earth of her gauzy, holiday morning-gown, and exposed her every-day petticoat of mud.

Our march to-day has been one of great difficulty, through a deep, brushy mountain gorge, through which it was almost impossible to force the field-pieces. In one place they were lowered with ropes down a steep and nearly perpendicular precipice of great height and depth. We encamped about 3 o'clock, P. M., in a small valley. Many of the horses gave out on the march, and were left behind by the men, who came straggling into camp until a late hour of the evening, bringing their saddles and baggage upon their shoulders. I noticed, while crossing an elevated ridge of hills, flakes of snow flying in the air, but melting before they reached the ground. The small spring-branch on which we encamped, empties into the Salinas river. The country surrounding us is elevated and broken, and the soil sandy, with but little timber or grass upon it. Distance 12 miles.

December 6.—Morning clear and cool. Crossed an undulating country, destitute of timber and water, and encamped in a circular valley surrounded by elevated hills, through which flows a small tributary of the Salinas. The summits of the mountains in sight are covered with snow, but the temperature in the valleys is pleasant. Distance 15 miles.

December 7.—Ice, the first I have seen since entering California, formed in the branch of the thickness of window-glass. We reached the valley of the Salinas about 11 o'clock, A. M., and encamped for the day. The river Salinas (laid down in some maps as Rio San Buenaventura) rises in the mountains to the south, and has a course of some sixty or eighty miles, emptying into the Pacific about twelve miles north of Monterey. The valley, as it approaches the ocean, is broad and fertile, and there are many fine ranchos upon it. But higher up, the stream becomes dry in the summer, and the soil of the valley is arid and sandy. The width of the stream at this point is about thirty yards. Its banks are skirted by narrow belts of small timber. A range of elevated mountains rises between this valley and the coast. A court-martial was held to-day, for the trial of sundry offenders. Distance 8 miles.

Dec. 8.—Morning cool, clear, and pleasant. Two Californians were arrested by the rear-guard near a deserted rancho, and brought into camp. One of them turned out to be a person known to be friendly to the Americans. There has been but little variation in the soil or scenery. But few attempts appear to have been made to settle this portion of California. The thefts and hostilities of the Tular Indians, are said to be one of the causes preventing its settlement. Distance 15 miles.

Dec. 9.—The mornings are cool, but the middle of the days are too warm to ride comfortably with our coats on. Our march has been fatiguing and difficult, through several brushy ravines and over steep and elevated hills. Many horses gave out as usual, and were left, from inability to travel. Our *caballada* is diminishing rapidly. Distance 10 miles.

Dec. 10.—Our march has been on the main beaten trail, dry and hard and over a comparatively level country. We passed the mission of San Miguel about 3 o'clock, and encamped in a grove of large oak timber three or four miles south of it. This mission is situated on the upper waters of the Salinas, in an extensive plain. Under the administration of the *padres* it was a wealthy establishment, and manufactures of various kinds were carried on. They raised immense numbers of sheep, the fleeces of which were manufactured by the Indians into blankets and coarse cloths. Their granaries were filled with an abundance of maize and frijoles, and their store-rooms with other necessaries of life from the ranchos belonging on the mission lands

in the vicinity. Now all the buildings, except the church and
the principal range of houses contiguous, have fallen into ruins,
and an Englishman, his wife and one small child, with two or
three Indian servants, are the sole inhabitants. The church is
the largest I have seen in the country, and its interior is in good
repair, although it has not probably been used for the purpose
of worship for many years. The Englishman professes to
have purchased the mission and all the lands belonging to it
for $300!

Our stock of cattle being exhausted, we feasted on Californian mutton, sheep being more abundant than cattle at this
mission. The wool, I noticed, was coarse, but the mutton was
of an excellent quality. The country over which we have travelled to-day, shows the marks of long drought previous to the
recent rains. The soil is sandy and gravelly, and the dead
vegetation upon it is thin and stunted. About eighty of our
horses are reported to have given out and been left behind.
Distance 20 miles.

Dec. 12.—To relieve our horses, which are constantly giving
out from exhaustion, the grass being insufficient for their sustenance while performing labor, the entire battalion, officers and
men, were ordered to march on foot, turning their horses, with
the saddles and bridles upon them, into the general *caballada*
to be driven along by the horse-guard. The day has been
drizzly, cold, and disagreeable. The country has a barren and
naked appearance, but this, I believe, is attributable to the extreme drought that has prevailed in this region for one or two
years past. We encamped near the rancho of a friendly Californian,—the man who was taken prisoner the other day and
set at large. An Indian, said to be the servant of Tortoria
Pico, was captured here by the advance party. A letter was
found upon him, but its contents I never learned. This being the first foot-march, there were, of course, many galled
and blistered feet in the battalion. My servant obtained, with
some difficulty, from the Indians at the rancho, a pint cup
of *pinole*, or parched corn-meal, and a quart or two of wheat,
which being boiled, furnished some variety in our viands

at supper, fresh beef having been our only subsistence since the commencement of the march from San Juan. Distance 12 miles.

Dec. 13.—A rainy disagreeable morning. Mr. Stanley, one of the volunteers, and one of the gentlemen who so kindly supplied us with provisions on Mary's river, died last night. He has been suffering from an attack of typhoid fever since the commencement of our march, and unable most of the time to sit upon his horse. He was buried this morning in a small circular opening in the timber near our camp. The battalion was formed in a hollow square surrounding the grave which had been excavated for the final resting-place of our deceased friend and comrade. There was neither bier, nor coffin, nor pall—

" Not a drum was heard, nor a funeral note."

The cold earth was heaped upon his mortal remains in silent solemnity, and the ashes of a braver or a better man will never repose in the lonely hills of California.

After the funeral the battalion was marched a short distance to witness another scene, not more mournful, but more harrowing than the last. The Indian captured at the rancho yesterday was condemned to die. He was brought from his place of confinement and tied to a tree. Here he stood some fifteen or twenty minutes, until the Indians from a neighboring *rancheria* could be brought to witness the execution. A file of soldiers were then ordered to fire upon him. He fell upon his knees, and remained in that position several minutes without uttering a groan, and then sank upon the earth. No human being could have met his fate with more composure, or with stronger manifestations of courage. It was a scene such as I desire never to witness again.

A cold rain fell upon us during the entire day's march. We encamped at four o'clock, P. M., but the rain poured down in such torrents that it was impossible to light our camp-fires and keep them burning. This continued nearly the whole night, and I have rarely passed a night more uncomfortably. A scouting party brought in two additional prisoners this evening.

32

Another returned, and reported the capture of a number of horses, and the destruction of a rancho by fire.   Distance 12 miles.

December 14.—The battalion commenced its march on foot and in a heavy rain. The mud is very deep, and we have been compelled to wade several streams of considerable depth, being swollen by the recent rains. At one o'clock a halt was ordered, and beef slaughtered and cooked for dinner. The march was resumed late in the afternoon, and the plain surrounding the mission of San Luis Obispo was reached in the pitchy darkness of the night, a family in the *cañada* having been taken prisoners by the advance party to prevent them giving the alarm. The battalion was so disposed as to surround the mission and take prisoners all contained within it. The place was entered in great confusion, on account of the darkness, about nine o'clock. There was no military force at the mission, and the few inhabitants were greatly alarmed, as may well be supposed, by this sudden invasion. They made no resistance, and were all taken prisoners except one or two, who managed to escape and fled in great terror, no one knew where or how. It being ascertained that Tortoria Pico, a man who has figured conspicuously in most of the Californian revolutions, was in the neighborhood, a party was dispatched immediately to the place, and he was brought in a prisoner. The night was rainy and boisterous, and the soldiers were quartered to the best advantage in the miserable mud houses, and no acts of violence or outrage of any kind were committed.

The men composing the California battalion, as I have before stated, have been drawn from many sources, and are roughly clad, and weather-beaten in their exterior appearance ; but I feel it but justice here to state my belief, that no military party ever passed through an enemy's country and observed the same strict regard for the rights of its population. I never heard of an outrage, or even a trespass being committed by one of the American volunteers during our entire march. Every American appeared to understand perfectly the duty which he owed to himself and others in this respect, and the deportment of the battalion might be cited as a model for imitation. Distance 18 miles.

CHAPTER XXXII.

DECEMBER 15.—The rain fell in cataracts the entire day. The
small streams which flow from the mountains through, and
water the valley of, San Luis Obispo, are swollen by the deluge
of water from the clouds into foaming unfordable torrents. In
order not to trespass upon the population at the mission, in their
miserable abodes of mud, the church was opened, and a large
number of the soldiers were quartered in it. A guard, however, was set day and night, over the chancel and all other
property contained in the building, to prevent its being injured
or disturbed. The decorations of the church are much the
same as I have before described. The edifice is large, and the.
interior in good repair. The floor is paved with square bricks.
I noticed a common hand-organ in the church, which played
the airs we usually hear from organ-grinders in the street.

Besides the main large buildings connected with the church,
there are standing, and partially occupied, several small squares
of adobe houses, belonging to this mission. The heaps of mud
and crumbling walls outside of these, are evidence that the
place was once of much greater extent, and probably one of
the most opulent and prosperous establishments of the kind in
the country. The lands surrounding the mission are finely situated for cultivation and irrigation if necessary. There are several large gardens, enclosed by high and substantial walls,

which now contain a great variety of fruit-trees and shrubbery. I noticed the orange, fig, palm, olive, and grape. There are also large enclosures hedged in by the prickly-pear, (cactus,) which grows to an enormous size, and makes an impervious barrier against man or beast. The stalks of some of these plants are of the thickness of a man's body, and grow to the height of fifteen feet. A juicy fruit is produced by the prickly-pear, named *tuna*, from which a beverage is sometimes made called *calinche*. It has a pleasant flavor, as has also the fruit, which, when ripe, is blood-red. A small quantity of pounded wheat was found here, which, being purchased, was served out to the troops, about a pound to the man. Frijoles and pumpkins were also obtained, delicacies of no common order.

December 16.—A court-martial was convened this morning for the trial of Pico, the principal prisoner, on the charge, I understood, of the forfeiture of his parole which had been taken on a former occasion. The sentence of the court was, that he should be shot or hung, I do not know which. A rumor is current among the population here, that there has been an engagement between a party of Americans and Californians, near Los Angeles, in which the former were defeated with the loss of thirty men killed.

December 17.—Cool, with a hazy sky. While standing in one of the corridors this morning, a procession of females passed by me, headed by a lady of fine appearance and dressed with remarkable taste and neatness, compared with those who followed her. Their *rebosos* concealed the faces of most of them, except the leader, whose beautiful features, I dare say, she thought (and justly) required no concealment. They proceeded to the quarters of Colonel Fremont, and their object, I understood, was to petition for the reprieve or pardon of Pico, who had been condemned to death by the court-martial yesterday, and whose execution was expected to take place this morning. Their intercession was successful, as no execution took place, and in a short time all the prisoners were discharged, and the order to saddle up and march given. We resumed our march at ten o'clock, and encamped just before sunset in a small but picturesque and fertile valley timbered with oak, so near the coast that the roar of the surf breaking against the shore could be heard distinctly. Distance 7 miles.

December 18.—Clear, with a delightful temperature. Before the sun rose the grass was covered with a white frost. The day throughout has been calm and beautiful. A march of four miles brought us to the shore of a small indentation in the coast of the Pacific, where vessels can anchor, and boats can land when the wind is not too fresh. The surf is now rolling and foaming with prodigious energy—breaking upon the beach in long lines one behind the other, and striking the shore like cataracts. The hills and plains are verdant with a carpet of fresh grass, and the scattered live-oaks on all sides appearing like orchards of fruit-trees, give to the country an old and cultivated aspect. The mountains bench away on our left, the low hills rising in gentle conical forms, beyond which are the more elevated and precipitous peaks covered with snow. We encamped about three o'clock near the rancho of Captain Dana, in a large and handsome valley well watered by an *arroyo*.

Captain Dana is a native of Massachusetts, and has resided in this country about thirty years. He is known and esteemed throughout California for his intelligence and private virtues, and his unbounded generosity and hospitality. I purchased here a few loaves of wheat bread, and distributed them among the men belonging to our company as far as they would go, a luxury which they have not indulged in since the commencement of the march. Distance 15 miles.

December 19.—The night was cold and tempestuous, with a slight fall of rain. The clouds broke away after sunrise, and the day became warm and pleasant. We continued our march up the valley and encamped near its head. The table-land and hills are generally gravelly, but appear to be productive of fine grass. The soil of the bottom is of the richest and most productive composition. We crossed in the course of the day a wide flat plain, upon which were grazing large herds of brood-mares (*manadas*) and cattle. In the distance they resembled large armies approaching us. The peaks of the elevated moun-

32*

tains in sight are covered with snow. A large number of horses gave out, strayed, and were left behind to-day, estimated at one hundred. The men came into camp bringing their saddles on their backs, and some of them arriving late in the evening. Distance 18 miles.

December 20.—Parties were sent back this morning to gather up horses and baggage left on the march yesterday, and it was one o'clock before the rear-guard, waiting for the return of those, left camp. The main body made a short march and encamped early, in a small hollow near the rancho of Mr. Faxon, through which flows an *arroyo*, the surrounding hills being timbered with evergreen oaks. The men amused themselves during the afternoon in target-shooting. Many of the battalion are fine marksmen with the rifle, and the average of shots could not easily be surpassed. The camp spread over an undulating surface of half a mile in diameter, and at night, when the fires were lighted, illuminating the grove, with its drapery of drooping Spanish moss, it presented a most picturesque appearance. Distance 3 miles.

December 21.—Clear and pleasant. A foot-march was ordered, with the exception of the horse and baggage guard. We marched several miles through a winding hollow, passing a deserted rancho, and ascending with much labor a steep ridge of hills, descending which we entered a handsome valley, and encamped upon a small stream about four miles from the mission of St. Ynes. The banks of the *arroyo* are strewn with dead and prostrate timber, the trees, large and small, having been overthrown by tornadoes. The plain has suffered, like much of the country we have passed through, by a long-continued drought, but the composition of the soil is such as indicates fertility, and from the effects of the late rains the grass is springing up with great luxuriance, from places which before were entirely denuded of vegetation. A party was sent from camp to inspect the mission, but returned without making any important discoveries. Our horses are so weak that many of them are unable to carry their saddles, and were left on the road as usual. A man had his leg broken on the march to-day, by the kick of a mule. He was sent back to the rancho of Mr. Faxon. Distance 15 miles.

December 22.—Clear and pleasant. Being of the party which performed rear-guard duty to-day, with orders to bring in all stragglers, we did not leave camp until several hours after the main body had left. The horses of the *caballada* and the pack-animals were continually giving out and refusing to proceed. Parties of men, exhausted, lay down upon the ground, and it was with much urging, and sometimes with peremptory commands only, that they could be prevailed upon to proceed. The country bears the same marks of drought heretofore described, but fresh vegetation is now springing up and appears vigorous. A large horse-trail leading into one of the *cañadas* of the mountains on our left, was discovered by the scouts, and a party was dispatched to trace it. We passed one deserted rancho, and reached camp between nine and ten o'clock at night, having forced in all the men and most of the horses and pack-mules. Distance 15 miles.

December 23.—Rain fell steadily and heavily the entire day. A small party of men was in advance. Discovering in a brushy valley two Indians armed with bows and arrows, they were taken prisoners. Learning from them that there was a *caballada* of horses secreted in one of the *cañadas*, they continued on about ten miles, and found about twenty-five fresh, fat horses, belonging to a Californian now among the insurgents below. They were taken and delivered at the camp near the eastern base of the St. Ynes mountain. Passed this morning a rancho inhabited by a foreigner, an Englishman.

December 24.—Cloudy and cool, with an occasional sprinkling rain. Our route to-day lay directly over the St. Ynes mountain, by an elevated and most difficult pass. The height of this mountain is several thousand feet. We reached the summit about twelve o'clock, and our company composing the advance-guard, we encamped about a mile and a half in advance of the main body of the battalion, at a point which overlooks the beautiful plain of Santa Barbara, of which, and the ocean beyond, we had a most extended and interesting view.

With the spyglass, we could see in the plain far below us, herds of cattle quietly grazing upon the green herbage that carpets its gentle undulations.   The plain is dotted with groves, surrounding the springs and belting the small water-courses, of which there are many flowing from this range of mountains. Ranchos are scattered far up and down the plain, but not one human being could be seen stirring.   About ten or twelve miles to the south, the white towers of the mission of Santa Barbara raise themselves.   Beyond, is the illimitable waste of waters. A more lovely and picturesque landscape I never beheld.   On the summit of the mountain, and surrounding us, there is a growth of hawthorn, manzanita, (in bloom,) and other small shrubbery.   The rock is soft sandstone and conglomerate, immense masses of which, piled one upon another, form a wall along the western brow of the mountain, through which there is a single pass or gateway about eight or ten feet in width. The descent on the western side is precipitous, and appears almost impassable.   Distance 4 miles.

December 25.—Christmas-day, and a memorable one to me. Owing to the difficulty in hauling the cannon up the steep acclivities of the mountain, the main body of the battalion did not come up with us until twelve o'clock, and before we commenced the descent of the mountain a furious storm commenced, raging with a violence rarely surpassed.   The rain fell in torrents and the wind blew almost with the force of a tornado.   This fierce strife of the elements continued without abatement the entire afternoon, and until two o'clock at night.   Driving our horses before us we were compelled to slide down the steep and slippery rocks, or wade through deep gullies and ravines filled with mud and foaming torrents of water, that rushed downwards with such force as to carry along the loose rocks and tear up the trees and shrubbery by the roots.   Many of the horses falling into the ravines refused to make an effort to extricate themselves, and were swept downwards and drowned. Others, bewildered by the fierceness and terrors of the storm, rushed or fell headlong over the steep precipices and were killed.   Others obstinately refused to proceed, but stood quaking with fear or shivering with cold, and many of these perished in the night from the severity of the storm. The advance party did not reach the foot of the mountain and find a place to encamp until night—and a night of more impenetrable and terrific darkness I never witnessed. The ground upon which our camp was made, although sloping from the hills to a small stream, was so saturated with water that men as well as horses sunk deep at every step. The rain fell in such quantities that fires with great difficulty could be lighted, and most of them were immediately extinguished.

The officers and men belonging to the company having the cannon in charge, labored until nine or ten o'clock to bring them down the mountain, but they were finally compelled to leave them. Much of the baggage also remained on the side of the mountain, with the pack-mules and horses conveying them; all efforts to force the animals down being fruitless. The men continued to straggle into the camp until a late hour of the night;—some crept under the shelving rocks and did not come in until the next morning. We were so fortunate as to find our tent, and after much difficulty pitched it under an oak-tree. All efforts to light a fire and keep it blazing proving abortive, we spread our blankets upon the ground and endeavored to sleep, although we could feel the cold streams of water running through the tent and between and around our bodies.

In this condition we remained until about two o'clock in the morning, when the storm having abated I rose, and shaking from my garments the dripping water, after many unsuccessful efforts succeeded in kindling a fire. Near our tent I found three soldiers who had reached camp at a late hour. They were fast asleep on the ground, the water around them being two or three inches deep ; but they had taken care to keep their heads above water by using a log of wood for a pillow. The fire beginning to blaze freely, I dug a ditch with my hands and a sharp stick of wood, which drained off the pool surrounding the tent. One of the men, when he felt the sensation consequent upon being "high and dry," roused himself, and sitting upright, looked around for some time with an expression of bewildered amazement. At length he seemed to realize the true state of the case, and exclaimed in a tone of energetic soliloquy :

"Well, who *wouldn't* be a soldier and fight for California ?"

"You are mistaken," I replied.

Rubbing his eyes he gazed at me with astonishment, as if having been entirely unconscious of my presence ; but reassuring himself he said :

"How mistaken ?"

"Why," I answered, "you are not fighting for California."

"What the d—l then am I fighting for ?" he inquired.

"For TEXAS."

"Texas be d—d ; but hurrah for General Jackson !" and with this exclamation he threw himself back again upon his wooden pillow, and was soon snoring in a profound slumber.

Making a platform composed of sticks of wood upon the soft mud, I stripped myself to the skin, wringing the water from each garment as I proceeded. I then commenced drying them by the fire in the order that they were replaced upon my body, an employment that occupied me until daylight, which sign, above the high mountain to the east, down which we had rolled rather than marched yesterday, I was truly rejoiced to see. Distance 3 miles.

Dec. 26.—Parties were detailed early this morning, and dispatched up the mountain to bring down the cannon, and collect the living horses and baggage. The destruction of horse-flesh, by those who witnessed the scene, by daylight, is described as frightful. In some places large numbers of dead horses were piled together. In others, horses half buried in the mud of the ravines, or among the rocks, were gasping in the agonies of death. The number of dead animals is variously estimated at from seventy-five to one hundred and fifty, by different persons. The cannon, most of the missing baggage, and the living horses, were all brought in by noon. The day was busily employed in cleansing our rifles and pistols, and drying our drenched baggage.

Dec. 27.—Preparations were commenced early for the resumption of our march ; but such was the condition of every thing around us, that it was two o'clock, P. M., before the battalion was in readiness; and then so great had been the loss of horses in various ways, that the number remaining was insufficient to mount the men. One or two companies, and portions of others, were compelled to march on foot. We were visited during the forenoon by Mr. Sparks, an American, Dr. Den, an Irishman, and Mr. Burton, another American, residents of Santa Barbara. They had been suffered by the Californians to remain in the place. Their information communicated to us was, that the town was deserted of nearly all its population. A few houses only were occupied. Passing down a beautiful and fertile undulating plain, we encamped just before sunset in a live-oak grove, about half a mile from the town of Santa Barbara. Strict orders were issued by Col. Fremont, that the property and the persons of Californians, not found in arms, should be sacredly respected. To prevent all collisions, no soldier was allowed to pass the lines of the camp without special permission, or orders from his officers.

I visited the town before dark; but found the houses, with few exceptions, closed, and the streets deserted. After hunting about some time we discovered a miserable dwelling, occupied by a shoemaker and his family, open. Entering it we were very kindly received by its occupants, who, with a princely supply of civility, possessed but a beggarly array of comforts. At our request they provided for us a supper of *tortillas, frijoles,* and stewed *carne,* seasoned with *chile colorado,* for which, paying them *dos pesos* for four, we bade them good-evening, all parties being well satisfied. The family consisted, exclusive of the shoemaker, of a dozen women and children, of all ages. The women, from the accounts they had received of the intentions of the Americans, were evidently unprepared for civil treatment from them. They expected to be dealt with in a very barbarous manner, *in all respects;* but they were disappointed, and invited us to visit them again. Distance eight miles.

CHAPTER XXXIII.

Santa Barbara—Picturesque situation—Fertility of the country—Climate— Population—Society—Leave Santa Barbara—Rincon—Grampus—Mission of St. Buenaventura—Fine gardens—Meet a party of mounted Californians—They retreat before us—Abundance of maize—Arrival of couriers from Com. Stockton—Effects of war upon the country—More of the enemy in sight—News of the capture of Los Angeles, by Gen. Kearny and Com. Stockton—Mission of San Fernando—The Maguey— Capitulation of the Californians—Arrive at Los Angeles—General reflections upon the march—Meet with old acquaintances.

THE battalion remained encamped at Santa Barbara, from the 27th of December to the 3d of January, 1847. The U. S. flag was raised in the public square of the town the day after our arrival.

The town of Santa Barbara is beautifully situated for the picturesque, about one mile from the shore of a roadstead, which affords anchorage for vessels of any size, and a landing for boats, in calm weather. During stormy weather, or the prevalence of strong winds from the southeast, vessels, for safety, are compelled to stand out to sea. A fertile plain extends some twenty or thirty miles up and down the coast, varying in breadth from two to ten miles, and bounded on the east by a range of high mountains. The population of the town, I should judge from the number of houses, to be about 1200 souls. Most of the houses are constructed of adobes, in the usual architectural style of Mexican buildings. Some of them, however, are more Americanized, and have some pretensions to tasteful architecture, and comfortable and convenient interior arrangement. Its commerce, I presume, is limited to the export of hides and tallow produced upon the surrounding plain; and the commodities received in exchange for these from the traders on the coast. Doubtless, new and yet undeveloped sources of wealth will be discovered hereafter, that will render this town of much greater importance than it is at present.

On the coast, a few miles above Santa Barbara, there are, I have been told, immense quantities of pure bitumen or mineral tar, which, rising in the ocean, has been thrown upon the shore by the waves, where in a concrete state, like rosin, it has accumulated in inexhaustible masses. There are, doubtless, many valuable minerals in the neighboring mountains, which, when developed by enterprise, will add greatly to the wealth and importance of the town. For intelligence, refinement, and civilization, the population, it is said, will compare advantageously with any in California. Some old and influential Spanish families are residents of this place ; but their *casas*, with the exception of that of Señor Don José Noriega, the largest house in the place, are now closed and deserted. Señor N. is one of the oldest and most respectable citizens of California, having filled the highest offices in the government of the country. One of his daughters is a resident of New York, having married ALFRED ROBINSON, Esq., of that city, author of " Life in California."

The climate, judging from the indications while we remained here, must be delightful, even in winter. With the exception of one day which was tempestuous, the temperature at night did not fall below 50°, and during the day the average was between 60° and 70°. The atmosphere was perfectly clear and serene, the weather resembling that of the pleasant days of April in the same latitude on the Atlantic side of the continent. It is a peculiarity of the Mexicans that they allow no shade or ornamental trees to grow near their houses. In none of the streets of the towns or missions through which I have passed, has there been a solitary tree standing. I noticed very few horticultural attempts in Santa Barbara. At the mission, about two miles distant, which is an extensive establishment and in good preservation, I was told that there were fine gardens, producing most of the varieties of fruits of the tropical and temperate climates.

Several Californians came into camp and offered to deliver themselves up. They were permitted to go at large. They represented that the Californian force at the south was daily

33

growing weaker from dissensions and desertions. The United States prize-schooner Julia, arrived on the 30th, from which was landed a cannon for the use of the battalion. It has, however, to be mounted on wheels, and the gear necessary for hauling it has to be made in the camp. Reports were current in camp on the 31st, that the Californians intended to meet and fight us at San Buenaventura, about thirty miles distant. On the 1st of January, the Indians of the mission and town celebrated new-year's day, by a procession, music, etc. etc. They marched from the mission to the town, and through most of the empty and otherwise silent streets. Among the airs they played was " Yankee Doodle."

January 3.—A beautiful spring-like day. We resumed our march at 11 o'clock, and encamped in a live-oak grove about ten miles south of Santa Barbara. Our route has been generally near the shore of the ocean. Timber is abundant, and the grass and other vegetation luxuriant. Distance 10 miles.

January 4.—At the " Rincon," or passage between two points of land jutting into the ocean, so narrow that at high tides the surf dashes against the nearly perpendicular bases of the mountains which bound the shore, it has been supposed the hostile Californians would make a stand, the position being so advantageous to them. The road, if road it can be called, where all marks of hoofs or wheels are erased by each succeeding tide, runs along a hard sand-beach, with occasional projections of small points of level ground, ten or fifteen miles, and the surf, even when the tide has fallen considerably, frequently reaches to the bellies of the horses. Some demonstration has been confidently expected here, but we encamped in this pass the first day without meeting an enemy or seeing a sign of one. Our camp is close to the ocean, and the roar of the surf, as it dashes against the shore, is like that of an immense cataract. Hundreds of the grampus whale are sporting a mile or two distant from the land, spouting up water and spray to a great height, in columns resembling steam from the escape-pipes of steamboats. Distance 6 miles.

Jan. 5.—The prize-schooner Julia was lying off in sight this morning, for the purpose of co-operating with us, should there be any attempt on the part of the enemy to interrupt the march of the battalion. We reached the mission of San Buenaventura, and encamped a short distance from it at two o'clock. Soon after, a small party of Californians exhibited themselves on an elevation just beyond the mission. The battalion was immediately called to arms, and marched out to meet them. But after the discharge of the two field-pieces, they scampered away like a flock of antelopes, and the battalion returned to camp, with none killed or wounded on either side. Under the belief that there was a larger force of Californians encamped at a distance of some five or six miles, and that during the night they might attempt a surprise, or plant cannon on the summit of a hill about a mile from camp, so as to annoy us, a party, of which I was one, was detached after dark to occupy the hill secretly. We marched around the mission as privately as possible, and took our position on the hill, where we remained all night without the least disturbance, except by the tempestuous wind, which blew a blast so cold and piercing as almost to congeal the blood. When the sun rose in the morning, I could see far out in the ocean, three vessels scudding before the gale like phantom-ships. One of these was the little schooner that had been waiting upon us while marching along the "Rincon." Distance 14 miles.

Jan. 6.—The wind has blown a gale in our faces all day, and the clouds of dust have been almost blinding. The mission of San Buenaventura does not differ, in its general features, from those of other establishments of the same kind heretofore described. There is a large garden, enclosed by a high wall, attached to the mission, in which I noticed a great variety of fruit-trees and ornamental shrubbery. There are also numerous enclosures, for cultivation, by willow hedges. The soil, when properly tilled, appears to be highly productive. This mission is situated about two miles from the shore of a small bay or indentation of the coast, on the edge of a plain or valley watered by the Rio Santa Clara, which empties into the Pacific at this point. A chain of small islands, from ten to twenty miles from the shore, commences at Santa Barbara, and extends south along the coast to the bay of San Pedro. These islands present to the eye a barren appearance. At present the only inhabitants of the mission are a few Indians, the white population having abandoned it on our approach, with the exception of one man, who met us yesterday and surrendered himself a prisoner.

Proceeding up the valley about seven miles from the mission, we discovered at a distance a party of sixty or seventy mounted Californians, drawn up in order on the bank of the river. This, it was conjectured, might be only a portion of a much larger force stationed here, and concealed in a deep ravine which runs across the valley, or in the *cañadas* of the hills on our left. Scouting-parties mounted the hills, for the purpose of ascertaining if such was the case. In the mean time, the party of Californians on our right scattered themselves over the plain, prancing their horses, waving their swords, banners, and lances, and performing a great variety of equestrian feats. They were mounted on fine horses, and there are no better horsemen, if as good, in the world, than Californians. They took special care, however, to keep beyond the reach of cannon-shot. The battalion wheeled to the left for the purpose of crossing a point of hills jutting into the plain, and taking the supposed concealed party of the enemy on their flank. It was, however, found impracticable to cross the hills with the cannon; and returning to the plain, the march was continued, the Californians still prancing and performing their antics in our faces. Our horses were so poor and feeble that it was impossible to chase them with any hope of success. As we proceeded they retreated. Some of the Indian scouts, among whom were a Delaware named Tom, who distinguished himself in the engagement near San Juan, and a Californian Indian named Gregorio, rode towards them; and two or three guns were discharged on both sides, but without any damage, the parties not being within dangerous gun-shot distance of each other. The Californians then formed themselves in a body, and soon disappeared behind some hills on our right. We encamped about four o'clock in the valley, the wind blowing almost a hurricane, and the dust flying so as nearly to blind us. Distance 9 miles.

Jan. 7.—Continuing our march up the valley, we encamped near the rancho of Carrillo, where we found an abundance of corn, wheat, and frijoles. The house was shut up, having been deserted by its proprietor, who is said to be connected with the rebellion. Californian scouts were seen occasionally to-day on the summits of the hills south of us. Distance 7 miles.

Jan. 8.—Another tempestuous day. I do not remember ever to have experienced such disagreeable effects from the wind and the clouds of dust in which we were constantly enveloped, driving into our faces without intermission. We encamped this afternoon in a grove of willows near a rancho, where, as yesterday, we found corn and beans in abundance. Our horses, consequently, fare well, and we fare better than we have done. One-fourth of the battalion, exclusive of the regular guard, is kept under arms during the night, to be prepared against surprises and night-attacks. Distance 12 miles.

January 9.—Early this morning Captain Hamley, accompanied by a Californian as a guide, came into camp, with dispatches from Commodore Stockton. The exact purport of these dispatches I never learned, but it was understood that the commodore, in conjunction with General Kearny, was marching upon Los Angeles, and that if they had not already reached and taken that town, (the present capital of California,) they were by this time in its neighborhood. Captain Hamley passed, last night, the encampment of a party of Californians in our rear. He landed from a vessel at Santa Barbara, and from thence followed us to this place by land. We encamped this afternoon at a rancho, situated on the edge of a fertile and finely-watered plain of considerable extent, where we found corn, wheat, and frijoles in great abundance. The rancho was owned and occupied by an aged Californian, of commanding and respectable appearance. I could not but feel compassion for the venerable old man, whose sons were now all absent and engaged in the war, while he, at home and unsupported, was suffering the unavoidable inconveniences and calamities resulting from an army being quartered upon him.

33*

As we march south there appears to be a larger supply of wheat, maize, beans, and barley, in the granaries of the ranchos. More attention is evidently given to the cultivation of the soil here than farther north, although neither the soil nor climate is so well adapted to the raising of crops. The Californian spies have shown themselves at various times to-day, on the summits of the hills on our right. Distance 12 miles.

January 10.—Crossing the plain we encamped, about two o'clock, P. M., in the mouth of a *cañada*, through which we ascend over a difficult pass in a range of elevated hills between us and the plain of San Fernando, or Couenga. Some forty or fifty mounted Californians exhibited themselves on the summit of the pass during the afternoon. They were doubtless a portion of the same party that we met several days ago, just below San Buenaventura. A large number of cattle were collected in the plain and corralled, to be driven along to-morrow for subsistence. Distance 10 miles.

January 11.—The battalion this morning was divided into two parties: the main body, on foot, marching over a ridge of hills to the right of the road or trail; and the artillery, horses, and baggage, with an advance-guard and escort, marching by the direct route. We found the pass narrow, and easily to be defended by brave and determined men against a greatly superior force; but when we had mounted the summit of the ridge there was no enemy, nor the sign of one, in sight. Descending into a *cañada* on the other side, we halted until the main body came up to us, and then the whole force was again reunited, and the march continued.

Emerging from the hills, the advance party, to which I was attached, met two Californians, bareheaded, riding in great haste. They stated that they were from the mission of San Fernando; that the Californian forces had met the American forces under the command of General Kearny and Commodore Stockton, and had been defeated after two days' fighting; and that the Americans had yesterday marched into Los Angeles. They requested to be conducted immediately to Colonel Fremont, which request was complied with. A little farther on we met a Frenchman, who stated that he was the bearer of a letter from General Kearny, at Los Angeles, to Colonel Fremont. He confirmed the statement we had just heard, and was permitted to pass. Continuing our march, we entered the mission of San Fernando at one o'clock, and in about two hours the main body arrived, and the whole battalion encamped in the mission buildings.

The buildings and gardens belonging to this mission are in better condition than those of any of these establishments I have seen. There are two extensive gardens, surrounded by high walls ; and a stroll through them afforded a most delightful contrast from the usually uncultivated landscape we have been travelling through for so long a time. Here were brought together most of the fruits and many of the plants of the temperate and tropical climates. Although not the season of flowers, still the roses were in bloom. Oranges, lemons, figs, and olives hung upon the trees, and the blood-red *tuna*, or prickly-pear, looked very tempting. Among the plants I noticed the American aloe, (*argave Americana*,) which is otherwise called *maguey*. From this plant, when it attains maturity, a saccharine liquor is extracted, which is manufactured into a beverage called *pulque*, and is much prized by Mexicans. The season of grapes has passed, but there are extensive vineyards at this mission. I drank, soon after my arrival, a glass of red wine manufactured here, of a good quality.

The mission of San Fernando is situated at the head of an extensive and very fertile plain, judging from the luxuriance of the grass and other vegetation now springing up. I noticed in the granary from which our horses were supplied with food, many thousand bushels of corn. The ear is smaller than that of the corn of the Southern States. It resembles the maize cultivated in the Northern States, the kernel being hard and polished. Large herds of cattle and sheep were grazing upon the plain in sight of the mission.

January 12.—This morning two Californian officers, accompanied by Tortoria Pico, who marched with us from San Luis Obispo, came to the mission to treat for peace. A consultation was held and terms were suggested, and, as I understand, partly agreed upon, but not concluded. The officers left in the afternoon.

January 13.—We continued our march, and encamped near a deserted rancho at the foot of Couenga plain. Soon after we halted the Californian peace-commissioners appeared, and the terms of peace and capitulation were finally agreed upon and signed by the respective parties. They were as follows:

ARTICLES OF CAPITULATION

Made and entered into at the Ranch of Couenga, this thirteenth day of January, eighteen hundred and forty-seven, between P. B. Reading, major; Louis McLane, jr., commanding 3rd Artillery; William H. Russell, ordnance officer—commissioners appointed by J. C. Fremont, Colonel United States Army, and Military Commandant of California; and José Antonio Carrillo, commandant esquadron; Augustin Olivera, deputado—commissioners appointed by Don Andres Pico, Commander-in-chief of the Californian forces under the Mexican flag.

Article 1st. The Commissioners on the part of the Californians agree that their entire force shall, on presentation of themselves to Lieutenant-colonel Fremont, deliver up their artillery and public arms, and that they shall return peaceably to their homes, conforming to the laws and regulations of the United States, and not again take up arms during the war between the United States and Mexico, but will assist and aid in placing the country in a state of peace and tranquillity.

Article 2nd. The Commissioners on the part of Lieutenant-colonel Fremont agree and bind themselves, on the fulfilment of the 1st Article by the Californians, that they shall be guarantied protection of life and property, whether on parole or otherwise.

Article 3d. That until a Treaty of Peace be made and signed between the United States of North America and the Republic of Mexico, no Californian or other Mexican citizen shall be bound to take the oath of allegiance.

Article 4th. That any Californian or citizen of Mexico, desiring, is permitted by this capitulation to leave the country without let or hinderance.

Article 5th. That in virtue of the aforesaid articles, equal rights and privileges are vouchsafed to every citizen of California, as are enjoyed by the citizens of the United States of North America.

Article 6th. All officers, citizens, foreigners or others, shall receive the protection guarantied by the 2d Article.

Article 7th. This capitulation is intended to be no bar in effecting such arrangements as may in future be in justice required by both parties.

ADDITIONAL ARTICLE.

CIUDAD DE LOS ANGELES, Jan. 16th, 1847.

That the paroles of all officers, citizens and others of the United States and of naturalized citizens of Mexico, are by this foregoing capitulation cancelled, and every condition of said paroles, from and after this date, are of no further force and effect, and all prisoners of both parties are hereby released.

> P. B. READING, Maj. Cal'a. Battalion.
> LOUIS MCLANE, Com'd. Artillery.
> WM. H. RUSSELL, Ordnance Officer.
> JOSE ANTONIO CARRILLO, Comd't of Squadron.
> AUGUSTIN OLIVERA, Deputado.

APPROVED,

J. C. FREMONT, Lieut.-Col. U. S. Army, and Military Commandant of California.

ANDRES PICO, Commandant of Squadron and Chief of the National forces of California.

[The next morning a brass howitzer was brought into camp, and delivered. What other arms were given up I cannot say, for I saw none. Nor can I speak as to the number of Californians who were in the field under the command of Andres Pico when the articles of capitulation were signed, for they were never in sight of us after we reached San Fernando.] Distance 12 miles.

January 14.—It commenced raining heavily this morning. Crossing a ridge of hills we entered the magnificent undulating plain surrounding the city of Angels, now verdant with a carpet of fresh vegetation. Among other plants I noticed the mustard, and an immense quantity of the common pepper-grass of our gardens. We passed several warm springs which throw up large quantities of bitumen or mineral tar. Urging our jaded animals through the mud and water, which in places was very deep, we reached the town about 3 o'clock.

A more miserably clad, wretchedly provided, and unprepossessing military host, probably never entered a civilized city. In all except our order, deportment, and arms, we might have been mistaken for a procession of tatterdemalions, or a tribe of Nomades from Tartary. There were not many of us so fortunate as to have in our possession an entire outside garment;

and several were without hats or shoes, or a complete covering to their bodies. But that we had at last reached the terminus of a long and laborious march, attended with hardships, exposure and privation rarely suffered, was a matter of such heartfelt congratulation, that these comparatively trifling inconveniences were not thought of. Men never, probably, in the entire history of military transactions, bore these privations with more fortitude or uttered fewer complaints.

We had now arrived at the abode of the *celestials*, if the interpretation of the name of the place could be considered as indicative of the character of its population, and drenched with rain and plastered with mud, we entered the " city of the Angels," and marched through its principal street to our temporary quarters. We found the town, as we expected, in the possession of the United States naval and military forces under the command of Commodore Stockton and General Kearny, who, after two engagements with six hundred mounted Californians on the 8th and 9th, had marched into the city on the 10th. The town was almost entirely deserted by its inhabitants, and most of the houses, except those belonging to foreigners, or occupied as quarters for the troops, were closed. I met here many of the naval officers whose agreeable acquaintance I had made at San Francisco. Among others were Lieutenants Thompson, Hunter, Gray, and Renshaw, and Captain Zeilin of the marines, all of whom had marched from San Diego. Distance 12 miles.

CHAPTER XXXIV.

Military operations of General Kearny and Commodore Stockton—Their reports to the Secretaries of War and Navy—Battles of San Pasqual and San Gabriel

THE operations of General Kearny in California, and afterwards the joint operations of Commodore Stockton and General

Kearny, which resulted in the defeat of the Californians on the 8th and 9th of January, and the capture of Los Angeles, are clearly and concisely stated in their official reports to the War Department, which were dispatched to Washington by Lieut. Gray of the navy, and Lieut. Emory of the army, immediately after our arrival at Los Angeles. The reports are subjoined.

HEADQUARTERS, ARMY OF THE WEST, }
San Diego, Upper California, Dec. 12, 1846. }

SIR : As I have previously reported to you, I left Santa Fé (New Mexico) for this country on the 25th September, with 300 of the 1st dragoons, under Major Sumner. We crossed to the bank of the Del Norte at Albuquerque, (65 miles below Santa Fé,) continuing down on that bank till the 6th October, when we met Mr. Kit Carson, with a party of sixteen men, on his way to Washington City, with a mail and papers, an express from Commodore Stockton and Lieut.-Col. Fremont, reporting that the Californias were already in possession of the Americans under their command ; that the American flag was flying from every important position in the territory, and that the country was forever free from Mexican control ; the war ended, and peace and harmony established among the people. In consequence of this information, I directed that 200 dragoons, under Major Sumner, should remain in New Mexico, and that the other 100, with two mountain-howitzers, under Captain Moore, should accompany me as a guard to Upper California. With this guard, we continued our march to the south, on the right bank of the Del Norte, to the distance of about 230 miles below Santa Fé, when, leaving that river on the 15th October, in about the 33d deg. of latitude, we marched westward for the Copper-mines, which we reached on the 18th, and on the 20th reached the river Gila, proceeded down the Gila, crossing and recrossing it as often as obstructions in our front rendered necessary ; on the 11th November reached the Pimos village, about 80 miles from the settlements in Sonora. These Indians we found honest, and living comfortably, having made a good crop this year ; and we remained with them two days, to rest our men, recruit our animals, and obtain provisions. On the 22d November, reached the mouth of the Gila, in latitude about 32 degrees —our whole march on this river having been nearly 500 miles, and, with but very little exception, between the 32d and 33d parallels of latitude.

This river, (the Gila,) more particularly the northern side, is bounded nearly the whole distance by a range of lofty mountains ; and if a tolerable wagon-road to its mouth from the Del Norte is ever discovered, it must be on the south side. The country is destitute of timber, producing but few cotton-wood and musquit-trees ; and though the soil on the bottom-lands is generally good, yet we found but very little grass or vegetation, in consequence of the dryness of the climate and the little rain which falls here. The Pimos Indians, who make good crops of wheat, corn, vegetables, &c., irrigate the land by water from the Gila, as did the Aztecs, (the former inhabitants of the country,) the remains of whose sequias, or little canals, were seen by us, as well as the position of many of their dwellings, and a large quantity of broken pottery and earthenware used by them.

We crossed the Colorado about 10 miles below the mouth of the Gila, and marching near it about 30 miles further, turned off and crossed the desert—a distance of about 60 miles—without water or grass

On the 2d December, reached Warner's rancho, (Agua Caliente,) the frontier settlement in California, on the route leading to Sonora. On the 4th we marched to Mr. Stokes's rancho, (San Isabella,) and on the 5th, were met by a small party of volunteers, under Captain Gillespie, sent out from San Diego by Commodore Stockton, to give us what information they possessed of the enemy, 600 or 700 of whom are now said to be in arms and in the field throughout the territory, determined upon opposing the Americans and resisting their authority in the country. Encamped that night near another rancho (San Maria) of Mr. Stokes, about 40 miles from San Diego.

The journals and maps, kept and prepared by Captain Johnston, (my aid-de-camp,) and those by Lieutenant Emory, topographical engineers, which will accompany or follow this report, will render any thing further from me, on this subject, unnecessary.

Very respectfully, your obedient servant,

S. W. KEARNY,
Brigadier-general, U. S. A.

BRIGADIER-GENERAL R. JONES, ⎰
Adjutant-general, U. S. A. ⎱

HEADQUARTERS, ARMY OF THE WEST, ⎰
San Diego, Upper California, Dec. 13, 1846. ⎱

SIR: In my communication to you of yesterday's date, I brought the reports of the movements of my guard up to the morning of the 5th instant, in camp near a rancho of Mr. Stokes, (Santa Maria,) about 40 miles from San Diego.

Having learned from Captain Gillespie, of the volunteers, that there was an armed party of Californians, with a number of extra horses at San Pasqual, three leagues distant on a road leading to this place, I sent Lieutenant Hammond, 1st dragoons with a few men to make a reconnoissance of them. He returned at two in the morning of the 6th instant, reporting that he had found the party in the place mentioned, and that he had been seen, though not pursued by them. I then determined that I would march for and attack them by break of day. Arrangements were accordingly made for the purpose. My aid-de-camp, Capt. Johnston, dragoons, was assigned to the command of the advanced guard of twelve dragoons, mounted on the best horses we had; then followed about fifty dragoons under Capt. Moore, mounted, with but few exceptions, on the tired mules they had ridden from Santa Fé, (New Mexico, 1,050 miles;) then about twenty volunteers of Captain Gibson's company under his command, and that of Captain Gillespie; then followed our two mountain-howitzers, with dragoons to manage them, and under the charge of Lieutenant Davidson of the 1st regiment. The remainder of the dragoons, volunteers, and citizens, employed by the officers of the staff, &c., were placed under the command of Major Swords, (quartermaster,) with orders to follow on our trail with the baggage, and to see to its safety.

As the day (December 6) dawned, we approached the enemy at San Pasqual, who was already in the saddle, when Captain Johnston made a furious charge upon them with his advance-guard, and was in a short time after supported by the dragoons; soon after which the enemy gave way, having kept up from the beginning a continued fire upon us. Upon the retreat of the enemy, Captain Moore led off rapidly in pursuit, accompanied by the dragoons, mounted on horses, and was followed, though slowly, by the others on their tired mules; the enemy, well mounted, and among the best horsemen in the world, after retreating about half a mile, and seeing an interval between Captain Moore and his advance and the dragoons coming to his support, rallied their whole force, charged with their lances, and, on account of their greatly superior numbers, but few of us in front remained untouched; for five minutes they held the ground from us, when our men coming up, we again drove them, and they fled from the field, not to return to it, which we occupied and encamped upon.

A most melancholy duty now remains for me: it is to report the death of my aid-de-camp, Captain Johnston, who was shot dead at the commencement of the action; of Captain Moore, who was lanced just previous to the final retreat of the enemy; and of Lieutenant Hammond, also lanced, and who survived but a few hours. We had also killed two sergeants, two corporals, and ten privates of the 1st dragoons; one private of the volunteers, and one man, an engagé in the topographical department. Among the wounded are myself, (in two places,) Lieutenant Warner, topographical engineers, (in three places,) Captains Gillespie and Gibson of the volunteers, (the former in three places,) one sergeant, one bugleman, and nine privates of the dragoons; many of these surviving from two to ten lance wounds, most of them when unhorsed and incapable of resistance.

Our howitzers were not brought into the action; but coming to the front at the close of it, before they were turned, so as to admit of being fired upon the retreating enemy, the two mules before one of them got alarmed, and freeing themselves from their drivers, ran off, and among the enemy, and was thus lost to us.

The enemy proved to be a party of 160 Californians under Andres Pico, brother of the late governor; the number of their dead and wounded must have been considerable, though I have no means of ascertaining how many, as just previous to their final retreat, they carried off all excepting six.

The great number of our killed and wounded proves that our officers and men have fully sustained the high character and reputation of our troops; and the victory thus gained over more than double our force, may assist in forming the wreath of our national glory.

I have to return my thanks to many for their gallantry and good conduct on the field, and particularly to Capt. Turner, first dragoons, (assistant acting adjutant-general,) and to Lieut. Emory, topographical engineers, who were active in the performance of their duties, and in conveying orders from me to the command.

On the morning of the 7th, having made ambulances for our wounded, and interred the dead, we proceeded on our march, when the enemy showed himself, occupying the hills in our front, but which they left as we approached; till, reaching San Bernado, a party of them took possession of a hill near to it, and maintained their position until attacked by our advance, who quickly drove them from it, killing and wounding five of their number, with no loss on our part.

On account of our wounded men, and upon the report of the surgeon that rest was necessary for them, we remained at this place till the morning of the 11th, when Lieut. Gray, of the navy, in command of a party of sailors and marines, sent out from San Diego by Com. Stockton, joined us. We proceeded at 10, A. M., the enemy no longer showing himself; and on the 12th, (yesterday,) we reached this place; and I have now to offer my thanks to Com. Stockton, and all of his gallant command, for the very many kind attentions we have received and continue to receive from them.

Very respectfully, your obedient servant,

S. W. KEARNY, *Brig. Gen. U. S. A.*

BRIGADIER-GENERAL R. JONES,
   Adjutant-general, U. S. A., Washington.

HEADQUARTERS, ARMY OF THE WEST, ⟩
   Ciudad de los Angeles, Upper California, Jan. 12, 1847. ⟨

SIR: I have the honor to report that, at the request of Com. R. F. Stockton, United States Navy, (who in September last assumed the title of governor of California,) I consented to take command of an expedition to this place, (the capital of the country,) and that, on the 29th December, I left San Diego with about 500 men, consisting of sixty dismounted dragoons under Capt. Turner, fifty California volunteers, and the remainder of marines and sailors, with a battery of artillery—Lieut. Emory (topographical engineers) acting as assistant adjutant-general. Com. Stockton accompanied us.

We proceeded on our route without seeing the enemy, till on the 8th instant, when they showed themselves in full force of 600 mounted men, with four pieces of artillery, under their governor, (Flores,) occupying the heights in front of us, which commanded the crossing of the river San Gabriel, and they ready to oppose our further progress. The necessary disposition of our troops was immediately made, by covering our front with a strong party of skirmishers, placing our wagons and baggage-train in rear of them, and protecting the flanks and rear with the remainder of the command. We then proceeded, forded the river, carried the heights, and drove the enemy from them, after an action of about an hour and a half, during which they made a charge upon our left flank, which was repulsed ; soon after which they retreated and left us in possession of the field, on which we encamped that night.

The next day (the 9th instant) we proceeded on our march at the usual hour, the enemy in our front and on our flanks : and when we reached the plains of the Mesa, their artillery again opened upon us, when their fire was returned by our guns as we advanced ; and after hovering around and near us for about two hours, occasionally skirmishing with us during that time, they concentrated their force and made another charge on our left flank, which was quickly repulsed. Shortly after which they retired, we continuing our march, and we (in the afternoon) encamped on the banks of the Mesa, three miles below this city, which we entered the following morning (the 10th instant) without further molestation.

Our loss in the actions of the 8th and 9th was small, being but one private killed, and two officers—Lieut. Rowan of the navy, and Capt. Gillespie, of the volunteers, and eleven privates wounded. The enemy, mounted on fine horses, and being the best riders in the world, carried off their killed and wounded, and we know not the number of them, though it must have been considerable.

Very respectfully, your obedient servant,
S. W. KEARNY, *Brigadier-general.*

BRIGADIER-GENERAL R. JONES,
    Adjutant-general, U. S. A., Washington.

Statement of killed and wounded in the action of the 8th January, 1847.

Killed.—Frederick Strauss, seaman, United States ship Portsmouth, artillery corps ; cannon-shot in neck.

Wounded.—1st. Jacob Hait, volunteer, artillery driver, wound in left breast ; died on evening of 9th. 2d. Thos. Smith, ordinary seaman, United States ship Cyane, company D, musketeers, shot, by accident, through the right thigh ; died on night of the 8th. 3d. William Cope, seaman, United States ship Savannah, company B, musketeers, wound in the right thigh and right arm ; severe. 4th. George Bantum, ordinary seaman, United States ship Cyane, pikeman, punctured wound of hand, accidental; slight. 5th. Patrick Campbell, seaman, United States ship Cyane, company D, musketeers, wound in thigh by spent ball; slight. 6th. William Scott, private, United States marine corps, ship Portsmouth, wound in the chest, spent ball; slight. 7th. James Hendry, seaman, United States ship Congress, company A, musketeers, spent ball, wound over stomach; slight. 8th. Joseph Wilson, seaman, United States ship Congress, company A, musketeers, wound in right thigh, spent ball; slight. 9th. Ivory Coffin, seaman, United States ship Savannah, company B, musketeers, contusion of right knee, spent ball; slight.

Wounded on the 9th.—1st. Mark A. Child, private, company C, 1st regiment United States dragoons, gunshot wound in right heel, penetrating upwards into the ankle-joint; severe. 2d. James Cambell, ordinary seaman, United States ship Congress, company D, carbineers, wound in right foot, second toe amputated; accidental discharge of his own carbine. 3d. George Crawford, boatswain's mate, United States ship Cyane, company D, musketeers, wound in left thigh; severe. Lieut. Rowan, United States navy, and Capt. Gillespie, California battalion, volunteers, contused slightly by spent balls.

I am, sir, most respectfully, your obedient servant,

JOHN S. GRIFFIN, *Assistant Surgeon, U. S. N.*

Capt. WM. H. EMORY,
    Assistant Adjutant-general, U. S. forces.
CIUDAD DE LOS ANGELES, *California, Jan.* 11, 1847.

HEADQUARTERS, ARMY OF THE WEST, }
    Ciudad de los Angeles, Upper California, Jan. 14, 1847. }

SIR: This morning, Lieutenant-colonel Fremont, of the regiment of mounted riflemen, reached here with 400 volunteers from the Sacramento; the enemy capitulated with him yesterday, near San Fernando, agreeing to lay down their arms, and we have now the prospect of having peace and quietness in this country, which I hope may not be interrupted again.

I have not yet received any information of the troops which were to come from New York, nor of those to follow me from New Mexico, but presume they will be here before long. On their arrival, I shall, agreeably to the instructions of the President of the United States, have the management of affairs in this country, and will endeavor to carry out his views in relation to it.

Very respectfully your obedient servant,

S. W. KEARNY *Brigadier-general.*

BRIGADIER-GENERAL R. JONES,
    Adjutant-general, U S. A., Washington.

HEADQUARTERS, CIUDAD DE LOS ANGELES, }
January 11, 1847. }

SIR : I have the honor to inform you that it has pleased God to crown our poor efforts to put down the rebellion, and to retrieve the credit of our arms, with the most complete success. The insurgents determined, with their whole force, to meet us on our march from San Diego to this place, and to decide the fate of the territory by a general battle.

Having made the best preparation I could, in the face of a boasting and vigilant enemy, we left San Diego on the 29th day of December, (that portion of the insurgent army who had been watching and annoying us, having left to join the main body,) with about six hundred fighting men, composed of detachments from the ships Congress, Savannah, Portsmouth, and Cyane, aided by General Kearny, with a detachment of sixty men on foot, from the first regiment of United States dragoons, and by Captain Gillespie, with sixty mounted riflemen.

We marched nearly one hundred and forty miles in ten days, and found the rebels, on the 8th day of January, in a strong position, on the high bank of the " Rio San Gabriel," with six hundred mounted men and four pieces of artillery, prepared to dispute our passage across the river.

We waded through the water, dragging our guns after us, against the galling fire of the enemy, without exchanging a shot, until we reached the opposite shore, when the fight became general, and our troops having repelled a charge of the enemy, charged up the bank in a most gallant manner, and gained a complete victory over the insurgent army.

The next day, on our march across the plains of the " Mesa" to this place, the insurgents made another desperate effort to save the capital and their own necks; they were concealed with their artillery in a ravine until we came within gunshot, when they opened a brisk fire from their field-pieces on our right flank, and at the same time charged both on our front and rear. We soon silenced their guns, and repelled the charge, when they fled, and permitted us the next morning to march into town without any further opposition.

We have rescued the country from the hands of the insurgents, but I fear that the absence of Colonel Fremont's battalion of mounted riflemen will enable most of the Mexican officers, who have broken their parole, to escape to Sonora.

I am happy to say that our loss in killed and wounded does not exceed twenty, whilst we are informed that the enemy has lost between seventy and eighty.

This dispatch must go immediately, and I will wait another opportunity

34*

to furnish you with the details of these two battles, and the gallant conduct of the officers and men under my command, with their names.

Faithfully, your obedient servant,

R. F. STOCKTON, *Commodore, &c*

To the Hon. GEORGE BANCROFT,
Secretary of the Navy, Washington, D. C.

P. S. Enclosed I have the honor to send to you a translation of the letter handed to me by the commissioners mentioned in another part of this dispatch, sent by José Ma. Flores, to negotiate peace honorable to both nations. The verbal answer, stated in another page of this letter, was sent to this renowned general and commander-in-chief. He had violated his honor, and I would not treat with him nor write to him.

General Flores' letter is here given—

[Translation.]

Civil and Military Government of the Department of California.

The undersigned, governor and commandant-general of the department, and commander-in-chief of the national troops, has the honor to address himself to the commander-in-chief of the naval and land forces of the United States of North America, to say that he has been informed by persons worthy of credit, that it is probable at this time the differences which have altered the relations of friendship between the Mexican republic and that of the United States of North America have ceased, and that you looked for the news of the arrangement between the two governments by the schooner Shark, expected every moment on this coast.

A number of days have elapsed since the undersigned was invited by several foreign gentlemen settled in the country, to enter into a communication with you, they acting as mediators, to obtain an honorable adjustment for both forces, in consequence of the evils which all feel are caused by the unjust war you wage; but the duty of the undersigned prohibited him from doing so, and if to-day he steps beyond the limits marked out by it, it is with the confidence inspired by the hope there exists a definitive arrangement between the two nations; for the undersigned being animated with the strongest wishes for the return of peace, it would be most painful to him not to have taken the means to avoid the useless effusion of human blood and its terrible consequences, during moments when the general peace might have been secured.

The undersigned flatters himself with this hope, and for that reason has thought it opportune to direct to you this note, which will be placed in your hands by Messrs. Julian Workman and Charles Fluge, who have voluntarily offered themselves to act as mediators. But if, unfortunately, the mentioned news should prove untrue, and you should not be disposed to grant a truce to the evils under which this unfortunate country suffers, of which you alone are the cause, may the terrible consequences of your want of consideration fall on your head. The citizens, all of whom compose the national forces of this department, are decided firmly to bury themselves under the ruins of their country, combating to the last moment, before consenting to the tyranny and ominous discretionary power of the agents of the government of the United States of North America.

This is no problem ; different deeds of arms prove that they know how to defend their rights on the field of battle.

The undersigned still confides you will give a satisfactory solution to this affair, and in the mean time has the honor of offering to you the assurance of his consideration and private esteem.

God and liberty !   JOSE MA. FLORES

HEADQUARTERS AT THE ANGELES,
     January 1, 1847.

General Order.

HEADQUARTERS, CIUDAD DE LOS ANGELES,
          January 11, 1847.

The commander-in-chief congratulates the officers and men of the southern division of the United States forces in California, on the brilliant victories obtained by them over the enemy on the 8th and 9th instants, and on once more taking possession of the " Ciudad de los Angeles."

He takes the earliest moment to commend their gallantry and good conduct, both in the battle fought on the 8th, on the banks of the " Rio San Gabriel," and on the 9th instant, on the plains of the " Mesa."

The steady courage of the troops in forcing their passage across the " Rio San Gabriel," where officers and men were alike employed in dragging the guns through the water against the galling fire of the enemy, without exchanging a shot, and their gallant charge up the banks against the enemy's cavalry, has perhaps never been surpassed ; and the cool determination with which, in the battle of the 9th, they repulsed the charge of cavalry made by the enemy at the same time on their front and rear, has extorted the admiration of the enemy, and deserves the best thanks of their countrymen.

R. F. STOCKTON,
     Governor and Commander-in-chief
          of the Territory of California.

On the 14th, Colonel Fremont had arrived, and Commodore Stockton wrote as follows—

HEADQUARTERS, CIUDAD DE LOS ANGELES, }
January 15, 1847.

SIR : Referring to my letter of the 11th, I have the honor to inform you of the arrival of Lieutenant-colonel Fremont at this place, with four hundred men—that some of the insurgents have made their escape to Sonora, and that the rest have surrendered to our arms.

Immediately after the battles of the 8th and 9th, they began to disperse ; and I am sorry to say that their leader, José Ma. Flores, made his escape, and that the others have been pardoned by a capitulation agreed upon by Lieutenant-colonel Fremont.

José Ma. Flores, the commander of the insurgent forces, two or three days previous to the 8th, sent two commissioners with a flag of truce to my camp, to make a " treaty of peace." I informed the commissioners that I could not recognise José Ma. Flores, who had broken his parole, as an honorable man, or as one having any rightful authority, or worthy to be treated with—that he was a rebel in arms, and if I caught him I would have him shot. It seems that not being able to negotiate with me, and having lost the battles of the 8th and 9th, they met Colonel Fremont on the 12th instant, on his way here, who, not knowing what had occurred, he entered into the capitulation with them, which I now send to you ; and, although I refused to do it myself, still I have thought it best to approve it.

The territory of California is again tranquil, and the civil government formed by me is again in operation in the places where it was interrupted by the insurgents.

Colonel Fremont has five hundred men in his battalion, which will be quite sufficient to preserve the peace of the territory ; and I will immediately withdraw my sailors and marines, and sail as soon as possible for the coast of Mexico, where I hope they will give a good account of themselves,

Faithfully, your obedient servant,

R. F. STOCKTON, *Commodore, &c.*

To the HON. GEORGE BANCROFT, }
Secretary of the Navy, Washington, D. C.

CHAPTER XXXV.

City of Angels—Gardens—Vineyards—Produce of the vine in California— General products of the country—Reputed personal charms of the females of Los Angeles—San Diego—Gold and quicksilver mines—Lower California—Bituminous springs—Wines—A Kentuckian among the angels—Missions of San Gabriel and San Luis Rey—Gen. Kearny and Com. Stockton leave for San Diego—Col. Fremont appointed Governor of California by Com. Stockton—Com. Shubrick's general order—Insurrection in the northern part of California suppressed—Arrival of Col. Cook at San Diego.

La Ciudad de los Angeles is the largest town in California, containing between fifteen hundred and two thousand inhabitants. Its streets are laid out without any regard to regularity. The buildings are generally constructed of adobes one and two stories high, with flat roofs. The public buildings are a church, quartel, and government house. Some of the dwelling-houses are frames, and large. Few of them, interiorly or exteriorly, have any pretensions to architectural taste, finish, or convenience of plan and arrangement. The town is situated about 20 miles from the ocean, in an extensive undulating plain, bounded on the north by a ridge of elevated hills, on the east by high mountains whose summits are now covered with snow, on the west by the ocean, and stretching to the south and southeast as far as the eye can reach. The Rio St. Gabriel flows near the town. This stream is skirted with numerous vineyards and gardens, enclosed by willow hedges. The gardens produce a great variety of tropical fruits and plants. The yield of the vineyards is very abundant; and a large quantity of wines of a good quality and flavor, and *aguardiénte*, are manufactured here. Some of the vineyards, I understand, contain as many as twenty thousand vines. The produce of the vine in California will, undoubtedly, in a short time form an important item in its exports and commerce. The soil and climate, especially of the southern portion of the country, appear to be peculiarly adapted to the culture of the grape.

We found in Los Angeles, an abundance of maize, wheat, and *frijoles*, showing that the surrounding country is highly productive of these important articles of subsistence. There are no mills, however, in this vicinity, the universal practice of Californian families being to grind their corn by hand; and consequently flour and bread are very scarce, and not to be obtained in any considerable quantities. The only garden vegetables which I saw while here, were onions, potatoes, and *chile colorado*, or red pepper, which enters very largely into the *cuisine* of the country. I do not doubt, however, that every description of garden vegetables can be produced here, in perfection and abundance.

While I remained at Los Angeles, I boarded with two or three other officers, at the house of a Mexican Californian, the late alcalde of the town, whose political functions had ceased. He was a thin, delicate, amiable, and very polite gentleman, treating us with much courtesy, for which we paid him, when his bill was presented, a very liberal compensation. In the morning we were served, on a common deal table, with a cup of coffee and a plate of *tortillas*. At eleven o'clock, a more substantial meal was provided, consisting of stewed beef, seasoned with *chile colorado*, a rib of roasted beef, and a plate of *frijoles*, with *tortillas*, and a bottle of native wine. Our supper was a second edition of the eleven o'clock entertainment.

The town being abandoned by most of its population, and especially by the better class of the female portion of it, those who remained, which I saw, could not, without injustice, be considered as fair specimens of *the angels*, which are reputed here to inhabit. I did not happen to see one beautiful or even comely-looking woman in the place; but as the fair descendants of Eve at Los Angeles have an exalted reputation for personal charms, doubtless the reason of the invisibility of those examples of feminine attractions, so far-famed and so much looked for by the sojourner, is to be ascribed to their "unavoidable absence," on account of the dangers and casualties of war. At this time, of course, every thing in regard to society, as it usually exists here, is in a state of confusion and disorganization, and no correct conclusions in reference to it, can be drawn from observation under such circumstances.

The Bay of San Pedro, about twenty-five miles south of Los Angeles, is the port of the town. The bay affords a good anchorage for vessels of any size, but it is not a safe harbor at all times, as I have been informed by experienced nautical men on this coast. The St. Gabriel river empties into the bay. The mission of San Gabriel is about twelve miles east of Los Angeles. It is represented as an extensive establishment of this kind, the lands surrounding and belonging to it being highly fertile. The mission of San Luis Rey is situated to the south, about midway between Los Angeles and San Diego. This mission, according to the descriptions which I have received of it, is more substantial and tasteful in its construction than any other in the country ; and the gardens and grounds belonging to it are now in a high state of cultivation.

San Diego is the most southern town in Upper California. It is situated on the Bay of San Diego, in latitude 33° north. The country back of it is described by those who have travelled through it as sandy and arid, and incapable of supporting any considerable population. There are, however, it is reported on authority regarded as reliable, rich mines of quicksilver, copper, gold, and coal, in the neighborhood, which, if such be the fact, will before long render the place one of considerable importance. The harbor, next to that of San Francisco, is the best on the Pacific coast of North America, between the Straits of Fuca and Acapulco.

For the following interesting account of Lower California I am indebted to RODMAN M. PRICE, Esq., purser of the U. S. sloop-of-war Cyane, who has been connected with most of the importants events which have recently taken place in Upper and Lower California, and whose observations and opinions are valuable and reliable. It will be seen that the observations of Mr. Price differ materially from the generally received opinions in reference to Lower California.

BURLINGTON, N. J., *June* 7, 1848.

DEAR SIR,—It affords me pleasure to give you all the information I have about Lower California, derived from personal observation at several of its ports that I have visited, in the U. S. ship Cyane, in 1846–47.

Cape St. Lucas, the southern extremity of the peninsula of Lower California, is in Lat. 22° 45′ N., has a bay that affords a good harbor and anchorage, perfectly safe nine months in the year ; but it is open to the eastward, and the hurricanes which sometimes occur during July, August, and September, blow the strongest from the southeast, so that vessels will not venture in the bay during the hurricane season. I have landed twice at the Cape in a small boat, and I think a breakwater can be built, at small cost, so as to make a safe harbor at all seasons. Stone can be obtained with great ease from three cones of rocks rising from the sea, and forming the extreme southerly point of the Cape, called the Frayles. Looking to the future trade and commerce of the Pacific ocean, this great headland must become a most important point as a depot for coal and merchandise, and a most convenient location for vessels trading on that coast to get their supplies. Mr. Ritchie, now residing there, supplies a large number of whale-ships that cruise off the Cape, annually, with fresh provisions, fruits, and water. The supplies are drawn from the valley of San José, twenty miles north of the Cape, as the land in its immediate vicinity is mountainous and sterile ; but the valley of San José is extensive and well cultivated, producing the greatest variety of vegetables and fruits. The sweet and Irish potato, tomato, cabbage, lettuce, beans, peas, beets, and carrots, are the vegetables ; oranges, lemons, bananas, plantains, figs, dates, grapes, pomegranates, and olives, are its fruits. Good beef and mutton are cheap. A large amount of sugar-cane is grown, from which is made *panoche*, a favorite sugar with the natives : it is the sirup from the cane boiled down, and run into cakes of a pound weight, and in appearance is like our maple-sugar.

Panoche, cheese, olives, raisins, dried figs, and dates, put up in ceroons of hide, with the great staples of the Californias—

hides and tallow—make the export of San José, which is carried to San Blas and Mazatlan, on the opposite coast. This commerce the presence of the Cyane interrupted, finding and capturing in the Bay of La Paz, just after the receipt of the news of war on that coast, in September, 1846, sixteen small craft, laid up during the stormy season, engaged in this trade.

I cannot dismiss the valley of San José, from which the crew of the Cyane have drawn so many luxuries, without alluding to the never-failing stream of excellent water that runs through it (to which it owes its productiveness) and empties into the Gulf here, and is easily obtained for shipping when the surf is low. It is now frequented by some of our whale-ships, and European vessels bound to Mazatlan with cargoes, usually stop here to get instructions from their consignees before appearing off the port; but vessels do not anchor during the three hurricane months. The view from seaward, up this valley, is beautiful indeed, being surrounded by high barren mountains, which is the general appearance of the whole peninsula, and gives the impression that the whole country is without soil, and unproductive. When your eye gets a view of this beautiful, fertile, cultivated, rich, green valley, producing all the fruits and vegetables of the earth, Lower California stock rises. To one that has been at sea for months, on salt grub, the sight of this bright spot of cultivated acres, with the turkeys, ducks, chickens, eggs, vegetables, and fruit, makes him believe the country an *Eldorado*. Following up the coast on the Gulf side, after passing Cape Palmo good anchorage is found between the peninsula and the island of Cerralbo. Immediately to the north of this island is the entrance to the great and beautiful bay of La Paz. It has two entrances, one to the north and one to the south of the island of Espiritu Santo. The northern one is the boldest and safest for all craft drawing over twelve feet. The town of La Paz is at the bottom or south side of the bay, about twenty miles from the mouth. The bay is a large and beautiful sheet of water. The harbor of Pichelinque, of perfect millpond stillness, is formed inside of this bay. The Cyane lay at this quiet anchorage several days. Pearl-fishing is the chief employment of the inhabitants about the bay, and the pearls are said to be of superior quality. I was shown a necklace, valued at two thousand dollars, taken in this water. They are all found by diving. The *Yaque* Indians are the best divers, going down in eight-fathom water. The pearl shells are sent to China, and are worth, at La Paz, one dollar and a half the *arroba*, or twenty-five pounds. Why it is a submarine diving apparatus has not been employed in this fishery, with all its advantages over Indian diving, I cannot say. Yankee enterprise has not yet reached this new world. I cannot say this either, as a countryman of ours, Mr. Davis, living at Loretta, has been a most successful pearl-fisher, employing more Indians than any one else engaged in the business. I am sorry to add that he has suffered greatly by the war. The country about La Paz is a good grazing country, but very dry. The mountains in the vicinity are said to be very rich in minerals. Some silver-mines near San Antonio, about forty miles south, are worked, and produce well. La Paz may export one hundred thousand dollars a year of *platapiña*. Gold-dust and virgin gold are brought to La Paz. The copper and lead mines are numerous and rich. To the north of La Paz are numerous safe and good harbors. Escondida, Loretta, and Muleje, are all good harbors, formed by the islands in front of the main land. The island of Carmen, lying in front of Loretta, has a large salt lake, which has a solid salt surface of several feet thickness. The salt is of good quality, is cut out like ice, and it could supply the world. It has heretofore been a monopoly to the governor of Lower California, who employed convicts to get out the salt and put it on the beach ready for shipping. It is carried about a quarter of a mile, and is sent to Mazatlan and San Blas. A large quantity of salt is used in producing silver. To the north of Muleje, which is nearly opposite Guymas, the gulf is so much narrower that it is a harbor itself. No accurate survey has ever been made of it—indeed, all the peninsula, as well as the coast of Upper California, is laid down wrong on the charts, being about twelve miles too far easterly. The English government now have two naval ships engaged in surveying the Gulf of California.

On the Pacific coast of the peninsula there is the great Bay of Magdalena, which has fine harbors, but no water, provisions, or inhabitants. Its shores are high, barren mountains, said to possess great mineral wealth. A fleet of whale-ships have been there during the winter months of the last two years, for a new species of whale that are found there, represented as rather a small whale, producing forty or fifty barrels of oil; and what is most singular, I was assured, by most respectable whaling captains, that the oil is a good paint-oil, (an entire new quality for fish-oil.) Geographically and commercially, Lower California must become very valuable. It will be a constant source of regret to this country, that it is not included in the treaty of peace just made with Mexico. We have held and governed it during the war, and the boundary of Upper California cuts the head of the Gulf of California, so that Lower California is left entirely disconnected with the Mexican territory.

Cape St. Lucas is the great headland of the Pacific ocean, and is destined to be the Gibraltar and entrepot of that coast, or perhaps La Paz may be preferred, on account of its superior harbor. As a possession to any foreign power, I think Lower California more valuable than the group of the Sandwich Islands. It has as many arable acres as that group of islands, with rich mines, pearl-fishing, fine bays and harbors, with equal health, and all their productions. As a country, it is dry, mountainous, and sterile, yet possessing many fine valleys like San José, as the old mission establishments indicate. I have heard Todas Santos, Comondee, Santa Guadalupe, and others, spoken of as being more extensive, and as productive as San José.

I am, most faithfully and truly, yours,
RODMAN M. PRICE,
Purser, U. S. Navy.

EDWIN BRYANT, Esq., *City Hotel, New York.*

In the vicinity of Los Angeles there are a number of warm springs which throw out and deposite large quantities of bitumen or mineral tar. This substance, when it cools, becomes hard and brittle, like rosin. Around some of these springs many acres of ground are covered with this deposite to the depth of several feet. It is a principal material in the roofing of houses. When thrown upon the fire it ignites immediately, emitting a smoke like that from turpentine, and an odor like that from bituminous coal. This mineral, so abundant in California, may one day become a valuable article of commerce.

There are no reliable statistics in California. The traveller is obliged to form his estimate of matters and things chiefly from his own observation. You can place but little reliance upon information derived from the population, even when they choose to answer your questions; and most generally the response to your inquiries is—" Quien sabe," (who knows?) No Californian troubles his brains about these matters. The quantity of wines and aguardiénte produced by the vineyards and distilleries, at and near Los Angeles, must be considerable—basing my estimate upon the statement of Mr. Wolfskill, an American gentleman residing here, and whose house and vineyard I visited. Mr. W.'s vineyard is young, and covers about forty acres of ground, the number of vines being 4,000 or 5,000. From the produce of these, he told me, that last year he made 180 casks of wine, and the same quantity of aguardiénte. A cask here is sixteen gallons. When the vines mature, their produce will be greatly increased. Mr. W.'s vineyard is doubtless a model of its kind. It was a delightful recreation to stroll through it, and among the tropical fruit-trees bordering its walks. His house, too, exhibited an air of cleanliness and comfort, and a convenience of arrangement not often met with in this country. He set out for our refreshment three or four specimens of his wines, some of which would compare favorably with the best French and Madeira wines. The aguardiénte and peach-brandy, which I tasted, of his manufacture, being mellowed by age, were of an excellent flavor. The quantity of wine and aguardiénte produced in California, I would suppose, amounted to 100,000 casks of sixteen gallons, or 1,600,000 gallons. This quantity, by culture, can be increased indefinitely.

It was not possible to obtain, at Los Angeles, a piece of woollen cloth sufficiently large for a pair of pantaloons, or a pair of shoes, which would last a week. I succeeded, after searching through all the shops of the town, in procuring some black cotton-velvet, for four yards of which I paid the sum of $12. In the United States the same article would probably have cost $1.50. For four dollars more I succeeded in getting the pantaloons made up by an American tailor, who came into the country with General Kearny's forces. A Rocky Mountain trapper and trader, (Mr. Goodyear,) who has established himself near the Salt Lake since I passed there last year, fortunately arrived at Los Angeles, bringing with him a quantity of dressed deer and elk skins, which were purchased for clothing for the nearly naked soldiers.

Among the houses I visited while here, was that of Mr. Pryor, an American, and a native of Louisville, Ky. He has been a resident of the country between twenty and thirty years, but his Kentucky manners, frankness, and hospitality still adhere to him.

I remained at Los Angeles from the 14th to the 29th of January. During this time, with the exception of three days, the weather and temperature were pleasant. It rained one day, and during two days the winds blew strong and cold from the northwest. The nights are cool, but fires are not requisite to comfort. The snow-clad mountains, about twenty-five or thirty miles to the east of us, contrast singularly with the brilliant fresh verdure of the plain.

On the 18th of January General Kearny, with the dragoons, left for San Diego. There was understood to be a difference between General Kearny and Commodore Stockton, and General Kearny and Colonel Fremont, in regard to their respective powers and duties ; which, as the whole subject has subsequently undergone a thorough investigation, and the result made public, it is unnecessary for me to allude to more particularly. I did not converse with General Kearny while he was at Los Angeles, and consequently possessed no other knowledge of his views and intentions, or of the powers with which he had been invested by the President, than what I derived from report.

On the 19th, Commodore Stockton and suite, with a small escort, left for San Diego. Soon after his departure the battalion was paraded, and the appointment of Colonel Fremont as governor of California, and Colonel W. H. Russell as secretary of state, by Commodore Stockton, was read to them by Colonel Russell. It was announced, also, that although Colonel Fremont had accepted the office of chief civil magistrate of California, he would still retain his military office, and command the battalion as heretofore.

From the date of the annexed circular, which I find published in the " Californian" newspaper of Feb. 6th, it was written three days after the public announcement of Colonel Fremont as governor, as above stated.

A CIRCULAR.

The peace of the country being restored, and future tranquillity vouchsafed by a treaty made and entered into by commissioners respectively appointed by the properly authorized California officers, on the one hand, and by myself, as military commandant of the United States forces in the district of California, on the other, by which a civil government is to take place of the military, an exchange of all prisoners, etc., etc., forthwith ensure to the end that order, and a wholesome civil police, should obtain throughout the land. A copy of which said treaty will be immediately published in the California newspaper, published at Monterey.

Therefore, in virtue of the aforesaid treaty, as well as the functional that in me rest as civil governor of California, I do hereby proclaim order and peace restored to the country, and require the immediate release of all prisoners, the return of the civil officers to their appropriate duties, and as strict an obedience of the military to the civil authority as is consistent with the security of peace, and the maintenance of good order when troops are garrisoned.

Done at the capitol of the territory of California, temporarily seated at the Ciudad de los Angeles, this 22d day of January, A. D. 1847.

J. C. FREMONT,

Governor and commander-in-chief of California.

Witness—WM. H. RUSSELL, Secretary of State.

Commodore Shubrick had, however, arrived at Monterey on the 23d of January, in the U. S. ship Independence, and ranking Commodore Stockton, had assumed the chief command in California, as appears by the date of the following general order, published in the " Californian" newspaper at Monterey :—

GENERAL ORDER.

The commander-in-chief has great satisfaction in announcing to the inhabitants of Monterey, that, from information received from various sources, he has every reason to believe that the disorders which have recently disturbed the territory of California are at an end, and that peace and security are restored to this district certainly, and he hopes to the whole territory.

The improved state of affairs in the district, and the arrival of a company of United States artillery, under Captain Tompkins, has enabled the commander-in-chief to dispense with the services of the company of mounted volunteers, under Lieutenant Maddox, of the marine corps. The patriotic settlers who composed this company nobly stepped forward in time of danger, and stood between the flag of the United States and the defenceless women and children of Monterey, on the one hand, and the bands of lawless disturbers of the peace on the other.

For such disinterested conduct, the company of mounted volunteers under Lieutenant Maddox, of the marine corps, (acting as captain,) is tendered the thanks of the commander-in-chief, and will without doubt receive commendation and due recompense from the general government.

Given on board the U. S. ship Independence, harbor of Monterey, February 1st, 1847.   W. BRANFORD SHUBRICK,
                                        Commander-in-chief.

To explain some of the allusions in the preceding " General Order" of Commodore Shubrick, it is necessary to state that an insurrection, headed by Don Francisco Sanchez, had broken out in the upper portion of California some time towards the last of December, which had been put down by a detachment of marines and volunteers. The insurgents had committed some outrages, and among other acts had taken prisoner Lieutenant W. A. Bartlett, acting Alcalde of San Francisco, with some other Americans. An account of the suppression of this affair, I find in the " Californian" newspaper of February 6th, 1847, from which it appears " that a party of one hundred and one men, commanded by Captain Ward Marston of the United States marines, marched from San Francisco on the 29th December in search of the enemy, whom they discovered on the 2d of January, about one hundred in number, on the plains of Santa Clara, under the command of Francisco Sanchez. An attack was immediately ordered. The enemy was forced to retire, which they were able to do in safety, after some resistance, in consequence of their superior horses. The affair lasted about an hour, during which time we had one marine slightly wounded in the head, one volunteer of Captain Weber's command in the leg; and the enemy had one horse killed, and some of their forces supposed to be killed or wounded. In the evening the enemy sent in a flag of truce, with a communication, requesting an interview with the commanding officer of the expedition the next day, which was granted, when an armistice was entered into, preparatory to a settlement of the difficulties. On the 3d, the expedition was reinforced by the mounted Monterey volunteers, fifty-five men, under command of Captain William A. T. Maddox, and on the 7th by the arrival of Lieutenant Grayson with fifteen men, attached to Captain Maddox's company. On the 8th a treaty was concluded, by which the enemy surrendered Lieutenant Bartlett, and the other prisoners, as well as all their arms, including one small field-piece, their ammunition and accoutrements; and were permitted to return peaceably to their homes, and the expedition to their respective posts."

A list of the expedition which marched from San Francisco is given as follows: Captain Ward Marston, commandant; Assistant-surgeon J. Duval, aid-de-camp. A detachment of United States marines under command of Lieutenant Tansil, thirty-four men; artillery consisting of one field-piece, under the charge of Master William F. De Iongh, assisted by Mid. John M. Kell, ten men; Interpreter John Pray; mounted company of San José volunteers, under command of Captain C. M. Weber, Lieutenant John Murphy, and acting Lieutenant John Reed, thirty-three men; mounted company of Yerba Buena volunteers, under command of Captain William M. Smith, Lieutenant John Rose, with a small detachment under Captain J. Martin, twelve men.

Thus ended the insurrections, if resistance against invasion can properly be so called, in Upper California.

On the 20th of January, the force of sailors and marines which had marched with Commodore Stockton and General Kearny, left Los Angeles to embark at San Pedro for San Diego. On the 21st a national salute was fired by the artillery company belonging to the battalion, in honor of Governor Fremont. On the 22d, letters were received from San Diego, stating that Colonel Cooke, who followed General Kearny from Santa Fé with a force of four hundred Mormon volunteers, had reached the neighborhood of that place. Having applied for my discharge from the battalion as soon as we reached Los Angeles, I received it on the 29th, on which day, in company with Captain Hastings, I set out on my return to San Francisco, designing to leave that place on the first favorable opportunity for the United States.

CHAPTER XXXVI.

Leave Los Angeles for San Francisco—Don Andres Pico—A Californian returning from the wars—Domestic life at a rancho—Women in favor of peace—Hospitable treatment—Fandango—Singular custom—Arrive at Santa Barbara—Lost in a fog—Valley of the Salinas—Californians wanting Yankee wives—High waters—Arrive at San Francisco.

WE left Los Angeles late in the afternoon of the 29th of January, with two Indian vaqueros, on miserable, broken-down horses, (the best we could obtain,) and encamped at the deserted rancho at the foot of Couenga plain, where the treaty of peace had been concluded. After we had been here some time, two Indians came to the house, who had been sent by the proprietor of the rancho to herd the cattle. Having nothing to eat with us, a tempting offer prevailed upon the Indians to milk one of the cows; and we made our supper and our breakfast next morning on milk. Both of our Indian vaqueros deserted in the night, carrying with them sundry articles of clothing placed in their charge. A few days have made a great change in the appearance of the country. The fresh grass is now several inches in height, and many flowers are in bloom. The sky is bright, and the temperature delightful.

On the 30th of January, leaving the mission of San Fernando on our right, at a distance of eight or ten miles, we followed the usually travelled trail next to the hills, on the western side of the plain.   As we were passing near a rancho, a well-dressed Californian rode out to us ; and after examining the horses of our miserable *caballada,* politely claimed one of them as his property. He was told that the horse was drawn from the public *caballada,* at Los Angeles, and could not be given up.   This seemed to satisfy him.   After some further conversation, he informed us that he was Don Andres Pico, the late leader and general of the Californians.   The expression of his countenance is intelligent and prepossessing ; and his address and manners courteous and pleasing.   Shaking hands and bidding us a very earnest *adios,* he put spurs to his horse and galloped away.

We were soon after overtaken by a young Californian, who appeared at first rather doubtful whether or not he should make our acquaintance.   The ice being broken, however, he became very loquacious and communicative.   He stated that he was returning to his home, near Santa Barbara, from the wars, in which he had been engaged against his will.   The language that he used was, that he with many others of his acquaintances, were forced to take up arms by the leading men of the country. He was in the two battles of the 8th and 9th of January, below Los Angeles ; and he desired never to be in any more battles. He was heartily rejoiced that there was peace, and hoped that there would never be any more wars.   He travelled along with us until afternoon, when he fell behind, and we did not see him again until the next day.

After passing two or three deserted houses, we reached an inhabited rancho, situated at the extremity of a valley, and near a narrow gorge in the hills, about four o'clock, and our jaded animals performing duty with reluctance, we determined to halt for the night, if the prospect of obtaining any thing to eat (of which we stood in much need) was flattering.   Riding up to the house, a small adobe, with one room, and a shed for a kitchen, the *ranchero* and the *ranchera* came out and greeted us with a hearty " *Buenas tardes Señores, paisanos, amigos,*" shaking hands, and inviting us at the same time to alight and remain for the night, which invitation we accepted. The kind-hearted *ranchera* immediately set about preparing supper for us. An Indian *muchacha* was seated at the *metáte*, (hand-mill,) which is one of the most important articles of the Californian culinary apparatus. While the *muchacha* ground, or rather crushed the wheat between the stones, the *ranchera*, with a platter-shaped basket, cleansed it of dust, chaff, and all impure particles, by tossing the grain in the basket. The flour being manufactured and sifted through a *cedazo*, or coarse sieve, the labor of kneeding the dough was performed by the *muchacha*. An iron plate was then placed over a rudely-constructed furnace, and the dough being beaten by hand into *tortillas*, (thin cakes,) was baked upon this. What would American housewives say to such a system as this? The viands being prepared, they were set out upon a small table, at which we were invited to seat ourselves. The meal consisted of *tortillas*, stewed jerked-beef, with *chile* seasoning, milk, and *quesadillas*, or cheesecakes, green and tough as leather. However, our appetites were excellent, and we enjoyed the repast with a high relish.

Our host and hostess were very inquisitive in regard to the news from below, and as to what would be the effects of the conquest of the country by the Americans. The man stated that he and all his family had refused to join in the late insurrection. We told them that all was peaceable now; that there would be no more wars in California; that we were all Americans, all Californians,—*hermanos, hermanas, amigos.* They expressed their delight at this information by numerous exclamations.

We asked the woman how much the dress which she wore, a miserable calico, cost her? She answered, " *Seis pesos,*" (six dollars.) When we told her that in a short time, under the American government, she could purchase as good a one "*por un peso,*" she threw up her hands in astonishment, expressing by her features at the same time the most unbounded delight. Her entire wardrobe was soon brought forth, and the price paid for every article named. She then inquired what would be the cost of similar clothing under the American government, which we told her. As we replied, exclamation followed upon exclamation, expressive of her surprise and pleasure, and the whole was concluded with "*Viva los Americanos—viva los Americanos !*" I wore a large coarse woollen pea-jacket, which the man was very desirous to obtain, offering for it a fine horse. I declined the trade.

In the evening several of the brothers, sisters, and brothers and sisters-in-law of the family collected, and the guitar and violin, which were suspended from a beam in the house, were taken down, and we were entertained by a concert of instrumental and vocal music. Most of the tunes were such as are performed at fandangos. Some plaintive airs were played and sung with much pathos and expression, the whole party joining in the choruses. Although invited to occupy the only room in the house, we declined it, and spread our blankets on the outside.

The next morning (January 31st) when we woke the sun was shining bright and warm, and the birds were singing gayly in the grove of evergreen oaks near the house. Having made ready to resume our journey, as delicately as possible we offered our kind hostess compensation for the trouble we had given her, which she declined, saying, that although they were not rich, they nevertheless had enough and to spare. We however insisted, and she finally accepted, with the condition that we would also accept of some of her *quesadillas* and *tortillas* to carry along with us. The ranchero mounted his horse and rode with us three or four miles, to place us on the right trail, when, after inviting us very earnestly to call and see him again, and bidding us an affectionate *adios*, he galloped away.

Travelling over a hilly country and passing the ruins of several deserted ranchos, the grounds surrounding which were strewn with the bones of slaughtered cattle, we reached, about five o'clock, P. M., a cluster of houses in the valley of Santa Clara river, ten miles east of the mission of San Buenaventura. Here we stopped at the house of a man named Sanchez. Our arrival was thought to be worthy of notice, and it was accordingly celebrated in the evening by a fandango given at one of the houses, to which we were invited. The company, to the number of some thirty or forty persons, young and old, were assembled in the largest room of the house, the floor being hard clay. The only furniture contained in the room was a bed and some benches, upon which the company seated themselves when not engaged in dancing.

Among the *señoritas* assembled, were two daughters of an American named Chapman, who has been a resident of the country for many years. They were fair-skinned, and might be called handsome. An elder and married sister was also present. They called themselves Americans, although they did not speak our language, and seemed to be more proud of their American than their Spanish blood.

A singular custom prevails at these fandangos. It is this : during the intervals between the waltzes, quadrilles, and other dances, when the company is seated, a young lady takes the floor *solus*, and after showing off her graces for general observation a few minutes, she approaches any gentleman she may select and performs a variety of pirouettes and other Terpsichorean movements before him for his especial amusement and admiration, until he places on her head his hat or cap, as the case may be, when she dances away with it. The hat or cap has afterwards to be redeemed by some present, and this usually is in money. Not dancing ourselves, we were favored with numerous special exhibitions of this kind, the cost of each of which was *un peso*. With a long journey before us, and with purses in a nearly collapsed condition, the drafts upon us became so frequent, that at an early hour, under a plea of fatigue and want of rest, we thought it prudent to beat a retreat, leaving our fair and partial *fandangueras* to bestow their favors upon others better able to bear them. The motions of the Californian females of all classes in the dance are highly graceful. The waltz is their favorite measure, and in this they appear to excel as much as the men do in horsemanship. During the progress of the dance, the males and females improvise doggerel rhymes complimentary of the personal beauties and graces

36

of those whom they admire, or expressive of their love and de-
votion, which are chanted with the music of the instruments,
and the whole company join in the general chorus at the end
of each verse. The din of voices is sometimes almost deafening.
Our host accompanied us to our lodgings on the opposite
side of the way. Beds were spread down under the small porch
outside, and we laid our bodies upon them, but not to sleep,
for the noise of the fandango dancers kept us awake until broad
daylight, at which time it broke up.

Hiring fresh horses here, and a vaquero to drive our tired
animals after us, we started about 9 o'clock in the morning, and
passing through San Buenaventura, reached Santa Barbara, 45
miles, a little after two in the afternoon. We stopped at the
house of Mr. Sparks, who received us with genuine hospitality. Santa Barbara presented a more lively appearance than
when we passed here on our way down, most of its population
having returned to their homes. Procuring fresh but miserably
poor horses, we resumed our journey on the afternoon of the 2d
of February, and encamped at the rancho of Dr. Den, situated
on the plain of Santa Barbara, near the seashore. The soil of this
plain is of the most fertile composition. The fresh grass is now
six or eight inches high, and the varieties are numerous. Many
of the early flowers are in bloom. I noticed a large wheat-field
near the house, and its appearance was such as to promise a
rich harvest.

The rain fell heavily on the morning of the 3d, but continuing our journey we crossed the St. Ynes mountain, and passing the mission by that name, reached the rancho of Mr. Faxon
after dark, where we halted for the night. Around the mission of St. Ynes I noticed, as we passed, immense quantities
of cattle-bones thickly strewn in all directions. Acres of ground
were white with these remains of the immense herds belonging
to this mission in the days of its prosperity, slaughtered for
their hides and tallow. We met two or three elegantly-dressed
Californians to-day, who accosted us with much civility and apparent friendliness.

Mr. Faxon is an Englishman by birth, and has resided in

California about thirty years. He is married to a Californian lady, and has a family of interesting and beautiful children. A large portion of the land belonging to his rancho is admirably adapted to agriculture, and he raises crops of corn and vegetables as well as wheat without irrigation. He informed me that the yield of wheat on his rancho was fully seventy bushels to the acre. Mr. F. showed me specimens of lead ore from which he moulds his bullets, taken from an inexhaustible mine in the Tular valley, some fifty miles distant from this. It is certainly the richest ore that I have ever seen, appearing almost like the pure metal. He also showed me a caustic alkali, produced by burning a plant or shrub which grows in great abundance in the Tular valley. This substance is used by him in the manufacture of soap.

About noon on the 4th, we halted at the rancho of Captain Dana, where we procured fresh horses, leaving our wretchedly lean and tired animals, and proceeding on, stopped for the night at the rancho of Mr. Branch, an intelligent American, originally from the state of New York, who has been settled in the country a number of years. His rancho is situated on what is called the *arroyo grande*, a small stream which empties into the Pacific some two or three miles from the house. The house is new, and constructed after American models of farm-houses, with neat and comfortable apartments, chimneys and fireplaces. The arable lands here are finely adapted to the culture of maize, wheat, and potatoes.

Our horses straying, it was twelve o'clock on the 5th before we found them. The rain had fallen steadily and heavily all night, and during the forenoon, and was pouring down when we started. We passed through the mission of San Luis Obispo just before sunset, intending to halt at a rancho about three miles distant in a *cañada*. But the storm increasing in strength, it became suddenly so dark in the mountain-gorge, that we could not distinguish the trail; and after wandering about some time, vainly attempting to find the house, we were compelled to bivouac, wet to our skins, without fire or shelter, and the rain pouring down in torrents.

The next morning, (Feb. 6,) in hunting up our loose horses, we discovered the house about half a mile distant from our camp. Continuing our journey, we halted about nine o'clock at a rancho near the ruins of Santa Margarita. A solitary Indian was the only occupant of the house, and only inhabitant of the place; and he could furnish us with no food. Passing two or three other deserted ranchos, we reached the house of a Mexican about one o'clock, where we obtained a meal of fried eggs and *tortillas*, after having been without food thirty hours. Late in the afternoon we arrived at the mission of San Miguel, now occupied by an Englishman named Reed, his *mestiza* wife, and one child, with two or three Indian vaqueros. Crossing the Salinas in the morning, (Feb. 7,) we continued down its eastern side, and encamped in a wide bottom under a large live-oak. A *quesadilla* was all we had to eat. This was divided, one half being reserved for breakfast. The fresh vegetation has so much changed the face of the country on this river since we passed along here in December, that I scarcely recognise it. The grass is six or eight inches high in the bottom, the blades standing so thick as to present a matted appearance, and the hills are brilliant with flowers—pink, purple, blue, and yellow.

On the 8th we continued down the eastern bank of the Salinas, passing through several large and fertile bottoms, and reaching the rancho of San Lorenzo about twelve o'clock. This rancho, as we learned from the proprietors, is owned by two bachelor brothers, one of whom told me that he had not been off his lands but once or twice for several years. Large herds of fat cattle and horses were grazing upon the luxuriant grasses of the plain, and there were several extensive enclosures sowed in wheat, which presented all the indications of an abundant harvest. But with all these natural resources surrounding him, the elder brother told us that he had nothing to eat in his house but fresh beef. A quantity of the choice pieces of a fat beef was roasted by an Indian boy, which we enjoyed with all the relish of hungry men. Our host, a gentleman of intelligence and politeness, made apology after apology for his rude style of living, a principal excuse being that he had no wife. He inquired, with apparent earnestness, if we could not send him two pretty, accomplished, and capable American women, whom they could marry; and then they would build a fine house, have bread, butter, cheese, and all the delicacies, luxuries, and elegancies of life in abundance. He appeared to be well pleased with the conquest of the country by the Americans, and desirous that they should not give it up. When we resumed our journey in the afternoon, he rode with us four or five miles to show us the way; and on taking his leave, invited us to return again, when he said he hoped his accommodations would be much improved. Riding 15 miles, we halted at a tule-cabin, where we remained until two o'clock in the morning, when, the moon shining brightly, we mounted our horses and continued our journey.

We reached the Monterey road just at daylight. My intention had been to visit Monterey; but the Salinas being unfordable, and there being no ferry, it was not possible to do it without swimming the river, which I did not feel inclined to do. Monterey is situated on the bay by that name, about 90 miles by water south of San Francisco. The bay affords a good anchorage and landing in calm weather, being exposed only to the northers, which blow violently. The town contains about 1,500 inhabitants, and is rapidly increasing in wealth and population. Arriving at the rancho of Don Joaquin Gomez, we found no one but a *mestiza* servant at home, and could obtain nothing to eat but a *quesadilla*. All the streams, large and small, are much swollen by late heavy rains, and the travelling is consequently very laborious and difficult. Resting our horses a short time, we crossed the mountains, and reached the mission of San Juan Bautista about noon.

At San Juan we met with Messrs. Grayson, Boggs, and a party of volunteers returning from Monterey to San Francisco, having been discharged since the suppression of the rebellion in this part of California, headed by Francisco Sanchez. Here we learned, for the first time, the arrival at Monterey of Commodore Shubrick in the ship Independence, and of the Lexington with Captain Tompkins's company of artillery, and freighted

36*

otherwise with munitions, stores, and tools necessary to the erection and defence of durable fortifications at Monterey and San Francisco.

Seven or eight miles beyond San Juan, we found that the waters of the *arroyo* had risen so as to inundate a wide valley which we were compelled to cross. After making several ineffectual attempts to reach the opposite side, wading through the water, and sometimes falling into deep holes from which it was difficult for either men or horses to extricate themselves, we encamped for the night on a small elevation in the valley, entirely surrounded by water. Our condition was miserable enough. Tired, wet, and hungry, we laid down for the night on the damp ground.

The next day, (Feb. 10,) about eleven o'clock, we succeeded in finding a ford across the valley and stream, and procured dinner at a soap-factory on the opposite side, belonging to T. O. Larkin, Esq. Continuing on, we encamped at a rancho occupied by an Englishman as *mayor domo*. He was very glad to see us, and treated us with unbounded hospitality, furnishing a superabundance of beef and *frijoles* for our consumption. On the 11th, about three P. M., we arrived at the Pueblo de San José ; and finding there a launch employed by Messrs. Howard & Mellus in collecting hides, bound for San Francisco, we embarked in her, and on the morning of the 13th, arrived at that place. We found lying here the U. S. sloop Warren, and Lieutenant Radford politely furnished us with a boat to land. In the afternoon the Cyane, Commander Dupont, with Gen. Kearny on board, and the store-ship Erie, with Col. Mason on board, arrived in the harbor. Col. Mason is from the U. States direct, via Panama, and brings late and interesting intelligence.

The Cyane and Warren have just returned from a cruise on the southern Pacific coast of Mexico. The town of Guymas had been taken by bombardment. The Cyane had captured, during her cruise, fourteen prizes, besides several guns at San Blas. The boats of the Warren, under the command of Lieut. Radford, performed the gallant feat of cutting out of the harbor of Mazatlan, the Mexican schooner Malek Abdel.

Landing in San Francisco I found my wardrobe which I had deposited in the care of Capt. Leidesdorff; and the first time for nearly five months dressed myself in a civilized costume. Having been during that time almost constantly in motion, and exposed to many hardships and privations, it was, as may be supposed, no small satisfaction to find once more a place where I could repose for a short time at least.

CHAPTER XXXVII.

Progress of the town of San Francisco—Capt. Dupont—Gen. Kearny—The presidio—Appointed Alcalde—Gen. Kearny's proclamation—Arrival of Col. Stevenson's regiment—Horse-thief Indians—Administration of justice in California—Sale of lots in San Francisco.

WHEREVER the Anglo-Saxon race plant themselves, progress is certain to be displayed in some form or other. Such is their "go-ahead" energy, that things cannot stand still where they are, whatever may be the circumstances surrounding them. Notwithstanding the wars and insurrections, I found the town of San Francisco, on my arrival here, visibly improved. An American population had flowed into it; lots, which heretofore have been considered almost valueless, were selling at high prices; new houses had been built, and were in progress; new commercial houses had been established; hotels had been opened for the accommodation of the travelling and business public; and the publication of a newspaper had been commenced. The little village of two hundred souls, when I arrived here in September last, is fast becoming a town of importance. Ships freighted with full cargoes are entering the port, and landing their merchandise to be disposed of at wholesale and retail on shore, instead of the former mode of vending them afloat in the harbor. There is a prevailing air of activity, enterprise, and energy; and men, in view of the advantageous position of the town for commerce, are making large calculations upon the future ; calculations which I believe will be fully realized.

On the 15th I dined on board the sloop-of-war Cyane, with Commander Dupont, to whom I had the good fortune to be the bearer from home of a letter of introduction. I say " good fortune," because I conceive it to be one of the greatest of social blessings, as well as pleasures, to be made acquainted with a truly upright and honorable man,—one whose integrity never bends to wrongful or pusillanimous expediency ;—one who, armed intellectually with the panoply of justice, has courage to sustain it under any and all circumstances ;—one whose ambition is, in a public capacity, to serve his country, and not to serve himself ;—one who waits for his country to judge of his acts, and if worthy, to place the laurel wreath upon his head, disdaining a self-wrought and self-assumed coronal. Capt. Dupont is a native of Delaware ; and that gallant and patriotic state should feel proud of such a son. He is one of whom all men, on sea or on land, with whom his duties as an officer or a citizen of our republic brings him in contact, speak well ; and whose private virtues, as well as professional merits, are deserving of the warmest admiration and the highest honors.

Although I have long known Gen. S. W. Kearny from reputation, and saw him at Los Angeles, I was here introduced to him for the first time. Gen. K. is a man rising fifty years of age. His height is about five feet ten or eleven inches. His figure is all that is required by symmetry. His features are regular, almost Grecian ; his eye is blue, and has an eagle-like expression, when excited by stern or angry emotion ; but in ordinary social intercourse, the whole expression of his countenance is mild and pleasing, and his manners and conversation are unaffected, urbane, and conciliatory, without the slightest exhibition of vanity or egotism. He appears the cool, brave, and energetic soldier ; the strict disciplinarian, without tyranny ; the man, in short, determined to perform his duty, in whatever situation he may be placed, leaving consequences to follow in their natural course. These, my first impressions, were fully confirmed by subsequent intercourse, in situations and under circumstances, which, by experience, I have found an unfailing alembic for the trial of character,—a crucible wherein, if the metal be impure, the drossy substances are sure to display themselves. It is not my province to extol or pronounce judgment upon his acts ; they are a part of the military and civil history of our country ; and as such will be applauded or condemned, according to the estimate that may be placed upon them. But I may be allowed to express the opinion, that no man, placed under the same circumstances, ever aimed to perform his duty with more uprightness and more fidelity to the interests and honor of his country; or who, to shed lustre upon his country, ever braved greater dangers, or endured more hardships and privations, and all without vaunting his performances and sacrifices.

On the 16th, in company of Gen. Kearny, Capt. Turner, and Lieuts. Warner and Hallock, of the U. S. Engineer Corps, I rode to the Presidio of San Francisco, and the old fortification at the mouth of the bay. The presidio is about three miles from the town, and consists of several blocks of adobe buildings, covered with tiles. The walls of most of the buildings are crumbling for the want of care in protecting them from the annual rains ; and without this care they will soon become heaps of mud. The fort is erected upon a commanding position, about a mile and a half from the entrance to the bay. Its walls are substantially constructed of burnt brick, and are of sufficient thickness and strength to resist heavy battering. There are nine or ten embrazures. Like every thing else in the country belonging to the public, the fort is fast falling into ruins. There has been no garrison here for several years ; the guns are dismounted, and half decomposed by exposure to the weather, and from want of care. Some of them have sunk into the ground.

On the 20th I was waited upon by Gen. Kearny, and requested to accept the office of alcalde, or chief magistrate of the district of San Francisco. There being no opportunity of returning to the United States immediately, I accepted of the proposed appointment, and on the 22d was sworn into office ; my predecessor, Lieut. W. A. Bartlett, of the navy, being

ordered to his ship, by the commanding officer of the squadron.

The annual salute in celebration of the birthday of the immor-
tal and illustrious founder of our republic, required by law from
all the ships of the navy in commission, in whatever part of the
world they may be at the time, strikes us more forcibly when
in a far-off country, as being a beautiful and appropriate tribute
to the unapproachable virtues and heroism of that great bene-
factor of the human race, than when we are nearer home, or
upon our own soil. The U. S. ships in the harbor, at 12
o'clock on the 22d, each fired a national salute ; and the day
being calm and beautiful, the reports bounded from hill to hill,
and were echoed and re-echoed until the sound died away,
apparently, in the distant gorges of the Sierra Nevada. This
was a voice from the soul of WASHINGTON, speaking in majestic
and thunder-tones to the green and flowery valleys, the gentle
hills and lofty mountains of California, and consecrating them as
the future abode of millions upon millions of the sons of liberty.
The merchant and whale ships lying at anchor, catching the enthusiasm, joined in the salute ; and for a time the harbor and bay
in front of the town were enveloped in clouds of gunpowder smoke.

General Kearny left San Francisco, in the frigate Savannah,
Captain Mervine, on the 23d, for Monterey, and soon after his
arrival at that place, the following circular and proclamation
were issued :

CIRCULAR.

To all whom it may concern, be it known—

That the President of the United States, desirous to give and secure to
the people of California a share of the good government and happy civil
organization enjoyed by the people of the United States, and to protect
them at the same time from the attacks of foreign foes, and from internal
commotions—has invested the undersigned with separate and distinct
powers, civil and military ; a cordial co-operation in the exercise of which,
it is hoped and believed, will have the happy results desired.

To the commander-in-chief of the naval forces the President has assigned the regulation of the import trade—the conditions on which vessels
of all nations, our own as well as foreign, may be admitted into the ports
of the territory, and the establishment of all port regulations.

To the commanding military officer the President has assigned the direction of the operations on land, and has invested him with administrative functions of government over the people and territory occupied by the forces of the United States.

Done at MONTEREY, capital of California, this 1st day of March, A. D. 1847.

W. BRANFORD SHUBRICK,
Commander-in-Chief of the Naval Forces.

S. W. KEARNY, *Brig. Gen. U. S. A.,*
and Governor of California

PROCLAMATION TO THE PEOPLE OF CALIFORNIA.

The President of the United States having instructed the undersigned to take charge of the civil government of California, he enters upon his duties with an ardent desire to promote, as far as he is able, the interests of the country and the welfare of its inhabitants.

The undersigned has instructions from the President to respect and protect the religious institutions of California, and to see that the religious rights of the people are in the amplest manner preserved to them, the constitution of the United States allowing every man to worship his Creator in such a manner as his own conscience may dictate to him.

The undersigned is also instructed to protect the persons and property of the quiet and peaceable inhabitants of the country against all or any of their enemies, whether from abroad or at home ; and when he now assures the Californians that it will be his duty and his pleasure to comply with those instructions, he calls upon them all to exert themselves in preserving order and tranquillity, in promoting harmony and concord, and in maintaining the authority and efficiency of the laws.

It is the wish and design of the United States to provide for California, with the least possible delay, a free government, similar to those in her other territories ; and the people will soon be called upon to exercise their rights as freemen, in electing their own representatives, to make such laws as may be deemed best for their interest and welfare. But until this can be done, the laws now in existence and not in conflict with the constitution of the United States, will be continued until changed by competent authority ; and those persons who hold office will continue in the same for the present, provided they swear to support that constitution, and to faithfully perform their duty.

The undersigned hereby absolves all the inhabitants of California from any further allegiance to the republic of Mexico, and will consider them as citizens of the United States ; those who remain quiet and peaceable will be respected in their rights and protected in them. Should any take up arms against, or oppose the government of this territory, or instigate others to do so, they will be considered as enemies, and treated accordingly.

When Mexico forced a war upon the United States, time did not permit the latter to invite the Californians as friends to join her standard, but compelled her to take possession of the country to prevent any European power from seizing upon it, and in doing so, some excesses and unauthorized acts were no doubt committed by persons employed in the service of the United States, by which a few of the inhabitants have met with a loss of property ; such losses will be duly investigated, and those entitled to remuneration will receive it.

California has for many years suffered greatly from domestic troubles ; civil wars have been the poisoned fountains which have sent forth trouble and pestilence over her beautiful land.   Now those fountains are dried up ; the star-spangled banner floats over California, and as long as the sun continues to shine upon her, so long will it float there, over the natives of the land, as well as others who have found a home in her bosom ; and under it agriculture must improve and the arts and sciences flourish, as seed in a rich and fertile soil.

The Americans and Californians are now but one people ; let us cherish one wish, one hope, and let that be for the peace and quiet of our country. Let us, as a band of brothers, unite and emulate each other in our exertions to benefit and improve this our beautiful, and which soon must be our happy and prosperous home.

Done at Monterey, capital of California, this first day of March, A. D. 1847, and in the seventy-first year of independence of the United States.

S. W. KEARNY, *Brig. Gen. U. S. A.,*

and Governor of California.

The proclamation of General Kearny gave great satisfaction to the native as well as the emigrant population of the country. Several of the alcaldes of the district of my jurisdiction, as well as private individuals, (natives of the country,) expressed by letter and orally, their approbation of the sentiments of the proclamation in the warmest terms.   They said that they were heartily willing to become Americans upon these terms, and hoped that there would be the least possible delay in admitting them to the rights of American citizenship.   There was a general expectation among natives as well as foreigners, that a representative form of territorial government would be immediately established by General Kearny.   The reason why this was not done, is explained by the recent publication of General Scott's letter to General Kearny, dated November

3d, 1846, of which Colonel Mason was the bearer, he having left the United States on the 7th of November. In this letter General Scott says :—

" As a guide to the civil governor of Upper California, in our hands, see the letter of June the 3d, (last,) addressed to you by the Secretary of War. You will not, however, formally declare the province to be annexed. Permanent incorporation of the territory must depend on the government of the United States.

" After occupying with our forces all necessary points in Upper California, and establishing a temporary civil government therein, as well as assuring yourself of its internal tranquillity, and the absence of any danger of reconquest on the part of Mexico, you may charge Col. Mason, United States first dragoons, the bearer of this open letter, or land officer next in rank to your own, with your several duties, and return yourself, with a sufficient escort of troops, to St. Louis, Missouri ; but the body of the United States dragoons that accompanied you to California, will remain there until further orders."

The transport ships Thomas H. Perkins, Loo Choo, Susan Drew, and Brutus, with Col. Stevenson's regiment, arrived at San Francisco during the months of March and April. These vessels were freighted with a vast quantity of munitions, stores, tools, saw-mills, grist-mills, etc. etc., to be employed·in the fortification of the principal harbors on the coast—San Francisco, Monterey, and San.Diego. The regiment of Col. Stevenson was separated into different commands, portions of it being stationed at San Francisco, Sonoma, Monterey, Santa Barbara, and Los Angeles, and some companies employed against the horse-thief Indians of the Sierra Nevada, and the Tulares.

As good an account of these horse-thief Indians, and their depredations, as I have seen, I find in the " California Star," of March 28th, 1847, written by a gentleman who has been a resident of California for a number of years, and who has been a sufferer. It is subjoined :

" During the Spanish regime, such a thing as a horse-thief was unknown in the country, but as soon as the Mexicans took possession, their characteristic anarchy began to prevail, and

37

the Indians to desert from the missions. The first Indian horse-thief known in this part of the country, was a neophyte of the mission of Santa Clara, George, who flourished about twenty years ago. He absconded from his mission to the river of Stanislaus, of which he was a native. From thence he returned to the settlements, and began to steal horses, which at that time were very numerous. After pursuing his depredations for some time, he was at last pursued and killed on his return from one of his forages. The mission of Santa Clara has been, from that time to the present day, the greatest nursery for horse-thieves, as the Stanislaus river has been, and is their principal rendezvous. I have taken some pains to inquire among some of the most intelligent and respectable of the native inhabitants, as to the probable number of horses that have been stolen between Monterey and San Francisco within the last twenty years, and the result has been that more than one hundred thousand can be distinctly enumerated, and that the total amount would probably be double that number. Nearly all these horses have been eaten ! From the river of Stanislaus, as a central point, the evil has spread to the north and south, and at present extends from the vicinity of the Mickelemes river on the north, to the sources of the St. Joaquin on the south. These Indians inhabit all the western declivity of the great snowy mountains, within these limits, and have become so habituated to living on horseflesh, that it is now with them the principal means of subsistence.

" In past time they have been repeatedly pursued, and many of them killed, and whole villages destroyed, but so far from being deterred, they are continually becoming more bold and daring in their robberies, as horses become scarcer and more carefully guarded. About twenty persons have been killed by them within the knowledge of the writer. Among others, Mr. Lindsay and Mr. Wilson were killed by them not long ago. Only about one month since, they shot and dangerously wounded four persons employed on the farm of Mr. Weber near the Pueblo of St. Joseph, and at the same time stole the horses of the farm, and those also from the farms of Captain Fisher, and

Mr. Burnal, in the same vicinity; in all, above two hundred head.   Within the last ten days, numerous parties of them have been committing depredations on many of the farms in the jurisdiction of the Contra Costa, and scarcely a night passes but we hear of their having stolen horses from some one.   Three days ago, a party of them were met by some young men who had been out catching wild horses on the plains of the St. Joaquin, but as they were mounted on tired animals, they were only able to recapture the stolen horses, but could not overtake the thieves."

It has not been within the scope of my design, in writing out these notes, to enter into the minute details of the conquest and occupation of California by the forces of the United States. To do so would require more space than I have allowed myself, and the matter would be more voluminous than interesting or important.   My intention has been to give such a sketch of the military operations in California, during my residence and travels in the country, as to afford to the reader a general and correct idea of the events transpiring at the time.   No important circumstance, I think, has escaped my attention.

Among the officers of the army stationed at San Francisco, with whom I became acquainted, were Major Hardie, in command of the troops, Captain Folsom, acting quartermaster-general in California, and Lieut. Warner of the engineer corps. Lieut. Warner marched with Gen. Kearny from the United States, and was at the battle of San Pasqual.   I have seen the coat which he wore on that occasion, pierced in seven different places by the lances of the enemy.   He did not make this exhibition himself, and I never heard him refer to the subject but once, and then it was with the modesty of a veteran campaigner.

The corps of topographical engineers accompanying Gen. Kearny, under the command of Captain Emory, will, doubtless, furnish in their report much interesting and valuable information.   Mr. Stanley, the artist of the expedition, completed his sketches in oil, at San Francisco; and a more truthful, interesting, and valuable series of paintings, delineating mountain scenery, the floral exhibitions on the route, the savage tribes between Santa Fé and California—combined with camp-life and marches through the desert and wilderness—has never been, and probably never will be exhibited. Mr. Stanley informed me that he was preparing a work on the savage tribes of North America, and of the islands of the Pacific, which, when completed on his plan, will be the most comprehensive and descriptive of the subject, of any that has been published.

Legal proceedings are much less complex in California than in the United States. There is no written statute law in the country. The only law-books I could find were a digested code entitled, "Laws of Spain and the Indies," published in Spain about one hundred years ago, and a small pamphlet defining the powers of various judicial officers, emanating from the Mexican government since the revolution. A late Mexican governor of California, on being required by a judicial magistrate to instruct him as to the manner in which he should administer the law within his jurisdiction, replied, "*Administer it in accordance with the principles of natural right and justice,*" and this is the foundation of Californian jurisprudence. The local *bandos,* or laws, are enacted, adjudicated, and executed by the local magistrates, or alcaldes. The alcalde has jurisdiction in all municipal matters, and in cases for minor offences, and for debt in sums not over one hundred dollars. In cases of heinous or capital offences, the alcalde has simply an examining power, the testimony being taken down in writing, and transmitted to the *juez de primera instancia,* or first judge of the district, before whom the case is tried. Civil actions, for sums over one hundred dollars, must also be tried before the *juez de primera instancia,* and from him there is an appeal to the prefect, or the governor of the province. The trial by *hombres buenos,* or good men, is one of the established legal tribunals when either of the parties demand it, and is similar to our trial by jury ; the difference being in the number, the *hombres buenos* usually consisting of three or five, as they may be ordered by the magistrate, or requested by the litigants, and our jury of twelve. With honest and intelligent magistrates the system operates advantageously, as justice is speedy and certain ; but the reverse of this, with corrupt and ignorant magistrates, too frequently in power, the consequences of the system are as bad as can well be imagined.

The policy of the Mexican government has been to encourage in certain localities the erection of pueblos, or towns, and for this purpose they have made grants of land to the local authorities, or municipalities, within certain defined limits, to be regranted upon application, in lots of fifty or one hundred varass, as the case may be, to persons declaring their intention to settle and to do business in the town. For these grants to individuals a certain sum of money is paid, which goes into the treasury of the municipality. The magistrates, however, without special permission, have no power to grant lots of land within a certain number of feet of or below high-water mark. This power is reserved to be exercised by the governor of the province. It being necessary for the convenient landing of ships, and for the discharging and receiving of their cargoes, that the beach in front of the town of San Francisco should be improved with wharves, etc. etc., and that titles should be granted to individuals who otherwise would make no durable improvements, as magistrate of the town, in compliance with the request of numerous citizens, I solicited from General Kearny, the acting governor, a relinquishment on the part of the general government of the beach lands in front of the town in favor of the municipality, under certain conditions. General Kearny made the following decree:

I, Brigadier-general S. W. KEARNY, Governor of California, by virtue of authority in me vested, by the President of the United States of America, do hereby grant, convey, and release unto the town of San Francisco, the people, or corporate authorities thereof, all the right, title, and interest of the Government of the United States, and of the Territory of California, in and to the beach and water lots on the east front of said town of San Francisco, included between the points known as the Rincon and Fort Montgomery, except such lots as may be selected for the use of the United States Government by the senior officers of the army and navy now there; Provided the said ground hereby ceded shall be divided into lots, and sold by public auction to the highest bidder, after three months' notice previously given: the proceeds of said sale to be for the benefit of the town of San Francisco.

Given at Monterey, capital of California, this 10th day of March, 1847, and the seventy-first year of the Independence of the United States.

S. W. KEARNY,
Brigadier-general and Governor of California.

These beach lots were advertised immediately, and having been surveyed subsequently, were sold at public auction by my successor. I subjoin the advertisement under which they were sold:

Great Sale of Valuable Real Estate in the Town of San Francisco, Upper California.

By the following decree of his Excellency, General S. W. Kearny, Governor of California, all the right, title, and interest of the United States, and of the Territory of California, to the beach and water lots on the east front of the town of San Francisco, have been granted, conveyed, and released, to the people or corporate authorities of said town.

(Here follows the decree copied above.)

In pursuance of, and in compliance with the conditions of the foregoing decree, all the ungranted tract of ground on the east front of the town of San Francisco, lying and situated between Fort Montgomery and the Rincon, and known as the water and beach lots, (the reservations by the general and town governments excepted,) will be surveyed and divided into convenient building lots for warehouses and stores, and offered at public sale, to the highest bidder, on Tuesday the 29th day of June next, at ten o'clock, A. M. A plan of lots in connection with a general map of the town, will be made out and exhibited on or before the day of sale.

Terms of sale, one fourth cash,—one fourth in six months,—one fourth in twelve months,—and one fourth in eighteen months, the purchaser giving approved security bearing an interest of ten per cent. per annum from the day of sale.

Other conditions will be made known on or before the day of sale.

The site of the town of San Francisco is known by all navigators and mercantile men acquainted with the subject, to be the most commanding commercial position on the entire eastern coast of the Pacific ocean, and the town itself is, no doubt, destined to become the commercial emporium of the western side of the North American continent. The property offered for sale is the most valuable in, or belonging to the town, and the acquisition of it is an object of deep interest to all mercantile houses in California and elsewhere engaged in the commerce of the Pacific.

EDWIN BRYANT,
Alcalde, or Chief Magistrate, Town and Dist. of San Francisco.
SAN FRANCISCO, UPPER CALIFORNIA, }
March 16, 1847.   }

While acting as magistrate of the district of San Francisco, a survey of the town, commenced under my predecessor, was completed under my directions, and the plan extended so as to include the pueblo lands contained in the grant of the general government to the municipality.   This survey was made by Mr. Jasper O'Farrell, the departmental-surveyor under the Mexican government, and a plan of the town, in connection with a map of the Bay of San Francisco and its environs, was admirably drawn by him.   After the survey, lots were granted to applicants in conformity with the Mexican laws and precedents. The following extracts from the "California Star," published at San Francisco, will afford the best idea of the thrift and progress of the place :

From the California Star, March 13, 1847.

The town of San Francisco, is now rapidly improving, and bids fair to rival, in rapidity of progress, the most thriving town or city on the American continent.   If the necessary labor and lumber can be obtained, from three to five hundred houses will probably go up in the course of the present year. There is room here for artisans, mechanics, and laborers of all kinds.   The highest wages are paid, and will continue to be paid ; and the highest price for lumber, brick, adobes, and every description of building materials, will be given upon their delivery here, payable in cash.

The town of San Francisco is no doubt destined to be the Liverpool or New York of the Pacific Ocean.   At this point will be concentrated nearly all the commercial enterprise and capital engaged and invested in the Pacific trade.   The position of the town for commerce is unrivalled, and never can be rivalled unless some great convulsion of nature shall produce a new harbor on the Pacific coast equalling in beauty and security our magnificent bay.   Without difficulty or danger, ships of any burden can at all times enter the harbor, which is capacious enough to contain the navies of the whole world.   The extensive and fertile countries, watered by the Sacramento and San Joaquin rivers, and the numerous navigable creeks emptying into the bay, must, when they are settled upon with an industrious population, as they soon will be, pour their produce into this place, and receive in exchange from our merchants, all their supplies of manufactures and luxuries.   All the products of the gold, silver, copper, iron, and quicksilver mines, with which the country abounds, must be concentrated here for manufacture and exportation.   In a few years our wharves and streets will present a scene of busy life, resembling those witnessed in Liverpool, New Orleans, and New York.   Mechanics and artisans from all parts of the world will flock here, and we shall be in the full enjoyment of all the elegancies and luxuries of the oldest and most polished countries of the globe. This is no fancy sketch ; but, on the contrary, all who now read may live and see it fully verified.

From the same.

Regular Mail.—Our readers will be pleased to learn, that Governor Kearny has established a semi-monthly mail, to run regularly between San Francisco and San Diego. This mail is to be carried on horseback, by a party consisting of two soldiers, and is to commence on the 19th instant. Starting every other Monday from San Diego and San Francisco, the parties to meet at Captain Dana's rancho the next Sunday, to exchange mails ; start back on their respective routes the next morning, and arrive at San Diego and San Francisco on the Sunday following, and so continuing. The mail will thus be carried once a fortnight from San Diego to San Francisco, and from San Francisco to San Diego.

From the same, May 8.

Public meeting—Church in San Francisco.—A meeting of the citizens of this place was called on Thursday evening last, for the purpose of ascertaining the prevailing sentiment in relation to the establishment of a church in the town of San Francisco.

We hail this as the first step towards planting the standard of our glorious institutions on the shores of the Pacific, and trust an energetic co-operation of our citizens will ensure success to the enterprise.

From the same, May 22.

A Sabbath-school, under the direction of Mr. J. H. Merrill, superintendent, has been organized, and will be held at the office of the Alcalde every Sunday, at the hour of 9 A. M., and at 2 P. M. All children, with their parents, are respectfully invited to attend. Donations will be thankfully received and appropriated to the use of the school. A library is to be presented by the Rev. W. Roberts, superintendent of the Oregon mission.

J. D. MARSTON, Secretary.

From the same, May 29.

Illumination.—The first grand illumination of the town of San Francisco, took place yesterday evening, in honor of General Taylor's glorious achievement. Every dwelling, store, and tavern, shone in a blaze of splendor, and never since the founding of the place were the qualities of *sperm* so fully tested, nor did the *tallow* of the country ever meet with such a home consumption.

From the same.

Our town.—The town of San Francisco is progressing in population with a rapidity almost without example, certainly with no example on the waters of the Pacific ocean. Not less than fifty houses have gone up within the last month. Every man now here finds constant employment, and if thousands more were here in search of labor, they would find it, and receive for their services as much as any reasonable man would require.

Lumber, adobes, brick and lime, are much wanted, and whoever embarks largely in the manufactory of these building materials, for consumption at this place, will reap a rich harvest of profits. The high price now demanded for them, renders building expensive ; and the houses now going up are consequently small. But another year we trust will remedy this difficulty.

Numerous merchant-vessels are arriving here almost daily, furnishing our wholesale and retail commercial houses with large supplies of merchandise of every description. San Francisco is now a point where many articles of merchandise can be furnished nearly as cheap as they can be in the United States, carriage and commissions excepted. Merchants along the seaboard to the south can do better by coming here to replenish their stock of merchandise, than by sending to the Islands.

CHAPTER XXXVIII.

GENERAL OBSERVATIONS UPON THE COUNTRY.

First settlement of the missionaries—Population—Characteristics of white population—Employments—Pleasures and amusements—Position of women—Soil—Grasses—Vegetable productions—Agriculture—Fruits—Cattle—Horses—Wild animals—Minerals—Climate—Flora—Water-power—Timber—Religion.

It was during the month of November 1602, the sun just retiring behind the distant highland which forms the background of a spacious harbor at the southernmost point of Alta California, that a small fleet of vessels might have been seen directing their course as if in search of a place of anchorage ; their light sails drawn up, while the larger ones swelling now and then to the action of the breeze, bore them majestically along, forcing their way through the immense and almost impenetrable barrier of sea-weed to a haven, which at the remote period stated was considered the unexplored region of the North. The fleet referred to hauled their wind to the shore, and passing a bluff point of land on their left, soon came to anchor ; but not until the shades of night had cast a gloom over the scene so recently lighted up with the gorgeous rays of a setting sun.

This was the commencement, or rather preliminary mark of civilization in this country, by the Spaniards, (if so it can be called,) and on the following morning a detachment was landed, accompanied by a friar, to make careful investigation of the long ridge of highland which serves as a protection to the harbor from the heavy northwest gales. They found, as reported, an abundance of small oak and other trees, together with a great variety of useful and aromatic herbs ; and from its summit they beheld the extent and beauty of the port, reaching as they said full three leagues from where the vessel lay at anchor. A large tent was erected on the sandy beach to answer the purposes of a church, where the friar might perform mass, and by directions of the commanding officers, the boats were drawn up for repairing, wells were dug, parties were sent off to cut wood, while guards were placed at convenient distances to give notice of the approach of any hostile force. The latter precaution was hardly carried into effect, ere a large body of naked Indians were seen moving along the shore, armed with bows and arrows. A friar, protected by six soldiers, was dispatched to meet them, who, making signs of peace by exhibiting a white flag and throwing handfuls of sand high into the air, influenced them to lay aside their arms, when affectionately embracing them, the good old friar distributed presents of beads and necklaces, with which they eagerly adorned their persons. This manifestation of good feeling induced them to draw near to where the commander had landed with his men, but perceiving so large a number, they retreated to a neighboring knoll, and from thence sent forward to the Spaniards ten aged females, who, possessing apparently so much affability, were presented immediately with gifts and instructed to go and inform their people of the friendly disposition cherished for them by the white strangers. This was sufficient to implant a free intercourse with the Indians, who daily visited the Spaniards and bartered off their skins and furs in exchange for bread and trinkets. But at length the time arrived for the fleet to depart, and they proceeded northward, visiting in their course Monterey and Mendocino, where the same favorable result attended the enterprise as at other places, and they returned in safety to New Spain.

So successful had been the character of this expedition throughout the entire period of its execution, that an enthusiasm prevailed in the minds of the Spaniards, which could only be assuaged by an attempt to conquer and Christianize the inhabitants of that distant portion of the American continent. Many were the fruitless results of the Spanish adventurer— numerous were the statements of his toil and labor, till at length a formidable attempt, under the patronage and direction of Don Gaspar de Portala and Father Junipero Serra, successfully achieved the desired object for which it was planned and executed.

At San Diego, where, a century and a half before, the primitive navigators under Cortez communed with the rude and unsophisticated native—there, where the zealous devotee erected his altar on the burning sand, and with offerings of incense and prayer hallowed it to God, as the birthplace of Christianity in that region—upon that sainted spot commenced the spiritual conquest, the cross was erected, and the holy missionaries who accompanied the expedition entered heart and soul upon their religious duties. Successful in all they undertook, their first establishment in a short time was completed, and drawing around it the converted Indians in large numbers, the rude and uncultivated fields gave place to agricultural improvement— the arts and sciences gradually obtained foundation where before all was darkness, and day after day hundreds were added to the folds of the holy and apostolic church. Thus triumphantly proceeded the labors of the Spanish conquerors! In course of time other institutions were founded at Santa Barbara, Monterey, and San Francisco, where at each place a military fortress was erected, which served for their protection, and to keep in check such of the natives who were disinclined to observe the regulations of the community.

The natives formed an ardent and almost adorable attachment for their spiritual fathers, and were happy, quite happy, under their jurisdiction. Ever ready to obey them, the labor in the field and workshop met with ready compliance, and so prosperous were the institutions that many of them became wealthy, in the increase of their cattle and great abundance of their granaries. It was no unusual sight to behold the plains for leagues literally spotted with bullocks, and large fields of corn and wheat covering acres of ground. This state of things continued until the period when Mexico underwent a change in its political form of government, which so disheartened the feelings of the loyal missionaries, that they became regardless of their establishments, and suffered them to decline for want of attention to their interests. At length, civil discord and anarchy among the Californians prepared a more effective measure for their destruction, and they were left to the superintendence of individuals who plundered them of all that was desirable or capable of removal. Thus, the government commenced the robbery, and its hirelings carried it out to the letter, destroying and laying waste wherever they were placed. In order to give the inhabitants a share of the spoils, some of them were permitted to slaughter the cattle by contract, which was an equal division of the proceeds, and the contractors were careful when they delivered one hide to a mission, to reserve *two* for themselves, in this way following up the example of their superiors.

This important revolution in the systematic order of the monastic institutions took place in 1836, at which period the most important of them possessed property, exclusive of their lands and tenements, to the value of two hundred and fifty thousand dollars. At the present day they have but a little more than dilapidated walls and restricted boundaries of territory. Notwithstanding this wanton devastation of property, contrary to the opinion of many who were strongly in favor of supporting these religious institutions, the result proved beneficial to the country at large. Individual enterprise succeeded as the lands became distributed, so that the Californian beheld himself no longer dependent on the bounty of his spiritual directors, but, on the contrary, he was enabled to give support to them, from the increase and abundance of his own possessions.

Subsequent to the expulsion of the Mexicans, numbers of new farms were created, and hundreds of Americans were scattered over the country. Previous to 1830, the actual possessions of horned cattle by the *rancheros* did not exceed one hundred thousand; but in 1842, according to a fair estimate, made by one on the spot, the number had increased to four hundred thousand; so that the aggregate is equal to that held by the missions when in their most flourishing condition. The present number is not much, if any, short of one million.

Presuming a statistical knowledge of this country, before and after the missionary institutions were secularized, may be interesting, I will insert the following returns of 1831 and 1842, to contrast the same with its present condition :—

1st. In 1831 the white population throughout Alta-California did not exceed 4,500, while the Indians of the twenty-one missions amounted to 19,000; in 1842, the former had increased to 7,000, and the latter decreased to about 5,000.

2d. In the former year, the number of horned cattle, including individual possessions, amounted to 500,000; in the latter, to 400,000.

3d. At the same period, the number of sheep, goats, and pigs, was 321,000; at the latter, 32,000.

4th. In 1831 the number of horses, asses, mules, etc., was 64,000; in 1842 it was 30,000.

5th. The produce in corn, etc., had decreased in a much greater proportion—that of seventy to four.

The amount of duties raised at the custom-house in Monterey, from 1839 to 1842, was as follows, viz. :—

1839................... $85,613
1840................... 72,308

1841 101,150
1842 73,729

The net amount of revenue seldom exceeding in any year, eighty thousand dollars ; so that when a deficiency took place, to supply the expenditures of government, it had been usual to call upon the missions for aid.

The value of the hides and tallow derived from the annual *matanzas*, may be estimated at $372,000. These two commodities, with the exception of some beaver, sea-otter, and other furs, comprise the most important part of the exportations, which, in addition, would augment the value of exports to $400,000.

The permanent population of that portion of Upper California situated between the Sierra Nevada and the Pacific, I estimate at 25,000. Of this number, 8,000 are Hispano-Americans, 5,000 foreigners, chiefly from the United Stâtes, and 12,000 christianized Indians. There are considerable numbers of wild or Gentile Indians inhabiting the valley of the San Joaquin, and the gorges of the Sierra, not included in this estimate. They are probably as numerous as the Christian Indians. The Indian population inhabiting the region of the Great Salt Lake, Mary's river, the oases of the Great Desert Basin, and the country bordering the Rio Colorado and its tributaries, being spread over a vast extent of territory, are scarcely seen, although the aggregate number is considerable.

The Californians do not differ materially from the Mexicans, from whom they are descended, in other provinces of that country. Physically and intellectually, the men, probably, are superior to the same race farther south, and inhabiting the countries contiguous to the city of Mexico. The intermixture of blood with the Indian and negro races has been less, although it is very perceptible.

The men, as a general fact, are well made, with pleasing, sprightly countenances, and possessing much grace and ease of manners, and vivacity of conversation. But hitherto they have had little knowledge of the world and of events, beyond what they have heard through Mexico, and derived from the supercargoes of merchant-ships and whalemen touching upon the coast. There are no public schools in the country—at least I never heard of one. There are but few books. General Valléjo has a library with many valuable books, and this is the only one I saw, although there are others; but they are rare, and confined to a few families.

The men are almost constantly on horseback, and as horsemen excel any I have seen in other parts of the world. From the nature of their pursuits and amusements, they have brought horsemanship to a perfection challenging admiration and exciting astonishment. They are trained to the horse and the use of the lasso, (*riata*, as it is here called,) from their infancy. The first act of a child, when he is able to stand alone, is to throw his toy-lasso around the neck of a kitten; his next feat is performed on the dog; his next upon a goat or calf; and so on, until he mounts the horse, and demonstrates his skill upon horses and cattle. The crowning feat of dexterity with the *riata*, and of horsemanship, combined with daring courage, is the lassoing of the grisly bear. This feat is performed frequently upon this large and ferocious animal, but it is sometimes fatal to the performer and his horse. Well drilled, with experienced military leaders, such as would inspire them with confidence in their skill and prowess, the Californians ought to be the finest cavalry in the world. The Californian saddle is, I venture to assert, the best that has been invented, for the horse and the rider. Seated in one of these, it is scarcely possible to be unseated by any ordinary casualty. The bridle-bit is clumsily made, but so constructed that the horse is compelled to obey the rider upon the slightest intimation. The spurs are of immense size, but they answer to an experienced horseman the double purpose of exciting the horse, and of maintaining the rider in his seat under difficult circumstances.

For the pleasures of the table they care but little. With his horse and trappings, his sarape and blanket, a piece of beef and a *tortilla*, the Californian is content, so far as his personal comforts are concerned. But he is ardent in his pursuit of amusement and pleasure, and these consist chiefly in the fandango, the game of monte, horse-racing, and bull and bear baiting. They gamble freely and desperately, but pay their losses with the most strict punctuality, at any and every sacrifice, and manifest but little concern about them. They are obedient to their magistrates; and in all disputed cases decided by them, acquiesce without uttering a word of complaint. They have been accused of treachery and insincerity. Whatever may have been the grounds for these accusations in particular instances, I know not; but judging from my own observation and experience, they are as free from these qualities as our own people.

While the men are employed in attending to the herds of cattle and horses, and engaged in their other amusements, the women (I speak of the middle classes on the ranchos) superintend and perform most of the drudgery appertaining to housekeeping, and the cultivation of the gardens, from whence are drawn such vegetables as are consumed at the table. These are few, consisting of *frijoles*, potatoes, onions, and *chiles*. The assistants in these labors are the Indian men and women, legally reduced to servitude.

The soil of that portion of California, between the Sierra Nevada and the Pacific, will compare, in point of fertility, with any that I have seen elsewhere. As I have already described such portions of it as have come under my observation, it is unnecessary for me here to descend to particulars. Wheat, barley, and other small grains, with hemp, flax, and tobacco, can be produced in all the valleys, without irrigation. To produce maize, potatoes, and other garden vegetables, irrigation is necessary. Oats and mustard grow spontaneously, with such rankness as to be considered nuisances upon the soil. I have forced my way through thousands of acres of these, higher than my head when mounted on a horse. The oats grow to the summits of the hills, but they are not here so tall and rank as in the valleys.

The varieties of grasses are greater than on the Atlantic side of the continent, and far more nutritious. I have seen seven different kinds of clover, several of them in a dry state, depositing a seed upon the ground so abundant as to cover it, which is lapped up by the cattle and horses and other animals, as corn or oats, when threshed, would be with us. All the grasses, and they cover the entire country, are heavily seeded, and when ripe, are as fattening to stock as the grains which we feed to our beef, horses, and hogs. Hence it is unnecessary to the sustenance or fattening of stock, to raise corn for their consumption.

Agriculture is in its rudest state. The farming implements which have been used by the Californians, with few exceptions, are the same as were used three hundred years ago, when Mexico was conquered by Cortez. A description of them would be tedious. The plough, however, which merely scratches the ground, is the fork of a small tree. It is the same pattern as the Roman plough, two thousand years ago. Other agricultural implements are of the same description. The Americans, and other foreigners, are, however, introducing the American plough, and other American farming tools, the consequence of which has already been, to some extent, to produce a revolution in agriculture. The crops of wheat and barley, which I saw about the 1st of June, while passing through the country on my journey to the United States, exceeded in promise any which I have seen in the United States. It was reported to me that Captain Sutter's crop of wheat, for 1847, would amount to 75,000 bushels.

The natural vegetable productions of California, have been sufficiently noticed in the course of this work, for the reader to form a correct estimate of the capabilities of the soil and climate. It is supposed by some, that cotton, sugar, and rice, could be produced here. I do not doubt but there are portions of the country where these crops would thrive; but I question whether, generally, they could be cultivated to advantage. Nearly all the fruits of the temperate and tropical climates are produced in perfection in California, as has before been stated.

The principal product of the country has been its cattle and horses. The cattle are, I think, the largest and finest I ever saw, and the beef is more delicious. There are immense herds of these, to which I have previously referred; and their hides and tallow, when slaughtered, have hitherto composed the principal exports from the country. If I were to hazard an estimate of the number of hides annually exported, it would be conjectural, and not worth much. I would suppose, however, at this time, (1847,) that the number would not fall much short of 150,000, and a correspondiug number of arrobas (25 pounds) of tallow. The average value of cattle is about five dollars per head.

The horses and mules are correspondingly numerous with the cattle ; and although the most of them are used in the country, considerable numbers are driven to Sonora, New Mexico, and other southern provinces, and some of them to the United States, for a market. They are smaller than the American horses, and I do not think them equal for continuous hard service ; but on short trips, for riding, their speed and endurance are not often, if ever, equalled by our breed of horses. The value of good horses is from $10 to $25 ; of mares, $5. The prices have, however, since the Americans came into the country, become fluctuating, and the value of both horses and cattle is increasing rapidly.

The wild animals of California are the wild-horse, the elk, the black-tailed deer, antelope, grisly bear, all in large numbers. Added to these are the beaver, otter, coyote, hare, squirrel, and the usual variety of other small animals. There is not so great a variety of small birds as I have seen elsewhere. I do not consider that the country presents strong attractions for the ornithologist. But what is wanting in variety is made up in numbers. The bays and indentations on the coast, as well as the rivers and lakes interior, swarm with myriads of wild-geese, ducks, swans, and other water birds. The geese and ducks are a mongrel race, their plumage being variegated, the same as our barnyard fowls. Some of the islands in the harbor, near San Francisco, are white with the *guano* deposited by these birds ; and boatloads of eggs are taken from them. The pheasant and partridge are abundant in the mountains.

In regard to the minerals of California, not much is yet known. It has been the policy of the owners of land upon which there existed minerals, to conceal them as much as possible. A reason for this has been, that the law of Mexico is such, that if one man discovers a mine of any kind upon another man's land, and the proprietor does not work it, the former may *denounce* the mine and take possession of it, and hold it so long as he continues to work it. Hence the proprietors of land upon which there are valuable mineral ores, conceal their existence as much as possible. While in California I saw quicksilver, silver, lead, and iron ores, and the specimens were taken from mines said to be inexhaustible. From good authority I learned the existence of gold and copper mines, the metals being combined ; and I saw specimens of coal taken from two or three different points, but I do not know what the indications were as to quality. Brimstone, saltpetre, muriate and carbonate of soda, and bitumen, are abundant. There is little doubt that California is as rich in minerals of all kinds as any portion of Mexico.

I have taken much pains to describe to the reader, from day to day, and at different points during my travels in California, the temperature and weather. It is rarely so cold in the settled portions of California as to congeal water. But twice only while here I saw ice ; and then not thicker than window-glass. I saw no snow resting upon the ground. The annual rains commence in November, and continue, with intervals of pleasant, spring-like weather, until May. From May to November, usually, no rain falls. There are, however, exceptions. Rain sometimes falls in August. The thermometer, at any season of the year, rarely sinks below 50° or rises above 80°. In certain positions on the coast, and especially at San Francisco, the winds rise diurnally, and blowing fresh upon the shore render the temperature cool in midsummer. In the winter the wind blows from the land, and the temperature at these points is warmer. These local peculiarities of climate are not descriptive of the general climate of the interior.

For salubrity I do not think there is any climate in the world superior to that of the coast of California. I was in the country nearly a year, exposed much of the time to great hardships and privations, sleeping, for the most part, in the open air, and

I never felt while there the first pang of disease, or the slightest indication of bad health. On some portions of the Sacramento and San Joaquin rivers, where vegetation is rank, and decays in the autumn, the malaria produces chills and fever, but generally the attacks are slight, and yield easily to medicine. The atmosphere is so pure and preservative along the coast, that I never saw putrified flesh, although I have seen, in midsummer, dead carcasses lying exposed to the sun and weather for months. They emitted no offensive smell. There is but little disease in the country arising from the climate.

The botany and flora of California are rich, and will hereafter form a fruitful field of discovery to the naturalist. There are numerous plants reported to possess extraordinary medical virtues. The "soap-plant" (*amóle*) is one which appears to be among the most serviceable. The root, which is the saponaceous portion of the plant, resembles the onion, but possesses the quality of cleansing linen equal to any "oleic soap" manufactured by my friends Cornwall & Brother, of Louisville, Ky.

There is another plant in high estimation with the Californians, called *canchalagua*, which is held by them as an antidote for all the diseases to which they are subject; but in particular for cases of fever and ague. For purifying the blood, and regulating the system, I think it surpasses all the medicinal herbs that have been brought into notice, and it must become, in time, one of the most important articles in the practice of medicine. In the season for flowers, which is generally during the months of May and June, its pretty pink-colored blossoms form a conspicuous display in the great variety which adorn the fields of California.

The water-power in California is ample for any required mill purposes. Timber for lumber is not so convenient as is desirable. There is, however, a sufficiency of it, which, when improvements are made, will be more accessible. The timber on the Sierra Nevada, the most magnificent in the world, cannot be, at present, available. The evergreen oak, that grows generally in the valleys, is not valuable, except for fuel. But in the *cañadas* of the hills, and at several places on the coast, particularly at Santa Cruz and Bodega, there is an amount of pine and fir, adapted for lumber, that will not be consumed for a long time.

The religion of the Californians is the Roman Catholic, and like the people of all Roman Catholic countries, they appear to be devotedly attached to the forms of their religion. That there are some, I will not say how many, paganish grafts upon the laws, formalities, and ceremonies, as prescribed by the " Holy Church Universal" for its government and observance, is undeniable, but these probably do not materially affect the system. The females, I noticed, were nearly all devoutly attached to their religious institutions. I have seen, on festival, or saint days, the entire floor of a church occupied by pious women, with their children, kneeling in devout worship, and chanting with much fervency some dismal hymn appertaining to the service. There are but few of the Jesuit fathers who established the missions now remaining in the country. The services are performed at several of the churches that I visited, by native Indians, educated by the *padres* previous to their expulsion by the Mexican government.

———

I left San Francisco on my return to the United States, on the 2d of June. On the 18th I joined, at Johnson's settlement on the Sacramento, the party of General Kearny, consisting of General K., Captain Turner, his aid-de-camp, Major Swords, Major Cooke, Dr. Saunderson, and the Honorable W. P. Hall. Colonel Fremont and his exploring party returned to the United States at the same time. We left the valley of the Sacramento on the 19th of June, and reached Fort Leavenworth on the 22d of August, making the journey in sixty-four days. The limits prescribed for this volume will not allow me to sketch the incidents of this journey. Should it appear desirable hereafter, it may be done.

Thermometrical Observations from Independence, Mo., to the Great Salt Lake.

		Thermometer.		Weather.	Wind.
		Sunrise.	Sunset.		
May	6	60°	—	Showery.	——
"	7	62	71°	Rain.	——
"	8	58	52	Cloudy.	Northwest.
"	9	52	64	Clear.	"
"	10	53	76	"	Calm.
"	11	56	69	"	"
"	12	54	72	"	"
"	13	64	66	Rainy.	——
"	14	62	61	Cloudy.	Northwest.
"	15	43	61	Clear.	"
"	16	69	72	"	Calm.
"	17	68	78	"	Southwest.
"	18	70	70	Fair.	Calm.
"	19	62	75	Cloudy.	N. E., strong.
"	20	71	74	Fair.	——
"	21	65	80	Clear.	N. E., fresh.
"	22	69	79	"	Northwest.
"	23	69	78	——	"
"	24	72	75	Cloudy.	N. E., strong
"	25	71	73	"	East.
"	26	69	78	Clear.	Calm.
"	27	64	64	Cloudy.	East.
"	28	62	80	Fair.	West.
"	29	58	72	Clear.	North.
"	30	58	74	"	West.
"	31	64	44	"	Calm.
June	1	46	57	Cloudy.	Northwest
"	2	48	61	Clear.	"
"	3	54	54	Fair.	Northeast
"	4	48	55	Clear.	Northwest.
"	5	44	54	"	"
"	6	54	62	"	West.
"	7	54	65	"	"
"	8	54	68	Cloudy.	Northwest
"	9	52	65	Clear.	Calm.
"	10	52	68	"	West.
"	11	58	65	"	East.
"	12	50	65	"	Southwest.
"	13	52	72	"	West.
"	14	52	—	"	East, fresh.
"	15	—	74	——	South.
"	16	52	74	Clear.	Southeast.
"	17	64	78	"	South.
"	18	58	72	Cloudy.	West, fresh.

	Thermometer.		Weather.	Wind.
	Sunrise.	Sunset.		
June 19	64°	70°	Clear.	Calm.
" 20	65	—	"	—
" 21	—	—	"	West.
" 22	—	—	Rainy.	—
" 23	—	—	——	——
" 24	—	—	Clear.	——
" 25	—	—	"	——
" 26	—	—	"	——
" 27	—	—	"	——
" 28	—	—	"	——
" 29	61	65	"	Calm.
" 30	60	53	"	"
July 1	54	67	Cloudy.	"
" 2	65	67	Clear.	West.
" 3	35	65	"	Calm.
" 4	44	63	"	"
" 5	51	72	"	——
" 6	56	64	"	——
" 7	49	68	——	——
" 8	51	72	Clear.	——
" 9	59	58	"	Calm.
" 10	51	68	"	East.
" 11	44	61	"	Southwest.
" 12	40	69	Fair.	Calm.
" 13	56	80	Clear.	N. w., strong.
" 14	58	78	"	Calm.
" 15	55	62	Cloudy.	——
" 16	52	39	Fair.	Calm.
" 17	47	46	Clear.	——
" 18	52	51	——	——
" 19	46	52	Fair.	West.
" 20	48	58	"	Calm.
" 21	31	66	Clear.	West.
" 22	36	56	"	——
" 23	27	64	"	Calm.
" 24	46	72	"	"
" 25	40	64	"	West, strong.
" 26	42	68	"	West.
" 27	48	64	"	Calm.
" 28	56	74	"	East, strong.
" 29	59	—	"	"

Broke thermometer.